1987

D0927668

THE
AMERICAN ALPINE
JOURNAL

1987

THE AMERICAN ALPINE CLUB
NEW YORK

ISSN 0065-6925
ISBN 0-930410-29-7

Manufactured in the United States of America

*Articles and notes submitted for publication
and other communications relating to*

THE AMERICAN ALPINE JOURNAL

should be sent to

THE AMERICAN ALPINE CLUB
113 EAST 90th STREET
NEW YORK, NEW YORK 10128-1589 USA

THE AMERICAN ALPINE JOURNAL

VOLUME 29 • ISSUE 61 • 1987

CONTENTS

COVER PHOTO: Kangtega from the Mingbo-Omoga Ridge. A subsidiary peak
is on the right (front cover). The main peak is in the rear center.
Photo by Henry W. Kendall

The August Catastrophe on K2

H. ADAMS CARTER

THE YEAR 1986 was a tragic one in the great mountains. It was not an influx of inexperienced mountaineers innocently straying into situations which were beyond their capacities. A shocking number of the world's most skilled climbers met death on the heights. Many climbers seem to have lost respect for hazards in the mountains, purposefully to cut the margin of safety to nearly zero, to risk total physical and mental exhaustion after too much time spent at excessively high altitude, to carry insufficient food and fuel, to show little team spirit or desire to help one's fellows, to be selfish, to engage in unhealthy competition. Many of these factors, together with terrible weather at crucial times, compounded the effects of inadequate food, water, shelter and of high altitude.

K2 was the scene of grim tragedy in early August. Already six deaths had occurred on the mountain in June and July as reported in the *Climbs and Expeditions* section. Another seven were soon to lose their lives. These last victims were members of five different expeditions, who happened to be on the mountain at the same time.

Koreans had been working on the route for some time, fixing ropes and installing camps. The full Korean account appears in the *Climbs and Expeditions* section. The Austrian expedition was composed of Alfred Imitzer, leader, Willi Bauer, Hannes Wieser, Michael Messner, Manfred Ehrengruber, Siegfried Wasserbauer and Helmut Steinmassl. They set up Base Camp on June 19 and for a few days made good progress on the Abruzzi Ridge. They continued to be active on the mountain although they were hampered by bad weather. For instance, on July 8 Imitzer made a solo attempt to 8000 meters, before having to descend in bad weather. However, the weather kept them mostly moving up high and then back down again. On July 26 material from Camp IV was found in avalanche debris at the foot of K2, which indicated the loss of valuable gear which had already been carried high. Yet, it appears that they did not carry up sufficient supplies to replace the loss when they made their summit try.

On July 28 and 29 all seven Austrians started out from Base Camp for a final attempt, but the group dwindled to Bauer, Wieser and Imitzer. On arriving at Camp III at 7300 meters, they found that the camp had also been partially destroyed and that a tent and its contents were missing. According to Kurt Diemberger, also Austrian but a member of a different expedition, the Austrians made a deal with the Koreans to carry up a Korean tent from Camp III to Camp

1

PLATE 2

Photo by H. Adams Carter

K2 from Base Camp.

IV at 8000 meters on August 1 and to make their summit bid on the 2nd. The Koreans would move up to use their own tent on the night of the 2nd while the Austrians descended to Camp III. In perfect weather on August 2, Imitzer, Bauer and Wieser started for the summit attempt. They took much time to fix ropes in the "Bottleneck" and on the icy traverse above it and had to turn back at 8400 meters.

Meanwhile Austrian Kurt Diemberger and Englishwoman Julie Tullis, who were a high-altitude film crew with the Italian Quota 8000 Expedition but were filming for German television, had been moving up for another summit bid. On July 6, they had reached the "Bottleneck" and had retreated because of unfavorable weather. They had left a carefully anchored rucksack at 7900 meters but on their return it was missing, possibly removed by the Koreans' high-altitude porters. By good planning, they had carried up another complete Camp IV, just in case the gear should be missing. They camped beside the Korean tent on August 2. Some 100 meters lower, within calling distance, Alan Rouse from the British northwest-ridge team and Dobrosława Miodowicz-Wolf from the Polish expedition had their tent. She was affectionately called Mrufka by all the climbers. The name means "ant" and is written "Mrówka" in Polish.

The Austrians descended from their summit attempt later than planned, but did not keep on going down to Camp III as they had agreed. After considerable argument, two of them squeezed in with the Koreans, five men in a three-man tent! Imitzer descended to crowd in with Rouse and Mrufka. Rouse said that he did not sleep at all that night and so was in no condition to try for the summit. The next day he and Mrufka moved their tent up with the other two.

On August 3, while the other climbers rested at Camp IV, South Koreans Jang Bong-Wan, Kim Chang-Sun and Jang Byong-Ho, the only climbers using supplementary oxygen, went to the summit. That same day, Poles Wojciech Wróż and Przemysław Piasecki and Czechoslovak Petr Božik completed the first ascent of the south-southwest ridge and began their descent down the Abruzzi Ridge. The Koreans and the Poles were caught in the dark. Wróż fell to his death, possibly having rappelled off the end of a fixed rope. Bauer shone his headlamp on the tent so that the descending climbers could see the camp. The first got to the camp at ten P.M. and the last at four A.M. Rouse and Mrufka took Piasecki and Božik in with them. Rouse tried to sleep half in and half out the entrance in a tiny snow hole.

On August 4 Piasecki, Božik and the Koreans began their difficult descent. Rouse and Mrufka started for the summit at 5:30 A.M., followed by Imitzer alone, then Julie Tullis and Diemberger and finally Bauer and Wieser. Wieser turned back after 100 meters, fearing frostbite because of damp mittens. Rouse broke trail to within 100 meters of the summit where Bauer took over. Bauer and Imitzer reached the top at 3:30 P.M. Mrufka, exhausted, quit at 8500 meters and descended with Rouse, who had got to the summit at four P.M. Diemberger and Julie Tullis reached the top at 5:30. Diemberger was leading the rope on the descent. Tullis slipped, pulling her companion off. They fell about 100 meters. Though not seriously hurt, they had to spend the night in the open at 8400 meters. Although a severe storm had begun further down the mountain, they were able to return to the others in Camp IV in a whiteout the next morning.

It then stormed unmercifully for five days and they were all trapped. Diemberger and Julie Tullis had to abandon their tiny tent, which kept being drifted over with snow. Diemberger joined Rouse and Mrufka, and Tullis went in with the Austrians. She weakened, lost her vision and finally died peacefully in her sleep on August 7. On August 8 they ran out of food and fuel and could no longer melt water. On August 10 it stopped snowing, but the wind was still at gale force. Diemberger and Mrufka tried in vain to get Rouse up, but he was hallucinating and near death.

Bauer stirred his companions Wieser and Imitzer into descending with him and Mrufka, but Wieser and Imitzer were so weak that a short distance below Camp IV both collapsed and died. Diemberger set out alone half an hour later. Bauer did most of the trail breaking in the deep snow. Camp III had been destroyed in the storm. Rope had been fixed almost all the way down from there and each went separately.

At nine P.M. Bauer got to Camp II, where he finally could melt snow and eat something. Diemberger arrived at ten P.M. Mrufka never did reach Camp II, probably having fallen between Camps III and II. They waited for her until noon before descending together past House's Chimney. Bauer went on ahead to Base Camp and alerted a rescue crew. Diemberger reached Advance Base at midnight where he met the rescuers. Michael Messner and Przemysław Piasecki climbed back up to 7100 meters but found no signs of Mrufka. Both Bauer and Diemberger were badly frostbitten and were helicoptered out on August 16. On August 4 the Korean success was marred by the death of their sirdar, Mohammad Ali, who was killed by rockfall near Camp I.

A total of 66 climbers have now stood on the summit of K2. Twenty-four climbers have died on the mountain, thirteen of them in 1986.

PLATE 1

Photo by H. Adams Carter

K2 from the Godwin Austen Glacier.
——— = South-Southwest Buttress;
– – – = South Face;
. . . = Yugoslav (Česen) Route.
Abruzzi Ridge lies farther right.

Death in High Places

CHARLES S. HOUSTON, M.D.

THE INCREDIBLE and the tragic were commonplace in the Himalayas during 1986. A world-class climber completed climbing all fourteen 8000 meter summits, two Swiss climbed Everest north face direct from base to summit—and back—in 43 hours, without oxygen, shelter, or food. Twenty-five persons summited K-2—but seven of them died, along with six others. On other high peaks some of the world's great climbers were also lost. Too many of the deaths were avoidable. . . .

Also commonplace were outrageous behavior, intense rivalry, and disregard of mountain ethics—which caused several deaths. Not many years ago some of the things that were done would have led to excommunication by the climbing fraternity. But this is for others to discuss: my concern is the violation of physiological principles and the odds of surviving such transgression.

Two years ago in this *Journal,* I discussed recent advances in what we knew and what we guessed and what we did not know about high-altitude wellness and illness. We have learned only a little more since then, but it is worth repeating some basics for those who wish to live longer to climb again.

Above 20,000 feet mountaineers face several potentially killer hazards. Lack of oxygen, cold, dehydration and exhaustion are the most subtle and the most dangerous. They are synergistic—each re-enforcing the impact of the others. They affect judgment, perception and coordination early and progressively, and while numbing the thinking brain, are free to kill, almost uncorrected. No one, not even the strongest and the best, is immune.

Almost everyone realizes that alcohol whittles away our higher faculties but fortunately most people have learned to enjoy its pleasures and to avoid the penalties of over-indulgence. Lack of oxygen is very similar—but since it is not something we experience every day, many climbers assume it will not affect them. But above 20,000 feet (and for many people much lower) every one is impaired by altitude, and usually is unaware of how much. Hypoxia slows the works and will wreck the lovely machinery of the body if the warnings are ignored.

What's less well recognized is that hypoxia increases the risk of cold injury—frostbite and hypothermia—putting the climber at altitude in double jeopardy. Like oxygen lack, hypothermia muffles the brain, dampens the reflexes, stiffens the muscles and causes hallucinations and erratic behavior. Both reduce the unwary to clumsy automatons, able to move about but unable to think clearly or to take care of basic needs—like water.

Dehydration is the third great enemy on high mountains. The thin dry air sucks moisture from lungs and skin insatiably but almost imperceptibly. Dehydration thickens the blood so it flows sluggishly, and the red blood cells stack together, surrendering their load of oxygen less readily, thus further aggravating the cells' lack of oxygen. The thicker blood tends to form clots which obstruct blood flow in legs or arms and may migrate to the lungs, fatally. Without adequate water, the kidneys cannot function well, and acclimatization is slowed. And if blood volume is decreased greatly, blood pressure falls, aggravating the effects of both hypoxia and of cold.

The higher the altitude the greater the volume of air breathed, indeed this is the body's best way of adjusting to oxygen lack. But every breath of the cold dry air drains both water and heat from the body—first to warm the inflowing air to body temperature, and second by evaporating water from the mucus membranes to saturate this air. So much heat is lost that it may be difficult or impossible to keep warm, regardless of what one wears.

The body must burn fuel for heat and activity and just to stay alive, and the fourth danger, also aggravated by hypoxia, is exhaustion. This too is compounded by lack of oxygen which causes loss of appetite and faulty absorption. It is difficult to make the effort to cook or even to find food. The body's stores are depleted. The climber who does not eat will burn his own tissues for a time, but as these are consumed, or when he needs rapid energy, fuel is not immediately available, and his muscles, like his mind, falter and fail.

Why are these obvious dangers so often ignored? Clearly, lack of oxygen, and cold so dull the mind that they are not only self-reinforcing, but their impact rapidly snowballs and becomes lethal. Though they affect every one above 20,000 feet, the climber who is at the limit, straining every nerve and sinew in alpine-style climbing, will be at greater risk, more likely not to sense or to heed the warning signs.

As one tries to analyze the terrible events on K-2, it takes no great wisdom or insight to realize that the victims—as well as many who survived—were terribly dehydrated, empty of body fuel, bemused by oxygen lack, and undoubtedly drained of heat. Cause of death: hypoxia, dehydration, hypothermia—an accumulation due to bad judgment, bad manners, and bad luck. They had not enough food and fuel. Unplanned sorties clustered too many people in too few tents; some crammed into small tents, others crouched in snow holes, sapping their strength from lack of sleep, cold, exhaustion and lack of oxygen.

Other parties or individuals poached fixed lines, cut rappel ropes to make slings, used supplies that others relied on, too often it appears, in a selfish grab for the summit. Quarrels divided too may parties and strangers found themelves climbing together. The weak were left to descend alone. Ironically, much of the tragedy played out during the same week and in the very place where we had coped with a similar situation in a different way in 1953.

Does this condemn alpine-style climbing? Not at all. The experienced team (and it must be more than one person), fit, well acclimatized and well fed and

PLATE 3

Photo by H. Adams Carter

K2 from the South.

rested and splashing with water, choosing wisely the right day and route can do far more than we dreamed a few years ago. The Swiss pair on Everest showed what such a team can do—but they were immensely lucky that no sudden storm, no small injury from a small fall, no failure of their tiny stove did not kill them. Somehow they escaped HAPE and HACE which killed Pete Thexton and Chris Chandler, and many others, not to mention scores of near misses.

This brings us to a big question: why do some people succumb to altitude illnesses while others trying something even more extreme are unscathed? Why are some world class climbers affected on one occasion and not on another, apparently similar? Can we predict, not only who can acclimatize well, but whether an individual will do well or badly today or tomorrow? Unfortunately not. These answers are yet to be found.

These incredible alpine-style climbs have taught us a great deal. Eighty years ago only a few persons believed a person could survive overnight above 20,000 feet. Twenty years ago most physiologists believed that slow ascent, with ample time for acclimatization was the only safe way to climb. Within the last ten years we have found that acclimatization develops, and perhaps develops best, if the climber spends weeks at 17,000 to 18,000 feet, making frequent climbs many thousand feet higher, returning to Base to minimize what we call altitude deterioration for lack of better understanding. I find the evidence now persuasive that climbing for many weeks from a comfortable Base Camp at moderate altitude will perfect acclimatization better than creeping slowly up a great mountain in siege style. But if the climber tries to cut short these weeks of acclimatization, he is in real danger of death from altitude sickness.

We must remember that siege tactics also have dangers. The same potential killers stalk those who inch their way higher, stockpiling as they go. Perhaps acclimatization may be more complete at first but at great altitude deterioration parallels or outstrips acclimatization. The party may burn out, lose enthusiasm, drive and strength unless they husband their reserves. Too much time at very high altitude may be as bad as too little. Which leads to the conclusion that each person, each party must find its own pace and rhythm. By being always aware of the dangers, by recognizing that judgment and perception are always dulled, and by choosing to retreat and try again, the real and great risks can be controlled by invoking the very faculties that are first to be dulled by cold, dehydration, hypoxia and exhaustion. The alpine-style climber who wishes to climb again must be aware of the hazards not in an abstract way, but how they are affecting him, at the time.

K2's Magic Line

JANUSZ MAJER, *Klub Wysokogórski, Katowice, Poland*

We dedicate our route to the memory of Americans Alan Pennington and John Smolich, Italian Renato Casarotto and Pole Wojciech Wróż, who died while struggling on this "Magic Line."

OUR EXPEDITION, organized by the Mountaineering Clubs of Katowice and Poznań and the Polish Mountaineering Association, consisted of three ladies, Anna Czerwińska, Krystyna Palmowska and Dobrosława Miodowicz-Wolf, and five men, Petr Božik from Czechoslovakia, Krzysztof Lang, Przemsław Piasecki, Wojciech Wróż and me as leader. Lang had to abandon the expedition before arriving at Base Camp.

We had difficulties and delays with the permission and further time lost because of the air-cargo shipment. We reached Skardu only on June 20. Our goal was the south-southwest pillar of K2, known as the "Magic Line." In 1979 it was attacked by a strong French expedition that reached 8400 meters. Also in 1979 Messner looked at the route and turned instead to the Abruzzi Ridge. In 1981 Japanese Eiho Ohtani and Pakistani Nazir Sabir ascended the upper part of the pillar from 8400 meters to the summit.

In the summer of 1986, aside from our team, there were three other expeditions with permission to try the route: Americans, the Italian Quota 8000 Expedition and the famous Italian solo climber, Renato Casarotto. The American and Italian expeditions got to 6800 meters before John Smolich and Alan Pennington were tragically killed in an avalanche at the foot of the slope below the Negrotto Col on June 20. The Americans gave up the attempt. The Italians also abandoned the pillar, turning to the Abruzzi Ridge instead. Renato Casarotto twice reached 8200 meters on the pillar and on a third attempt also had to retreat. While descending to Base Camp, he perished in a crevasse fall, fifteen minutes above safe ground. Details appear elsewhere in this *Journal*.

We began climbing on June 22. Working in two groups, one a four-man and the other a three-woman team, we established three camps: Camp I on June 24 on the Negrotto Col at 6300 meters, Camp II on July 6 at 6900 meters and Camp III on July 17 at 7400 meters. The route ascended the De Filippi Glacier and a snow-and-ice slope of 50° to 60° to the Negrotto Col. From there it ascended the pillar on rocky terrain of UIAA IV to V difficulty, interlaced with small snowfields, up to a small hanging glacier at 7400 meters. Steep snow and ice with several rock steps led further to the bottom of a huge couloir on the right edge of the pillar. From the top of the couloir, we climbed 60° ice and snow to mixed terrain. From the top of the buttress at 8500 meters, the route ascended a snow ridge to the summit of K2.

PLATE 4

Photo by Krystyna Palmowska

Couloir at 8100 meters on the Magic Line of K2 (South-Southwest Buttress.)

We used the fixed ropes left earlier by the American and Italian expeditions. On July 18 and 19 the four-man team climbed up and fixed rope from Camp III to 7600 meters. We were forced back by the weather. After a spell of bad weather, on the night of July 29 we all left Base Camp for the summit try. Božik, Piasecki and Wróż spent nights at Camps II and III and on August 1 bivouacked at 8000 meters, after fixing ropes from 7600 to 7800 meters. After a night in a bivouac sack and another at 8400 meters, they reached the summit of K2 on August 3 at six P.M. Because of the difficulty of the ascent, they decided to descend the Abruzzi Ridge. The route was partially secured by fixed ropes and there were several camps on the ridge.

At about 11:30 P.M. a tragic accident occurred at 8100 meters. While rappelling on the fixed ropes in the Bottleneck, Wróż fell to his death. The exact cause of the accident is not known. There was a one-meter gap in the fixed ropes between the last two sections of the line. The team was descending in the following order; Piasecki, Božik and Wróż. Only the first had an efficient headlamp. They told each other about the gap in the ropes. Piasecki rappelled the last 50 meters and Božik followed him. They waited for Wróż in order to descend together the remaining section of the route to Camp IV, which had no fixed ropes. Suddenly they heard the noise of a fall. They feared the worst but, exhausted, could do nothing more than to wait. An hour and a half later, a member of the Korean team, which had also reached the summit on August 3, appeared. He had started down after Wróż but never saw him again. At two P.M. Piasecki and Božik got to Camp IV on the Abruzzi Ridge.

Meanwhile, I had joined two of the women, Czerwińska and Palmowska. We bivouacked at 8200 meters with the intention of attacking the peak the next day. Early on the morning of August 4, we received a message about our other group reaching the summit and of the tragedy. We decided to abandon further climbing and to return to Base Camp, evacuating the camps on the descent. The weather suddenly deteriorated. Both teams worked our way down in dreadful conditions: Božik and Piasecki down the Abruzzi Ridge and our group down the pillar. The winds blew a whirling, blinding hurricane: masses of snow constantly threatened to bury us. It was frigidly cold. Both teams returned to Base Camp on August 6 and 8 respectively. Czerwińska and Božik had frozen feet. We were all so exhausted that a few days passed before we recuperated.

Meanwhile, a series of tragic events was taking place on the Abruzzi Ridge, as related elsewhere in this *Journal*. Dobrosława Miodowicz-Wolf, whom we called Mrówka [pronounced "Mrufka" and meaning "ant"], had joined with the British climber Alan Rouse on the Abruzzi Ridge, regarding the pillar as too difficult. Without news of the climbers on the ridge, we were preparing a rescue operation in Base Camp. The foul weather and the bad condition of the potential rescuers made it impossible at first. Czerwińska and Božik had frozen feet. Piasecki was exhausted and suffering from retinal hemorrhages. Just as the rescue party was to enter the action, Bauer struggled in from above with the message that Diemberger and Mrufka were following. Palmowska, Englishman Jim Curran and I got up to Advance Base at eleven P.M. and found the completely exhausted Diemberger. The next day Piasecki and Austrian Michael Messner set out to search for Mrufka. Pushing steadily ahead all night and all the next day, they finally climbed to 7100 meters, where she had last been seen. Alas, they came upon no trace of her. Hurricane winds and falling snow, the lack of bivouac gear and the lack of hope that Dobrosława Miodowicz-Wolf could still be alive caused the rescue operation to be given up. Early on the morning of August 13, Piasecki, Messner and I penetrated the icefields at the foot of the face but found nothing. On August 15, the expedition sadly abandoned Base Camp.

Alas, the new route had been a costly victory. These accidents placed our expedition under a dark and bitter shadow.

Summary of Statistics:

AREA: Baltoro Mustagh, Karakoram, Pakistan.

NEW ROUTE: K2, First complete ascent of the South-Southwest Ridge; summit reached on August 3, 1986; first traverse of the mountain (Božik, Piasecki, Wróż). Wróż died on the descent.

PERSONNEL: Janusz Majer, leader, Anna Czerwińska, Krystyna Palmowska, Dobrosława Miodowicz-Wolf, Petr Božik, Krzysztof Lang, Przemysław Piasecki, Wojciech Wróż.

K2's South Face

JERZY KUKUCZKA, *Klub Wysokogórski Katowice, Poland*
Translated by INGEBORGA DOWBRAWA-COCHLIN

OGETHER WITH Tadeusz Piotrowski, I found myself beneath K2 as a member of a large international expedition, organized by Karl Maria Herrligkoffer from Munich. For me, the invitation to participate in this expedition was a sheer delight. Not only could I try to climb the second highest peak in the world, I was also relieved of the onerous task of organizing the expedition. We had a permit to climb Broad Peak and the south face of K2. Unfortunately, most of the members did not show enough sporting spirit to attempt even K2's normal route, let alone anything new. I couldn't believe this since on Polish expeditions we always try to attempt something different.

We split into two groups with two separate Base Camps. One was for Broad Peak. Ours for K2 was set up on June 7 at 5070 meters. We found a huge crowd of people already there below K2 since the mountain was being attempted simultaneously by Italians, French, Americans, English, Poles, Austrians and Koreans.

We decided to attack the center of the south face. The first part of this I already knew from a previous attempt in 1982 with Wojciech Kurtyka, when we had tried it alpine-style. This year there were three Swiss and German Toni Freudig, who were to climb with Tadeusz Piotrowski and me. They had wanted to go up the Abruzzi Ridge, but not having permission, Dr. Herrligkoffer was on our side and forbade it. And so, on June 9 we started on the face and reached 6000 meters, where we set up Camp I. From there on, the real problems began. Two Swiss climbers, Beda Fuster and Rolf Zemp, pulled out. The next day four of us fixed some rope on the sharp, snowy ridge and deposited equipment at 6200 meters. At this point the third Swiss, Diego Wellig, withdrew too.

On June 19, only three of us set off from Base Camp, each carrying 25 kilos. Under the first sérac at 6400 meters we got to the site of Camp II and the following day carried up ropes and food. We saw we could climb around the sérac up a steep ridge alongside it. On June 21 we fixed 500 meters of rope on the ridge. Unfortunately, at this point Toni Freudig gave up too. There were now just two of us. On June 22, carrying two days' food and bivouac gear, we started up the fixed ropes. By midday we had reached the steep, snow-covered icefields. They were an absolute torture to climb. We bivouacked at 6950 meters and the following day got to 7400 meters, where we bivouacked again. On June 24 the excellent weather began to deteriorate and black clouds gathered. At midday we hung our equipment from pitons and descended to Base Camp in a raging snow storm.

Bad weather held us one week in Base Camp. We were determined that on the next attempt we would reach the summit. When the sun came out on June 3, the two of us set off again. We reached Camp II without difficulty and the next day got to the place at 7400 meters where we had cached our gear. The 1000-meter climb at that altitude left us exhausted. On the 5th we were on snow-covered icefields which led into an enormous couloir. Because of its shape, we called it "The Hockey Stick." After a bivouac at 7800 meters, we climbed the couloir and confronted a steep headwall, not visible from below. We set up our next bivouac at 8200 meters, hoping to find a route over this barrier. Where the wall rose about 100 meters, it seemed the most logical place to ascend. The first 30 meters were the most grueling.

On July 7 we started the day's climbing with the idea that we would overcome this difficult obstacle and reach the summit that very day. Our hopes were quickly dashed. We rated that section as V + difficulty. If that takes a maximum of strength and concentration in the Polish Tatra, imagine what it demands at 8000 meters! Moreover, to economize on weight, we had taken with us only four pitons and one 30-meter rope. It took me the whole day just to scale this one rope-length. Instead of reaching the summit, we had to bivouac a second time at 8200 meters. That evening we ran out of gas with which to melt water; through carelessness we had dropped a gas canister a few hours before. The next morning we had to make do each one with a small cup of water melted on a candle!

With all these problems, we obviously couldn't reach the summit with our complete rucksacks and so we left behind the tent, sleeping bags, mattresses, food, everything. With only bivouac sacks and cameras, we started upwards. Since the section we had climbed the day before was followed by forty meters of easier climbing, at noon we reached the Abruzzi Ridge at 8300 meters, at the spot where Wanda Rutkiewicz and her French companions had bivouacked in June. Although the route was easier now, it was covered with loose snow, slowing our progress. At about six P.M. I wondered if we would ever get to the summit. It was now or never. The weather was beginning to change and mist hid everything. Under a sérac we found some litter, including empty French soup packets. Was this another of their camps? As I moved around the sérac, I saw the ground begin to flatten. At 6:25 I finally reached the top! I took from my pack two small scarves which my sons had given me and hung them on my ice-axe together with the red-and-white flag of Poland. I took a few pictures. Just then Tadeusz appeared. We congratulated each other and took some more pictures. We were both ecstatic, I, because my dream of climbing the south face of K2, my twelfth 8000er, had come true, and Tadeusz, because he had climbed an 8000er, one of the highest and most difficult in the world.

Dusk closed in at 8300 meters. I took out my flashlight and we kept on. Suddenly the bulb burned out and we were plunged into darkness. We dug a hole in the snow and bivouacked in our bivouac sacks, shaking with cold until the morning.

At the first light we started the descent. The heavy snow sloughed off in small avalanches. Often unable to find our way, we found ourselves on very difficult terrain where we had to rappel. During the day we managed to descend only 400 meters. As darkness fell, we reached easier terrain. Our bivouac was even worse than the night before. For two days we had not even had a drop of water and our bivouac sacks were worn and full of holes. The night was absolute torture as we shivered in the frigid cold and snow penetrated every nook and cranny. We got only snatches of sleep.

In the morning the weather had cleared a little and we were able to see a route down. Worried that the break in the weather was only temporary, I got ready quickly and set out, but Tadeusz tarried. Shortly I was able to see that we were on the route; I could make out Korean tents below at 7300 meters. I waited for Tadeusz and finally he joined me. It was about half past ten o'clock. Immediately below us was a very steep slope. This was the spot where in 1953 Art Gilkey died. When I asked Tadeusz for the rope, I discovered that he had forgotten to bring it with him from the bivouac. I started down first with Tadeusz behind me. The ice was harder than usual. Just after I warned Tadeusz to go a little to my left, I saw one of his crampons slip off. When he tried to bang his other foot into the ice, the crampon shot off his other boot. I was directly below him. He fell full force onto me. I braced and could barely keep my footing, but I was totally unable to catch him. He hurtled down over the edge.

I climbed down very slowly and took five-and-a-half hours to cover the 200 meters to the Korean camp. I was under the strange illusion that somehow I might see Tadeusz there alive. I found a radio in one of the tents but it was dead. There was a little gas cookstove and I drank and ate. Then I fell into a deep sleep and woke up the following afternoon. I had slept for 20 hours. Just after four P.M., I started down, meeting two Koreans on the way up. I stopped at the next Korean camp at 6800 meters where I was looked after by a solitary Korean host. From there I was at last able to make contact with Base Camp. I told Janusz Majer about the accident, but he already knew, having heard from the two Koreans I had met. He told me that two rescue teams had gone out to search in vain for Tadeusz under the face where he had fallen.

The next day I returned to Base Camp to the large group of people there where congratulations were intermingled with condolences. Everybody was very kind to me. Our Italian doctor inquired about my physical condition, some one tried to film me and somebody else recorded my story on tape.

Four days later I flew by helicopter to Skardu. I had my last sight of K2, but I felt no joy at having conquered its magnificent face, just two of us, partly in alpine-style, and without supplementary oxygen. My experiences on that mountain were too tragic and the price we paid for victory was too high.

Summary of Statistics:

AREA: Baltoro Karakoram, Pakistan.

NEW ROUTE: K2, 8611 meters or 28,250 feet, via South Face; summit reached on July 8, 1986 (Jerzy Kukuczka, Tadeusz Piotrowski). Piotrowski fell to his death on the descent on July 10, 1986.

Gasherbrum IV's Northwest Ridge

GREG CHILD

O N MOST EXPEDITIONS, you are invited along, agree to go, often without knowing much about the peak, get swept along in the choas of organization, travel and penury, then arrive at the mountain. Only then does the mountain begin to possess you. When I think of the origins for the seven of us going to Gasherbrum IV, I have to say that though this was true for some, others already had a kind of "investment" in the mountain.

Geoff Radford had attempted the northwest ridge in 1984 and had reached a highpoint of 23,800 feet. This time, he was determined to be part of a successful expedition. My own motive was, for want of a better term, to settle a score. With what, I'm not sure—probably myself. My first view of the northwest ridge of Gasherbrum IV had been in 1983, from Broad Peak. Peter Thexton and I were standing on the col before the main summit, looking directly onto the ridge. We discussed what a fine climb it would be, and even picked out a line of snow ramps through the steep headwall, knowing that a team of Americans were at that time attempting the ridge. A few hours later Pete contracted pulmonary edema, and despite an all-night struggle to shed altitude, he died. I vowed I would never return to the Himalaya after that.

As years passed, the seed of Gasherbrum IV planted itself in the heads of several friends and before I knew exactly why, I found myself with the unenviable task of leading an expedition to it. Never returning to the Himalaya was a vow I always knew I would break. Never leading another expedition is another matter.

Gasherbrum IV has justly earned a reputation as one of the most elusive summits. Since the first ascent by Bonnatti and Mauri in 1958, Japanese, British, American and Polish-Austrian attempts had all fallen short of the summit. The closest anyone had come to the summit were Wojciech Kurtyka and Robert Schauer, who made perhaps the most serious climb in the great mountains of the world by climbing the west face. Though a brilliantly conceived and executed alpine-style climb, they were without food and fuel for six days. In an extreme state, they had exited from the face near the south summit and descended the northwest ridge, missing the true summit.

The northwest ridge had been the focus of two strong American attempts in 1983 and 1984. In 1983 a team led by Steve Swenson had reached 23,000 feet

PLATE 5

Photo by H. Adams Carter

GASHERBRUM IV from Concordia.
Northwest Ridge on left.

but was halted by deep and unstable snow. In 1984 Werner Landry led a team (on which Geoff was a member) to the same route; they reached 24,000 feet, but ran out of steam after overcoming the first of two difficult rockbands that comprise the headwall of the upper ridge. In 1984 the Poles Kurtyka and Jerzy Kukuczka used the fixed ropes of the Americans to go high on the route, but mostly as a reconnaissance for the west face. In 1985 Kurtyka returned with Schauer. They used the deteriorating ropes on the northwest ridge to acclimatize to about 23,000 feet, and to make a cache of gear for their descent of this ridge from the west face. The ropes must have aided them greatly as they descended in their exhausted states.

So, in 1986, there wasn't a great deal that was unknown about the northwest ridge: it had been climbed to 24,000 feet; Kurtyka and Schauer had descended its headwall; I had seen a path through the upper rockband. The obsession was that obscure object of desire, the summit. Though our successful ascent of the mountain stood on the shoulders of those who went before us, it was no stepladder to the summit. Gasherbrum IV had sting in it till the very end and the outcome was always uncertain. Tim Macartney-Snape, who had climbed Everest by a new route and without oxygen, said that "G4" was harder than even that.

On May 17, Base Camp on the West Gasherbrum Glacier was established. We were Americans Tom Hargis, Randy Leavitt, Geoff Radford, Dr. Steve Risse, Andy Tuthill, and Australians Tim Macartney-Snape, and I as climbers, and Phil Balston as cameraman. The trek along the Baltoro was bitterly cold this year, and at least five Balti porters with various expeditions died due to complications arising from cold. Expeditions were also amazed to see helicopter-supported military bases at Gore and Concordia, which support armed camps at key passes such as Sia La, Gyong La and Bilafond La. All this is part of the Pakistani response to Indian "invasions" of the Siachen Glacier area. This bizarre conflict over mountainous terrain useless for anything except climbing or trekking is costing the Indian and Pakistani governments fortunes in human life and money.

Winter was slow to leave the Baltoro this spring. During our first thirty days in Base Camp it snowed for all but six. Nevertheless, we established Camp I in the huge cwm beneath the northwest ridge at 18,500 feet on May 25 and Camp II in a cramped spot at the top of a 3500-foot couloir at 21,800 feet on June 5. Geoff recalled bare ice in the couloir in 1984. This year we found deep snow. Trail-breaking was soul-destroying. We recorded temperatures of $-25°$ F in Camp I and $-15°$ during rope-fixing in the couloir.

To reach Camp III we deviated from earlier attempts. Instead of following the tattered ropes in the diagonal couloirs of the west side, we dropped over the col, east, onto the easier slopes of China.

On June 10, the site for Camp III, at 23,100 feet, was reached in high winds. After five hours of digging, Hargis, Macartney-Snape and I occupied a snow cave just in time for a massive storm to pin us down for three days. After two days in the cave, Hargis began to cough up infected matter, so he decided to descend alone. His descent to Camp I was, in his words, "The most desperate

PLATE 6

Photo by Greg Child

Tim Macartney-Snape at 24,500 feet on the Northwest Ridge of Gasherbrum IV.

thing I've ever done." The next day Macartney-Snape and I also descended and shared his experience of being tossed about on fixed ropes and crawling from one rope to another through deep, shifting snowdrifts.

Back in Base Camp, we waited till June 17 until signs of good weather returned. During that time the British who were attempting the horrifyingly loose west face spur abandoned their attempt.

By June 19 we were all back on the mountain, Leavitt and Risse in Camp II and all others in the snow cave. With the wind turning from an unfavorable sou'wester to a nor'easter blowing clear skies from China, we made our move.

Our hope on June 20 was to get to the high point at 24,100 feet of the 1984 attempt, and reach the summit the next day. The five in Camp III set off early, with Geoff and Andy breaking trail. At 23,600 feet we arrived at the first rock-band. Torn and sun-bleached ropes marked the 1984 attempt. We re-fixed some lines here, following an ice chute where the other attempt had apparently climbed steep rock, and at dusk pulled onto a flat promontory, at exactly 24,140 feet, the 1984 highpoint. Here we bivouacked.

The 21st dawned perfectly clear, yet windy. The only visible clouds on the vast horizon were monsoon thunderheads over distant Indian Kashmir. The most difficult section awaited. To move quickly, we economized on weight, taking four sleeping bags, two stoves, two 300-foot 7mm-ropes, a few pitons and a movie camera.

Two hundred feet above the bivouac Andy, leading the way, dropped neck-deep into a slot. Minutes later he stepped on a windslab which boomed sick-eningly under our weight. This drove us onto the ridge crest where we found firm névé and ice up to 65°. We moved unroped over this section for some 800 feet, until we reached the base of the second rockband at ten in the morning. Feeling optimistic, we ditched everything except climbing gear and the movie camera and set off up the rock wall. At this point Geoff decided to turn back, feeling that he had reached his own personal summit. Since this was his second try at the mountain, it was sad to see him descending.

Kurtyka had written to me describing what he had found on the descent of the ridge in 1985. "Do not fear the rock band. It's a nice surprise," he had written. As I slipped about on the first steep marble fist-crack, gasping and expecting to fall at any second, I wasn't so sure. But the difficulties relented as we reached the snow ramps I had seen from Broad Peak.

We were all feeling the strain of technical climbing at altitude. Tim, irre-pressible in his stamina, did more than his share of the leads. At four P.M. we reached the top of the rock band, at 25,800 feet, in a howling wind. The main summit was still some 1500 feet horizontally south. Clearly, we would not make the summit before dark, and rappelling the rocks by moonlight seemed like lunacy.

We had a brief, yet urgent discussion over a bivouac in the open with only the clothes on our backs. Tim and I were for it, and so, eventually, was Tom, despite a racking cough. Andy decided that the gamble with frostbite was not worth the risk. He took a rope and descended alone, while the rest of us found a suitable place on the ridge to scratch out a tiny snow cave.

Digging the cave was almost more than we could manage. Handful by handful we clawed away. Framed in the entrance I could see Broad Peak. The sight of it and the thought of Pete still there made me determined to reach the summit of Gasherbrum IV. Yet I was also conscious of the bridge we had burned, and wondered if recklessness was not taking the helm. But as the sun set and the moon rose, the fantastic sky convinced us that we had chosen the right place. The pearly tusks of Gasherbrums I and II stood stark against an indigo horizon capped by a band of pink. In the upper band a full moon beat out its eerie light. A landscape from another planet. As we entered the cave I felt like a stranded astronaut bedding down for the night on a strange, and possibly hostile planet.

It was a desperately cold night, full of Tom's coughing and chattering of teeth, Tim's nocturnal singing, my mumblings and groanings. Our brains were too cloudy to really feel the true agony of it, which was a blessing. When the sun rose we found ourselves crawling out the cave and moving over the north summit, along the icy gap to the rocky pinnacles of the south summit. We moved like robots, battered by the wind that rammed Gasherbrum IV's east face and poured over the gap like surf pounding into a seawall. Even when I climbed to the wrong summit our brains were too numb to feel frustration; subsequent ascents may see a sling on a spike on one of the first towers.

Tim, more *compos mentis* than Tom or I, led on, across the snowfield capping the west face. He soloed across a treacherous fifty feet of verglased limestone. Here, I insisted on a rope. This was to prove wise in another hour.

From there it was a short distance, up an easy slope and a 60° rock slab sprinkled with large holds, to the summit. At ten in the morning on June 22, the obscure object of desire was reached. It was supremely clear. Not a single cloud interrupted the endless view of mountains in Sinkiang, China and the Karakoram. The summit was a small dome of snow clinging to a narrow, rocky fin. We stood atop it, shot some movie-film and felt grateful that our punch-drunk bodies would not have to climb up anymore. I think we were all too spent to really feel elation.

Bonatti had described descending from a piton driven into the summit. We searched for it everywhere. Nothing. We left our own sling around a chockstone and rappelled. As I descended I saw Tim shimmying along the summit-fin, like a mad, lost thing. After forty feet he returned to our anchor and descended. When he reached me, he was excited.

"I saw it! Fifty feet away. Bonatti's pin, with a carabiner and an old rope hanging from it!" We later theorized that twenty-eight years earlier, the summit cone of snow may have been fifty feet to the north.

Tom had already crossed the verglased traverse, racing to shed altitude. Again, I called for the rope, led across the awful rocks, and made a boot-axe belay for Tim. He paused to remove a piton at the start, and began levering it out with the pick of his ice-axe. The next thing I saw was his axe flying through the air, followed by him, hurtling backwards, a red ball bouncing down the west face. He seemed to fall in slow motion. I could hear my heart thumping, preparing itself for a grand tour of the west face. I yarded in slack, watched him

PLATE 7

Photo by Greg Child

**BROAD PEAK'S Main and Middle
Summits seen from the Northwest
Ridge of Gasherbrum IV.**

disappear behind a prow of rock, then a jolt torpedoed boot and axe into the slope.

I called his name. No answer! I tried to pull him up. Impossible! It occurred to me that if he was dead, with nowhere to anchor the rope to, I would be stuck here for eternity, as *in situ* as Bonatti's piton. And if I cut the rope, then Tom and I would have no way to descend the mountain.

Then the rope came in, and in and in. He appeared, dazed, his own suit leaking feathers as if both barrels of a shotgun had been blasted into it. He thanked me for saving him from the biggest tumble of his life. I thanked him for saving me from the longest wait of mine.

Time lost all meaning as we rappelled the headwall. Every anchor in the compact marble and the shattered diorite took an age to set. Soon, we ran out of slings and pitons. Cords on Jümars were removed and knots jammed into cracks. At the foot of the rocks we found the gear we had stashed. We lit the Scorpion stove, desperate for water. Propane spurted out and the stove exploded. We kicked it away.

"This is like a pub with no beer. Let's go," I said, and we continued rappelling, into the night.

As we hung on the belays, sleep would overtake us and strange dreams would fill our heads. The call to descend would propel us out of this netherworld. Just as we used our last piece of gear, a frozen sling of Wojciech's was found hanging on a horn.

At ten in the night we reached the tents and our first water in thirty-six hours. As we dropped into sleep I thought of the summit. I had originally wanted to leave something up there in memory of Pete, to make up for the summit we never reached. But I had left nothing, except for a fond thought. It was the best thing I could leave.

It's still there.

Summary of Statistics:

AREA: Karakoram, Pakistan.

NEW ROUTE: Gasherbrum IV, 7925 meters, 26,000 feet, via the northwest ridge, summit reached on June 22, 1986 (Child, Hargis, Macartney-Snape).

PERSONNEL: Thomas Hargis, Randy Leavitt, Dr. Stephen Risse, Geoffrey Radford, Andrew Tuthill, *Americans;* Greg Child, Timothy Macartney-Snape, Philip Balston, *Australians.*

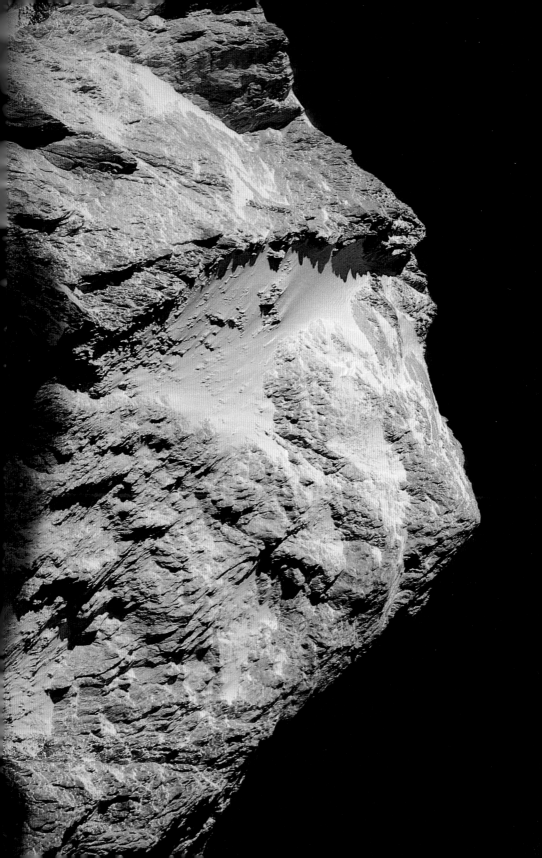

Canadian Light Everest Expedition

Sharon Wood, *Alpine Club of Canada*

I T WAS ONLY a few days after Dwayne Congdon and I had stumbled off the summit of Mount Everest when Barry Blanchard roused me from my semi-conscious void within the sanctuary of my sleeping bag. "Hey, Woody! I have this climb I'd like to do with you on the Rupal Face of Nanga Parbat. The biggest vertical face in the world, no sponsors, small team, alpine style, unclimbed line, 8000 meters. . . ." I responded with a groan and a few words of protest. "But it's a small 8000er." I didn't know there were any small 8000-meter peaks. I was operating on a much different frequency at the time. I had been dreaming of learning how to rock climb again; I mean really rock climb with a sleeveless tee-shirt and a pair of gaudy lycra tights. To enter a rock-climbing season sun-tanned and minus the atrophied appearance I am so accustomed to after high-altitude adventures that are exclusively mind-and-lung expanding. "Hey, Bubba, ask me later."

Barry's source of energy and enthusiasm had always been an admirable enigma to most of us mortals. He and Albi Sole had been the victims of my biggest regret of the Everest Light experience, which still looms very large in my mind. They had been slotted for the second summit team, due to begin their bid once Dwayne and I were safely down. In spite of being healthy, strong, and chafing at the bit, they were called down off the mountain. Circumstances had denied them the opportunity they deserved. Dwayne and I hadn't helped their chances by cutting it close to the line. Of course all eleven of us came on this trip aiming for the top. We came with the awareness that our odds were slim on an expedition-style ascent on a very big brand-name mountain.

Back on the 19th of March we were the first expedition to arrive. We selected the choice location for our Base Camp at the foot of the Rongbuk Glacier at 16,800 feet. The Americans who closely paralleled our schedule, route, and style, arrived a day later with a permit to climb the Great Couloir. The Spanish arrived approximately a week later with permission to attempt the North Ridge. Base Camp offered colorful and diverse entertainment.

The price of luxury is quickly paid when you drive to 17,000 feet. Donning nearly every layer of clothing we owned, and under the influence of a condition close to the worst hangover I've ever experienced, we attempted to create order out of our six tons of supplies. Within hours, amidst total chaos, Jane Fearing, our cook, had succeeded in turning out a fine meal, a demonstration of only one small quality that remained consistent throughout our sojourn. It is an illusion to believe that climbing is the feature attraction on a project of this nature. One day James Blench defined the role of an expedition member rather succinctly: "You go with a group of people you believe in, you give it all you have, you throw it all into one pot, and with the direction of a good leader you see what you come up with." I'm sure at times we may have all looked like good little Socialists. However, in reality, every one of us was a strong-willed, single-minded individual, who was not accustomed to aligning his or her purpose with more than one or two people at best. The one thing we did share in common was a recognition of the need to channel the diversity in this situation in order to accomplish our objective. Jim Elzinga was unanimously accepted as the leader. The cooperation and compliance that ensued was a source of constant wonderment.

Camp II at 19,500 feet was established at the base of the spur by the end of March. Camp III was established halfway up the spur, and reclaimed several times before it was successfully occupied by mid April. Due to the blessing of some good weather and relatively straightforward climbing and fixing, Camp IV at 24,000 feet was ready for occupation by the third week in April. Old abandoned caches and carcasses of box tents were grim reminders of the wrath of this mountain. I recalled reading an account of a team loaded with big guns who were defeated by the next section because of the winds and the sustained work load above 24,000 feet. We too were beginning to wear. All but Albi Sole and I had been stricken by a virus which attacked the respiratory tract that crippled our force and pace. Interestingly enough all but Annie Whitehouse on the American team had been afflicted by the same virus.

We spent days building our camps, spurred on by the sight of the tattered remains of efforts before us and of past horror stories of expeditions losing up to fifteen tents to the winds. I will never forget that dramatic photograph from Tom Hornbeins' book of climbers leaning 45° into the wind attempting to salvage the remains of their Camp IV. We also spent many extra days laying down and maintaining fixed ropes on easy ground to ensure we remained intact when the winds picked up. As the season advanced, our fears materialized. I remember one day watching Jim Elzinga, who weighs 200 pounds or better, get lifted off his feet and hurtled back down to the next anchor.

By April 20, Camp V was installed through the tenacious efforts of Barry Blanchard and Dwayne Congdon in three days of block cutting and shelter construction. By this time it felt as if we were beginning to spin our wheels. There is a paradox that exists in an expedition-style ascent. The multitude of incremental steps that promote a slow but strong and consistent progress tend to block the attainment of the ultimate objective. In securing the platforms from which to extend, long exposure to altitude burns you out by the time you're in position to make a summit bid. Our work force above 24,000 feet was down to half. We had to change our original objective of climbing the West Ridge Direct to traversing out onto the north face and climbing the Hornbein Couloir. To some this appeared the only viable alternative. To others it was a hard blow, a

PLATE 8

Canadian Light Everest Expedition Photo

**MOUNT EVEREST from the North.
Altitude of Camps in feet: II =
19,400; III = 21,600; IV = 24,000;
V = 25,000; VI = 26,800.**

compromise. They would have rather failed on the hard way than succeed by a less technical route. After reading Tom Hornbein's account and given the mountain we were on, I was not confident we had anything in the bag.

A week later on the 6th of May, another crucial decision was made. The summit teams were selected. This painful process was made easier by the mountain having already pared us down to four. Dwayne Congdon and I were to be the first assault team and Barry Blanchard and Albi Sole the second. The strategy from here would go as follows: two teams of two would fix from Camp V across the north face to the bottom of the couloir in four days. Meanwhile, whoever was capable would ferry the remainder of supplies necessary for Camp VI to Camp V. Within the week, following a rest, Dwayne and I would commence our summit bid. Being the first summit team we would install Camp VI at 27,000 feet and go for the summit the next day. If we failed to reach the summit, we would at least fix as much of the technical sections as possible with 6mm Kevlar rope for the second team to move through on.

With a concrete plan now in place, the hulking expedition machine began making steps forward. Everyone put out to his maximum capacity even when his cards were played out. Jim had contracted a bad viral infection which permanently bound him to Camp II and below. From there he continued to maintain a relentless grip on the orchestration of the strategy. Over the next week we succeeded in carrying out the initial stages of our plan.

On May 15, on parting from Camp I to begin our summit bid, Todd Bibler, a member of our American neighbors, shouted out some parting words of wisdom, "Glory or Death!." Coleen, Dwayne's long-time mate, failed to grasp the nature of Todd's humor. Later that day, Jim Elzinga took us aside for a little pep talk. He said that no matter what, make sure you treat this climb just like any other mountain; don't die for it.

Barry and Kevin Boyle joined Dwayne and me. They would carry in support through to Camp VI. At Camp II, we waited out two days of storms before we started up in spite of unsettled weather. On this day, halfway up our 5000-foot carry, when the conditions were especially compromising, I tried this little tidbit of Jim Elzinga philosophy out on Kevin. It didn't wash. If the truth be known, one's bearing on reality and the margin one leaves for longevity is altered significantly in a place like this.

On May 19, at Camp V, we strapped on the oxygen for the first time. Our circulation improved almost immediately. However, with two oxygen bottles on top of all the supplies for Camp VI and above, our packs were pushing 70 pounds. The pace was discouragingly slow and painful. I didn't dare take my pack off for fear of dropping it or losing energy needed to put it back on. As the four of us crept across the face, every now and then someone was toppled over by the wind. An ominous lenticular cloud capped the summit. Late in the afternoon we left the ropes and entered the couloir. It was constantly being flushed by surface avalanches from thousands of feet above. Periodically, rocks dislodged by the raging winds ricocheted down off the walls of the couloir. Near misses were stripping away our resolve. At eight P.M., I saw Barry step out of

the couloir into an alcove. This would be our Camp VI, at approximately 26,800 feet. Barry and Kevin remained with us and did everything they could to help us get settled. It was painful to watch them turn their backs to return to Camp V. This day had been a far more demanding test of their commitment than of ours, as we had the sweet incentive of the summit luring us on the next day. We remained outside preparing our equipment and securing our tent until after midnight, reducing ourselves to a devastating level of exhaustion.

On May 20, at five A.M., we arose covered in spindrift that had been driven through the walls of the tent during our few hours of respite. We made the first and one of the only radio calls of the day. The boys indicated that the lenticular cloud was holding its ground and obscuring the summit from 28,000 feet and above. Their words were barely audible over the screaming wind. We stepped out of the tent at nine A.M., eight hours behind schedule, and loaded up our packs with one oxygen bottle, 600 feet of 6mm Kevlar rope, and a few pitons. I tucked a portable radio on full volume deep inside my jackets. Our oxygen would last ten hours on a low flow rate of two litres per minute. All was not in our favour as we plodded up the icy couloir where trailings of old ropes hauntingly dangled on the walls. In the initial stages of the day, Dwayne's sense of conviction was considerably stronger than mine. As the day wore on, when his energy waned, mine would surge. We played off one another's fluctuating strengths throughout the day. To save time, we elected to climb unroped. When we reached the rock pitches at the Yellow Band, we began to string the rope out. A few hundred feet later we came together, having both assumed a much different mode of operation. The climbing had consumed our disappointment and pessimism. A very intense level of concentration and commitment prevailed. Every now and then I'd get a boost from the voices that crackled over the radio inside my jacket from our anxious onlookers 10,000 feet below. By five o'clock in the afternoon we had covered half the elevation to the summit. With no verbal communication necessary, we continued on. We seemed to be operating in perfect synchronism, matched in thought, determination, and decision. The voices that wafted up from the depths of my jacket had a marked change in tone. Now I was hearing the odd broken phrase with the words, bivouac, or benighted and speculations of where we would spend the night. We were unquestionably on our way to the top, and we certainly didn't have any intentions of spending the night out. The wind had died to a low roar confining us to the protection of the face on the summit pyramid. One final step of fifth-class climbing and we gained the endless ridge.

We stepped onto the summit at sunset, nine P.M. We wrestled with flags and cameras for twenty minutes, then turned our attention to the descent. Unfortunately the conditions would not allow us to sit on our backsides and surrender to a quick slide back home and live to see our friends' smiles the next day. Darkness intercepted us at about 28,500 feet on the traverse back into the couloir. We were separated about halfway down where we reached our fixed ropes. We both continued alone under the assumption that everything was under control but not particularly fun. We were slipping deeper and deeper into a very efficient state of function, that of survival. Meanwhile downstairs, the team helplessly watched as our head lamps grew further and further apart. I was too preoccupied to realize the radio had ceased working before the summit.

I arrived at Camp VI ninety minutes before Dwayne. During the wait, my mind had its first chance to register anything beyond putting one foot below the other. I thought of the implications of having separated from Dwayne; my thoughts raced randomly, entertaining everything from the best to the worst of scenarios. One of the most pleasant memories I recall was the sound of Dwayne's footsteps outside the tent at 3:30 A.M. During the interim before dawn we managed to create a few more exciting moments for ourselves when a mishandled stove blew up, leaving us quite cold and thirsty, and me with little facial hair.

At dawn, we reassembled the radio, and pushed the button to re-establish contact with the rest of the team. There was no question as to whether it was a team success. Dwayne and I were lucky enough to climb off their shoulders to reach the pinnacle of everyone's efforts.

Summary of Statistics:

AREA: Tibet

ASCENT: Mount Everest, 8848 meters, 29,028 feet, via West Ridge and Hornbein Couloir; First Ascent by a North American Woman, May 20, 1986 (Congdon, Wood).

PERSONNEL: Jim Elzinga, leader, James Blench, Barry Blanchard, Kevin Doyle, Dwayne Congdon, Dave McNab, Chris Shank, Dan Griffin, Laurie Skreslet, Albi Sole, Sharon Wood, Jane Fearing, Dr. Robert Lee.

IWA TO YUKI *is a Japanese climbing magazine that covers news and photos about mountaineering all over the world, climbing gear, high-altitude medicine and much more. Although it is published in Japanese, it has a summary, photo captions and maps in English. The yearly subscription for six issues is 7380 yen, including sea mail. Send to* **IWA TO YUKI,** *Yama To Keikoku Sha Co. Ltd., 1-1-33 Shiba Daimon, Minato-ku, Tokyo, 105 Japan.*

A Hidden Gem—Ama Dablam's Northeast Face

MICHAEL KENNEDY

SUNSHINE, light, and warmth were all I wanted after Ama Dablam. But memory plays its tricks. The cold, the wind, the frustration of moving too slowly through soft, deep snow, the long, dark nights, all seem rather vague in retrospect. And what of the concrete recollections? They are of laughing through the green lowlands of Nepal, long afternoon hill walks in the upper Khumbu, and a few brief moments of inspiration and power on the climb itself.

We started with a simple enough idea. Carlos Buhler had gotten a permit to climb on the north side of Ama Dablam in the 1985/86 winter season. We hoped to climb a new route on the northeast face, which I had seen from nearby Island Peak in 1981. This face, invisible from most viewpoints, hadn't ever been attempted, although the ridges on either side had been climbed.

On the right, the north ridge was an attractive alternative should a new route prove excessively dangerous or otherwise unfeasible. A second pair of climbers, operating independently, would have this as their main objective. Not only would the party as a whole have greater self-rescue capability, but the relatively high fixed costs of a climbing trip to Nepal could be shared among four rather than just two people. We agreed that the trip should be a low-key one, self-financed as much as possible. It would be a climbing holiday. In the modern idiom, we would go light and fast. By acclimatizing during the approach in November, and starting on December 1, the beginning of the official winter season, we hoped to complete the climb and be home by Christmas.

In the end, things were as simple as we could have hoped for. The second climbing team dropped out a few months before departure. While easing the organizational burden, this put additional strain on our already-extended finances, but we eventually arrived at a budget that we could live with. Carlos' 60-year-old mother Julie Dougherty, his brother Roman, and my wife Julie decided to walk into the Khumbu with us, giving the whole trip the feel of a family outing.

Many regard a Himalayan approach as a necessary evil, something to be dispensed with as rapidly as possible so that the real task of climbing can be attended to. I know that I have often felt this way. But it is also a wonderful time to relax and unwind from the pressures of work, to acclimatize and prepare

PLATE 10

Photo by Michael Kennedy

**Northeast Face of AMA DABLAM
from Island Peak. (See Plate 62 in
A.A.J., 1986 for route.)**

yourself for the climb ahead. We were doubly fortunate in having family along for this particular journey. Not only could we share an integral part of the whole experience with them, but the presence of loved ones, more concerned with the wonder of the mountains than with their performance in this particular arena, helped defuse the intensity which so often accompanies a climbing trip.

As we made our preparations in Kathmandu, we learned that an unseasonally severe storm in mid-October had forced many post-monsoon parties off their routes. There had been several deaths, and reports of deep snow at the higher elevations. This caused us some concern. Not only were we contemplating a steep and potentially dangerous ice route, but our Base Camp would most probaby be inaccessible to yaks. As we passed through Lukla and Namche a few weeks later, our fears diminished. A large guided party had succeeded on the southwest ridge of Ama Dablam, reporting plentiful snow but good conditions overall. The skies were clear, and the weather appeared stable.

The days on our walk had fallen into a delightfully predictable pattern. Rising early to steaming mugs of tea, we'd gobble down a quick breakfast while the loads were packed. Strolling along the well-travelled paths, each at our own pace, we'd eventually reach the night's camp by early afternoon, having stopped along the way numerous times to snack, drink, or simply take in the view. After lunch, the slothful among us would read and nap for a few hours—those few hours often extending into twilight.

Late afternoons were spent taking long, lazy walks up the hillsides near our camps, gaining a few thousand feet in elevation, hoping for an edge in the acclimatization game. Julie and I had a particularly fine experience in reaching Kala Pattar, the trekker's viewpoint opposite the Khumbu Icefall on Everest. Having moved camp that day to Lobuje, we originally planned to spend the night there before going on. But after consuming an embarrassingly large lunch, we both felt surprisingly good and decided to proceed that afternoon.

Reaching the top late in the day, we were entranced by sunset colors bathing Everest, Nuptse, and Pumori. We lingered on until twilight, but all too soon the evening's chill and the prospect of a long walk home drove us back down to the trail. Bathed in moonlight, we stumbled back to camp late that night, tired but overjoyed by the magic of a perfect late fall day.

After reaching their own summit the next day on Kala Pattar, Julie Dougherty and Roman headed back to the pleasures of Kathmandu. Carlos, Julie, and I established ourselves in the meadows of Shango, a seasonal pasture ground at 14,500 feet below the north side of Ama Dablam. With the help of our sirdar Ang Jangbo and two porters, we took food, climbing gear, and a tent to the normal Base-Camp site some 2000 feet higher. Deep snow there made us appreciate our lower and warmer camp.

The greatest danger of climbing in the winter season was in evidence as we studied Ama Dablam. Wind scoured the upper reaches of the mountain, ripping massive plumes of snow from the cornices and flinging them off into the clearest of skies. But the route itself, an elegant line of snow flutings rising up the center of the face, appeared far more reasonable than we had hoped. The threatening

PLATE 11

Photo by Michael Kennedy

Carlos Buhler traverses into the first steep ice pitch on AMA DABLAM'S Northeast Ridge.

sérac barrier below the top looked fairly stable, and the crest we planned to follow was prominent enough that all but the most monstrous avalanches could be avoided. Nevertheless, we would be exposed to significant danger at several points. Fast climbing would be essential to both success and survival.

Having spent nearly a month walking in from Jiri, we were reasonably fit and acclimatized. Nevertheless, we hadn't been above 18,000 feet, and had planned a final acclimatization exercise before going onto Ama Dablam. Travelling light, the three of us spent a cold and windy three-day round trip from Shango on Island Peak's regular route, reaching the 20,285-foot summit early on November 24.

At midday on November 25, Julie left for Lukla and the flight home. It was a sad parting, but far better than the usual rushed farewell at the airport, after having worked seven days a week for months in preparation for the trip. We'd spent a very good month together, laughing and playing more than ever seems possible at home. And we'd only be separated for a few weeks if all went as planned.

The weather was superb, and the winds that plagued us on Island Peak had died out. After a few days' rest, Carlos and I left for our camp beneath the face. We spent parts of two more days finding an easy route through the lower snow ramps, leaving a cache of food and equipment at the base of the difficult climbing at about 18,000 feet.

Late afternoon on November 30 saw us back at the site of the cache, hacking a tent platform out of a rib of snow and settling in for the first of seven cold nights. Having followed our most optimistic schedule to the day, and having no good excuses for not continuing, it seemed inevitable that we should actually get on with the climb.

Starting out the next morning was as difficult as always. Visions of the comforts of home, and the relative ease with which they might be obtained, always intrude on my thoughts during the first few days of a big climb. Fear of the unknown, uncertainty about how I might perform, the nagging questions about weather, illness, if we've brought enough food, all conspire to pull me back to the safety of Base Camp.

But there is always that little demon inside, wondering what might be ahead, prodding me to go a little higher, to see what's around the next corner. All too soon, any potential descent becomes far more problematic than continuing on. At that point, doubts and fears vanish—there is no room for them in a life that, temporarily at least, is reduced to those activities directly related to climbing.

Because of the shortness of the winter days, one of us would awake early and start the lengthy process of brewing up in the cold, dark hours before daybreak. We rotated this thankless task each day so that the other could enjoy the luxury of uninterrupted sleep. The sun usually arrived just as we were ready to emerge from the tent, fully clothed and ready for the day's work.

We never had more than four hours of direct sun before the shadow of the east ridge on our left plunged the face into intense cold. Although tolerable for the first two days, the shadowed afternoons became increasingly bitter as we

gained elevation. Toes and fingers required constant attention to prevent frost-bite. We could seldom climb more than eight hours a day, and would always search for the night's camp well before dark.

Setting up a bivouac in these arctic conditions was a race against the even colder nighttime temperatures to come. An hour of digging a platform out of the soft snow usually sufficed. One night we had to chip away at the ice of a sérac for five hours to make enough space, finally crawling exhausted into the tent at ten P.M. Three or four hours of melting snow, eating, and rearranging socks, hats, gloves, cameras, water bottles, pee bottles, food bags, and all the other paraphernalia of a winter ascent followed. Eventually, we would fall into a state of semiconsciousness until the alarm watch awoke him whose duty it was to start the next day.

These nightly eternities were not without their humorous moments. The most amusing, at least for me, was awakening momentarily at 20,000 feet to hear Carlos fumbling about in his sleeping bag, cursing everything holy on this earth. I quickly dozed off, wanting no part of whatever problem he might be having. When I queried him the next morning, he sheepishly admitted that he had woken up with an urgent need to urinate, but had only done half the job into his pee bottle before falling back asleep, thus dousing himself, his clothing, and his sleeping bag. Miraculously enough, the half-filled one-liter bottle remained upright between his legs until he awoke some time later. Suffice it to say that modern synthetics, noted for their wicking properties, worked well.

The route was entirely on snow and proved surprisingly sustained and difficult. For a medium which most climbers regard as boring, snow displays an incredible variety of form, texture, and consistency. And the techniques required, while perhaps not as elegant or as artistic as those on rock, are never-theless complex and engaging in their own right.

A good example is 5.10 snow. Usually found plastered over a hopefully-short band of steep rock, it generally has the consistency of wet sugar. Modern tools, for all their advantages on steep ice, are of absolutely no use here. The preferred method is to punch the hands as far down into the snow as possible. The feet then are used to pack down a nebulous platform on which to stand. Distributing his weight as evenly as possible over all four appendages, as well as any other part of the body coming into contact with this repellent surface, the climber progresses by a combination of delicate balance moves and dynamic readjustments as holds collapse unexpectedly. Since the underlying rock is often smooth or completely rotten, protection is usually far below at the belay, which may not be any good itself. Having surmounted such a pitch, sinking tools into 165 feet of perfect, vertical styrofoam ice is pure pleasure—a simple technical trick, spectacular but not particularly demanding. There was a savage joy in this sort of climbing, a feeling of light, quick flowing across steep, hollow onion skins of ice, thousands of feet below and the sky a blue vault above. At times, I wanted the climb to be longer, harder. Everest, Lhotse, Nuptse, and Makalu towered close at hand, and Kanchenjunga winked out in the hazy distance. Each rope-length was a challenge, but what more satisfying toil could we ask for?

PLATE 13

Photo by Michael Kennedy

AMA DABLAM. Buhler on thin-ice traverse at 21,000 feet.

Most of the climbing on Ama Dablam's northeast face wasn't at these extremes. It started with three pitches of very steep ice, tucked in the back of a gash in the lower rockband. Anything that fell from the upper part of the face would funnel directly through the gash—fortunately, nothing came down. Above this, we followed a crest of snow flutings in the center of the face as it slowly steepened and eventually faded out several hundred feet below the sérac barrier.

Here, another three pitches of steep ice led to our most spectacular bivouac, atop a fin of ice next to the upper rockband. A short step of rotten rock forced a traverse right for most of a rope-length on thin ice over rock. More thin ice gained us a cramped tent site below a sérac, followed by easier ground to the big sérac barrier at 21,500 feet. Weaving through this, we encountered a final spectacular pitch, with the Nuptse-Lhotse wall and Everest spread out in the background, before reaching the easy snow slopes above the séracs and a final windy bivouac at almost 22,000 feet.

The final morning was as cold as any I've yet encountered. Despite the most perfectly clear day imaginable, the wind was raging around the north ridge, and it was all we could do to stave off frostbite. A few tea bags and half a gas cylinder were all that remained of our supplies, but fatigue made the packs seem as heavy as when we'd started up the last few hundred feet of the north ridge.

The summit itself was almost anticlimatic. The wind had died to a whisper when we arrived at ten A.M. greeted by a patch of flat snow the size of a football field and a cloudless panorama of the Himalaya stretching as far as the eye could see. We were happy to have put the pieces of this particular puzzle together, and after 45 minutes on top, wearily turned our thoughts homeward.

With many fixed ropes still in place from ascents earlier in the fall, the descent of the southwest ridge was uneventful. We arrived at the bottom well after dark, having lost over 5000 feet in elevation, and stayed in the tents of the New Zealanders attempting a winter ascent of that route.

There had been much soul-destroying wading through soft snow, and every variety of ice imaginable. Tools were dulled by intimate contact with rock, ice screws were dropped, precious water was spilled over an already food-encrusted sleeping bag. A careless step ripped the tent. The food was adequate, if not exciting. Shoulders ached from too-heavy packs, and insufficiently-large lungs wheezed in the cold, dry air.

Summary of Statistics:

AREA: Mahalangur, Himal, Nepal.

NEW ROUTE: Ama Dablam, 6812 meters, 22,350 feet, via Northeast Face, December 1 to 7, 1985 (Carlos Buhler, Michael Kennedy).

Kangtega's Northeast Buttress

JAY SMITH

MY OVERBOOTS WERE rapidly disintegrating before my eyes. No matter how I kicked and stomped, no warmth was generated to thaw the freezing Lincoln Logs where my toes were supposed to be.

"My goddamn toes are freezing! I won't have them for another route if you don't do something bloody quick." But Wally was engaged in his own life-threatening battle, 130 feet out from his only piece of protection: a number-three wire lodged between a quartz crystal and a snow flake. The rope vibrated in space, the final frontier which he had no inclination to explore. But my words never reached him, lost in a barrage of snow and ice that exploded endlessly around Mark and me.

Mark had plastered himself against a towering snow mushroom, the last relatively sheltered spot before my exposed belay. Twenty feet from my stance, he was desperately trying to cram his six-foot-two frame under a ten-inch brim.

"Can I jümar?" was just audible from Craig below. Much verbal abuse and an unquestionable "No" were the response. We told Craig to sit tight but understood his impatience, having been in the same situation many times during the past week: shivering at a stance while the action above moved at a snail's pace.

It was our seventh day on Kangtega's northeast buttress and the summit seemed light-years away. How far *were* we from the summit plateau? It could be only a few nightmare pitches above. However, our limited view from the depths of the couloir was keeping us in the dark in more ways than one.

We had had to make a critical decision at the previous belay which Craig still occupied. The couloir we had been following since noon yesterday was the key to the summit. Its 1500-foot length had seemed to make a beautiful 65° straight shot to the top. However, the gully now forked, twisted and steepened with its walls closing in on us. The right branch continued directly above, but appeared blocked by overhanging rock headwalls, bordered by huge cotton-candy towers. Wally's "premonition" that the hidden left fork was the line of least resistance was rapidly becoming more questionable.

The left fork curved out of view after 100 feet but it headed in the right direction: up. The climbing was again on plastic, blue ice, just as it had been for the last 650 feet. Full rope runouts led to whatever belay anchors were available.

41

PLATE 14

Photo by Mark Hesse
KANGTEGA'S Northeast Buttress.

The passage above involved spectacular chimneying between a vertical rock wall and the overhanging ice cliff on its right margin. Wally had negotiated the corner with the enthusiasm of a Great Dane chasing a female in heat, but he was now desperately wallowing in the snow overhangs at the chimney's top. I was hoping he would send down some encouragement from above, but all he sent down was more snow and ice with an occasional rock.

*   *   *   *

Our first day on the route had gone quite smoothly. We all soloed the easy snow slopes and short rock sections until a small roof and chimney forced us to tie in. Above, Mark and Craig began carving tent platforms on the arête proper while Wally and I started work on the first headwall: 250 feet of mixed free and aid climbing on excellent granite. Near dark, we descended and crawled into the tent for the night.

The second day we made slow progress after a late start, climbing only five pitches. Two were traverses that linked up weaknesses in the rock bands. We needed to get moving earlier in the morning. The sun left the face at noon and progress slowed in the afternoon's deep freeze.

It took hours to melt even the most meager amount of water. Knowing the importance of fluid consumption, we had to start brewing at 3:30 A.M. By 6:30 we had exhausted our fuel ration with two tepid brews and a half cup of slightly saturated Wheat Hearts.

One team would swap leads while the other would get a leisurely start and then come up to the belay to moan about slow progress. As darkness came upon us, we would hack ice into the night until the tents were up. Then another three-hour brewing session would commence.

Days three, four and five were very much the same: excellent climbing on deep snow, rotten ice and superior rock. Once we three were hanging in a belay while Craig led onto the sidewall of the gully above. All we could see were the power strokes of his tools, his feet wildly kicking and the continuous river of snow pouring out from the canal he was digging. He finally gained what looked like a broad, easy snow slope. Why was he going so slowly? It looked nearly flat compared with what he had just climbed.

"How much rope?" he shouted.

"You're almost out."

"Tie another one on. I need fifty feet more."

Soon he was at the fourth and final rock headwall and banged in three knife-blades for the belay. "Tomorrow we'll gain the great couloir. It will be a cruise. We'll be on top before we know it." But things aren't always what they seem. His "easy-angle" pitch turned out to be overhanging with the last sixty feet treading a dragon's back. It was an impressive lead up a snow fin so thin and steep that you'd swear the wind would have blown it away years ago. Not only that, but it was home for the night. After hours of hacking, the tents still overhung the void.

Difficult mixed climbing on the final rock headwall consumed half the next day and brought us to the "Land of the Shrooms."

*   *   *   *

Wally led another difficult mixed pitch in an attempt to traverse to the huge couloir. Yet all we were doing was weaving between towering conglomerates of whipped cream into which you sank until nothing was visible but a trough with a rope leading out. You had to climb the deep gullies that came and went between them.

He reluctantly belayed me up while carefully explaining the consequences of a fall. Suddenly, both my tools ripped. I started to pitch off backwards but my pack bumped the wall to my left and I somehow maintained my balance on my frontpoints. It was desperate with a pack, but the winding nature of the route and the unconsolidated snow did not allow the luxury of hauling.

Upon reaching his belay, I instantly saw why he had been so concerned. I began searching for a "real" anchor before we both departed from the mountain-side. "How does it look up and right?" I asked.

"It drops off 3000 feet down the north face."

"Oh!"

"How about traversing over to that ledge, that little crease in the mush-room?"

"O.K. I'll check it out, but I need a better belay."

"I've got this screw in. See?" and he pulled it out to show me.

With a little excavating I discovered a somewhat consolidated pillar two feet in diameter consisting of mostly oxygen-starved air. I wrapped an aider around it, clipped in and began a belly-crawl across to the "ledge." Luckily, a singular patch of ice lay just beyond and slightly above the next overlap of snow. With two solid thunks of my tools, I cut my feet loose and cranked over the snow roof and onto the narrow fluting thirty feet above Wally. This was the only possible bivouac site.

I was back on the prow, perched on top of a shroom with the route above consisting of snow fins overhanging the north face. To the left, flutings dipped a hundred feet into the next gully before jutting back into the darkening sky. I peeked out over the edge to the right. An icy blast of spindrift flew up and tore at my face. The Hinku Glacier, miles below in the void, was still and lifeless. I began tunneling into the snow to find anything solid. Anything! Anything that even closely resembled a firm consistency. Twenty minutes later, I had two pickets equalized in the back of a four-foot cave. Still not trusting the anchors, I had Wally jümar off my waist.

We had a terrible time of it. The rope sliced into the mushroom, pouring a steady stream of snow into his face. Every time he moved, he created an even larger roof to overcome. Finally he carved a deep trough ending under the points of my crampons. By the time he arrived, it was dark. We immediately began hacking out a platform.

PLATE 15

Photo by Jay Smith

Mark Hesse on KANGTEGA'S Northeast Buttress.

Craig and Mark 185 feet below had exhausted all possibilities for a bivy site. Craig seemed content just to sit out the night on his pack, but Mark would have nothing to do with it.

"Can we come up now?"

"Wait! Let me work on the anchors." Fifteen minutes later, I had a third picket in and all three equalized. I was hesitant to allow them to trust it, but we had no choice. Down there they would freeze to death. "O.K. You can jümar."

It wasn't till morning that I heard they had both jümared on the rope together. Forty feet up, Craig's headlamp battery kissed him goodbye; Mark's crampon fell loose four times. With the protection removed, they spun wildly in space with tons of snow pouring down. They didn't arrive until nearly ten o'clock, having been in the dark for almost four hours. Another hour was spent chipping a ledge and a second preparing a brew. This was their second night without a meal.

Craig mentioned rappelling off. I could understand his point of view. We had brought only enough food and fuel for six days, supposedly stretchable to ten. It was now the morning of the fifth and our remaining food could be carried in a one-quart ziplock. The fuel situation was even grimmer.

But there was no way that we were going to give up yet. In 1985 I had to turn back from a summit attempt on Mount Everest's direct west ridge because of my partner's failing oxygen equipment. Mark and Wally had similar Himalayan experiences in 1985. Wally was forced to abandon an attempt on Gangapurna's north face due to deep snow, avalanche hazard and high winds, while Mark was nearly blown off Dhaulagiri by the jet stream. The three of us were dangerously determined to bag a Himalayan summit and the closest one was looming somewhere overhead. After a brief discussion, Craig grabbed the rope and put Mark on belay. Nothing more was ever said.

After an eternity, Wally completed the chimney pitch and we all came up to join him. I led one last wild section through more cream rolls, surmounting a three-foot roof with my arms driven in to the shoulders. We had completed the buttress and an easy-angled slope led to the summit plateau. By six o'clock we were all stamping platforms in deep powder only a few hundred feet below the summit. Everest, Lhotse and Makalu still bathed in the sun's last rays. We downed our last meal, consisting of whatever was left in the corners of our food sack.

During the night the winds picked up and buffeted our little tents. By dawn our bags were soaked, but at least the winds appeared to be abating. We hadn't bothered to scrape out last night's pots and had to drink a half cup of a concoction of cocoa, shrimp, coffee and noodles. With that, we broke camp and waded through deep snow toward the summit.

After two hours of breaking trail alternately, we reached a point just short of the top where we could drop our packs and pick them up on the descent. Craig decided to call it quits. He felt it would be better to save what little energy he had left for the descent. We three kept on and a half hour later we were yelling and screaming on the wind-swept summit. Our cries of joy were heard a mile and a half away by my girlfriend Jo, who had been watching our progress for the last eight days.

We descended the southeast glacier in six hours and were back in Base Camp before dark, much to our surprise. We stuffed ourselves with crab hors d'oeuvre and other assorted goodies and indulged ourselves in our very adequate liquor supply. By eleven we stretched out with the pride of knowing we had completed the most demanding climb of our lives.

Summary of Statistics:

AREA: Khumbu Himalaya, Nepal.

NEW ROUTE: Kangtega, 6779 meters or 22,241 feet, first ascent of the Northeast Buttress, first traverse of the mountain, alpine-style, October 22 to 29, 1986.

PERSONNEL: Jay Smith, leader, Mark Hesse, Craig Reason, Paul (Wally) Teare.

The Last Unclimbed Peak

Leigh N. Ortenburger

CLIMBING HISTORY is not a subject that appeals to everyone. Many mountaineers are content in their climbs of today, without a need to reflect on where such climbs fit into the larger picture defined not only by the important dimensions of difficulty and style, but also by the less tangible scale of time. This brief article quarrels not with their approach, but provides from a broader outlook an overview of climbing in one region.

Every activity, be it science or art or climbing, is necessarily confined to the environment of the time in which it is practiced. Progress is made, but, with rare exceptions, it is achieved incrementally. Bold new strokes, where man has never gone before, are made, but not by most of the practicing artists or scientists or mountaineers. There is a wide variation in how we perceive our individual relation to what has gone before. Some climbers are sure that their knowledge and skills are purely the product of their own capabilities. Others are more appreciative of the contributions that the pioneers have made. These pioneers have advanced in various dimensions of mountaineering, such as simple mental courage to penetrate the unknown, or climbing equipment, or technical climbing skills. But each made his mark within the confines of his time.

Mountaineering evolution may be analyzed and clearly displayed within single regions, such as the Teton range in Wyoming. Here is a compact and spectacular mountain group apparently holding considerable challenge. Two centuries ago such a challenge was probably not perceived by the first passersby, the indigenous Indians of the region. Yet their culture did apparently contribute to the first Teton climb of which there is a record, that of the Enclosure, the western sub-summit of the Grand Teton. One sees this impressive accomplishment not so much as an acceptance of the basic challenge of the high places, but as an esthetic selection of a religious site. Nor did the fur trappers of the first half of the nineteenth century respond to the latent challenge of the Teton peaks. We find no record in this era of any mountaineering in the Tetons beyond the simple crossings of easy passes.

This lack of interest in the high mountains carried over to the first generation of settlers who arrived in the adjacent valleys during the last half of the century. To engage in the foolishness of mountain climbing requires both the opportunity and the right frame of mind. The first groups to satisfy both of these requirements were the government reconnaissance expeditions which penetrated the Teton region as early as 1859. The scientific curiosity brought west by these

PLATE 16

Photo by Leigh N. Ortenburger

Last Unclimbed Peak in the Tetons, Wyoming, from the Southeast.

exploring expeditions culminated in 1872 with the first substantial (and publicized) set of important climbs in the range. The attempted climb—or ascent as the case may be—of the Grand Teton by Langford and Stevenson initiated the era of pioneering exploration, soon to be followed in 1877 and 1878 by subsequent Hayden expeditions whose members reached several of the easy sedimentary peaks along the western slopes.

The attraction of the highest peak in the range was accepted and met in 1898 by the indefatigable William Owen who, after attempts in two previous years and aided by the crucial technical skills of Franklin Spalding, succeeded in reaching the summit of the Grand Teton. This reknowned ascent, curiously enough, failed to encourage other explorations. Almost a quarter century passed before any extensive additional climbing took place.

The need, not of local origin, for mapping of the region led to the arrival of surveyors and their paraphernalia in the 1880s and 1890s; they reached a handful of additional summits, easy peaks in the north and south ends of the range. The single major exception was the climb of Buck Mountain in 1898 by the topographer Bannon and his assistant. With completion of Bannon's efforts at the start of the twentieth century, full knowledge of the mountains and canyons of the Teton range could be claimed, since a detailed quadrangle map had been produced by application of the instruments of science. What more could be required? There was little or no need for any further efforts by man in the Teton mountains.

But civilization was moving forward. In fifty years from 1875 to 1925 the population of Wyoming and adjacent states was growing, becoming sufficiently large and affluent to contain a small number of enterprising individuals who saw in the mountains not only physical challenges but a splendid region full of beauty and wonder. In 1912 the Colorado Mountain Club was formed by a group of such visionary climbers. Mountain climbing in the American west was finally being done for its own sake and did not have to be scientifically or economically justified. This was an extremely important, but unwitting, conceptual breakthrough, a release from the past bondage of practicality.

Much mountaineering progress was being made in the Colorado Rockies during those years. The early climb by the enthusiast LeRoy Jeffers of the north summit of Mount Moran in 1919 diverted some attention from Colorado to the distant and remote Tetons. The decade from 1922 to 1931 was to be the primary period of magnificent pioneering by the most important Teton explorers and climbers. The main summit of Mount Moran fell in 1922 and the next year the outstanding Colorado mountaineer, A. R. Ellingwood, and his group made the much publicized third ascent of the Grand Teton, reaching the summits of both the South and the Middle Tetons as well. These were watershed climbs that brought awareness of this spectacular region to the American public.

The major event in attracting attention of the mountaineers of the United States to these splendid peaks was the establishment of the Grand Teton National Park in 1929. A few years before that political act with unexpected mountaineering consequences, the two great Teton pioneers were already on the scene, having come out of their own inner motivations to see the range. Fritiof Fryxell and Phil Smith had in common the love of the mountain scene, the curiosity to know its secrets, and the energy and ability to reach hitherto unknown places. Between them most of the major Teton summits were attained, including the first-rank peaks of Wister, Nez Perce, Cloudveil Dome, Disappointment, Teewinot, Symmetry Spire, St. John, Rockchuck, Woodring, East Horn, and Bivouac. In all they reached 18 new summits, an extraordinary and unrepeatable accomplishment. The considerable technical skills of Underhill and Henderson were essential in 1930 to the conquest of Mount Owen, the last major summit, and the pinnacle of Teepe's Pillar. Petzoldt, as professional guide, found two new peaks, while surveyors reached three new high points in the north end.

The next decade leading to World War II, while providing numerous first ascents, did not see much climbing that was both new and difficult. Nearly two dozen new high points were attained in 1934 and 1935 by the surveying team that produced the topographic map of the national park, but these were all technically easy ascents. Fryxell and Smith, still active, found no records on the summits of Prospectors, Veiled, Rolling Thunder, and Eagles Rest. The sharp eye of Fred Ayres sought out such prizes as Icecream Cone, West Horn, Traverse Peak, and several towers above Hanging Canyon including Rock of Ages. The remote and attractive Cleaver Peak was the last new peak ascended before the war reinstated the priority of practicality.

The notion that there was lasting significance associated with first ascents rose to the top of climbers' minds in the two decades following the war. This led to a rather methodical elimination of all obviously unclimbed peaks and pinnacles, some of which were genuinely difficult and had been either deliberately avoided by pre-war climbers, or had been the subject of failed attempts. This era finally saw the end to unclimbed pinnacles above Hanging Canyon (1954), about Mount Moran (1957), and the Grand Teton (1957). A dozen or more remote but easy sedimentary peaks were also accounted for in this productive period. Of all of these climbs—almost four dozen in all—serious difficulty, for the time, was found only in the pinnacles such as Red Sentinel, Hangover, Baxter's, Schoolhouse, Okie's Thorn, Second Tower, Rabbit Ears, Camel's Head, and Unsoeld's Needle. Teton climbing in the 1960s provided few surprises in new ascents. The last of the unclimbed high points in the south and north ends of the range were visited. Only Matternaught Peak and Fourteen Hour Pinnacle seem important from the current vantage point.

Thus the last two decades were entered with the unspoken belief that the Tetons were finished as a source of first ascents. Certainly the primary thrust of significant climbing had long since been in the search of new routes, not unclimbed peaks. On rare occasions small unclimbed towers were found in the canyons of Granite, Avalanche, and even Cascade; a few were, indeed, of serious difficulty. The last of these, a substantial pinnacle not far from the mouth of Cascade Canyon, was not found and climbed (F9, A1) until September of 1984. But the game appeared to be over.

Not so. This past summer a minor peak was recognized simultaneously by two veteran Teton climbers as probably unclimbed. And so it was. Rising directly above the west shore of Grizzly Bear Lake, not far from the well used trail of Indian Paintbrush Canyon, are cliffs guarding a summit that remained unclimbed until July 29, 1986. It was found to have no easy way to the summit; three pitches, one F7, were required to reach the virgin summit. Some sixty years after Ellingwood's first visit, the exploration of the Teton range,—"a practically inexhaustible studio for the mountaineer"—was finally completed. The climb of last summer combined with detailed knowledge accumulated through the past century, permits the statement that the end of the first-ascent era is at hand. There are no more.

This historical event for the Tetons raises the intriguing question of where else is there a climbing record sufficiently complete to show that no unclimbed point remains? It seems fair to presume that the Alps passed this threshold many years ago. But can this be said for the other American ranges? Has every point in Colorado now been reached? Have all the peaks and towers of the Cascades been climbed? Has someone stood on top of all the mountains and pinnacles of the Sierra Nevada? What about the ranges of Montana, Idaho, South Dakota, Nevada, Utah, New Mexico, Arizona? Are there unclimbed points anywhere?

When will the last unclimbed peak be taken? All are fascinating questions, but perhaps of only academic interest. Questions such as these may well be of significance only to those knowledgeable in mountaineering history. As was observed at the beginning, not all climbers have this interest. But for those who still feel driven to find new places, the expanses of Canada and Alaska must surely contain a good supply of summits yet unreached. And the Andes, the Karakoram, the Himalaya should all provide source material well into the next century. The game will surely continue but the court changes.

Summary of Statistics:

AREA: Teton Range.

FIRST ASCENT: Peak 10,080+, via west face and north ridge, on July 29, 1986 (Tom Kimbrough and Leigh Ortenburger).

Same Board, Different Rules

MICHAEL KENNEDY *and* JOHN STEIGER

"Gee, in the old days people used aid to make things easier, nowadays they use aid to make things harder."

— *Juanita Donini, comment on the debate*

ROCK CLIMBING in the U.S. has been in a state of flux over the past several years. European climbers, particularly the French with their very high standards of gymnastic rock climbing, have had great influence on the methods deemed acceptable in this country for pioneering new routes. Both in print and through their actions on the crags, America's leading climbers have also sought to influence the direction of U.S. free climbing as we move into the latter half of the decade.

There appear to be two conflicting areas of style in the country today. In *traditional style,* the climber starts from the bottom of the proposed route, with the eventual goal of free climbing to the top without falling. When falls are taken, the leader typically lowers to the ground or to a no-hands or similarly-relaxed stance, commonly leaving the rope through the last piece of protection. This is known as *yo-yoing.* All protection is placed on lead.

Similarly, the goal in *French style* is to free climb the route from the bottom to the top with no falls. However, anything goes to figure out the moves. This includes inspecting the proposed route from rappel, placing fixed protection from rappel, and rehearsing.

Rehearsing may be from a toprope or on lead. Lead rehearsal is often referred to as *hangdogging,* which denotes using direct aid or the rope to rest while figuring out individual moves or sequences. The final ascent, where the leader climbs the route from the bottom to the top without weighting the rope or any protection, and commonly placing and clipping all non-fixed protection, is known as a *redpoint* ascent.

Several other terms are being widely used to differentiate style, primarily for repeat ascents. *A vue* or *on-sight* denotes absolutely no prior knowledge of the route. *First try* implies that a previous attempt by another climber has given the leader crucial move information.

The term *flash,* originally coined by Jim Bridwell in an early issue of *Mountain,* has been used to describe both on-sight and first try ascents. Most climbers now use *on-sight flash* to describe what all styles view as a perfect ascent: on-sight, with no falls.

In an effort to promote a reasonable dialogue on this subject, the American Alpine Club sponsored "The Great Debate (Or, Is 5.14 Worth It?)", which took place last December during the 84th Annual Meeting in Denver. This was certainly a political coup for the Club, but as could have been expected, nothing was resolved. Perhaps a more appropriate title would have been "Great Opinions—For Those Who Don't Know Already, Or Can't Guess."

Still, it was impressive to have John Bachar, Henry Barber, Christian Griffith, Lynn Hill, Ron Kauk, Rob Robinson, Todd Skinner, Randy Vogel, and Alan Watts sitting together at the same table, having an amiable discussion on rock climbing's "new style"—namely, bolting on rappel and hangdogging.

The debate turned out to be a loose-knit slinging of ideals rather than a point-by-point analysis. Not surprisingly, the 400-strong audience displayed a clear preference for the traditionalist side of the table, and the out-manned "eurodogs" (a term coined by Russ Raffa and Lynn Hill earlier in the day) seemed destined to be overwhelmed during the question-answer period following each panelist's statement of position. Nevertheless, all concerned held their positions well, first through a pointed, one-by-one grilling by AAC President Jim McCarthy, and later through questioning by the audience.

Clearly, no side "won," but the points raised appear to have summed up virtually all the concerns voiced throughout the country, as European tactics are slowly but surely becoming accepted, and traditionalists struggle to maintain "The Way."

Issues of climbing style reflected the broadest range of opinion, although most seemed to agree that style is a personal matter. Tactics such as hangdogging, previewing on rappel, and toprope rehearsal were wholeheartedly embraced by Griffith, Skinner and Alan Watts, who was perhaps the most eloquent spokesman for these neoeuropean traditions:

"Personally, I am strongly a proponent of European tactics. Hangdogging is essential to acquire the skills necessary to succeed on today's hardest climbs. Traditional tactics, as commendable as they are, simply are not a means to succeed on 5.14.

"Many critics of European tactics feel that high numbers are not everything—they point to adventure, danger, and inner growth as vital components of the sport. Indeed, numbers are not everything, but difficulty has always been an important part of climbing tradition.

"The Europeans are way ahead of us in the free climbing game. The world's hardest routes, the boldest solos, and the most remarkable flashes have all been accomplished by Europeans. Throughout the 1960's and 1970's, the U.S. was on top of the rock-climbing world, and I've always been proud of this. Frankly, it bothers me when I hear the top French climbers referring to U.S. climbing as a 'myth.' The only way for us to improve enough to climb their hardest routes is to adopt their style.

"Climbing the hardest routes is not important to everyone, and there's no reason why it should be. But for those of us who have made it our goal to put the

U.S. on top again, the path to take is clear. Among these individuals, there is no debate."

In sharp contrast, Bachar, Barber and Kauk took the strongest stands against these European tactics. Henry Barber disagreed with the importance Watts put on competing in the international climbing arena:

"I don't really see climbing as competition. I see climbing as an activity that is sensitive to the environment. It's an activity in which we can develop ethics and style, and where we can develop long-lasting friendships, experiences, and camraderie.

"I've been climbing for 18 years, I've been fortunate to travel all over, and I have a really good feel for the history of rock climbing throughout the world. I have never used Friends for protection. I don't hangdog, I don't toprope. I rely on doing a lot of climbing with a lot less.

"Since 1975, when confronted with a possible fall, I've either downclimbed to a restpoint or to the belay, and then started back up. In the event of a fall, or if I have to be lowered to a restpoint or the belay, I go down and pull the rope back through.

"I think that style matters in life. I think that tomorrow is another day. We should leave some of these gems of climbs and real challenges for climbers who will be really inspired to do them in the best possible style."

Hill, Robinson, and Vogel all took a more moderate position on matters of style, primarily from the viewpoint that differences in style do not affect others directly. Rob Robinson, speaking about the relatively-recent development of the Southeastern Sanstone Belt, summed up the attitudes of many:

"The South is a sanctuary where climbers could care less whether you are a eurodogger, redpointer, or believe that the earth is flat. It is enough that you are a climber who shares in the spirit, power, and aesthetics that guide us in our dream-like existence in the vertical world. That you love the sport is, in the final analysis, enough for us.

Lynn Hill commented, "With my background as a gymnast, I view hang-dogging as a technique for training, not climbing. Clearly, it has produced some very hard routes. I don't see anything wrong with it—it doesn't hurt anyone else."

Vogel continued along the same lines: "Hangdogging and previewing may erode a climber's personal integrity, but once that person is gone, I can still experience the rock the way it was before."

This statement reflected the stand-off on style very concisely. Although most of the panelists felt that other's style didn't interfere in their own climbing, they were quick to criticize. Either the others weren't climbing as hard because they were too attached to an antiquated style or the others weren't reaping the full benefits of experience because they were adopting styles with no basis in adventure.

Comparing the two styles is difficult, to say the least. To Robinson, the question that sums it up is, "What is harder, doing a 5.12c/d on-sight in traditional style, or doing a 5.14 hangdog?" This feeling that higher numbers don't

represent a higher quality of experience is a point well taken by climbers of all standards, 5.4 to 5.14. Traditionalists maintained that the traditional quality of experience is higher, as can be seen by Kauk's statement: "To truly raise the standards of freeclimbing, you can't sacrifice style or purity for a higher number."

Issues concerning climbing ethics elicited far more disagreement. Even the definition of the term seemed hard to pin down: do ethics involve only the physical alteration of the rock, or do ethics include actions which infringe upon the rights of others? Or both?

Probably the biggest area of contention centered around the gray area where personal style and community ethics overlap, very specifically the practice of placing bolts on rappel. Todd Skinner summed up the essential new-wave argument: "Ethically, drilling bolts on the lead, bolts however they are drilled, it doesn't matter. The performance is the end."

Watts again brought the place of the American climber in the world scene to the forefront: "Bolting on rappel is the only way to protect (these) futuristic routes. Denying the validity of hangdogging and pre-placing bolts closes one's eyes to one of the best tools available to improve. Simply put, (these tactics) allow a climber to do a hard route faster, and I feel that the more hard routes you do, the better climber you will be. Time is spent facing new challenges, rather than wiring the same old problem. But if this fails to convince you, I suggest a trip to Smith Rock to attempt America's first 5.14, the Sunshine Wall, a route recently pioneered by Frenchman J. B. Tribout. This one route does more to show the benefits of European tactics than any amount of debate."

In contrast, John Bachar summed up the traditionalist's argument that routes should be started from the ground: "I don't really believe bolts should be placed on rappel—it offends the guys who are out to do first ascents (from the ground up). I travel around looking for virgin rock; I'm looking for gymnastically-difficult stuff. But I like to do it on the lead. I don't know anything about it; I'm up there pushing gymnastics; I'm trying to put it all together for that first ascent.

"For example, I've worked on routes before, fallen off, gotten hurt, then came back to find that some guy put bolts in on rappel and did the 'first ascent.' It seems that he copped out on the challenge by walking around the back. I would have more respect if the guy drilled a bolt ladder and freed it—at least he faced up to the fact that he had to climb the route.

"Another reason for not bolting on rappel is that after someone has toproped it, the bolts might be too far apart for someone to attempt it on-sight. For example, if I got into this business of placing bolts on rappel after toproping, I could produce some death routes.

"Should I expect a person to walk up and climb something on-sight, after I had it thoroughly wired? That would be unfair. So the only way to bolt is on the lead, on-sight, without prior knowledge of the route. And if you can't do it, leave it for someone else."

And what of the difference between bolts placed on hooks and those placed on rappel? Although Bachar acknowledged that a bolt placed on hook is aid, the similarities stop there. "The big difference is whether or not you start from the ground. A lot of these new routes placed on rappel are really abstract, in the sense that the methods used have no practical sense in the world of alpinism. Placing a bolt on rappel is not a choice in the mountains."

Randy Vogel sees an analogy between what industry is doing to the environment and what the current trend of placing bolts on rappel is doing to the rock. "The oil industry is saying, 'We need to exploit our environment so we can insure our great status as a nation, do what ever it takes to stay ahead.' They're looking at the short term, not the long term."

This theme, that first ascentionists who place bolts on rappel are depleting the potential for first ascents too quickly, was echoed by Robinson. "Too me it looks like they the Europeans are burning the rock reserves up. They're not going to have anything left."

Henry Barber added an interesting tack to the traditionalist argument, invoking the name of diversity. "I really don't want to tell people how to climb, but I really believe that when you are in Rome, you do as the Romans do—and I don't want to build Rome here. I want to go to Rome, I want to travel all over the world and experience the different types of climbing available in different areas. I don't want to make it all the same."

Lynn Hill took perhaps the most moderate position on the issue of rappel-placed bolts. "I don't look down on people who place bolts. There are obviously different types of rock, limestone in France, welded tuff in Smith Rocks, and I have enjoyed doing routes that have been bolted on rappel. . . . Each area is unique and it is the responsibility of the local climbers to organize themselves and decide what should be done."

Certainly, this deference to local practice weaved through many of the panelists' comments. Not surprisingly, the question of community enforcement, namely chopping bolts, soon came up.

If there was a unanimous agreement on anything, it was on manufacturing holds. Virtually every panelist denounced this practice, despite style. Griffith, who apparently embraced the concept in his opinion article "Manifesto" *(Climbing* no. 98), addressed McCarthy's query on the issue: "Most people up here consider chipping holds as being completely disadvantageous. I really agree with that right now." He further qualified his position by stating, "I consider extreme difficulty as being relatively unnatural. You have to have just enough that you can climb it but not so much that it is easy, and the variation in between is very, very limited. There may come a time when there isn't a natural place for a 5.15, or 5.16."

Others were far more vocal on this issue. Skinner stated that manufacturing holds is where the quest for ultimate difficulty ceases. "That is the point where you admit the route is too hard for you." Vogel summed up the traditionalist's argument against alteration of the rock itself: "People think, 'Well, nobody really chops holds,' but there are some very revered climbers who have been known to participate in this activity. What those climbers were saying is that they were the best climbers in the world, and that nobody would ever be any better.

"People are justifying what they're doing because of the extreme level of climbing they're participating in. They're doing a 5.13, therefore it is justifiable to do something a little quasi-ethical. However, five or ten years from now, dozens of people will be doing 5.13's every day—to think otherwise is very naïve."

Bachar reiterated the idea of leaving the rock intact for future generations, pointing out that in Buoux, "Chiseling is commonplace. Some 7c's that were the hardest routes of the time were chiseled, manufactured to make them go. Now 7c's are commonplace, and they're looking for 8b's and 8c's to do. They had them—they chiseled them to make the 7c's—and now the new 8b's are (being) manufactured."

Another area of agreement was on the need for communication and honesty in reporting new routes. A concensus to respect local traditions was also reached, although tradition is subject to change. Watts pointed out: "Change is inevitable. When a majority of the local climbers in each area decide it's time for a transition, then change will occur, despite tradition. Change, as much as anything, is what tradition in climbing is about."

Clearly, every panelist came to the podium hoping to explain their position and sway attitudes. Equally clear, however, was the feeling of community as the panelists lined up for photographs shortly after. Barber's closing remark seemed to be dead-center on the proverbial nail:

"Together, the old chumsters like me and these guys today, we can all walk away from here talking the same language even though we don't agree. I think this is really where the future of the sport lies."

Lost in America*

GREG CHILD

NIGHT HAD FALLEN. Randy Leavitt and I were high on the overhanging east face of El Capitan, at the end of a new route, setting up our last hanging bivouac. Behind us lay nine days of difficult climbing and 2700 feet of granite. As I sat on my porta-ledge I chanced to look over my shoulder.

"Christ! Look!"

Leavitt turned toward an exploding sky. In the west two white-hot pinpoints of light traversed the heavens, heading east. In their wake a silver tail trailed off for dozens of miles before dissipating to a lingering evanescent blue against the mauve dusk. The dots climbed into the upper atmosphere, then vanished, leaving ghostly contrails. It was an eerie conclusion to our climb.

"What the hell was that?"

Speculations: Comet, UFO, ICBM, WW3, LA and San Francisco up in smoke. We scanned the skies for mushroom clouds.

"What a pity to be vaporised now, just as we're about to finish. Maybe we'd be the only survivors. We'd reach the top on scorched ropes and stumble out of the valley onto the plains. Cars melted to roads, roads glazed to earth. Nowhere to go, nothing to do, no one to give a damn about our climb. We'd be lost in America."

Later we would learn that this was a test of a Tomahawk Missile, self destructing in a ball of flame, but on that last night of our climb it fired our imaginations.

* * * * *

The beginning of this idea to climb a new route on El Cap began in the fall of 1984 and a meeting with Randy Leavitt in Yosemite.

Grasping the fin of his Cadillac like a handrail, he limped across the parking lot toward me. His dislocated knee crackled like a bowl of rice crispies as it dragged weary feet through thick drifts of pine needles piled against flat tires of long dead vans. He looked thinner for eight solitary days on *Aurora*, a route on El Cap created by Peter Mayfield and me back in 1981, unrepeated till Randy's solo ascent. We shook hands. I asked about his knee. He had taken a short fall,

---

* This article was first published in *Climbing* of June 1986.

caught his foot in a sling, and hung upside down, like a cowboy fallen from a horse with his boot caught in the stirrup.

"Too bad about your route," he said.

I agreed. I'd driven to California to complete an El Cap route I'd attempted twice before, to find that someone had done the jump on me. Not only had I lost a route but a name as well. *Heart of Darkness,* a fine Conradian piece of nomenclature heavy with intimations of soul searching in a sinister realm, as well as geologic applicability to boot, namely an arrow-straight line bisecting the jet-black diorite of the North American Wall, was now named *Sheep Ranch of Wyoming,* a gauche slap in the face nightmare of bestial images.

Sheep Ranch's main protagonist, parachutist/climber Rob Slater, had snatched the route as his swan song before embarking on a high-powered career as a Wall Street broker. His sole regret in leaving Yosemite to seal this Faustian pact with money was forfeiting the chance to climb the sister-line to the *Sheep Ranch,* pre-named *Iowa Pig Farm.* I recalled a long-silent outcry by sage Royal Robbins against names like *Tangerine Trip, Mescalito* and *Magic Mushroom* due to their druggy connotations. What would he say about atrocities such as these?

After talk of climbs past we spoke of climbs future. Leavitt suggested a jaunt into the Arctic Circle, to Baffin Island, to climb some alpine monstrosity.

"Climb it, and . . . . ?" I asked warily.

"Jump."

This is the problem with Leavitt. Not content to climb a steep wall he must parachute it as well. Its all part of the up-down fixation among these hybrids of climbing and BASE jumping, BASE jumpers being those who jump from Buildings, Antennae, Spans (bridges) and Edges (cliffs).

"You'd leave me on the summit, all alone?"

"You could jump too."

"Thanks, but I don't jump."

He offered to teach me. I repeated I don't jump. He suggested I toss the haulbags off and descend the back side solo. I countered that he'd be an airdrop for a polar bear and I'd get lonely. Impasse reached, I proposed an alternative: El Cap, via the second-last good new route.

"Where?" asked Leavitt, sceptically.

We spoke in the arcane tongues of climbing and unfolded our mental roadmaps of El Capitan. Flakes and chunks of rock were our landmarks on these blue highways.

"Between *Tangerine Trip* and *Zenyatta Mendatta.*"

"When?"

"Next spring."

* * * * *

Our correspondence that year agreed that this route would rewrite the book on big-wall climbing. With the combined experience of thirty walls we knew

PLATE 19

Photo by Greg Child

**Leavitt on A4 Pitch on Day Two on
LOST IN AMERICA, El Capitan.**

precisely what luxuries were needed. This hedonistic desire to attain un-surpassed levels of comfort on an overhanging environment accounts for the overkill wattage of our ghetto-blaster, pillows for porta-ledges, changes of un-derwear, shaving kit and pre-moistened towelettes, books, newspapers, gour-met food and other excesses totalling 400 pounds. If we were going to live on a rock for ten days we were going to do it in style.

Arriving to a Yosemite of thundering waterfalls and overcrowded, heavily policed campgrounds, we headed directly to the base of El Cap to fix the first pitch, mindfully avoiding the greatest single danger to the route, the Mountain Room Bar. Greater climbers than we had been sucked into this intellectual vacuum, to spend all their money on drink and talk nonsense for nights on end, only to see their ambitions and brains turn to mush. On those too-comfy stools, surrounded by empty bottles of over-priced beer and sneaky-strong cocktails, the timelessness of the valley stretches like saran-wrap over the season, so that by the time the victim finally escapes this climate-controlled vortex, winter has set in and he kicks himself, wondering where went the dream.

Leavitt won the toss for first lead. He joyed to the therapeutic chime of hammered steel and dull thwack of copperheads, I could see it in his eyes. At a perfect ledge we fix a rope, haul our bags (we call them pigs), and rappel to the rattlesnake-crawling scree, gazing at a daunting sheet of rock above a swaying nylon strand hanging fifteen feet free of the wall for 150 feet of height. Every pitch as steep or steeper, each fifteen feet will join the next to total 250 feet of tilt from ground to summit, making retreat an unlikely possibility.

At dawn next day, we cut all ties with the ground, beginning our ten-day ascent. Only three days in the Valley and we are on the wall. We haven't even seen the bar: An unheard of achievement.

My lead begins with a handcrack that fades to blank after sixty feet. A silver, bulging wall surrounds me, interrupted by occasional thin overlaps. Only 200 feet off the ground and already exposure consumes us. A few rivets reach over-lapping onion-skin flakes. They expand as I hammer knifeblades underneath them. Too much hammering and the natural elasticity in the rock is lost, not enough and the piton won't grip. Chouinard chrome-moly rings like a tuning fork as it slides between leaves of granite. Wait for the right note, stop ham-mering, clip in, step up. At rope's end, in the middle of the featureless wall, I drill a bolt belay. All day for one pitch, a mere 150 feet, but that's the pace. We name the pitch "The Big Country," gateway to the vertical prairie.

To haul the pigs through a pulley demands our combined weight and sweat. By nightfall we are spent, prostrate on porta-ledges. Leavitt slips a tape into the machine, constructs tuna sandwiches. The wind drops. Perfect acoustics.

* * * * *

The climbing rack for this route; a jangling juggernaut of scrap metal bris-tling with hooks, pitons, cabled devices, even masking tape to stick hooks to flakes as runners and to pad sharp edges from gnawing the rope.

Now, when it comes to the hardware of climbing, Leavitt combines a propensity for invention with the aquisitiveness of a bower bird, while on rock the compact, thoughtful Californian is a bantam-weight with yardbird reflexes.

Incipient flakes on the third pitch gives him a chance to use his "Stars," tiny pointed hatchet-pitons, a tenth the size of a RURP, with the fall-holding power of a paper-clip.

Then he spies something totally out of place on our virgin climb: a fixed nut twenty blank feet above us. Nausea overwhelms me. Has someone been here before? But no, relief, its part of the unfinished girdle traverse of El Cap. The only thing more abstract than climbing up a wall is to traverse it from one end to the other.

Leavitt snags the nut with his cheat-stick, a sectioned tent-pole with a hook on the end and a ladder of cabled loops attached to the hook. He clips up the cable and avoids an hour of drilling. We dub the pitch "The Astral Lassoo."

Our bivouac that night hangs level with the great arch of the *Tangerine Trip*. Bats drop from its dark interior and we recall tales of tragedy, bad taste and black humour born beneath that arch. Shadowy and oppressive, it has the look of a bad place, where "things happen." A severed rope, a death; a climber becomes unclipped from her Jümars, another death. Death cloaks a route with a sinister shroud, until fools eager to shatter the aura rushed in where angels feared to tread, and crossed the tainted arch clad in Ghostbuster T-shirts and devil masks procured from a Fresno magic store.

Next day we enter the brittle quartz of "The Badlands." Hanging from hooks perched on crumbling flakes I reach an enormous detached scimitar of rock. To beat pitons into it would pry it from the face, slicing Leavitt and me from the wall like stalks of wheat felled by a scythe, so I slip nuts behind it, moving cautiously, slowly and silently as a man crossing a frozen lake.

The vibrating flake mesmerizes me. Serious climbing treads a thin line between recklessness and calculated risk, the path marked only by intuition, a capricious and often flawed instinct. Like a house of cards, every placement must be exact. The mind computes the right move, finds the way out, but only by pushing you deeper into it, until, in the end, the ice is so thin that there is no choice but to trust intuition. This bridge-burning paradox of willingly climbing into a hazardous situation that you are then forced to climb out of stinks of adrenalin. But intuition, or luck, holds out, and puts me at a hanging belay.

On the fourth day Leavitt drops a nut behind a distant flake with the cheater-stick, swings onto it and proceeds to meld copperheads into an arch. At its end the wall tilts back, abruptly turning from orange to moody black. Finding no crack he begins to hook upwards. Dead ended, he gingerly hooks back down. Bits of grit pop under the weight of his hooks and strike him in the eye. Treading his own patch of thin ice, he tries a hook traverse out right, but it too goes nowhere so he makes a belay.

"Too hard to hook. Maybe it has to be freeclimbed."

He's right. The sixth pitch runs it out thirty feet on 5.10 face, relents to fistcrack, then hits a ledge.

Hauling the pigs to this place is a cursed ordeal. The five bags have developed separate personalities and dangle entangled like a family of suckling hogs crowding the belly of an enormous central sow. The hog-mother and her cluster are herded onto the ledge. We name it "The Bay of Pigs."

Leavitt throws his hip into an offwidth, levitates past a huge loose block and nails a sweeping arch. Belay. With daylight left, I put some time into the 8th pitch, an A4+ hook traverse to a blade crack that splits the blank wall. Now in the mode of doing 1.4 pitches a day we see the ground fall behind, the pines become pencils and the peregrine falcons, nesting far below, accept us as fact.

Hunting to feed their newly-hatched young, they rip the air in dives aimed at swallows and pigeons, smashing them in explosions of feathers, then catching their stunned prey mid-air. High pitched shrieks from the male signal a successful catch. The female rises on an updraft, collects the swallow from her mate's talons, then accelerates with folded wings, pulling out of the 3000-foot dive to land light as a tuft of down on the rim of her eyrie to feed the catch to squawking offspring.

The eighth evening sees us on a foot-ledge beneath the headwall, a looming bulge that surpasses all else on El Cap for steepness. Leavitt peers down glassy eyed. I would have restrained him were he not clipped to the belay.

"What a place to jump!"

"But we're only two-thirds of the way up. Don't you need more height?"

He who had jumped off antennae low as 500 feet eyed me with pity, a poor uninitiate who had never known the rush of free-fall.

"It isn't quantity, its quality. There are parts of El Cap worth jumping that are nowhere near the top. I've considered doing certain climbs just to reach these spots." He meant grand ledges like El Cap Tower or The Continental Shelf, to name but two. The usual place to jump was atop the Dawn Wall, a sloping prow of rock that beckons one to the edge. And right at that hour was the best time to jump, when the evening stillness had set in and El Cap was saturated in soft light.

"Nothing beats seeing the landmarks of El Cap that you know as a climber rush past at 32 feet per second squared. You dive, spread your limbs and feel the acceleration build. Reaching terminal velocity is like hitting a pillow. You don't go any faster. The illusion is to float, to fly, but you're moving fast, and have to snap out of the trance to open your chute. There's a crack as silk hits air, a pull upwards, and a slow ride to the ground. Free-fall: Thats where it's at.

It. Quintessential. Definitive, yet undefined.

I felt the suction of the space below begin to pull like a current.

"It's addictive. You get hooked. You forget fear. You feel immortal. That's why I retired. I was getting too blasé. Yeah, it gets under your skin, like a terrible rash that just has to be scratched. Slater calls it Bad Craziness."

Then Leavitt told about the time he jumped into the Black Canyon of the Gunnison, the worst craziness I'd ever heard.

"Rob Slater and I planned to jump in, then climb out. While we were waiting for the wind to drop he mentioned that the buzz was wearing thin with jumping,

PLATE 20

Photo by Greg Child

Leavitt leading the *Fly or Die* Pitch (A5).

so I suggested we try something different and jump hand in hand. Whenever you jump tandem you pre-plan to release, veer off in different directions, and for one person to open his chute before the other. To avoid collision.

"So Rob is flying in front and to my left, looking over his shoulder for my open chute while trying to track the right path, because it's a narrow gorge with only one place to land. But he doesn't see me. He just keeps looking over his shoulder, falling, falling. Split seconds pass. I open my chute, but he's still falling, still trying to spot me. 300 feet above the ground he finally opens. Last thing I see before I land is Rob flying toward the cliffs. On the landing zone I look around, certain he's dead, but there he is, landing safely, but on the wrong side of the Gunnison River. The river was a torrent. He nearly drowned getting over. All that happened in seconds. The story takes longer than the jump. We never did climb out . . ."

In all Leavitt's hundreds of jumps he'd accumulated just a few minutes of free-fall. It was a very dangerous drug.

"If it wasn't illegal to jump El Cap I'd still do it."

His third jump from the Dawn Wall marked the end of his career. Arrested by Park Rangers for this victimless non-crime and crucified by the internal justice system of Yosemite, he languished in a Valley cell like some political prisoner of a regime against fun, and only escaped a lengthy prison term because a lawyer detected violations of his constitutional rights. But bureaucracy had won. No one was jumping anymore.

He stares at me. "Someday you gotta jump. You gotta."

Next day Leavitt climbs to beneath the headwall and traverses right, jamming everything from Friends to blades into the crack until it blanks out before reaching the summit corners. As he drills through the headwall bulge toward these corners I hear a strangled shriek, feel a tug on the rope and look up to see him dangling. A snapped rivet hanger floats to the ground. Back up again he inches up the bottomless corner on RURPs, blade-tips and copperheads.

"If this pops . . ." he says shaky voiced, "Its fly or die . . ."

Darkness. He belays, I jümar. Sparks shower the face like flint asizzle as I clean the pitch. I pluck the final RURP out with my fingers. In the final eighty feet of his lead every placement was barely capable of supporting body weight. If one had popped he would have ripped the entire string and fallen 160 feet.

Another morning breaks and grows blustery as sunlight swamps the wall. Anticipating the summit, we break out the shaving cream, mount our sunglasses in front of us as mirrors and mow down a week's stubble. Leavitt even changes his underwear. But the pitch is long and slow and consumes every one of our 35 bent and beaten blades. Beneath me the antenna of the radio glints in the sun while Leavitt thumbs through a week-old *Wall Street Journal*. The wind carries a San Jose traffic report up the wall. Rush hour and the freeway is jammed.

The corner stops twenty feet from *Zenyatta Mendatta*. I sink four bolts into the wall, belay. The line has ended, like a place of dead roads. Tomorrow we'll swing into the last 300 feet of *Zenyatta*, and be off by night.

Leavitt reaches me as alpenglow saturates the High Sierra so close we could touch it. The shapes of Yosemite's skyline stand like black cutouts on the horizon. The peregrine makes a last dive back to its nest, while below headlights map the valley loop. And far away a military mind presses a button and launches a Tomahawk missile that paves the sky with fire, annihilating the alpenglow and, in our blackest dreams, man himself.

Summary: An account of the first ascent of *Lost in America,* 5.10, A5, a 2700-foot route on El Capitan, climbed over ten days in May 1985 by Greg Child and Randy Leavitt.

PLATE 21

Photo by Greg Child

Leavitt leading A4 on Rurps, Stars and Copperheads.

Desert Climbing

ERIC BJØRNSTAD

IN 1986 THERE was a surge of climbing on the southwest desert that exceeded any year since the initiation of technical desert ascents with the climbing of Shiprock in 1939. Several dozen first ascents and new routes were done in the Moab, Utah area alone. The increased activity is dramatically illustrated by the fact that the 825th ascent of Castleton Tower was recorded by the end of 1986, the last 200 ascents having been done within the previous 12 months.

Much of the popularity of desert climbing is no doubt due to the numerous magazine and journal articles that have been written over the years. John Harlin's inclusion of a Canyonlands section in Volume II of *The Climber's Guide to North America* has sparked considerable interest in the area, but perhaps the most far reaching exposure has been the inclusion of three desert routes in the rigorously pursued Steck and Roper's *Fifty Classic Climbs of North America*. Increased published mention and media coverage of desert climbing, coupled with advances in equipment which have made these standards of climbing possible and relatively safe, have all contributed to the astonishing growth. Let us hope clean climbing and an ecologically sound approach to desert moutaineering will continue also to grow.

Four new sandstone routes have been established in Colorado National Monument near Grand Junction, Colorado. Details on approach, equipment, etc. may be obtained by asking to see the loose-leaf binder of climbs kept at the front desk of the visitor's center.

The northeast face of Independence Monument was climbed by Ed Webster and Pete Athens (III, 5.11, A-1). *Medicine Man* was put up on Sentinel Spire (Watusi Tower) in the spring by Andy Petefish and Tom Bratton (IV, 5.10, A-2, 4 pitches). *Special Verdict* was climbed by Steve Johnson and Tom Blake (I, 5.8 +). In April Steve Kolarik and David Kozak climbed *Hairboatin'* (I, 5.10b).

Primal Yawn was put up on Pope Tower in April by Todd Gordon and Dave Evans (III, 5.10, A-3 + , 5 pitches). The route is on the south southwest side of the tower which is located near Chinle Spire in northeastern Arizona by the small Navajo towns of Rock Point, Lukachukai and Many Farms.

In Canyonlands National Park Chuck Grossman and Kent Wheeler climbed the west face of Traracian Knightmare in April (III, 5.11, 3 pitches). The first ascent, via the north face, was made in 1983 by Ron Olevsky solo (III, 5.8, A-3,

3 pitches). The tower is directly west of Moses. Chris Begue, Kent Wheeler and Chuck Grossman climbed *Seven-Up Crack* (I, 5.10 −) in April. The route is on the right wall just inside the first canyon branching to the left (north) from Taylor Canyon on the way to Moses and Zeus from the Green River approach.

Jim Dunn and Maureen Gallagher climbed *Sorcerer's Apprentice Left* July 21 (III, 5.11c, 3 pitches), located opposite the 1-Mile Marker on the River Road (State Highway 128) near Moab, Utah.

March Hare Flare was climbed by Bill Robins and Kirsten Davis in Negro Bill Canyon just past Mile Marker 3 on the River Road (I, 5.11 −). The route is identified by rappel slings ½ mile up the canyon on the left.

In the River Road Dihedrals area *Oxygen Debt* was climbed September 30 by Paul Gagner and Rich Perch (I, 5.11, A-0). The route is four crack systems right of The Molar at the entrance to Sheep Canyon just before Mile Marker 3.

December 18-20, 1985, *Rasta Wall* was climbed by Jim Beyer solo siege (IV, 5.7, A-4). It is on the southwest corner of River Tower located east of Mile Marker 22, one mile beyond (east of the Fisher Towers turn off. On the same tower Jim Beyer soloed *Savage Master* September 30 (III, 5.8, A-5). The route is on the north face.

Dark Spire was climbed December 22, 1985 from the north solo by Jim Beyer (II, 5.7, A-4). Dark Spire is the farthest right (south) tower in an amphitheater east of the River Road Mile Marker 23.

Raven's Delight was put up on Barney Rumble Tower across the river from Mile Marker 4 on the River Road on November 28 by Bego Gerhart, Jeff Widen and Tony Valdes (II, 5.9 +) from the east.

For better than a decade routes have been turned into climbing magazines and journals and articles written where climbs were described as being done on the Nuns. These routes were in fact located on the Rectory, the mesa north of Castleton Tower and south of the true Nuns formation. This landform was named by Harvey T. Carter and Cleve McCarthy when they made the first ascent in 1962. Ironically the Nuns had not been climbed until December 28, 1986 when a route was put up by Charlie Fowler, Jim Dunn, Maureen Gallagher (I, 5.11). The route ascends the left crack that divides the two Nuns on the west side of the formation.

On November 15 Jeff Widen made the first solo ascent of The Priest located just north of the Nuns. (This was not the first ascent of the tower; the other solos mentioned are also first ascents.)

In the Fisher Towers *The Jagged Edge* on King Fisher Tower was climbed October 28-30 in a solo siege by Jim Beyer (V, 5.9, A-4, 8 pitches) via the southeast ridge. On Echo Tower *Phantom Sprint* was established on February 25-26 by Jim Beyer solo. The route is 60 feet left of the original north-face chimney route (IV, 5.9, A-3). Also on Echo Tower Jim Beyer (perhaps not reported before) had soloed a major line on the south face. *Run Amok* was rated V, 5.9, A-4 and established March, 1979.

PLATE 22

Photo by Eric Bjørnstad

Kyle Copeland on _Hall of Flame_ on Candalabrum Tower, Arches National Park, Utah.

Ron Olevsky, Dave Mondeau and Dan McGee climbed a new route on Merrimac Butte in May. *Merrymaker* (II, A-3) is the first crack system left of the Hyper-Crack Route on the east side of the landform.

On the Monitor Butte southeast of the Merrimac Butte, Ron Olevsky and Dave Mondeau made the first ascent in May when they climbed a right-facing corner on the south side of the southwest buttress (II, 5.7, A-3).

Funnel Arch was soloed by Lin Ottinger in October. It is above Kane Springs Canyon between Pritchett and Hunter Canyons south of Moab.

Charlie Fowler and Sue Wint climbed the *Toco Bender* in November (I, 5.9). It is located at the 2.5-Mile Mark on Highway 279 (the Potash Mine road), a few miles west of Moab.

Jeff Widen and Tony Valdes climbed *Song of the Canyon Wren* on November 27 (I, 5.11a, A-O). This is an hour's drive from Moab via Little Canyon and then the Dry Fork of Bull Canyon. The route faces south on a prominent head-wall. Rappel slings are visible from the ground.

In Arches National Park, 22 new routes were established in the spring and fall of 1986 including first ascents on the three remaining unclimbed major towers in the park: Sheep Rock, Tower of Babel and Organ Tower. The location and equipment list etc. may be obtained from the loose-leaf binder of climbs kept at the front desk of the visitor's center. Many of the restrictions imposed on climbing in the park in the past have been lifted, but registration before climbing is requested.

Stronger Than Dirt was climbed by Charlie Fowler and Chris Goplerud in November (I, 5.12). *Libbis Maximus* was climbed on September 14 by Tony Valdes, Sonja Paspal and Bob Milton with the second pitch being done in November by Tony Valdes and Jeff Widen (I, 5.10d). *The Dumpster* by Charlie Fowler was belayed by Eric Bjørnstad (I, 5.11). *Cinnamon Rose* was climbed by Charlie Fowler solo (I, 5.9). *Sand Tears* was climbed by Charlie Fowler belayed by Eric Bjørnstad (I, 5.11). *Dusty Shadows* was climbed in November by Charlie Fowler and Dan Grandusky (III, A-2 +). *Sand Bag* was climbed by Kyle Copeland and Sue Kemp. (I, 5.10b). On the Candelabrum Tower *Hall of Flame* was climbed by Kyle Copeland and Alison Sheets (I, 5.11c). *Soft Parade* was climbed by Charlie Fowler and Sue Wint in November (I, 5.10 +, A-4).

The Organ Tower was climbed in March by Pete Gallagher and Steve Sommers. The route was named *Death By Hands* and is on the southwest tower (III, 5.11, A-2, 7 pitches). In April *Dune* was established by Duane Raleigh solo on the southwest tower (III, 5.10, A-3 +, 5 pitches). Raleigh's night descent from the 500-foot tower turned into an epic when he became disconnected from the rope while on the second rappel. He free-fell about 160 feet. Miraculously his 9mm haul line, which was clipped to an equipment sling, jammed in a crack during the fall and brought him to a tenuous arrest. The impact bent a carabiner and badly damaged the rope. Steve Swanke, the park's climbing ranger, assisted by lighting the way for the remaining descent. A jammed carabiner gate is the probable cause of Duane's fall which, had it not checked itself, would have continued another 200 feet to the ground. In October Pete Gallagher and John

Photo by Rob Robinson

**The 5.12 Crux on *Journey from the
Future*, Snow Canyon, Utah.**

Gatto made the first ascent of the northeast tower of Organ Tower. The route, *Gates of Hell,* is rated IV, 5.10, A-3.

The Tower of Babel was climbed by Charlie Fowler on October 14-17. Eric Bjørnstad worked on four of the six pitches of the 550-foot monolith. Lin Ottinger prusiked the entire tower. The route was named *Zenyatta Entrada* and was IV, 5.4, A-4.

Sheep Rock, 440 feet high, was climbed by the west face on October 2 by Charlie Fowler and Kyle Copeland via the west face. The route was named *Buggers Banquet* (III, 5.7, A-3, 5 pitches). *Virgin Wool* was put up in November by Jim Bodenhamer and Sandy Fleming on the east face of Sheep Rock (III, 5.7, A-3). The first pitch of Buggers Banquet had been climbed by Layton Kor in the early 1960s. At that time his ascent was curtailed by the Arches National Monument park rangers. All climbs done in 1986 in the park were sanctioned by the park authorities. They do, however, request climbers to register at the visitors center.

The Lamb Tower was climbed by Charlie Fowler solo. The route was named *The Sheepish Grin* (I, 5.10). In the fall Charlie Fowler soloed *Wolf In Sheep's Clothing* on the Lamb Tower (I, 5.10).

The Hideout was soloed by Charlie Fowler (I, 5.9), and *Chinese Eyes* was climbed by Charlie Fowler and Dan Grandusky (I, 5.10).

Industrial Disease was put up by Scott Reynolds and Max Kendall in October (I, 5.11).

Queen Victoria Rock was climbed by Charlie Fowler and Alison Sheets. The route, *Queen For A Day,* was rated (I, A-2).

In the remote Klondike Bluffs area of the park, Cuddlebunny Tower was climbed by Charlie Fowler, Rob Slater and Geoff Tabin. The route was dubbed *Givin' The Dog A Bone* (I, 5.11).

On January 1, 1987 Terrel Lashier and Steve Swanke climbed *The Fledgling* (I, 5.4). The route is in Arches National Park, two formations left of the Doll route.

All routes done in Arches National Park are composed of Entrada Sandstone.

The Monitor and the Merrimac

RON OLEVSKY

THERE ARE JUST two seasons for climbing in the canyon country of the desert, too hot and too cold. Often they are separated by a matter of minutes and one does not necessarily find them when one expects. While there are, of course, exceptions to this rule, when climbing in the desert the name of the game is fluctuation and intensity.

With this lesson well learned, I arrived in Moab in early May mentally and physically prepared for anything.

Well . . . almost anything.

I had placed my camp on the slickrock gap between the Monitor and Merrimac Buttes, two easily visible landmarks twenty kilometers north of town. As far as was known the very summits of both were untrodden although the Merrimac, the more substantial of the two, sported the Hyper Crack, a two-pitch route established the previous year by John Bouchard, Jim Dunn, Eric Bjørnstad and Lin Ottinger.

It was, however, the Monitor that held my interest as it offered an aesthetic dihedral on its south side that I had eyed from the state highway two kilometers distant. With the weather still wintry the sunny climbing would be welcome.

The next few days were rewarding and serene as I was treated to beautiful views of wilderness and wildlife. Birds cried overhead as the wind traced new wave patterns in the desert sand. At one point a coyote bitch perhaps in heat spent several hours within a hundred meters of camp attempting to entice my hound, Bat Hook, into a romp in the sand with yips and howls, but at two years he was still a bit young fully to pursue the invitation although he ventured more than halfway out to her both scared and excited. It was a display I have never seen equalled in an area where coyotes are unfortunately so intensively hunted.

After nearly three days I had transported piles of hardware to the base but had only managed to solo twenty-five meters of thin crack in the blustery cold weather before heading back into town to rendezvous with my friend and climbing partner, Dave Mondeau. Together, we returned, Dave driving his two-wheel-drive up the four-wheel-drive trail.

Soon after the instalation of two drilled angles at a hanging belay just over halfway up our perfect dihedral crack, the first pitch was fixed. The ascent the following day went quickly and smoothly. It began with the discovery and avoidance of a rattlesnake near the base of the route. (As it was not near camp, I elected not to shoot it.) Later Dave was forced to drill where the dihedral crack

76

PLATE 24

Photo by Ron Olevsky

MONITOR from the base of Merrimac.

went offwidth. Unable to watch well from my bolts I grew impatient and called up to find out whether Dave had placed his bolt yet and was informed with a defiant laugh that he had already placed two! The Entrada sandstone is much softer than the Wingate, Navaho and Aztec that I usually climb on, which is good or bad depending upon how one looks at it.

Shortly, we belayed each other onto the summit knob, left a register, explored the top of the butte, rappelled back to the base and, wanting to return to town, quickly packed our gear into two enormous loads. Opting for an alternate route down the talus to avoid the rattlesnake, I staggered a few steps only to discover that the snake had moved!

It all happened very fast but it seemed like slow motion. I heard the snake under the rock right behind my foot. Dave cried out a warning. I jumped two meters onto a boulder downhill, and as I sprang, I remember feeling relieved that the snake had not effected a strike.

Silly me!

The boulder began to roll down the talus and I flew sprawling headlong in front of it. Although I flung my hands in front of me, I was so overloaded that I couldn't keep from going face first into another boulder. There was no time for recovery! Dave yelled a useless warning. The boulder I had jumped onto headed for me. I rolled partially clear and ineffectually held out my hand again to block the half-ton rock that stopped next to me.

Then pain surged. My face throbbed with a warm numbness, my arm burned, my knee seared. Most painful of all, badly torn ligaments made my left ankle useless. With Dave's help I moved clear of the loose rock (and the snake) and unloaded the gear. With difficulty I explained to Dave that I was going into shock and needed my sleeping bag to maintain core temperature but ice from the cooler to reduce the swelling of my injuries. As Dave hurried back to the trucks, I lay in agony, staring at the wisps of clouds and feeling the wind blow down the cold sweat that had formed on my back.

Somehow I made it back to town (shifting gears was a problem) where I was scheduled to give a slide show at the Rim Cyclery. I imagine I didn't quite live up to my image after limping in wincing.

Two days later Dave began working on a new line just left of the Hyper Crack on the Merrimac with Dan McGee as I watched from below. The following morning, while the others were finishing breakfast, I limped up to the base with the help of a crutch (discovering another rattler which I failed to hit with a large rock). I managed the one-legged jümar to the high point where I racked up and waited for a belayer. It took a half hour to nail eight meters before I relinquished the lead to Dave. A good thing too, as it turned out to be the crux! Soon we were on the rim looking down on the upper rappel bolts of the Hyper Crack.

The "too hot" season had arrived and I limped over to the summit knobs to find a cool spot for the champagne. Soon the others joined me with some gear and we climbed to the true summit (low fifth-class made more interesting by the inclusion of my crutch). We popped the cork amidst the usual formalities, and during a calm moment I scanned the horizon. There, shimmering on the horizon, were more rocks waiting to be climbed.

Summary of Statistics:

AREA: Desert near Moab, Utah.

ASCENTS: Monitor Butte, via *Class Monitor,* First Ascent, II, 5.9, A2, May, 1986 (Dave Mondeau, Ron Olevsky).

Merrimac Butte, via *Merrymakers' Route,* First Ascent to the Highest Point, II, A3, May, 1986 (Dan McGee, Dave Mondeau, Ron Olevsky).

PLATE 25

Photo by David Mondeau

McGee and Olevsky descending from Merrimac. Hyper Crack is right of the climbers. Olevsky has the crutch.

Foraker—Denali's Neglected Wife

DONALD J. GOODMAN

Mount Foraker is a formidable mountain, and the route followed looked to be the only practical one. Its average standard is at least as high as that of a first-class alpine peak, and some of the passages were difficult, while much of the exposure was very great.

—*T. Graham Brown, following the first ascent of Mount Foraker in 1934.*

MOUNT FORAKER, Alaska Range, 17,400 feet, was named in 1899 by Lieutenant Joseph S. Herron for Senator Joseph B. Foraker of Ohio. Senator Foraker was re-elected in 1902 but some time later exposed by the Hearst Papers for accepting fees and loans from Standard Oil Co. and driven from public life. Not a very happy connotation for so great a mountain. The Tanaina Indians of Lake Minchumena called Foraker "Sultana" meaning "His Wife" (Denali's). Foraker is the sixth highest peak in North America (Denali [McKinley], Logan, St. Elias, Orizaba, Popocatéptl, Foraker).

Since Foraker's first ascent in 1934, through the 1986 climbing season, twelve routes have been completed with two major start variations. Of the twelve routes seven have seen only one ascent. Table A summarizes the number of successful individuals by route and year. The 131 successful individuals to the summit compares to over 4000 for Mount McKinley. From 1976 to 1986 the success ratio on Foraker was 30% compared to McKinley's 55%. Why such great differences in activity and successes between the two mountains? Certainly it is not because Foraker is not a worthwhile objective! Although second in shear mass to McKinley, Foraker dominates its nearest neighbor, Mount Hunter, by 3000 feet, possessing a myriad of ridges and buttresses. Foraker's north face, rising 11,500 vertical feet from the Foraker Glacier, is comparable to McKinley's Wickersham Wall.

In my opinion there are three reasons Mount McKinley sees so much greater activity. 1) McKinley is the highest point in North America; for that reason alone it sees much more activity. 2) Unlike McKinley, there is no "walk-up" route on Foraker. The least technical routes on Foraker are extremely long or

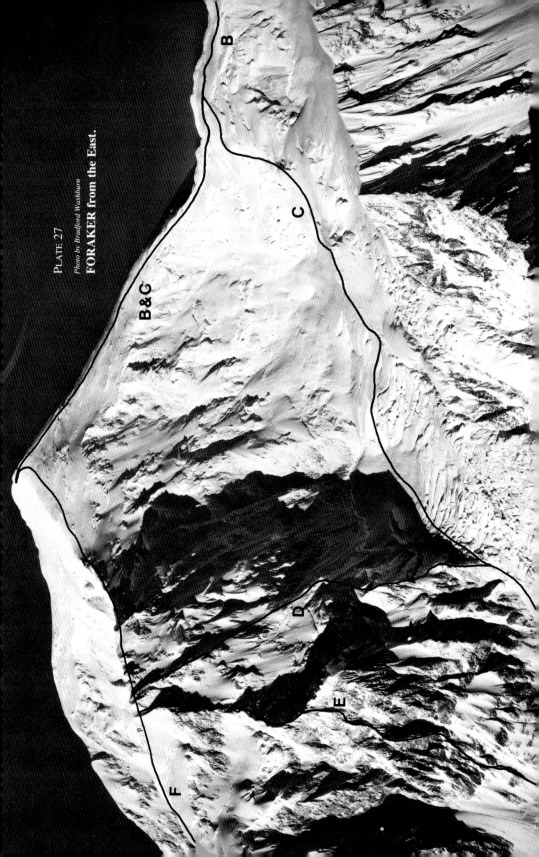

PLATE 27

Photo by Bradford Washburn

FORAKER from the East.

B

C

B&C

D

E

F

PLATE 28

Photo by Bradford Washburn

FORAKER from the Southeast.

involve lengthy approaches. 3) The Bradford Washburn map of Mount Mc-Kinley does not include Foraker. This may seem a minor point until one tries to obtain detailed topographic information on Foraker, information necessary for approach and route details. The Mount McKinley National Park map is very poor in this regard. The best source is U.S.G.S. 15-minute topographic maps. Unfortunately the summit of Foraker lies very near the corner of one of the sheets, hence four are required (U.S.G.S. McKinley A3, A4 and Talkeetna D3, D4).

Below is a summation and brief description of all existing completed routes through 1986 starting with the Archangel Ridge on the north face and going around the mountain clockwise (reference map).

(A) *North Face—East Spur—Archangel Ridge, 1975.* Party used horses from Wonder Lake for approach up true right bank of the Herron Glacier then crossed over a pass to the Foraker Glacier. In my opinion, the finest line on the mountain. Still only one ascent. Ref. *AAJ* 1976, pgs. 277-284

(B) *Northeast Ridge—Sultana Ridge, 1979.* Very long route that climbs Mount Crosson first. Gains over 14,000 feet and loses 4000 feet. Subject to slab avalanche. Several ascents. Ref. *AAJ* 1980, pg. 521.

(C) *Northeast Icefall—Japanese route, 1966.* Route joins Sultana Ridge. Several ascents (third-ascent route). Very subject to ice and snow avalanches. Ref. *AAJ* 1967, pgs. 343-344.

(D) *East Face—Czechoslovakian route, 1986.* The second route on the difficult east face. Like many of the routes in this vicinity a prime attraction is the very short approach. Joins the upper southeast ridge. Ref. *AAJ* 1987.

(E) *East Face—Pink Panther Route, 1984.* The first route on the east face. Also joins the upper southeast ridge. One ascent. Ref. *AAJ* 1985, pgs. 14-19.

(F) *Southeast Ridge, 1963. Second-ascent route (F1).* Has become the "standard" route (although no ascents were recorded in 1985 or 1986). F2 variation (Southwest Toe of Southeast Ridge), completed in 1974, reduces the ice avalanche hazard on the normal route. Ref. *AAJ*s 1964, pgs. 52-55, and 1975, pg. 116.

(G) *South/Southeast Ridge—French Ridge, 1976.* Party placed cumulatively 24,000 feet of fixed rope. One ascent. Long, superb, difficult. Ref. *AAJ* 1977, pgs. 149-152.

(H) *Central Spur of South Face—Infinite Spur, 1977.* Most difficult and technical sustained route to date. First traverse of Foraker (descent via southeast ridge). Difficult approach from Kahiltna Glacier. One ascent. Ref. *AAJ* 1978, pgs. 352-358.

(I) *South Ridge—Talkeetna Ridge, 1968.* Fourth-ascent route. First severely technical route. Second ascent in 1986 (second traverse of Foraker with descent via southeast ridge). Ref. *AAJ*s 1969, pgs. 289-294, and 1987.

(J) *Southwest Ridge, 1977.* This longest and most complex ridge on Foraker has been the subject of numerous attempts. Prior to the success in 1977 no fewer than five attempts were made with none starting from the same point. Approach may be as difficult as the climb itself. Existing route has a 1500-vertical-foot

PLATE 30

Photo by Bradford Washburn

FORAKER from the Southwest. The Southwest Ridge Route (J) ascends the triangular face at the bottom left and follows the ridge over the Fin to the summit, which is out of the picture to the right.

PLATE 31

Photo by Bradford Washburn

FORAKER from the North. Left sky-line is upper part of the Southeast Ridge (F). The route over the Fin (J) is partially visible on the right skyline.

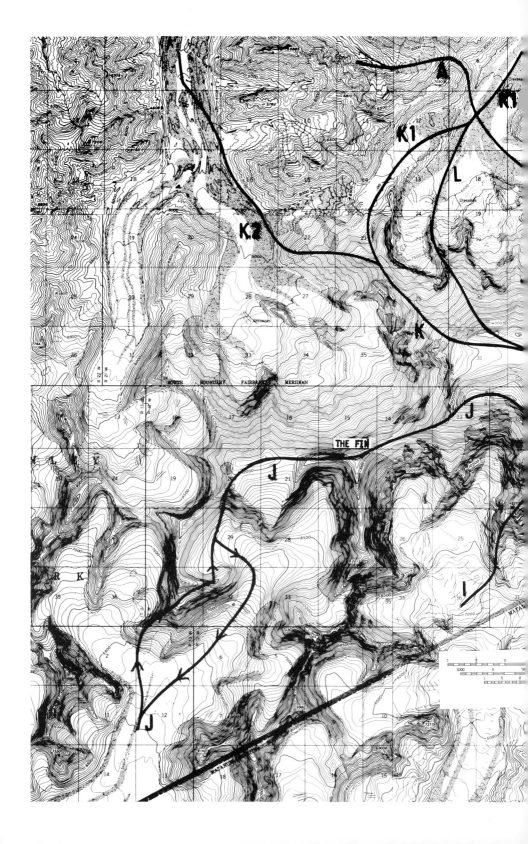

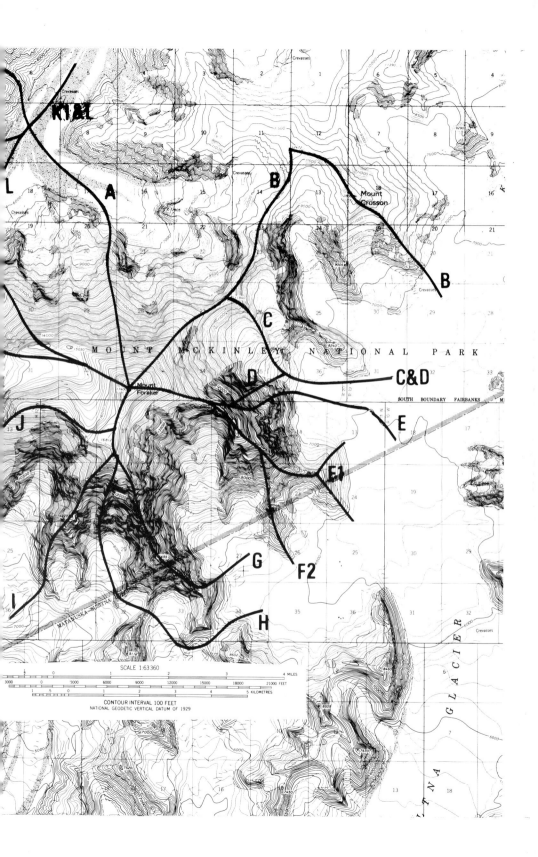

SCALE 1:63360

CONTOUR INTERVAL 100 FEET
NATIONAL GEODETIC VERTICAL DATUM OF 1929

drop-off the ridge at one point. Prominent feature on this ridge is "The Fin," a 13,300-foot point named by the 1934 West Ridge party. One ascent. Ref. *AAJ* 1978, pgs. 359-365.

(K) *West Ridge, 1934.* First-ascent route (K1). Original approach from McKinley Park using horses then up Foraker Glacier. Major variation in 1977 approaches via the Herron Glacier and joins the original route at 11,000 feet (K2). Three ascents in total. Ref. *AAJ*s 1935, pgs. 285-297 and 1978, pgs. 508-509.

(L) *North Face—West Spur—Highway of Diamonds, 1983.* The western spur of the three prominent spurs on the massive north face. Approach was via Kantishna on skis. Difficult route. One ascent. Ref. *AAJ* 1984, pgs. 87-93.

Additional activity of note includes (1) the first winter ascent, March 13, 1975 via the southeast ridge, (Ref. *AAJ* 1976, pg. 430), (2) first ski descent (alpine gear), 1981 via the southeast ridge, (Ref. *AAJ*s 1982, pg. 133 and 1983, pgs. 146-147), and (3) first circumambulation, 1981 (Ref. *AAJ* 1982, pgs. 132-133).

The author wishes to acknowledge the assistance of Mr. David Hirst, of the U.S. Geologic Survey—Ice and Climate Project, and Mr. Robert Seibert, Mountaineering Ranger, Denali National Park.

Table A

SUMMARY OF ASCENTS—FORAKER

NUMBER OF SUCCESSFUL INDIVIDUALS

Year	No. Face East Spur Archangel	N.E. Ridge Sultana	N.E. Icefall Japanese Rt.	East Face Czech Rt.	East Face Pink Panther	S.E. Ridge + Variation	S./S.E. Ridge French Rt.	Central Spur of So. Face Infinite Spur	So. Rdg. Talkeetna Ridge	S.W. Ridge	West Ridge + Variation	North Face West Spur Hwy. of Diamonds	Total Successful Individuals
1934											3		3
1963						2							2
1966			3										3
1968									3				3
1969			4			2							6
1974						8							8
1975	6		5			6							17
1976							7						7
1977						4		2		4	5		15
1978						4							4
1979		8											8
1980		5				8							13
1981						6							6
1982						4							4
1983						13						2	15
1984		4			3	3							10
1985													0
1986				2					2		3		7
TOTALS	6	17	12	2	3	60	7	2	5	4	11	2	131

SOURCES: *American Alpine Journal* and Denali National Park Records

The Tusk

GARY SPEER

I WAS PSYCHED. The loose holds, a slippery wet gully, and rockfall had taken its toll. How did Paul lead this thing? It wasn't very hard, maybe 5.7, but it was nasty—loose and wet. It was here that Paul took a twenty-foot leader fall on a bolt left by a previous party.

I reached for the only decent-looking hold with my left hand. In horror, I watched a melon-sized rock rip loose and crash onto my thigh. I cursed at top volume. Paul asked if I was all right.

It hurt, but it was nothing worse than a bruise. Hurriedly, I clipped the haul rope into Paul's pack, and thrashed my way to the top of what we were calling Elephant Gully.

Once out, I breathed a sigh of relief and began hauling the pack. I'd pulled in about 30 feet when the rope went slack and I heard a crashing sound below: the pack was gone. I instantly was flooded with guilt and self-anger. In my fear-induced haste, I had clipped the haul rope into the accessory straps—not the stronger shoulder straps. I told Paul what had happened and apologized profusely. Not only was the day's climbing at an end, but also, I suspected, was Paul's camera and binoculars which were in the pack.

Paul was forgiving. I was hoping that the Tusk would be forgiving on a second attempt. I had visions of being "gored" by this giant horn of rock.

We fixed a rope to a bolt near the top of Elephant Gully and rappelled the route. Down-climbing the 50° couloir was as nerve-racking as the loose rock had been in the gully. Having left crampons and ice-axes near the bottom of the Tusk, we had planned the day as only a "reconnaissance." Having turned the day into a full-scale attempt, we now yearned for the security of an ice-axe.

At the bottom of the couloir I looked up at the route. At the top of the couloir is a jagged finger of a rock, pointing savagely at the Alaskan sky. At the moment, it struck me as signaling a particularly obscene gesture.

The Tusk had certainly given it to other parties. It was first attempted in 1971 by a strong team led by Alaskan Steve Hackett. We had seen a "note-bottle" stashed at what Hackett termed "Disappointment Col" at the top of Elephant Gully. They were stopped cold by a blank headwall on what we called Walrus Buttress. We had a good look at it that first day, and it looked as if it was going to be bolts and thin placements in flared cracks. In short, it looked slow.

When I interviewed Fred Beckey for a profile last year, I ran across a story about the Tusk in the book *World Climbing*. Beckey, Craig Martinson and Eric

PLATE 32

Photo by Robert Smith

**The TUSK from the Northeast. The
route ascended the right couloir to
the upper col and then the left
skyline.**

Bjørnstad in 1977 hadn't succeeded, yet it was easy to see why they wanted to climb this remote fang of rock: it looked like something out of Patagonia. Though not nearly as high as Fitz Roy, the Tusk bore obvious resemblance to that or perhaps Bugaboo Spire. When I confronted Beckey with questions about this prize, he reluctantly admitted that it had never been climbed.

I soon found that there were good reasons for failure. The rock was bad. Beckey had described it as "the worst rock I've been on in twenty years." Hackett's party made the same comments.

Bjørnstad told me that at one point a ledge had broken loose, and a rock "the size of a TV set" had tumbled down, nearly hitting him. Both he and Beckey had been hit by rockfall, but weren't injured. When I pressed Bjørnstad about why they hadn't at least tried to continue, Bjørnstad confided that the party was "pretty psyched out" by loose holds and deadly rockfall.

Nonetheless, I saw the Tusk as an irresistible challenge. Besides that, the rock didn't *look* all that bad in the photos. Maybe, I optimistically told myself, there is another route.

By far the most impressive alpine challenge in the area is the west face of the Tusk. Rising vertically some 2500 feet, it will someday give fine Grade V or VI routes on Yosemite-like granite. Numerous crack systems tempted us, but the summit—by whatever route—was our goal and the south arête appeared most feasible. And our first attempt had failed.

Paul and I returned to our Base Camp on the west side of the Tusk. Since this trip had the added company of my wife it was a pleasure I'd never experienced on longer expeditions. Far from loved ones, I often developed a hard shell (or so I've been told) that wasn't easily cracked by homesickness. Though she is a capable climber, we felt it was best for Jennifer to stay at Base with our CB radio and do the thinking for us in case the unthinkable happened. I related the events of the day to her as the evening sun lit up the great west wall of the Tusk.

The next day—the summer solstice—we awoke to another beautiful sunny sky. We ate a quick breakfast and were off at 6:30 A.M. Paul's pack was undamaged when we found it in the moat of the couloir, some 800 feet below where I'd dropped it. His camera, binoculars, and light meter, however, were a total loss. It showed me how quickly things can go wrong when fear gets the upper hand.

Controlling fear was foremost on my mind as we hiked around to the east couloir—the start of our route. We had considered other possibilities while studying the aerial photos taken by Bob Smith of the Hackett party. From the comfort of a living room chair, it's easy to draw ambitious lines of possible routes up huge walls of granite. But when you arrive on the scene, the lines disappear, leaving only impossible-looking faces that can be left for some future challenge. We wanted the virgin summit, and it was quite clear that Hackett and Beckey had picked the best possible route.

About midway up the east couloir we heard a reassuring sound: Lowell Thomas's Heliocourier. He had come to check on us, and we waved as he made the first of several passes. Climbing the couloir with ice-axes was infinitely more

The TUSK, Lake Clark National Park, Alaska

secure. We ascended some 500 feet up the east couloir and where it narrowed scrambled into a horizontal moat where we began climbing the rock on the right. Feeling more secure because of Lowell, I led toward Elephant Gully. The first pitch ascends parallel to the couloir (Class 4). The second pitch bears up and right into a dihedral (5.5). The third pitch enters what we called Elephant Gully (because you *feel* like an elephant when your in it—awkward and clumsy). There is a bolt about halfway up the pitch, which is fortunate: the protection is dubious and the rock is very bad here. There is another bolt for a belay at the top of the pitch (5.7). The day before, we had fixed a rope on this bolt. About halfway up the fixed rope, I heard Paul yell. His arm had been hit by a baseball-sized rock. As I hung from my Jümar, he told me he wasn't sure if it was broken.

"No," yelled Paul. "I don't feel any protruding bones. Let's try for the col and we'll see how I feel."

At the col we had a bite to eat and took a nap. Paul said I even started snoring. Upon my waking, he said what I wanted to hear: "Let's give it a try."

Despite a big swelling knot near his elbow, he stoically decided to continue. After sorting out an arsenal of bolts, pitons, rurps, bashies, and hooks (along with my regular "free" rack), I scrambled up the exposed, knife-edged ridge to the Walrus Headwall.

"Why don't you have a look around to the right?" Paul called out, before I could even drive one pin.

"Well," I responded, "I guess we've got nothing to lose."

The left (west) side of the Buttress looked loose and improbable. I was skeptical about the prospects to the right, but thought anything sounded better than trying to attack the headwall straight on. A forty-foot horizontal traverse took me to a small ledge. I looked up into a reasonable-looking dihedral and smiled.

"Yeah," I yelled. "This is it!"

I led what was the first pitch of untouched granite on the Tusk. I'd expected more of the same loose, dangerous rock. Instead I found superbly sound alpine granite. I was elated. I led to a small alcove and brought Paul up. The following two pitches were moderate class 5 with a few harder (5.8) moves here and there. In less than an hour we had solved the major crux of the Tusk: the Walrus Buttress. Lucky route-finding made it three pitches of 5.8.

The top of the buttress was a spacious, airy place. There was room for four or five to comfortably bivouac, and we stopped here to admire the view. The remaining south ridge looked like cake.

Paul is a man of science (a research associate at Washington State University). Still, he has these odd moments of superstitious sentiment.

"Paul," I declared, "I'm going to make the summit even if I have to bolt it from here. I can feel it."

"Now, don't say that," Paul cautioned, half chuckling.

I just smiled and grabbed the rack, walking across the top of the buttress, so hyped-up and excited I could hardly contain myself.

The remaining six pitches were very enjoyable but quite easy (Class 3 to mid-Class 5) on more superb granite. I often climbed a whole rope length with only one or two pieces of protection. About 200 feet below the summit we unroped and scrambled together to the top—the first virgin summit I had ever attained.

All around was a sea of mountains and glaciers, most of them untouched as the Tusk. Several peaks stood out as having excellent climbing possibilities. Among them were Goldpan Peak, the Mammaries (as we called those twin towers), and the Pyramid. We took a dozen or so photos, shook hands, and built a cairn. I was nearly overwhelmed by the joyful glow of the moment, but tempered my emotions with the fact that we still had to descend the route—some 2000 feet.

The 20 or so rappels were tiring but uneventful—except for one detail: our camera was left on the top of the buttress. Shades of Cesare Maestri and Cerro Torre? No proof that we made the summit? Maybe such doubts can entice a second party up the Tusk. They can have the camera—I just want the film.

At the bottom of the route I looked up at the spire that yesterday I had thought was flipping obscenities at us.

"Paul," I said, "Look at it. It looks like a salute!"

Summary of Statistics:

AREA: Chigmit Mountains, Alaska

FIRST ASCENT: The Tusk, 1674 meters, 5820 feet, Summit reached on June 21, 1986 (Gary Speer, Paul Bellamy), Grade IV, 5.8.

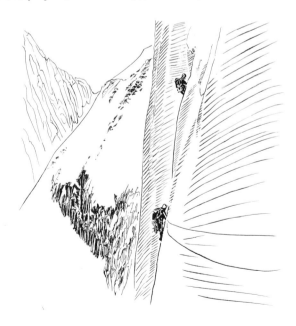

A Calling—Cayesh

JERRY M. GORE, *Alpine Club*

NEVADO CAYESH IS a pinnacle in the Peruvian Andes. The name itself is derived from the Quechua word *caye,* meaning "to call," and indeed for me it did just that. Described by John Ricker as "possibly the most spectacular peak in the Cordillera Blanca," I first saw a shot of the mountain whilst leafing through his guidebook to the range. I became captivated and decided to make it the basis of a climbing documentary film for the BBC's *Mick Burke Award*.

Cayesh had had only two full ascents. Both of these would have easily qualified for the title "Epic." The first ascent, in 1960, involved a truly horrendous climb by three intrepid New Zealanders along the peak's overhung, corniced and heavily mushroomed south ridge. The second ascent took place in 1984, with a superbly technical and serious route up the east face by Mark Richey and two friends. The crux of the five-day horror-show was centred around tiers of ice ceilings projecting out horizontally thirty feet, at mid height on the face. The suspended icicles which decorated these tiers were surmounted amidst graphic details of axe hooking on pockets with icicle tie-offs for protection!

The whole of the northwest face lay untouched and was quite clearly up for grabs. In 1985, I decided to keep the idea in mind but make a final decision when we got there. As usual the conditions on the hill dictated events. Our film team reached Base Camp at the bottom of Cayesh around early June, 1985. We soon realised that the face was still badly choked with early season snowfall. Since it would take at least two weeks to clear, we went for the unclimbed west face of Milpocraju and filmed it in its entirety. By the time we had returned to Cayesh, the weather had come in again. We initiated two major assaults but were soundly repulsed both times. That was the conclusion of events for 1985.

* * * * *

The long trudge up the glacier in early July of 1986 is endurable. We had left gear for the wall climb four days before and our packs are light for the first time in a week. Terry Moore is obviously well rid of the dysentery that has been troubling him and he storms ahead, the old glacial rhythm well established. I stumble on behind, trying deperately to find mine, but to no avail.

We reach the bergschrund at the foot of the face by early afternoon, time enough to fix the first pitches across the gap and up to the first *rognon*. This will

97

—— **British Route**
· · · **Czechoslovakian Route**
– – – **Yellow Italian Fixed Ropes**

NEVADO CAYESH

DMOLENAAR

allow us access to the ice couloir and the start of the real difficulties. We are well pleased with our work and retire to our palatial bivy tent, floating amidst a sea of whiteness in a hollow curving from the baked névé. The hardened snow is testimony to the appalling fact that the Blanca has recently come through five weeks of perfect weather. We have missed it all and know only too well that time is not on our side. It will surely break up soon. The sunsets each night play mercilessly with our fantasies. We brew and drink mechanically. Each is lost in his own private world and the discussion remains short and clipped until our bivy sack finally enshrouds us, together with our worries.

In the first full day on the face, we reach the col after six hours' struggle. I find a good ledge, protected from the icicles above by an overhang and we prepare for the night. The drinks, a mixture of Duocal Carbohydrate and re-hydrated baby food is passed back and forth and we slowly regain the valuable fluid lost during the day.

I begin to think about tomorrow and what it might bring. We should reach, or get close enough to, last year's high point to determine whether or not the rock will go. I am convinced there is a line there somewhere, and have gambled this whole saga on that lone hope. Have I only been deceiving myself? I look across at Terry and grin. He is immersed in his own thoughts and ignores me totally. I hope for his sake I am right.

Day three arrives. We leave our little nest like vermin scurrying from the lair, and furtively stalk our prey. Long pitches are run out to the left, across the face, over very steep, mixed ground. The high point is reached finally, and dismay quickly replaces expected hope. There is no sense here and we recover our steps. Back to square one. I have no choice but to go for our only other option, a vague line of weakness above the bivy site, and one that we think will penetrate the rock band.

I shoulder my rucksack and begin work on the shattered dyke that splits the roof over 200 feet above me. Almost immediately I am spat out like some unwanted, indigestible scrap, and I lie sprawling at Terry's feet. The sack is ditched, and I reascend.

The first pitch goes well enough, with some aiding to start, followed by wide bridging up fairly solid rock with good protection. Terry jümars up, and I begin again. This time the problems are more intricate. A tension balance across the face of a giant block leads me to the bottom of another vertical crack system, which splits the main overhang in the band. We anticipate that this will be the crux. Above, it will be possible to gain access to the huge amphitheatre in the middle of the face. From reconnaissance shots taken on early New Zealand attempts we can identify a series of ice ramps that appear to lead up to the top sérac barrier. Although extremely steep, this "staircase" of ice seems a key element in the jig-saw of pieces needed to complete the picture. Above this, however, is No-Man's Land. Whether we encounter those same tiers of ice ceilings that Richey so vividly described, is impossible to ascertain. It would definitely be a case of suck it and see!

From below the roof I look up at a large block of suspended icicles, one of the many that litter the face. The simplicity of the analogy suddenly strikes me and I move off quickly. The crack yields begrudgingly until I am back to face-climbing on small incuts. The line leads up to a little niche between a large overhang on my left and a further crack system up to my right. I rest awkwardly, feeling the strain slowly build and the long run-out beginning to affect me. I place a small knife-blade and tension once more across the rock. Fifteen feet of toeing and I am across. The ground suddenly eases and I become immersed in a sort of open chimney. Relief floods in as I make safe and prepare for the abseil. Darkness stops play. It is a useful excuse because I am really knackered anyway. We scuttle back to last night's lair, pleased with our work.

Day four is unzipped to reveal the usual concoction of mist, cold and wind. It is Terry's turn to cook, so it's an evil chuckle and back into the pit, *rápido*! A late, late start and a series of long exhausting hauls sees us ensconced in the chimney, yesterday's highpoint.

Terry leads out a couple of fine pitches. We are in the amphitheatre, gaping at the amazing Gothic architecture that surrounds us. Huge walls of rock lie suspended, interspersed with graceful arches and columns of ice. Bach would definitely have had a field day up here, if he could only work out the organ arrangements!

Out to the left, a traverse across rock slabs leads to easy ground and a beautiful sight. The start of the ice ramps is right around the corner, guaranteeing further progress. A gift from heaven, and not the last on this route by any means. Terry miraculously finds a tiny ledge big enough for two bums, and we set up shop once more. Ropes fixed, gear racked and hung, bodies tied off and we're in and sitting pretty. I relax for the first time that day. The exposure and general situation makes for a fantastic bivy, more like front-row seats at the Albert Hall. We sit captivitated as the theatre of light and colour happens before us. Sunset yields hope, but the cold and blackness take its place, and we soon tire of the entertainment. Cracked hands and faces are encased in folds of fibre pile, and the night wears on, the ritual pattern of restlessness, shifting and shivering enacted to the full.

Summit Day, and we are up early for a change. I begin work on the ramp straight away, equipped only for ice, no sack, just a small one for the second. We lead out pitch after pitch of perfect 70°-85° green ice. Eventually I come up against a short rock wall, behind which the dreaded ice ceilings dramatically appear. A veritable "Creag-y-Rhaeadr" at 18,000 feet, but without the Vaynol Arms lurking beneath.

Terry joins me at the stance and we decide on a plan of action. The first option is tried, and quickly terminated as I retreat very carefully from a thin snow bridge, giving a brief glimpse of the North Face—horrendous! No way, no how! Option two is less threatening; in fact it's nothing short of sheer bloody genius. After carefully searching the morasse of icicles and séracs that now confront us, Terry has managed to discern a route up, and through, the barrier itself. He points it out, and I begin to trace his route over the ground. Hope flickers again and I set off.

PLATE 35

Photo by Leigh N. Ortenburger

NEVADO CAYESH, Peru. The British and Czechoslovakian Routes ascended the face in profile on the left.

The first problem is a shattered rock band, either side of which lie thick ice flows. The rock is verglased, but at a fairly easy angle. Grivels are whipped off at the edge, and I climb very slowly across on sloping holds, desperately regretting our decision to leave the rock gear behind. The pitch ends abruptly at the start of a honeycombed wall of ice, and the start of our journey through the séracs. Although initially low-angled, the ice rises up at me, and then strangely leads off and around a window of ice, ending in two very nice tied-off screws. The first good protection for some time, and with it comes the realisation that I am now on the summit snowfields.

I am surrounded by fantastic ice formations, but by the time Terry has joined me I can see the route ahead, and feel the certainty of success rising within. He leads through and races for the top. The sensation at the summit is too much and I sink to my knees—three years' ambition fulfilled.

The abseils back through the ice ramps are lengthy and expensive, as we gaily kiss goodbye to drilled stakes and titanium screws. We reach the start of the ramps by early evening and resolve to spend another night on the face. The wind that had continually plagued us each evening is strangely absent. We enjoy an hour's relaxation, sitting above the sea of cloud which lies lapping at the face 1000 feet below. Ambition has been halted, if only temporarily, and a sense of real contentment seeps in. Day becomes night once more. All sound has gone and some words from another world come slowly to mind:

> *Love silence, even in the mind . . .*
> *True silence is the rest of the mind; and is to   the   spirit,*
> *what sleep is to the body, nourishment and*
> *refreshment.*

> —*William Penn*

Summary of Statistics:

AREA: Cordillera Blanca, Peru.

NEW ROUTE: Nevado Cayesh, 5721 meters, 18,770 feet, via the Northwest Face; Fourth Ascent of the Peak; July 8 to 13, 1986 (Jerry M. Gore, Terry Moore).

Cerro Torre Solo

MARCO PEDRINI, *Club Alpino Svizzero* *

THE ENORMOUS advances in free climbing achieved in the last ten years have also raised the standard of classic alpinism, especially in regard to light expeditions and major ascents undertaken in alpine style. Fortunately in Patagonia as well, expeditions of the "Himalayan" type are becoming increasingly rare, even though this year there was a Yugoslav group which climbed a new route on the east face of Cerro Torre with fixed ropes all the way to the summit and an unsuccessful Italian group on the south face of the Aguja Poincenot.

In January 1984, during an attempt on the 1970 Maestri route on Cerro Torre, Romulo Notaris and I were blocked at the altitude of the ice towers by an unusual and difficult layer of spongy ice, which, covering the smooth vertical plates, hid Maestri's bolts, essential to further progress. For eight hours we vainly tried to continue before renouncing the attempt. Only a few weeks earlier Thomas Wüschner[1] and Daniel Anker had passed this point without any problem: *cosas patagónicas*!

On returning to Switzerland, I resumed free climbing, my preference in mountaineering. However, I could not forget my defeat on Cerro Torre and so I decided to try again, only this time alone. Since the difficulties were relatively moderate (5.9) on rock, 85° to 90° through an ice gully and A3 on the parts nailed by Jim Bridwell, it was above all a psychological problem. I particularly dedicated myself, therefore, to climbing brief, difficult rock routes without rope.

Before me, the solo climb of Cerro Torre had been tried by Bill Denz and Pierre Farges. Denz had reached the ice towers, where he was pinned down for five days by a storm. On the buttress below the shoulder where the Maestri route begins, he had fallen 250 meters while descending. Great fright and a dislocated shoulder! Farges had set out from Base Camp, and after a week of fine weather

---

* Tragically killed August 16, 1986 on the American Direttissima on the Petit Dru above Chamonix, France.

[1] With Daniel Danker, Wüschner climbed in December 1983 the 1970 Maestri route on Cerro Torre, the Chouinard route on Fitz Roy, the Aguja Mermoz and other small peaks. In November 1984 with Martin Moosberger he ascended the English route on Poincenot and the Buscaini route on Saint Exupéry. He was killed with his daughter in a snowslide during a walk on the Alpstein in Switzerland in December 1985.

he was found dead, killed by the collapse of a sérac on the glacier halfway between Base Camp and Cerro Torre. Was he climbing toward his snow cave when he was struck by the sérac, or was he returning after a victorious ascent?

Inspired by a feat like Bridwell's[2] and in keeping with my customary habit of solo climbing, I decided to aim at speed and lightness, seeking to limit self-belaying as much as possible. No stove, therefore, nor bivouac gear, but rock shoes for the rock and plastic outers to wear over them for the ice, one 8mm rope and another of 6mm for rappels. What was involved was climbing the 900 vertical meters from the shoulder to the summit (to reach the shoulder, one has to overcome a mixed buttress of 400 meters) and then redescending in 24 or at most 36 hours without sleeping and almost without eating. If something didn't go, I'd have to descend as fast as possible.

Swiss Television was interested in my attempt. I left in company with Fulvio Mariani, a movie-cameraman and professional photographer, as well as a superlative climbing companion, and his wife Lucia. If I succeeded on the solo, we would reclimb Cerro Torre together to reconstruct the climb and film it in 16mm.

By mid November I had made a first attempt, but 400 meters from the top excessive winds drove me down. Notwithstanding, I could now see that everything was functioning well and I was convinced that the tactic of speed and lightness was doubtless the best. Then I had to wait for good weather. When it cleared, I immediately set off during the night for the snow cave. At 7:30 A.M. on November 26 I began to reclimb the two fixed ropes left by who-knows-what expedition and the third I had placed the week before. On each long, difficult pitch, I climbed without my rucksack, which I left hanging on a skyhook. From the top I hauled it up with the 6mm rope.

It was very warm—indeed too warm. I climbed in T-shirt, trying to avoid the ice chunks that fell from the wall. Thanks to the rock shoes, I could climb quickly and do the aid pitches without using stirrups, going from bolt to bolt. In a few hours I reached the ice traverse, followed by the gully. At four in the afternoon I attacked the final wall and reached Maestri's compressor. This was certainly the strangest thing I have ever seen in the mountains. Anyone who would throw it off the slope after having climbed up to here solely thanks to the bolts driven by it would be a hypocrite.

For the next 30 meters Maestri had chopped his bolts while descending. Bridwell replaced them with aluminum dowels, knifeblades and copperheads. I drew out the other rope and belayed myself. After 25 meters of A3 on various rugosities and bits of rotten rope, I reached the snow tongue that descends from the summit mushroom. I found the rest of Maestri's broken bolts, which proves

---

[2] In February 1979 Jim Bridwell and Steve Brewer tackled the southeast buttress (the Maestri route of 1970) alpine-style, aiming for lightness and therefore speed. They ascended and descended in only three days, an exceptional exploit.

PLATE 36

Photo by Fulvio Mariani

Marco Pedrini in rock-climbing shoes and T-shirt on the "Banana Crack" (5.10) on Cerro Torre.

to me that in 1970 he reached the summit of Cerro Torre[3]. For the umpty-umpth time I put on the outerboots and crampons over my rock shoes. Then everything became soft and I exited onto the snow with crampons and ice axe and climbed onto the frightful ice mushroom which covers the summit of Cerro Torre.

At 8:30 in the evening I was at the top. The sun set behind the Hielo Continental, the boundless, level glacier which is more than 400 kilometers long. Six hours of rappels during a marvelous night with full moon brought me back to the snow cave. A little later, at dawn, the weather turned foul.

A week later, with Fulvio Mariani, I returned to the snow cave to climb Cerro Torre again and film a reconstruction of the climb. There we found Kurt Lochner and Martin Moosberger, two Swiss who had just descended from the summit. In the middle of the night the roof of the snow cave collapsed, burying us. Fulvio and I still had our heads out but Kurt and Martin had a meter and a half of snow on top of them and could not even breathe. Fulvio and I struggled out of our down sacks and, half nude in the dark, began to grub among the blocks of snow. After a couple of minutes we freed their heads. They were as red as peppers and their eyes were popping out of their sockets. Coughing and choking, they barely could gasp, "Thanks, thanks!"

The following morning Fulvio and I climbed up to bivouac near the top, under the edge of the mushroom. We descended in bad weather without filming anything but fog.

On another try on December 12, we began at two A.M. By noon we were on top. Even though it was not snowing, the mist had returned. We decided to film anyhow. At nine that night we were again at the snow cave; I was beginning to know the route like the back of my hand. We shot a few more meters of film on the first part of the ascent and returned to Base Camp. We had finished.

On December 28 the weather became beautiful again. Fulvio and his wife left. At Río Blanco, the Fitz Roy Base Camp, I found Kurt, who with Martin, had just returned from a luckless attempt on the Chouinard route on Fitz Roy. I agreed to do the north buttress with him. We planned to ascend the Casarotto route and descend by the French-Argentine route, thus traversing the mountain from north to south, all in 24 hours without a bivouac, naturally.

On December 29 we began the mixed gully (400 meters of 60° ice and UIAA Grade IV rock) and then the buttress. We ended by putting up a new variant[4] in rock shoes and with chalk. At eight P.M. we were on the top of the buttress,

---

[3] Bridwell, in his account published on pages 375 to 386 of the *American Alpine Journal* of 1980, expressed the opinion that Maestri may have halted 30 meters from the top of the summit mushroom. (See also *2000 Metri della nostra vita* by Fernanda and Cesare Maestri, published by Garzanti.)

[4] After the approach gully, our route climbed 100 meters in common with the Casarotto route. Then it continued for another 200 meters on the line of the ridge, finally traversing slightly in the second pitch behind and to the right of the ridge itself. It rises 700 meters and was entirely free climbing without pitons and with only nuts and Friends. It presented constant difficulties of 5.10 and had several pitches of 5.11a. It is actually the most difficult route technically on Fitz Roy.

PLATE 38

Photo by Marco Pedrini

Fulvio Mariani jümaring toward the Maestri compressor on Pedrini's second ascent of the route.

PLATE 37

Photo by Fulvio Mariani

Marco Pedrini on the ice traverse below the gully on CERRO TORRE. Fitz Roy's West Face is in the background.

having to cross the small col which separates it from the final 300-meter-high wall. We still had three hours of light and so we continued, planning to descend by night.

Since the traverse was easy, I told Kurt to stop belaying. Beneath me was the ugly gully climbed by the Slovenes the previous year. Just then I slipped on verglas and plunged down 20 meters of the gully. The result: a dislocated shoulder, a dysfunctional leg and blood everywhere.

Kurt helped me back up and we decided to bivouac and descend from there the next day. How I longed to see the stars through the cloud-covered sky. At dawn we set out and took four hours to climb back the 60 meters to the top of the buttress, then 32 rappels to descend. We bivouacked again on the glacier at the upper col and on the evening of December 31, we were at Base Camp for the eve of Saint Silvester. The next morning everything hurt: a bad end of the old year and a worse beginning of the new.

Summary of Statistics:

AREA: Patagonia, Argentina.

ASCENTS: Cerro Torre, 3020 meters, 9908 feet*, via the Southeast Buttress (1970 Maestri Route), November 26, 1985 (Marco Pedrini solo in less than 24 hours); December 3 and 12, 1985 (Pedrini, Fulvio Mariani).

Fitz Roy, 3375 meters, 11,072 feet*, attempt via a variant on the North Buttress to the top of the buttress about 1000 feet from the summit, December 29, 1985 (Pedrini, Kurt Lochner).

---

* It is often difficult to be sure of which altitudes are the most reliable. The altitudes given above are those which have for many years been accepted. However the Spanish Catalán Servei d'Informació de Muntanya has made a careful survey of existing maps and publishes in its monograph, *Cuadernos de alpinismo—Chaltel,* an altitude of 3128 meters or 10,263 feet for Cerro Torre and 3441 meters or 11,289 feet for Fitz Roy.

Fitz Roy's Simončič Route

MATEVŽ LENARČIČ, *Planinska Zveza Slovenije, Yugoslavia*

FITZ ROY, a colossus of granite and ice, is remarkable from every side. From far out to the east, from the flat, dry pampa, its dominant silhouette appears, defying comparison. Even the unearthly beauty of Cerro Torre loses its grandeur in its company. During most of the year this peak hides in a mobile dome of clouds, which continuously changes in color and shape. The few cloudless days shine in such glory that they remain forever in your memory.

If there weren't bad weather, there wouldn't be splendid weather either, since the latter would lose much of its meaning. Paradoxically, if Patagonian weather were worse, it would appeal even more to climbers. Everybody wishes to succeed. The more difficult it is to succeed, the more it means. Patagonian weather increases the difficulty and so climbing there can bring added satisfaction.

Bogdan Biščak, Rado Fabjan and I came there with the same desire. We made the plan, which seemed somewhat utopian, to climb the two beauties and to make a new route on one of them.

All the way to the Río Blanco Base Camp below Fitz Roy we hadn't decided which way to go. There were various suggestions about which route to take. We had to remember that in Patagonia the weather doesn't necessarily permit success.

The result of our discussions was the decision to try a new route on the south face of Fitz Roy. We would have problems with the cold since, being in the southern hemisphere, south walls get about as much sun as the north faces do with us. Also, the south face is exposed to hurricane winds from the west. The conditions are usually poor and the rock cracks are filled with ice. There was the problem of our being three. Even to get to the French Saddle (Silla), there is rather serious climbing. We had to bring a lot of food and equipment there, which meant losing some fine days doing that rather than climbing. All three of us climbed together. We had to descend every time we ran out of supplies, no matter how good the weather was. If there had been four of us, two could have brought the supplies up to the French Saddle while the other two were climbing.

During the first days of December we had bad luck with the weather. Quick changes led to a number of unsuccessful attempts. We dug a snow cave on the pass, Paso Superior (2000 meters). There we stored equipment and also found a perfect shelter during stormy days. This pass makes a relatively simple ap-

PLATE 39

Photo by Matevž Lenarčič

On the upper part of FITZ ROY.

PLATE 40

Photo by Matevž Lenarčič

Decending in storm from FITZ ROY.

proach to the glacier under the east face of Fitz Roy. A main depot was placed about 80 meters below the French Saddle on the wind-protected east side under a granite block frozen into the iced wall.

During two fine days we fixed rope 400 meters up the south face. Before dawn on the third, there were bright stars in a clear sky, but by morning the weather changed completely. Strong winds blew; the sky was covered with clouds. All thoughts of the summit disappeared. Even so, we expected only a short period of bad weather. Wrapped in sleeping bags, we sat in a small crack under the boulder in the middle of the icy wall below the French Saddle. Hope for quick improvement kept morale high, but the storm raged with much more force than expected. After two days, we hitched our bodies, stiff from long hours of lying in the ice, back to the valley, escaping into the green world. New snow covered our equipment, which we left right there, hoping to come back soon.

A few days later we were back on the French Saddle. Early morning sun found us high on the ropes of the south wall. We had already come a long way. We had left Base Camp the previous evening, walked all night and climbed the bottom of the wall. Today we'd get all the way to the summit! We had to make it to the top since while we were gone from the valley, our food had been stolen and we were left with just enough for this last try.

Since the weather was fine, we made good progress on the fixed ropes and soon reached the top of our previous attempt. The wind picked up. We lost a lot of time searching for the best route in the smooth and overhanging wall, but by four P.M. we reached the easier part. The weather was getting rapidly worse: snow, wind, fog. We did manage to get to the double-headed summit of Fitz Roy within the next hour, struggling hard against the wind and growing fear. We were seriously worried about the descent.

And rightly so. Our escape of the wall was a true adventure. Without the luck which was our constant companion, we would never have reached the bottom. At midnight we were finally in our bivouac: dry sleeping bags and insufficient protection from a granite block in the Brecha de los Italianos. The expensive equipment left in the higher bivouac on the first attempt lost all its value; our lives were much more precious. Base Camp welcomed us only late the next afternoon after 44 hours on the go. We were totally exhausted, famished but wildly happy and excited.

I kept wanting to name the route after my best friend, Boris Simončič, with whom we had tried this peak two years before. The weather then had turned us back 150 meters below the top. Three months after returning from Patagonia, an avalanche in the French Alps took his life. Somehow, I feared to make this very personal suggestion to my friends. My fears proved wrong. Bogdan and Rado had had the same idea.

We still had a month before heading for home. We hoped to climb Cerro Torre by the Maestri route. Our food shortage was solved by friends from another Slovene expedition which was attempting the east face of Cerro Torre.

On our first try, we got to within 200 meters from the top and were turned back by the weather. Two weeks of rain and snow followed. Just when our hopes were flickering out, the weather improved. Luck was with us again. We climbed all afternoon. The next day it took us 18 hours to reach the summit, where we bivouacked. In the morning we descended the upper wall, where we met six climbers from the other Slovene expedition. We used their ropes to descend.

Summary of Statistics:

AREA: Patagonia, Argentina.

ASCENTS: Fitz Roy, 3441 meters, 11,289 feet, via a new route on the South Face between the Californian (1968), and the Anglo-American (1972); summit reached on December 22, 1985 (whole party).

Cerro Torre, 3128 meters, 10,263 feet, via the Southeast Ridge; summit reached on January 15, 1986 (whole party).

PERSONNEL: Bogdan Biščak, Rado Fabjan, Matevž Lenarčič.

PLATE 41

Photo by Matevž Lenarčič

Aguja Poincenot and Fitz Roy. The Yugoslav Route on Fitz Roy ascended the face in shadow at the left.

East Face of Cerro Torre

STANE KLEMENC, *Planiska Zveza Slovenije, Yugoslavia*

ANYONE WHO HAS experienced Patagonian weather cannot fail to have doubts, and to fear each day more and more, that good weather will never come.

The clouds swirled in, covering what only minutes before had been a star-lit sky. Winds howled around the edge of the buttress. Half an hour later it was snowing hard and the wind grew to hurricane force. It was hard for the three of us to cling to a narrow shelf below the top of the buttress. The snow kept piling between us and the wall, pushing us toward the 800-meter drop. Our fourth member huddled nearby. The night was endless. Though only three hours from the top of route, we had to retreat to survive. The hurricane dance continued for three days. On the fourth, my three friends returned to the bivouac and successfully completed the climb. This happened two years before on the northeast buttress of Fitz Roy. [See *A.A.J.*, 1984, pages 218-219.]

* * * * *

How often my thoughts returned to Fitz Roy as I listened for eleven days in a row to heavy rain drumming on the tent. The last good weather had been on New Year's Eve. We had been in Patagonia for a month and had climbed 750 meters of the wall. The most difficult part was behind us. We had been lucky with the weather in December; out of 18 days, nine had been good. The hard rain brought discouraging thoughts. What was the use of good weather in December if we didn't get at least some in January for the summit climb?

In doubtful weather on December 14, Knez and Karo started toward the great couloir on the east face of Cerro Torre, where they found traces of a previous attempt on the first two rope-lengths. High up, it was snowing and the snow was piling up in the couloir and on the steep slabs below it. It took them five hours to climb the slabs, to fix rope to the overhanging entrance of the couloir and to rappel to the bottom of the wall. Thirty meters away, Jeglič and Svetičič had dug a bivouac, a snow cave. It snowed the next day. We brought a few loads of food and equipment to the bivouac. The sun hit the wall again on the 16th. Kozjek and Podgornik attacked the twenty meters of overhang blocking the entrance to the 500-meter-high couloir. The overhang was plastered with ice and snow, and melt-water poured down from the couloir. Without scuba-diving equipment, they were soaking wet and cold after the four, long hours it took them to climb the overhanging waterfall.

PLATE 42

Photo by Matevž Lenarčič

CERRO TORRE.

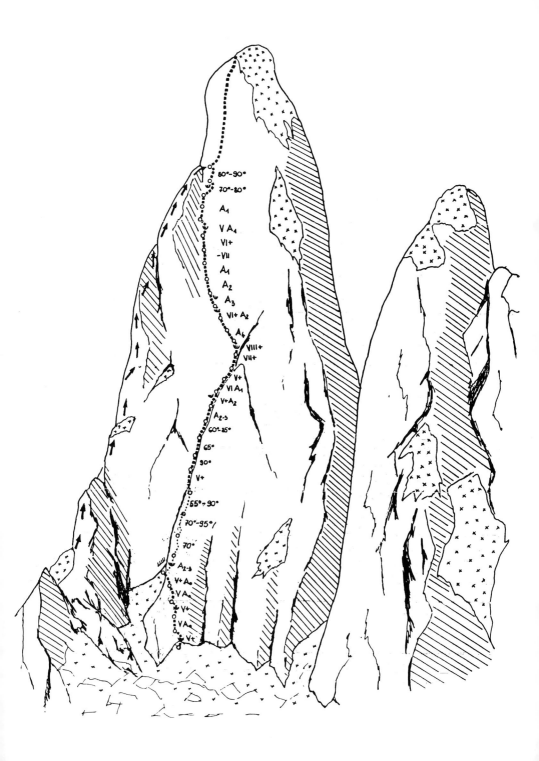

The next day Jeglič and Svetičič started to climb the couloir, polished smooth by continuous rain and snowfall and covered with vertical ice. By ten o'clock when it began to rain, they had climbed 50 meters. They felt as if they were in the mouth of a cannon, raked by ice breaking from the upper part of the wall. Luckily they were not hurt. As the weather got worse in the afternoon, we all retreated to Base Camp.

A three-day pause was useful. We arranged Base Camp and organized supplies. On December 20, Cerro Torre reappeared in full majestic greatness, its walls covered with pristine snow. Since the face had first to be blown clean, it was a day for photography. In the evening we celebrated my birthday, joined by climbers from several lands. With wine, guitar and songs in many languages, the unforgettable evening passed quickly.

On the following day the invasion of Cerro Torre began. Eight of us carried food and supplies to the bivouac. During the last of the approach, the snow lay deep. We knew our bivouac must be there, but it was buried under new snow. After probing with ski poles, we finally found it. Within an hour we had dug a new entrance tunnel 12 feet long. December 22 was beautiful. Knez and Karo climbed 145 meters of the couloir, luckily surviving a half-day of bombing by ice chunks. Most of the climbing was on icicles and frozen waterfalls with short bits of rock. In the afternoon the weather went bad again and they retreated, sopping wet.

Again it stormed for five days. Podgornik and Kozjek were waiting at the bivouac. Every morning they had to dig themselves out. More and more snow and ice coated the face day by day. Although December 27 dawned beautiful, they couldn't start climbing until eleven A.M. because continuous avalanches thundered down the couloir. The fixed ropes were frozen, in places a foot, into the ice. It took them four-and-a-half hours just to get to the top of the ropes. They managed to climb another two rope-lengths of 60° to 80° ice.

The day after, they climbed three more difficult pitches. While the lead climbers worked upwards, Jeglič and Svetičič started up the wall. Their task was to knock out all the pitons and pull up the ropes to the top of the buttress about 100 meters below the upper end of the couloir. After 16 hours of hard work, they had fixed the 500 meters of rope on the right side of the couloir down the slabs. No longer would we be exposed to the continual danger in the couloir. Climbing the fixed line would be much faster since the rope would not be frozen in day after day.

The weather continued to cooperate. Jeglič and Svetičič took over the lead. They could now ascend the fixed ropes much faster. Above them were two relatively easy pitches of rock to the top of the couloir. Then came the middle of the wall, the part we feared most. It looked horrifyingly compact and smooth, but luck was on our side. An overhanging chimney led from the couloir to the Red Band. Both had considerable overhang and the climbing was very technical.

We made good use of the last days of good weather and were 700 meters up the face. On December 30 Knez and Karo climbed an additional 80 meters of

PLATE 44

Photo by Stane Klemenc

Below the East Face of CERRO TORRE.

overhanging, crumbling slabs and flakes, the most difficult aid pitches. They had to place four bolts, the only ones we used.

New Year's Eve was unique. Only Knez and Karo were missing, above in the bivouac. First we toasted the European New Year, and then later, the Argentine one. In the last days of the old year, Patagonia had treated us well, much better than two years before.

The weather changed again on January 1. Two climbers continuously manned the bivouac. For eleven days it stormed. The bivouac was snowed in nearly every night. The entrance tunnel grew by several meters. Avalanches poured off the face. Our friends had to fight day and night with enormous quantities of snow.

On January 12, the mountains started peering out of the clouds. I set out to renew our food supplies leaving by bus from the Hostería for El Calafate. Twenty-four hours later I was back with a large supply of bread, meat, cheese, butter and jam. I rode up in a truck with the workers who during the season had built the bridge over the Fitz Roy River. This meant we no longer had to wade through icy water, but I still don't feel happy about this advance of "civilization." The romance is disappearing. The road will continue deep into the national park. A number of bridges are planned over the Río de las Vueltas, a town will be built next to Fitz Roy and a little further, under Cerro Rosado, a mining town will be set up. At the end of the valley large reserves of coal and uranium have been found.

I arrived at midnight to a totally dark Base Camp. As I was trying to get through the kitchen, I woke my friends nearby. They thought it must be a fox which had visited the kitchen a few times before to "wash" the dishes. There was the bad news that Svetičič had dislocated his thumb, practicing on the cliffs in the vicinity. Our doctor reduced it and put it into a cast.

Since the weather had been good for two days and the face had blown clear, Podgornik and Kozjek started jümaring early in the morning. They had to get up 700 meters of fixed ropes before they could begin to climb further. They did three difficult aid pitches in the last overhanging part and returned to the bivouac. Jeglič, Karo, Knez and cameraman Fistravec meanwhile ascended to the bivouac. On January 15 at four A.M. Jeglič and Karo set out, followed later by Knez and Fistrovec with the bivouac equipment. The lead pair climbed two more extremely difficult pitches (UIAA Grade VII, A1), and then another five rope-lengths between the two pillars, which involved 90° ice. In the last light of day, from below with binoculars, I spotted the two about 50 meters below the top of the pillars. At ten P.M. Jeglič finished this last pitch. A new route had been climbed. On the southeast ridge it joins the Maestri route. The climbers bivouacked just below this point.

During the night Kozjek and Podgornik started to climb the fixed ropes from the snow-cave bivouac. They had joined their friends by seven in the morning. Since they were warmed up from jümaring, they led the route up the gallery of pitons toward the summit. My five-year-old dreams were coming true. A Slovene route on this magnificent wall had been climbed. Six climbers were

PLATE 45

Photo by Peter Podgornik

Couloir on the lower part of the East Face of CERRO TORRE.

PLATE 46

Photo by Peter Podgornik

**Pavle Kazjek just below the top of
CERRO TORRE.**

right below the top. I was only sorry I wasn't there with them, but just before the expedition I had had a finger amputated. The top wall was rather crowded that morning. The six climbers were heading up while our friends Lenarčič, Biščak and Fabjan were starting down. The latter had climbed the mountain via the southeast (Maestri) route a day before and spent the night on the summit. At exactly 12:36 A.M. on January 16 the last of the six climbers stepped onto the top of the ice mushroom which decorates the summit of Cerro Torre. This was fantastic; in a single day nine Slovene climbers had stood on the summit.

On January 17 we were all back in Base Camp. The weather changed again that afternoon. We still had 14 days, but alas, it stormed for another full 12 days. It rained down low every day, and it snowed in the mountains. We needed one more good day to get the rest of our equipment from the bivouac. We made a vain attempt. After we had struggled back up in bottomless snow, strong winds drifted everything over as quickly as we dug. We couldn't save the equipment.

The next day we left the mountains, now all coated with snow, in beautiful clear weather. The last view of the east walls of Fitz Roy and Cerro Torre was unforgettable. My thoughts went back to the last night in 1983. It was past midnight and I was picking *calafate* [a blue berry found in Patagonia] with Ermanno Salvaterra and Maurizio Giarolli, friends from Italy. An old saying says that he who eats calafate berries returns to Patagonia. I ate them again this time. Shall I return?

Summary of Statistics:

AREA: Patagonia, Argentina.

NEW ROUTE: Cerro Torre, 3218 meters, 10,263 feet, via a route on the East Face to the right of the Southeast Ridge; summit reached on January 16, 1986 (Knez, Karo, Jeglič, Podgornik, Kozjek, Fistravec).

PERSONNEL: Stane Klemenc, leader; Franc Knez, Silvo Karo, Johan Jeglič, Slavko Svetičič, Peter Podgornik, Pavle Kozjek, Dr. Borut Belehar, Matjaž Fistravec.

The Sacred Himalaya

JOHAN REINHARD

H IMALAYAN EXPEDITION accounts often mention a fascination with the local people and their culture. Many climbers have felt that their experiences going to and from the mountains were more meaningful than those on the peaks themselves. Thus, it's surprising how little interest there has been in trying to understand the beliefs that Himalayan peoples have about their mountains. True, time factors, language barriers, and the like, help explain this, but there are many cases where these excuses wouldn't hold . . . my own, for example.

Despite spending several years in the Himalaya and being an anthropologist to boot, I barely asked a question about mountain beliefs. Looking back, I suppose it had to do in part with my viewing the mountains as simply physical challenges to be overcome. What other people thought of them seemed to be of little import, since my concerns were on more mundane things like logistics and getting through the day. Partly, too, it may have been due to thinking in terms of the broader aspects of Tibetan Buddhism and Hinduism. The occasional story about a god residing on a peak seemed to be just a tiny part of the whole. Such stories looked at times like patchwork mythology—the mountains are there so let's put some god on them.

Out of plain ignorance, I wasn't aware of how beliefs about mountains were closely linked with traditional religion and even daily life. Indeed, as far as I am aware, there is still no book that directly focuses on mountain worship across the Himalaya. This is a pity, since by tying together and analyzing such worship, patterns emerge that aid in understanding the people living not only near the mountains but often far distant.

We tend to be impressed when we hear that a religious cult has over a million followers. Imagine, then, that close to a *billion* people believe the Himalaya to be sacred and these include followers of two of the world's major religions: Buddhism and Hinduism. Nowhere in the world does a mountain range figure so prominently in the religious beliefs of such a large and diverse population. For these people mountains are the dwelling places of deities and saints, and for some they are the very embodiments of the gods themselves.

Such beliefs date back thousands of years, being noted in the oldest legends and epics. For example, the *Mahabharata*—eight times the length of the *Iliad* and *Odyssey* combined—was reportedly composed over 2500 years ago, and it makes clear the sacredness of the Himalaya. Mountain worship must predate the development of the established religions, since mountains doubtless would have been worshipped by primitive groups living near them. In the Himalaya—and in mountainous regions throughout the world as well—we find a common ground for such worship. The mountains influence weather and are the sources of rivers. In short, they affect the economic welfare of agriculturists and pastoralists alike. Due to their dominating positions, they unite the earth and sky and are perceived as the guardians of the land, people and animals within their domains.

This can even be the case for an entire country. Sikkim has Kanchenjunga as its protector deity. Kanchenjunga is worshipped annually in a ceremony in which he appears as a masked dancer. A similar belief underlies *Mani-Rimdu,* the famous Sherpa dance-drama undertaken principally to appease the local protector deities. At the beginning of the ceremony a yak is consecrated to a mountain god and allowed to roam free as a living offering to the deity.

The mountain protector deities are often given visual form in monasteries. For the layman, they are difficult to distinguish from other deities since they are depicted in the same general fashion. Thus the protector god Numbur was painted on a wall near the main entrance to Chiwong Monastery in north-central Nepal. At Ganden Monastery in Tibet there was (still is?) a life-size statue of the mountain Amne Machen, since he was seen to be one of its special protectors.

According to Tibetan Buddhist beliefs, mountains were the most important of the pre-Buddhist Bon deities. They were the warrior-protector gods, and the original kings of Tibet were closely associated with them. Some scholars claim that the early kings were believed to be incarnations or manifestations of the mountain gods.

When Padmasambhava established Buddhism in Tibet during the eighth century, he is believed to have defeated these deities and turned them into protectors of the Buddhist doctrine—an obvious means of syncretizing the new and old religions. Thus several of the main protector deities of Tibet, such as Nyanchenthangla, Amne Machen (Machenpomra) and the Tshering mchedlnga (the Five Long-Life Sisters) are mountain gods. Many place names refer to these battles, e.g. Darjeeling (from Dorje-ling) is said to be named for the place (ling) that Padmasambhava defeated the mountain goddess Chenchigma with his magical scepter (*dorje*). Rituals are still being performed to persuade Padmasambhava to continue using his powers to divert the anger of the mountain gods.

Nyanchenthanglha is also thought to be the protector deity of Marpori, the hill in Lhasa on which the Potala Palace stands. Marpori hill itself was a local god and the cairn originally devoted to it was maintained in a room of the Potala.

Everest is believed by many Sherpas to be one of the Five Long-Life Sisters: But not the most important one. The most revered of the Five Sisters is Tsheringma, identified by most Sherpas with the peak we know mainly by its Hindu name Gauri-Shankar (Shiva and his consort Parvati). At 23,406 feet, it is much lower than Everest but dominates an area that figures prominently in Tibetan religion and also oversees an important trade route. The great saint Milarepa was active in this region and, like Padmasambhava, believed to have defeated the

Plate 47

Photo by Johan Reinhard

MACHAPUCHARE, still off-limits to climbers because of religious beliefs of the Nepalese.

Five Sisters and turned them into protectors of Buddhism. The Five Sisters are even the guardians of an entire religious order, that of the Kargyupa of Tibetan Buddhism.

Everest is only one of several mountains worshipped in Solu Khumbu today. One important "country god" *(yul lha)* is the mountain Khumbu yul-lha that rises above Namche Bazaar. These country gods oversee the welfare of communities and may become offended by violations of social norms and environmental destruction. For example, grazing and wood cutting would not be allowed on the mountains associated with the principal clans of Khumbu. If this taboo was violated, it was believed the mountain god would cause the people responsible to become ill. In this way beliefs in mountain gods helped in the maintenance of an ecological equilibrium.

Mountain gods are also associated with riches. Kuber, the Hindu god of wealth, is believed to keep a treasure in the mountains of northwest India. Tibetan Buddhists believe that mountain gods protect the legendary "hidden valleys" *(beyul)* and "hidden treasures" *(ter)* of sacred texts and objects meant to be revealed only at special times of need.

The locations of important monasteries and other sacred places and objects (e.g. holy springs, caves and boulders) can often be traced to a direct or legendary association with a sacred mountain. To provide just one example, legend has it that the location of Thami Monastery in Khumbu was selected after a rainbow led from the summit of Khumbu yul-lha to the spot.

As protectors of animals, mountain gods might also take their forms or use them as their steeds. There are stories of the gods transforming themselves into yaks and one tells of Tsheringma (Gauri Shankar) riding on a snow leopard. If angered, mountain gods may send yetis to cause harm. Some villagers believe that yetis are actually the manifestations of these gods.

Mountain deities are believed to protect people against malevolent spirits, and shamans may call them when illnesses and other misfortunes occur. Among the Sherpas, these local deities (and not the high gods of Tibetan Buddhism) are the ones called. They provide spiritual empowerment during trances. Water from these mountains possesses healing qualities. In some areas the shamans are said to undertake magical flights to the sacred mountains in order to communicate with the gods. Even Tibet's famous state oracles became possessed by mountain gods.

Not infrequently, mountain worship can take place as part of a ritual which outwardly might seem to have little to do with it. For example, in Helambu (north-central Nepal) a *yul sang* ("country incense") ceremony is held twice a year to help increase the fertility of crops and livestock, prevent hail, etc., for the village as a whole. Village lamas preside and read a Tibetan text for the ritual, which includes the usual food, incense and liquid offerings along with traditional items, such as bells, drums, conch shells, peacock feathers. The local country gods are invoked and these include, of course, those of the mountains.

For religious reasons a number of Himalayan peaks are still not open to expeditions. Whereas the climbers see only the physical aspects of the moun-

PLATE 48

Photo by Johan Reinhard

Mani Rimdu dance-drama at Thami Monastery near Everest. This relates to worship of local protector gods, including those of the mountains. (Reinhold Messner is among the onlookers.)

tains and worry about risks during the ascents, the villagers have to worry about the long-term consequences if the gods become angry. Even in the case of Everest, now so regularly ascended, many Sherpa climbers make offerings to the goddess to appease her. Since climbing sacred mountains is often offensive to the gods, some high-altitude Sherpas resent doing it, and only are engaged in climbing because it pays so much better than any other work open to them.

If angered, mountain gods might not only cause accidents on the mountain, but can provoke more serious catastrophes to an entire region, e.g. by causing floods, bad weather and avalanches. In 1954 people near Manaslu prevented climbers from attempting the peak because an avalanche had partly destroyed their temple following an earlier ascent.

When Gauri Shankar was opened to expeditions, villagers living near it sent a delegation to Kathmandu to protest. As with any action of this sort, non-religious factors often play roles, and some climbers point to these as examples of the lack of a serious religious concern on the part of the villagers. In fairness, many expeditions have obtained the blessings of local religious authorities and paid for offerings to the mountain gods. On one expedition this came to no small expense, several hundred dollars being given for such offerings while we were on the mountain. And, of course, many mountains are being repeatedly climbed without anyone being particularly bothered. In some cases the villagers think the gods won't pay any attention, since non-believing mountain climbers aren't worthy of it in the first place! But as a general rule, climbers should at least attempt to find out what they can about villagers' beliefs and give serious consideration to how they can avoid offending them.

Climbers usually see little outward expression of mountain worship. In Buddhist areas a small altar of stones might be built at Base Camp. The burning of juniper boughs often serves as an incense offering. This pleases the mountain gods and, when inhaled by climbers, helps to purify their bodies. The gods are thus less offended by them and less apt to attack. Prayer flags also help to avert misfortune. Rice blessed by a lama may be offered at the altar and at dangerous places encountered on the mountain. The low chanting of *mantras* (spells) is often heard, especially before leaving in the mornings. It is a haunting and unforgettable experience to set out onto a glacier in the stillness of the night with dozens of chanting Sherpas.

Certainly the most sacred peak in the Himalaya is Kailash. This mountain is of central importance both in Hindu and Buddhist beliefs. Although only 22,028 feet, Kailash stands alone at a high point of the Tibetan plateau from which four major rivers of South and Central Asia originate: The Indus, Brahmaputra, Sutlej and Karnali. Its religious importance is obviously linked to its being a major geographical center of South Asia. The Karnali is a main tributary of the sacred Ganges River, which helps feed a third of India's population and whose own source lies not far away on the other side of the Himalaya. The Ganges' origin is near the foot of a peak considered one of the lesser abodes of the great Hindu god Shiva. Kailash is Shiva's principal home and he resides there with his consort Parvati. For Buddhists Kailash is the abode of the important pro-

Photo by Johan Reinhard

PLATE 49

Burning juniper as incense to the Goddess of Everest at an altar below the Khumbu Icefall.

tector deities Demchog and Dorje Phangmo and is also associated with Padmasambhava and Milarepa, not to mention numerous other deities and saints. It is here where the legendary contest between Milarepa and a great Bon shaman took place. The line down the south face of Kailash is thought to have been caused by the fall of the shaman's drum after he failed to be the first to the summit. This line gave rise to the name "swastika mountain," the swastika being also a talisman of spiritual strength.

Kailash came to be perceived as the physical manifestation of the cosmic mountain Meru and this symbolized for many the axis of the spiritual universe and center of the universal mandala. Several scholars feel that the forms of pagodas and stupas are based upon the concept of this cosmic mountain.

Mountain symbolism even can play a role in yoga. One yogic exercise is to imagine the spinal column to be one with Mount Meru, thereby gaining one a strengthening of earth consciousness. Of course, Shiva is the lord of the yogis and is believed to chiefly reside in the Himalaya.

The cairns of stones which are such common sights in the Himalaya are usually in honor of mountain gods in the Buddhist region. Some Hindus associate them with their main gods, while Muslims may explain them as being shrines or tombs of their saints.

Whereas Buddhists tend to view the mountains as being individual gods in their own right, Hindus more often claim them as associated in some way with major gods of the Hindu pantheon, e.g. as being their residences. Numerous of the most sacred shrines and pilgrimage sites of Hinduism, e.g. Badrinath, Kedarnath and Amarnath, are located amidst the Himalaya. Virtually every major Hindu deity and saint has been associated in some way with these mountains. One of the most sacred shrines of the great god Vishnu, for example, is found at Badrinath and the principal deified saints (*nathas*) are guardian spirits of mountains. Some believe that Goraknath, patron saint of the royal family of Nepal, still lives on Kailash.

There is an especially sacred mountain in the center of the cluster of peaks that make up the Gangotri-Kedarnath-Badrinath group. It is "Mahadeoka linga," the lingam (phallic symbol) of Shiva, today simply called Shivling. (It's one of the lesser abodes of Shiva, Kailash being the most important.)

Shiva's consort is Devi (meaning goddess), who in a gentler form is Parvati (one "from the mountains"). The mountain Nanda Devi is a manifestation of Parvati. When Nanda Devi Unsoeld died on the mountain she had been named for, local accounts invariably attributed this in some way to actions of the goddess.

The Sikhs make pilgrimages to a sacred place high in the mountains. They believe the great teacher Govind Singh was commanded by God at the lake Hem Kund (15,000 feet), to be reborn in order to combat lawlessness and help the poor. The lake is said to be surrounded by seven (a ritual number) mountains which protect it.

Muslims, too, can consider mountains to have sacred aspects. Thus in Swat-Kohistan in Pakistan they call one mountain, Musaka Musalla, the "prayer mat of Moses," for he is expected to land there when he returns to earth.

It is only logical that tribes living in the Himalaya would have worshipped mountains prior to the establishment of the major religions. After all, we know that primitive tribes throughout Asia believed mountains, lakes and rivers to be inhabited by spirits. If that wasn't enough, further evidence comes from the many accounts of Padmasambhavas' battles with local deities. These battles took place over an extensive area, and there is little doubt that beliefs in mountain gods existed prior to the introduction of Hinduism in the western Himalaya. Some groups, such as the Lepchas, appear to have maintained some of this ancient worship up to recent times.

"In a hundred ages of the gods I could not tell thee of the glories of the Himalaya" goes one saying. Despite the differences that exist between the peoples of the Himalaya, they all share a respect for the sacred mountains. As we have seen, these peaks are the homes of deities and saints believed to directly affect the well-being of millions of people. They can be associated with crop and livestock fertility, environmental catastrophes, illnesses, climbing accidents, pilgrimage places, meditational exercises, architecture, gods of major religions, protection of religious doctrines, even wildlife and legendary beings such as the yeti. Although now assimilated into major religious systems, they still maintain their powers for the peoples of the Himalaya.

APPENDIX

Mountains, Gods and Names—the Case of Everest

The information on the indigenous name for Everest can be summarized in a word—confusing. Some Sherpas perceive Everest to be Miyo (or Miyul) Langsangma. (This is the pronunciation of the more correct transliteration mi-gyo-glang-bzang-ma.) Miyul Langsangma is one of the famous Five Long-Life Sisters (Tshering mched-lnga) of Tibetan Buddhism. However, there are also Sherpas and many Tibetans who do not make this identification. Although he couldn't prove it, Johannes Schubert in his *Mount Everest—Das Namensproblem* (1956) felt that all the Five Sisters were grouped close to the mountain Gauri Shankar. If true, this would exclude Everest as being one of them. Friedrich Funke in *Religiöses Leben der Sherpa* (1969) made the following breakdown of Miyul Langsangma: *mi*-people, *yul*-place, *langsang*-sitting on summit and *ma*-mother goddess. Some Tibetans call this goddess Miyo Lobsangma (mi gyo blo bzang ma) which Funke translated as: *miyo*-unmovable, *sang*-good, *lob*-intellect, *ma*-mother goddess. To complicate things, one Sherpa specialist translated this as "unmovable good ox!" It would take someone knowledgeable not only in Tibetan but also how Tibetans and Sherpas perceive the terms to come up with a correct definition.

Many Tibetans, e.g. in Rongbuk Monastery at the foot of Everest, did not name Everest for one of the sisters, but rather called it Jomo glangma. Tibetans in the region of Khumbu used Jomo (Chomo) lungma. Now Chomo means "goddess" and lung is "valley" so we would have "mother goddess of the valley." This seems simple. However, according to Schubert, Chomolungma wouldn't be grammatically correct in Tibetan. On the other hand, he noted this name appearing on a Tibetan map of 1717. Funke translates Chomolungma as "mother goddess, wind mother," although it is unclear where he got "wind" from.

At least we can say that Everest is perceived as a goddess and a protector deity of nearby regions—not exactly the "goddess mother of the world" as some writers would have it. So which of the indigenous names would seem appropriate for Everest? Chomolungma is a neutral term, but Sherpas apparently do not use it much. Then again, there is no uniformity with Miyul Langsangma either, and it has more specific connotations being the name of one of the Five Sisters. All things considered, if one name had to be chosen, Chomolungma would seem to be the winner—but not by a landslide.

PLATE 50

Photo by Friedrich Funke

**The face of Everest as depicted in a
Sherpa mask.**

The Possible Altitude of K2

GEORGE WALLERSTEIN, *AAC* and *Astronomy Department,*
University of Washington

Editor's Note. The *Journal* is publishing the brief article which appears below because the Editor feels that it is most important for it to appear verbatim in this issue. It is important to note, however, that this does not mean in any sense that by so doing the AAC is announcing that, in essence, K2 is higher than Everest!

These figures are derived from extremely brief and cursory observations made by a mountaineering expedition—not a survey party. We hope they will create a challenge to others to return to the Karakoram soon and establish, once and for all, exactly where K2 is, and how high it is. However, in order to do this with the sort of validity that would be accepted by the world-wide surveying fraternity it would require:

1) An expedition whose prime purpose was to establish the position and altitude of K2.

2) A professional surveyor of high technical competence should either lead this party or be its deputy leader.

3) Assuming that the position is to be based on observations of GPS (Global Positioning System) Satellites, the equipment used should be recommended and approved by the FGCC (The Federal Geodetic Control Committee). Today there are four excellent producers of this equipment.

4) At least three base-stations should be occupied to do this, preferably four, if there appears to be any chance of K2 being higher than Everest.

5) The array of triangles relating these GPS stations to the summit of K2 should involve no angles smaller than 15° and the theodolite that observes these angles should be a Wild T-3, a Kern DKM3 or the equivalent. This is in part because the summit of K2 is not a sharp spire and a substantial "triangle of error" may result from these observations.

6) If laser prisms could be set up on the exact top of K2 (like the Chinese aluminum survey target on Everest) and sights could be made to them from one or more of the base stations, the results of this work would be much more conclusive.

7) The same sort of "final" determinations of the position and altitude of Mount Everest would be equally interesting, particularly if the observations were made from precise survey stations in both China and Nepal.

T HE ALTITUDES usually quoted for most peaks of the Himalaya and Karakoram ranges were determined by triangulation measurements completed during the 19th century by the Grand Trigonometric Survey of India. Hence, it is worthwhile to improve the control of the altitudes of major peaks by entirely independent methods. The best such method is undoubtedly Doppler measurements of the Transit Navigational Satellites.

During the 1986 American K2 Expedition to the north ridge of the mountain, a JMR-1 satellite receiver was brought to Base Camp at Sughet Jangal near the junctions of the Sarpo Laggo outwash stream and the K2 River, latitude = 36°4' N, longitude = 70°23' E. One satellite pass was recorded successfully to obtain the altitude of the site. The single pass was very favorable and yielded both the latitude and longitude to within 1' of arc. The data were reduced at Edo Canada in Calgary. The fact that the latitude was recovered correctly shows that the local oscillator was stable and the high altitude of the pass—83°—greatly reduces any ambiguity between longitude and altitude. The derived altitude of the receiver was 4164 meters above mean sea level.

Since K2 was not visible from Base Camp, it was necessary to tie the station altitude to various altitudes determined by Spender[1] in 1938. All of the altitudes on Spender's map are tied to K2, hence the mean difference between our altitudes and those of Spender's map may be taken as indicative of a correction to the previously quoted altitude of K2 of 8611 meters.

Two base lines, roughly N–S and E–W, 374.4 m and 366.5 m, respectively, were set up and their lengths determined with a Topcon laser range finder. Sightings were made with a Zeiss theodolite on several peaks and other points of established altitude on the Spender map. The results are shown in the following table, in which corrections for refraction and earth curvature have been included.

TABLE 1

DERIVED ALTITUDES NEAR SUGHET JANGAL

Point	Map Altitude	Our Altitude	Difference	Notes
6050 m	6050 m	6312 m	264 m	(1)
6030 m	6030 m	6115 m	95 m	(2)
outcrop	3890 m	4205 m	328 m	(3)
river baseline	3857 m	4155 m	298 m	(4)

Notes:

(1) Peak 5.5 km SSE of Sughet Jangal, mean of observation from both base-lines
(2) Peak 13.0 km SW of Sughet Jangal
(3) Bedrock outcropping at the junction of the Sarpo Laggo and Shaksgam Rivers
(4) Point 379.4 m N of base camp; map altitude interpolated between survey points at 3915 and 3730 m on the Sarpo Laggo River.

The mean correction is 247 ± 51 m, making the altitude of K2 8858 m, or 29,064 ft. If the sighting on peak 6030 is incorrect, *i.e.*, if I sighted a foreground and

---

[1] Spender, M. 1938, *The Himalayan Journal*, 10, 22.

hence lower point, which is quite likely, the mean correction from the other three points is 297 ± 16 m, yielding an altitude for K2 of $29,228 \pm 52$ ft. In that case, K2 is higher than the usually quoted altitude of Mount Everest. If our correction is confirmed it will apply to many peaks in the K2 area, and move several of them to heights above 8000 meters.

Our measurement must be considered to be indicative only, since it is based on a single satellite pass. In their determination of the altitude of Ulugh Muztagh, R. Bates reports (private communication) that of 21 passes at one station and 15 passes at a second station, the maximum deviation from the mean altitude of any single pass was 18 meters. This is a good estimate of the uncertainty in our altitude determination, though an error as large as 50 m is possible for a single satellite pass. In addition, we are uncertain as to the height reference system to which the canonical altitude of K2, 8611 m, refers. Our value refers to the Goddard Earth Model, GEM 10B (Lerch[2] *et al.* 1978), which is a global reference surface. It is essential that a full-fledged effort be made by experienced geodesists to redetermine the altitude of K2. There are rather few sites on the north side of the mountain that are favorable for satellite Doppler reception and have an unobstructed line-of-sight to K2. The most likely location is near the junction of the Sarpo Laggo and Shaksgam Rivers. On the Baltoro Glacier in Pakistan, Concordia is an obvious choice.

The JMR-1 was purchased by the Department of Civil Engineering of the University of Washington with partial support from the Putnam Research Fund of the AAC. The receiver is available for scientific use by AAC members for up to three months per year upon four months' notice to the C.E. Department. I am indebted to Dr. Delf Egge for showing me how to use the JMR-1 and Muhamed Hatem Eid for refreshing my memory on the use of the Zeiss theodolite. Assistance in the field was provided by Dan Bean and George Duffy. Mr. Henry Ayers reduced the satellite data at Edo Canada. The encouragement and support of the expedition leader, Lance S. Owens, is greatly appreciated. The American 1986 K2 Expedition was sponsored by the Coleman Corporation.

---

[2] Lerch, F. J., Wagner, C. A., Klosko, S. M., Belott, R. P., Laubscher, R. E., Taylor, W. A. 1978, Spring Annual Meeting, Am. Geophys. Union, Miami, Florida.

Aconcagua

CARLES CAPELLAS *and* JOSEP PAYTUBI, *Servei General d'Informació de Muntanya*

The idea of a new map of Aconcagua was partly inspired as a continuation of the *Cuadernos de Alpinismo* ("Mountaineering Notebooks")* and partly because of the difficulty of getting good maps of the region. Excellent work by Robert Helbing (1919) was later adapted by Federico Reichert in *Exploración de la Alta Cordillera de Mendoza* (Buenos Aires, 1929). Another good source is Luis Lliboutry's *Nieves y Glaciares de Chile* (Santiago, 1956). Maps of less quality and accuracy are published by the Instituto Geográfico Militar Argentino. In addition to their limited availability, Aconcagua is placed where the four 1:50 000 sheets (3369-7-4, 3369-8-3, 3369-13-2 and 3369-14-1) come together. A small topographic map appears in *Berge der Welt VII* (1952), later adapted by Mario Fantin in his works and by Kenji Yairi in *Sangaku LXII* (1967). A detailed study of this region would not omit reference also to the works of Martin Conway, Edward FitzGerald, Luis Risopatrón, Evelio Echevarría.

To make this a serious, concise study, we have collaborated with the expert Polish cartographer Jerzy Wala, who has carried out the main part of the cartographic work, using the wealth of photographic material from the Polish expeditions of 1934 and 1985, and with Evelio Echevarría for his advice and revisions. Basic cartographic material was also supplied by the Servei General d'Informació de Muntanya in collaboration with Dr. Zdzisław Ryn, who helped coordinate the work in Poland.

Routes. At this time Aconcagua has been climbed by fourteen routes which vary in difficulty from the Normal Route to the Slovene Route to the south summit. (The names of those who made the first ascent and the date appear in parentheses at the end of each route.)

1. Normal Route: This starts from the Plaza de Mulas at the head of the Horcones valley and heads northwest beside the Upper Horcones Glacier. At the foot of Cerro Manso it turns right, leaving the Gran Acarreo on the right, to gain the large plateau on the north ridge. The ridge descends to here from the summit. It winds east and then west towards the ridge which connects Aconcagua's two

---

* The *Cuadernos de Alpinismo* are monographs that deal with a peak or region. To date the following have been published: *Aconcagua* (1982), *Chaltel (Fitz Roy)* (1985) and *Garet el Djenoun* (1987). They are available from Servei General d'Informació de Muntanya, Apartat Correus 330, 08200 Sabadell, Barcelona, Spain.

summits (the *Guanaco* ridge). The ridge is reached by a 260-meter-high couloir (the *Canaleta)*. Once on the ridge, the summit is easily reached. (Matthias Zurbriggen, 1897.)

2. *Glaciar de los Polacos (Polish Glacier):* After heading towards, but not to, the Ameghino Col, one starts up the left edge of the glacier to reach the summit ridge, which leads easily to the summit. This is now considered the normal route from the east. (Wiktor Ostrowski, Stefan Daszyński, Konstanty Jodko-Narkiewicz, Stefan Osiecki, 1934.)

3. *Ibáñez-Marmillod Route*. This complicated and little-used route slabs around the west side of the mountain to reach the south ridge by traverses and gullies. Although it is difficult to follow, it gives you a complete idea of the mountain, particularly when combined with a traverse made by descending the Normal or Polish Glacier Route. (Franciso Ibáñez, Frédéric and Doris Marmillod, Fernando Grajales, 1953.) *3a. 1979 Variant*. This variant is more direct and no more difficult than the Ibáñez-Marmillod Route. (Martín Zabaleta, Xavier Erro, Joan Hugas, 1979.) *3b. Mendocino Route*. This variant in getting to the south ridge passes over Cerro Piramidal, which is reached by ascending the Quebrada Sargento Mas. At 6100 meters it joins the Ibáñez-Marmillod Route. (Carlos Sansoni, Sergio Buglio, 1982.)

4. *French Route on South Face*. This route ascends the central spur. The two principal problems are the great towers and the icefall of the upper glacier. (Pierre Lesueur, Adrien Dagory, Edmond Denis, Lucien Bernardini, Guy Poulet, 1954.) *4a. South Tirolean Route*. This badly named *direttissima* is only a variant of the French Route, with a different entry and a different ending. It is faster and safer and is at present the commonest route on the south face. (Reinhold Messner, 1974.) *4b. Japanese Variant*. From the upper glacier this variant exits by the right wall of the French Spur on rotten rock. (Hironobu Kamuro, Masayoshi Yamamoto, 1981.)

5. *West Ridge*. From the Plaza de Mulas, instead of following the Gran Acarreo, this route heads right and ascends two rocky gullies and joins the Normal Route at 5800 meters. Although a more direct and more interesting route, there is much rotten rock. (Gene Mason, Ralph Mackey, Richard Hill, 1965.)

6. *Argentina (Pasic) Route*. Although this is the easiest south-face route, it is also the longest. It traverses the whole south face from right to left and exits by the final spur of the French Route. (Omar Pellegrini, Jorge Aikes, 1966.)

7. *Central South Face*. This route ascends the couloir to the right of the French spur until it reaches the central glacier, which it crosses by its entire breadth, to join the French route below the icefall. This route is not recommended because of rock- and icefall. (José Luis Fonrouge, Hans Schönberger, 1966.)

8. *Argentine East-Face Route*. This route climbs directly the whole of the east glacier, which is in three separate parts connected by two narrows. It ascends to the top of the glacier and continues up a rock wall which puts one above

ACONCAGUA

Scale 1:50 000

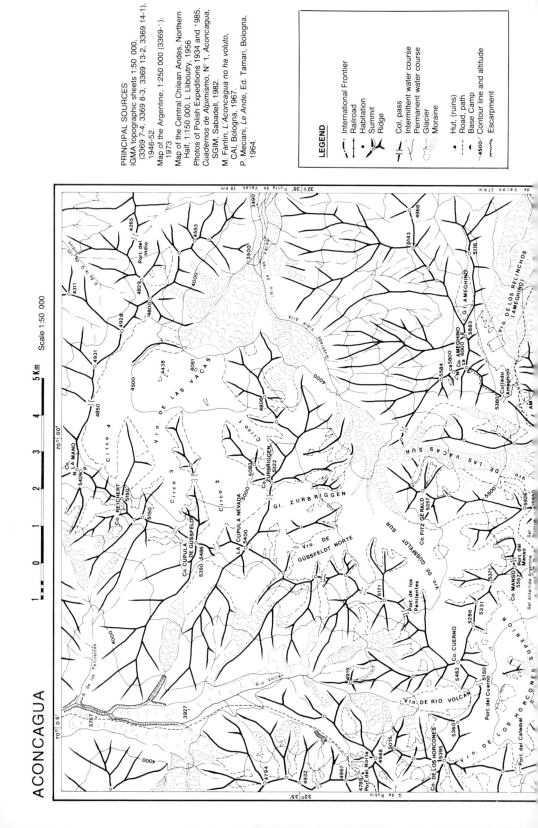

PRINCIPAL SOURCES

IGMA topographic sheets 1:50 000,
(3369 7-4, 3369 8-3, 3369 13-2, 3369 14-1),
1946-52.

Map of the Argentine, 1:250 000 (3369-1),
1973

Map of the Central Chilean Andes, Northern
Half, 1:150 000, L. Lliboutry, 1956

Photos of Polish Expeditions 1934 and 1985.

Cuadernos de Alpinismo, N° 1, Aconcagua,
SGIM, Sabadell, 1982.

M. Fantin, *L'Aconcagua no ha voluto*,
CAI, Bologna, 1967.

P. Meciani, *Le Ande*, Ed. Tamari, Bologna,
1964.

LEGEND

	International Frontier
	Railroad
	Habitation
	Summit
	Ridge
	Col, pass
	Intermittent water course
	Permanent water course
	Glacier
	Moraine
	Hut, (ruins)
	Road, path
	Base Camp
4500	Contour line and altitude
	Escarpment

ABBREVIATIONS

Co. –Cerro (peak)
Port.–Portezuelo (pass)
Ref. –Refugio (hut)
Vro. –Ventisquero (glacier)
gl –glaciar (glacier)
Q. –Quebrada (valley)

R. –Río (river)
A. –Arroyo (stream)
Pt. –Punta (point)
Cr. –Circo (cirque)
T. –Torre (tower)

ACONCAGUA SOUTH FACE

GI –gl Inferior (lower glacier)
GC –gl Central (central glacier)
GS –gl Superior (upper glacier)
AM –Aguja el Monje
PM –Peñón Martínez
PB –Piedra Bandera

SUMMIT

P. –Principal (main)
N. –Norte (north)
S. –Sur (south)
E. –Este (east)
W.–Oeste (west)
C. –Central

ELABORATION

JERZY WALA KRAKOW (POLAND)
SERVEI GENERAL D'INFORMACIÓ DE MUNTANYA
P.O. BOX 310 08200 SABADELL (SPAIN)

DRAFTING

JERZY WALA
XAVI. LLONGUERAS

CARTA OROGRAFICA DEL ACONCAGUA. EDICIÓN ENERO 1986

the Glaciar de los Polacos. It then joins the Polish Glacier Route to the summit. (Guillermo Vieiro, Edgar Porcellana, Jorge Jasson, 1978.)

9. Slovene South-Face Route. This beautiful, difficult, imaginative route ascends the whole south spur of the south face. It is very demanding both because of its length and its difficulty. (Zlatko Ganter, Ivan Rejc, Pavel Podgornik, Peter Podgornik, 1982.)

10. French Direct South-Face Route. This route ascends the right spur of the south face with serious technical difficulties until it joins the Argentine (Pasic) Route just before getting to the upper glacier. (Jean Paul Chassagne, Pierre Raveneau, 1985.)

Altitude of Peaks in Meters

Peak	J.W.	SGIM.	E.E.	L.Ll.	M.F.	P.M.
Aconcagua North	6959	6959	6960	6957	6959	6960
Aconcagua South	6930	6930	—	6886	6930	6955
Almacenes North	5120					
Almacenes South	4510	4510	5060	—	5060	5212
Ameghino North	5800					
Ameghino Main	6000	5883	5883	—	5883	6300
Ameghino East	5883					
Bonete	5100	—	5000	—	5000	—
Catedral	5335	5335	5310	5335	5335	5335
Cuerno	5462	5520	5520	5462	5462	5462
Cúpula Güssfeldt	5350/5486	5486	5350	5350	5350	5486
Cúpula Nevada	5400	—	—	—	—	—
De Los Dedos	5018	5018	4960	—	4960	5018
Fitz Gerald	5357	5357	5550	5550	5550	5357
De Los Horcones	5395	—	—	—	—	—
Ibáñez	5650	—	—	—	—	—
La Mano	5426	5426	5600	5600	5600	5426
Manso	5557	5557	—	—	5557	5557
Mirador	6089	—	—	—	5500	5500
Piramidal	6009	—	—	—	—	—
Reichert	5150	5296	5150	5150	5150	5296
Rico	5380	—	—	—	—	—
Tolosa	5432	5430	5370	5432	5370	5432
W. Schiller	4850	—	—	—	—	—
Zurbriggen	5322	5322	5550	5550	5550	5322

J.W.   = Jerzy Wala and Polish expeditions to Aconcagua 1934 and 1985
SGIM = Servei General d'Informació de Muntanya
E.E.   = Evelio Echevarría
L.Ll = Lliboutry
M.F. = Mario Fantin
P.M. = Pietro Meciani

Note: The same map published here but printed in a larger scale (c.12 x 19 inches or 30 x 50 cms) with the other information may be purchased from the American Alpine Club or the Servei General d'Informació de Muntanya.

Climbs and Expeditions,1986

The Editorial Board is extremely grateful to the many people who have done so much to make this section possible. Among those who have been very helpful, we should like to thank in particular Michael J. Cheney, Kamal K. Guha, Harish Kapadia, Mohan C. Motwani, H.C. Sarin, Józef Nyka, Tsunemichi Ikeda, Muneeruddin, Trevor Braham, Renato Moro, César Morales Arnao, Vojslav Arko, Franci Savenc, Paul Nunn, Xavier Eguskitza, Doug Scott, José Manuel Anglada, Josep Paytubi, Elmer Landes, Robert Renzler, Sadao Tambe, Annie Bertholet, Fridebert Widder, Silvia Metzeltin Buscaini, Luciano Ghigo, Zhou Zhen, Ying Dao Shui and Anders Bolinder.

METERS TO FEET

Unfortunately the American public seems to be resisting the change from feet to meters. To assist readers from the more enlightened countries, where meters are universally used, we give the following conversion chart:

meters	feet	meters	feet	meters	feet	meters	feet
3300	10,827	4700	15,420	6100	20,013	7500	24,607
3400	11,155	4800	15,748	6200	20,342	7600	24,935
3500	11,483	4900	16,076	6300	20,670	7700	25,263
3600	11,811	5000	16,404	6400	20,998	7800	25,591
3700	12,139	5100	16,733	6500	21,326	7900	25,919
3800	12,467	5200	17,061	6600	21,654	8000	26,247
3900	12,795	5300	17,389	6700	21,982	8100	26,575
4000	13,124	5400	17,717	6800	22,310	8200	26,903
4100	13,452	5500	18,045	6900	22,638	8300	27,231
4200	13,780	5600	18,373	7000	22,966	8400	27,560
4300	14,108	5700	18,701	7100	23,294	8500	27,888
4400	14,436	5800	19,029	7200	23,622	8600	28,216
4500	14,764	5900	19,357	7300	23,951	8700	28,544
4600	15,092	6000	19,685	7400	24,279	8800	28,872

NOTE: All dates in this section refer to 1986 unless otherwise stated. Normally, accounts signed by a name alone (no club) indicate membership in the American Alpine Club.

UNITED STATES

Alaska

Denali National Park and Preserve Mountaineering Summary, 1986. Record numbers of mountaineers, unusual weather patterns, light winter snow pack and volcanic eruptions set the scene for an interesting mountaineering season in the Alaska Range. The 1985-86 winter was extremely mild with many sunny days and few major winter storms. As a result, snow accumulation was far below normal for both Talkeetna and the entire Alaska Range. During the spring, Mount Augustine volcano, located in the Cook Inlet approximately 125 miles southwest of Anchorage, erupted. Ash from the eruption was carried by prevailing winds and deposited throughout much of south central Alaska, including parts of the Alaska Range. As the already reduced snowpack melted during the spring, the grey ash layer was eventually exposed. The ash absorbed more heat from the sun which further accelerated the snow melt. The surface of the glaciers melted with an exaggerated cup-shaped surface pattern, making ski-equipped aircraft landings difficult. By early July, the 7200-foot Base Camp airstrip was unusable. Since a number of expeditions were still on the mountain, special authorization was given for the air-taxi operators to land at 9700 feet on the Kahiltna Glacier to pick up those remaining expeditions. No drop-offs were permitted. There was one winter ascent attempted in 1986. Dave Johnston, a member of the first successful group winter ascent in 1967, made a solo attempt on the West Buttress which included a ski approach from his cabin in the Trapper Creek area. Dave reached Windy Corner (13,200 feet) before he frostbit the toes he froze during his first winter ascent. He skied all the way back to his cabin without assistance. The High Latitude Research Project was not funded this season, but a short research project was conducted by several of the project's medical personnel in conjunction with the U.S. Army's Northern Warfare Training Center. A group of military volunteers were flown directly to 14,200 feet where the medical personnel studied the effect of the drug Decadron upon the unacclimatized men. The project lasted approximately 1½ weeks. Afterward, the Mountaineering Rangers staffed the camp for the remainder of the season. Once again, the transportation of the camp to and from the mountain was provided by the U.S. Army, 242nd Aviation Company, Fort Wainwright, Alaska. The National Park Service conducted three, three-week expeditions on Mount McKinley. All were on the West Buttress route. We continue to emphasize environmentally sound expeditionary climbing and sanitation practices. In addition, mountaineers are encouraged to conduct their own evacuations when ever possible. During emergencies, the 14,200-foot medical/rescue camp provides an excellent base from which rescue operations can be staged. Possibly the greatest operational benefit derived from the camp is the improved communications with other mountaineering expeditions and the Talkeetna Ranger Station. We are more reliably able to determine if a rescue is really needed, and if so, the urgency and the appropriate level of the response. Two Americans and one New Zealander were issued citations for guiding without a permit. In 1986, new all-time records were set for the number of persons attempting to climb Mount McKinley. 1978 = 539; 1979 = 533; 1980 = 659; 1981 = 612; 1982 = 696; 1983 = 709; 1984 = 695; 1985 = 645; 1986 = 755.

Interesting Statistics. *Success Rate*: 406 (54%) of those attempting the summit of Mount McKinley were successful. 7 (33%) of those attempting Mount Foraker were successful. *Acute Mountain Sickness:* 105 (14%) had symptoms; of these 58 (8%) were mild, 30 (4%) were moderate and 16 (2%) were severe. *Frostbite*: 41 (5%) reported some degree of frostbite. None of these required hospitalization. *West Buttress route:* 597 (79%) of the climbers were on the popular West Buttress route. *Guiding:* More climbers were guided on McKinley than ever before. 319 (42%) of the climbers were with one of the authorized guiding companies. The overall success of these groups was 61%. Most of these were on the West Buttress, but other guided trips were attempted on the Muldrow, Cassin and South Buttress routes. *Foreign climbers:* 187 (25%) of the climbers were from foreign countries. 23 nationalities were represented: Australia 2, Austria 16, Brazil 2, Canada 14, Chile 1, Czechoslovakia 6, Finland 1, France 9, Great Britain 14, Iceland 5, Italy 9, Japan 24, Korea 10, Liechtenstein 6, Netherlands 4, New Zealand 1, Norway 2, Rumania 1, South Vietnam 1, Soviet Union 9, Spain 4, Switzerland 12, West Germany 33. *Temperatures*: On July 10, a party reported the summit temperature to be 30°F! For the second year, a minimum recording thermometer was left at 17,200 feet on the West Buttress route. It recorded a low reading of − 58°F for the previous winter. This is the exact reading recorded the previous winter. During the 1987 season, the Mountaineering Rangers will place a second minimum recording thermometer to check the accuracy of these readings. *Record number during a given week*: A new all-time high of 308 climbers were on the slopes of Mount McKinley for the week ending May 20.

Accidents. The season began on a tragic note when one of the first expeditions lost two members in a crevasse fall on April 20. A four-person French team was ascending the Kahiltna Glacier at about 9000 feet. The team was traveling up the west side of the glacier (the "normal" route was further to the east). The two members involved in the accident had decided to travel side-by-side with their ropes attached to a single sled so they could both pull the sled. A large snowbridge collapsed under them. Both were killed in the resulting 75-foot fall. During the investigation, it was determined that the two had used standard glacier travel techniques during the first two days of travel, but had decided to forego the safety of roped travel for the convenience of pulling the sled. The survivors said the safety aspect of the decision was discussed, but the victims felt there was no crevasse hazard. One of the victims was a professional mountain guide in his homeland.

In the middle of May, a four-person expedition began a descent of the South Buttress from their high point of 15,000 feet. Conditions were icy and one person would belay from above while the others descended. At the end of one of these belays, the rope became tangled in the belayer's ice tools. He unclipped from his anchors to clear the rope. While he was unprotected, the ice knob he was standing on sheared off. He sustained a tumbling fall for the entire rope-length and then another 150 feet until the rope stopped the fall. No intermediate anchors were placed by those descending. During the fall, his crampons caught in the ice severely injuring his ankle. The party lowered the victim to a saddle at 12,500 feet, but felt they could not safely proceed further and requested, via CB radio, a rescue. The victim was flown off the mountain via helicopter. In mid May, a member of a large German party was skiing from 15,000 feet to the 14,200-foot basin on the West Buttress route. During the descent he fell and severely twisted his knee. He was flown from 14,200 feet via fixed wing aircraft at his own expense. In mid June, four members of a Swiss team were camped at the 14,200-foot basin on the West Buttress. They had just completed a carry to 17,200 feet. Weather was deteriorating, everyone was tired from his long day's carry, so they retired to their tents (two men to each of two tents) to cook dinner. The storm continued throughout the night and into the next day. It broke later that afternoon. Two left their tent and noticed the other tent was sagging. There was no response from within the tent. When they opened the tent to investigate, they discovered the two young men dead. Investigation showed the two died from carbon monoxide poisoning from their butane cook stove. Their tent was made in Europe of a coated nylon with a full coverage rainfly (including a complete vestibule). The roof vents were closed and snow had either been packed around the bottom of the fly or had slid off the tent during the storm. Thus, there had been no allowance made for fresh air exchange. It appears the two had prepared and eaten dinner the first night, then were in the process of cooking soup when they were overcome by carbon monoxide. The survivors stated the group had discussed the importance of providing ventilation while operating the stoves prior to the accident. Also in the middle of June, two members of a seven-member Korean team began a rapid ascent of the Cassin Ridge. One of the team members began to develop a headache at 16,500 feet but decided to continue on to their high camp at 19,700 feet which they reached on day four. Here, the headache became severe, so they decided to rest the follow-ing day (day 5). On day 6, they broke camp but discovered both were too weak to ascend and one was showing definite signs of cerebral edema. They felt descent was impossible because they carried only a single rope. On the 7th day they began broadcasting for help, but the language barrier prevented their mes-sage from being understood until day 9. What followed was three days of one of the most logistically complex rescues to be conducted during the past five years. Volunteers were selected from climbers already acclimatized who were either on the mountain or who had just come off. The team was flown to 14,200 feet (weather prohibited the planned drop off at 17,200 feet). Of the four mem-bers in the advance team, two contracted altitude illness by the time they reached 17,200 feet. The remaining two were able to reach the summit ridge, descend the upper Cassin and assist the two Koreans back to the summit ridge. Fortu-nately, the Koreans were able to make the ascent with minimal assistance. Once at the ridge, the Korean suffering from CE collapsed, became comatose and did not regain consciousness for the remainder of the rescue. The team descended to 18,000 feet, where they spent the night with a large guided party. The following day, they met the support rescue team which lowered the comatose Korean down Denali Pass to 17,200 feet where he was eventually helicoptered to a hospital. The remaining Korean and the rescuers descended to 14,200 feet and were flown back to Talkeetna. The entire rescue took only three days. No one was injured and both Koreans recovered from their ordeal. The success of this mission must be attributed to a supreme effort on the part of the rescuers and a great deal of good luck.

Trends and items of special concern: *Percentage of foreigners requiring rescues:* Ten persons required some sort of organized rescue effort during 1986. Four of the evacuations were body recoveries. Nine of the ten (90%) were mountaineers from foreign countries. Even though foreign mountaineers comprised only 25% of all climbers, they accounted for 90% of all Search and Rescue incidents. All four of the fatalities were foreigners. In 1985, foreigners accounted for 19% of the climbers, but 50% of the fatalities (there were two) and 40% of the SAR incidents. In 1984, foreigners accounted for 28% of the climbers, but 100% (there were two) of the fatalities and 57% of the SAR incidents. For 1987, we are planning to expand the slide/tape mountaineering orientation to include French and Spanish in addition to the German, Japanese and English versions which are currently available. The information brochure *Mountaineering* will also be available soon in the same languages. It is difficult to state the exact causes of the disparity in SAR incidents between the foreign and American climbers. I believe that the majority of foreign mountaineers are leaving Talkeetna for their climb with a fairly good grasp on what the National Park Service recommends pertaining to high altitude, cold and crevasse related hazards. It seems more likely the higher accident rate is a result of many of the foreigner's seeming willingness to accept a higher level of risk in their mountaineering. Year after year, we see foreign parties traveling unroped on the lower glaciers or traveling Denali Pass without ropes and ice axes, or making rapid ascents which result in altitude illness. Clearly, for the majority of these groups, they have made a conscious decision to adopt specific techniques even after extended discussions with the mountaineering rangers in Talkeetna. *Solo ascents:* We have been seeing increased interest in solo ascents. During 1986, there were approximately six different solo ascents attempted. A number of other climbers arrived in Talkeetna with the intention of climbing solo but were convinced otherwise by the mountaineering rangers. It is clear that the majority of the persons attempting solo climbs have made no allowance for nor have given much thought to their safety while traveling the heavily crevassed lower glaciers. *Carbon monoxide poisoning:* In 1985, cooking in poorly ventilated areas such as tents with all doors and vents closed, or old ice-glazed igloos and snow caves caused two serious cases of CO poisoning. In 1986, two young Swiss mountaineers died of CO poisoning while cooking in a tent. It is very likely that mild cases of CO poisoning are a contributing factor to Acute Mountain Sickness especially pulmonary edema. CO poisoning might very well be a greater threat to mountaineers using the new tents with full coverage water-proof rain flies especially those with vestibules which encourage cooking in the tent while the coated vestibule can be kept closed. It is imperative for personal health and safety to allow adequate ventilation when cooking with stoves in enclosed areas. For more information, or to request mountaineering information or registration forms, please contact me, South District Mountaineering Ranger, Talkeetna Ranger Station, P.O. Box 327, Talkeetna, Alaska 99676.

ROBERT R. SEIBERT, *National Park Service*

DENALI NATIONAL PARK AND PRESERVE
1986 MOUNTAINEERING SUMMARY

Mount McKinley	Expeditions	Climbers	Successful Climbers
West Buttress	111	361	181
West Buttress (Guided)	30	236	152
Muldrow	3	9	4
Muldrow (Guided)	3	40	22
West Rib	12	38	27
Cassin	10	28	15
Cassin (Guided)	2	9	3
South Buttress	3	9	0
South Buttress (Guided)	2	18	0
East Buttress	1	3	2
Messner Couloir	2	4	0
	179	755	406 (54%)
Mount Foraker	5	21	7
Mount Hunter	10	27	2
Mount Huntington	1	2	0
Little Switzerland	4	13	N/A
Mount Dicky	2	7	7
Mount Barrille	5	16	15
Mount Dan Beard	3	9	U/K
Moose's Tooth	11	34	14
Broken Tooth	1	2	U/K
Kitchatna Spires	1	2	2
Miscellaneous Ski Trips	15	70	N/A
	58	173	

NOTE: Since registration is required only for Mount McKinley and Mount Foraker climbs, statistics for other climbs represent those climbers who voluntarily checked in with the Mountaineering Rangers. Other climbs, especially in the area of the Ruth Glacier, are likely to have occurred.

PLATE 51

Photo by Bradford Washburn

McKINLEY'S East Buttress. The route rose up the middle of the photo.

McKinley, East Buttress. On May 29, Don Lee flew Scott Hartle, Joe Terravecchia and me to 7700 feet on the northwest fork of the Ruth Glacier. For the next week during unstable weather, we ascended the 1963 ramp to Thayer Basin. Rather than to attack the dangerous icefall at 11,800 feet directly, as was done on the 1963 climb, we traversed to the right into a beautiful couloir for six pitches of moderate ice up to 50°. The couloir ended at a prominent pinnacle along the ridge. We followed this ridge to rejoin the 1963 route above the icefall at 13,000 feet. After five days of poor conditions in Thayer Basin, the weather cleared on June 11 and we summitted in a long day by climbing the upper section of the South Buttress route. We then descended the lower South Buttress to Kahiltna Base. The lower East Buttress, is more difficult and committing than the lower South Buttress, but is better protected from objective hazards. In our ascent, we did 19 belayed pitches, but with careful route-finding found no rappels necessary on the South Buttress. On the lower East Buttress, on the route we took, only in the easy section around 10,500 feet is there much objective danger. We climbed alpine-style with two weeks of food and saw no other climbers the entire time, except for two on the summit. There has been some confusion about climbs on the East Buttress. The *A.A.J.*, 1983, lists the "fourth" ascent. I talked with Bill Krause of that expedition. He said that they went up the lower section of the South Buttress and the upper part of the East Buttress, the opposite of what we did. Although both routes have been listed as "East Buttress," they start miles apart on different glacial systems.

GEORGE BELL, JR.

Soviet-American Exchange on Mount McKinley. In the spring of 1986 the Soviet-American Climbing Exchange resumed. Five of the ten members of the Soviet team had been members of the Soviet-American expedition which climbed Pik Pobedy in 1985. (See *A.A.J.*, 1986, pages 21-26.) They were Team Captain Nikolai Chorny, Sergei Bugomolov, Vladimir Puchkov, Oleg Borisyonok and Yuri Golodov. On the 1982 Soviet Everest expedition, Chorny reached Camp IV but had to descend to rescue another climber. Puchkov and Golodov reached the summit. The other climbers were Vitaly Bakhtigozin, Leonid Troshinenko, Yury Borodkin and Viktor Baibara. Troshinenko was logistics director on Everest. Non-climber Valery Epov was the Team Leader in Alaska. Joined by William Garner, the nine Soviet climbers started up through the icefalls between the Cassin Ridge and the West Rib. (See *A.A.J.*, 1973, pages 282-288.) We climbed to 16,500 feet and traversed onto the rib. The summit was reached on mid-morning of May 18 in superb weather. Though this was rigorous climbing by some standards, it was normal for this group. After the climb, Lowell Thomas, Jr., Charlie Sassara and John Markel orchestrated an Alaskan odyssey which is now legend in the Soviet Union. From Point Barrow to Halibut Cove, they displayed for the Soviets' joy all that is breathtaking and generous about Alaska and its people. They worked hard and long. Like the Alaskan section of the American Alpine Club, the New York and Blue Ridge

PLATE 52

Photo by George Bell, Jr.

East Buttress of McKinley between 10,000 and 14,000 feet.
—— = 1986 route;
– – – = 1963 route.

sections warmly greeted and magnificently entertained them on their month-long stay in America. Several corporate sponsors and many members of the Club contributed a lot to this exchange, for which we are very grateful.

WILLIAM GARNER *and* RANDALL M. STARRETT

Foraker. Our expedition to Foraker via the west ridge consisted of Mark Dale, Juan Esteban Lira, John Mason and me. Foraker was first ascended in August 1934 by the west ridge with an approach via the Foraker Glacier. The second ascent of the west ridge was done in July 1977 but it was actually a variation with the approach being made by the Herron Glacier. This second group on the west ridge spent five weeks pioneering this route, having started their trek at a hunting camp west of the Swift Fork River. Including equipment shuttles, they traveled over 200 miles on foot. We intended essentially to follow their route except to go in much earlier to take advantage of better snow cover on the tundra and traditionally clearer weather in April and May. There is a large lake, just outside the original park boundary, where we hoped to land to cut some 30 miles off the walking distance. We arrived in Talkeetna on April 11 and were successfully flown to the frozen lake on the 12th. We immediately began ferrying equipment across the tundra in the direction of the Somber Creek valley, which we knew from the 1977 party to be a shortcut to the Herron Glacier. A very light winter snowpack made pulling the sleds across brushy tundra difficult. Nine days were spent shuttling food and equipment to our Advance Base Camp at 5000 feet on the true right bank of the Herron Glacier at the foot of the west ridge. We took a much needed rest-and-organization day on the 21st and then on the 22nd began the ascent of the west ridge proper. The weather had been generally good but was getting colder as we ascended. We camped at 7800 and 9800 feet and had an equipment cache at 13,500 feet by April 26. Temperatures were dropping below 0°F and unfortuanately Mason frostnipped his toes and could not continue the ascent. On the 28th Dale, Lira and I headed off to establish Camp III while Mason stayed at Camp II. We had hoped to place the camp at 13,500 feet but a lack of tent platforms forced us to go on to 14,100 feet. The morning of April 29 dawned clear, though windy, with a temperature of −15°F. We left the tents at 11:30 A.M. with −5° and a 15-mph wind. We got to the summit (5303 meters, 17,400 feet) at 5:30 P.M. with 30- to 40-mph winds. We were reunited with Mason on the 30th and all members were back at Advance Base on May 1. We spent three days returning to the lake and were flown out on May 6.

DONALD J. GOODMAN

Foraker East Face. To acclimatize, Jaroslav Jaško and I climbed Mount Crosson. From there, we planned our route, which was to the right of the Pink Panther route on the east face of Foraker. For the climb we took five days of food, a Salewa Sierra tent without the fly, a 50-meter rope, 8 rock pitons, 6 ice screws, and a set of excentrics. We felt the ascent would not be too dangerous

PLATE 53

Photo by H. Adams Carter

FORAKER'S East Face. Pink
Panther Route (——) is left.
Czechoslovakian ascent route (— —)
is in center and their descent (· · · ·)
on right. Bivouacs are marked.

despite some snowy séracs. We left Base Camp on the Kahiltna Glacier in the afternoon of May 19, although the snow was avalanching off the face down onto the glacier. In four hours we were in a badly broken section of the glacier below the east face of Foraker. Finding the route through the crevasses to the bottom of the face was complicated but we managed it before bivouacking. On the morning of May 20 snow was falling and we climbed the glacier looking for a place to cross the bergschrund, which was ten meters wide. We were relieved when we could cross a weak snowbridge and get onto the face. Crevasses and weak snowbridges there were unnerving. On the fourth pitch, a snow avalanche passed over us from above. We were racing against time. Snow slides made us stop climbing after 12 hours. We bivouacked in a snow cave under a big rock at the edge of the buttress. On May 21 we tried to climb as fast as possible. We were in 50° knee-deep snow. When it was rock, it was verglas-covered. Since there was no place to bivouac, we kept on climbing until midnight, when we chopped a ledge in a snow ridge. We had surmounted difficult rock and much steep ice; one pitch was 85° and another 75°. We waked up on May 22 to lovely weather. We really enjoyed the mixed terrain. By two o'clock we were finally at the last nearly overhanging snow pitch before emerging onto the southeast ridge. After an hour's rest, it took us five hours to get to the summit. We began our descent down the Sultana Ridge and after sleeping a few hours, we finished by descending the Japanese route. Again, crevasses were a major problem, but we crawled through, belaying carefully. At nine P.M. we were back at our first bivouac. We rested until the cold froze our tracks across the Kahiltna Glacier. In the pale light of the night, we greeted our friends at Base Camp at 1:30 A.M. on May 23.

DUŠAN BECÍK, *Iames, Bratislava, Czechoslovakia*

Foraker, Talkeetna Ridge. On May 3, Dave Auble and I left the Kahiltna Glacier to attempt the second ascent of Foraker's Talkeetna Ridge, first climbed by Bertulis, Bleser, Baer, and Williamson in 1968 (*A.A.J.,* 1969, pp. 289-294). Our approach took two days, and unfortunately required us to cross two passes before we could set a camp at the base of the ridge. The first three days of climbing were spectacular: the mixed terrain among the gendarmes on May 5 led to a 500-foot wall of beautiful granite (5.7) on the second day. This was followed by several pitches of steep blue ice before we reached Camp III, a level tent site at about 12,000 feet, and a pleasant change from the cramped bivouac ledges that served as Camps I and II. A storm pinned us down for three days beneath the serpentine "Peruvian Way." Described by Bleser as "a thin suspension of ridge," this part of the climb offered us the same hair-raising experience his party had endured eighteen years earlier. The ice climbing was difficult and disturbing at best, and it occupied us for the next two days. Our fifth camp was carved from the very crest of the ridge itself, where it ended abruptly at a steep granite headwall; a strenuous pitch up hard blue ice took us from there to the interminable upper slopes of the mountain. Horrific conditions forced us to camp a few hundred feet from the top on May 13, but the next day we headed across the summit in the still-raging gale. We followed vague compass bearings to the edge of the plateau in a whiteout, finally settling for the welcome shelter of a huge hanging sérac while the storm continued until May 16. Our descent of the south-southeast ridge was less than pleasant: we nipped off a few giant cornices, had a remarkably close call with an avalanche, lost another day to bad weather, and Dave suffered from seriously frostbitten feet and a broken tooth. The innumerable rappels only served to prolong the ordeal. However, fueled by a herculean effort on Dave's part on the final day, we reached our Base Camp at last on May 19. With its 10,000 feet of vertical relief, varied and technical climbing, and spectacular positions, the Talkeetna Ridge receives our strong recommendation to anyone seeking a truly committing Alaskan outing.

CHARLES TOWNSEND, *Unaffiliated*

Hunter, South Ridge. During May, Ed Hart and I climbed the south ridge of Hunter, partly by the 1973 Waterman-Carman-Black route, traversed the mountain and descended the west ridge in a 12-day alpine-style ascent. We were flown to the Tokositna Glacier by Jim Okonek on April 26 and ferried loads through two icefalls to gain the south col at about 10,000 feet at the foot of the south ridge on April 29. We spent four days there, waiting for settled weather before starting the route on May 4. We climbed a variation to the lower 3000 feet of the ridge by climbing the mixed face to its left which avoided most of the rock climbing on the 1973 route. We then followed the fragile and sometimes double-corniced ridge for nearly a mile to reach a col below the final steep 800-foot ice arête that led to the summit plateau. We managed to traverse around the "Happy Cowboy Pinnacles" on the east side rather than straddle them as the previous south-ridge and southeast-spur parties had done. A storm kept us at the col for the next two days and the weather, which had been perfect until now, continued very unsettled for the rest of our time on the mountain. We resumed climbing on the seventh day but after two pitches we avoided climbing the rest of the badly corniced ice arête by traversing across the mixed face to its left to reach the sérac line just below the plateau. The following day we crossed the summit plateau in a whiteout on a compass bearing and established ourselves on the west ridge as it cleared that evening. Early on May 12 we climbed back up the ridge and up to the north summit—our ninth day on the mountain. The descent down the west ridge was hampered by poor visibility and took 2½ days. We reached the Kahiltna Glacier at dusk on May 4 and arrived at the landing site early next morning.

SIMON RICHARDSON, *Alpine Climbing Group*

Hayes Range Ski Traverse. Mike Brown, Richard Cooper, David Williams and I made a ski traverse of the Hayes Range during the spring of 1986, climbing six minor peaks on the way. Leaving the George Parks Highway at mile 229 on March 29, we arrived at the Black Rapids Roadhouse on April 18. For the first four days, as far as the moraine on the Yanert Glacier, we had dog-team support. The temperatures dropped to $-40°$ at night and two members, Paddy O'Neill and Steve Thomas, had to turn back with frostbitten fingers. (They have suffered no permanent damage.) After a further four days of hard work relaying loads through deep snow up onto the Yanert Glacier, we both climbed and traveled on most days. We were helped by excellent weather with only three days too poor to travel, although on one of these the wind was so violent that we had to drop the tents and take refuge in a hastily-dug snow cave. Crevasses were never a problem, but with recent heavy snowfall and strong winds, slab avalanches were a definite hazard. From camp at 5900 feet on the Yanert, we climbed P 8245 from the north. Crossing a low col to the south, we climbed P 7440 and P 8345 the same afternoon, and the following morning climbed an attractive peak of 8000 feet to the east before traveling to a 6000-foot col south of Deborah, helped by wind-hardened sastrugi. From there we attempted P 8020 by its north ridge, turning back after releasing a small avalanche. We continued east to camp beneath P 8240. This we climbed the next day by the west ridge and we moved on northeast to camp beneath a 7300-foot col. Back-tracking slightly, we visited the col northeast of P 9280 and enjoyed a view onto the Gillam Glacier, but we decided against an attempt on the 9000-foot peak to the east. Crossing the col above our camp, steep but short on both sides, we were delayed by a day of heavy snowfall, which gave us fine powder skiing when we continued down to the Susitna Glacier. From the Susitna-Black Rapids divide, we climbed Aurora Peak (10,065 feet) by its long southwest ridge and then skied down to Black Rapids in just over a day, relieved to find the Delta River still well frozen.

ROB COLLISTER, *Alpine Climbing Group*

Hayes Range Speed Traverse. On the first weekend of May, U.S. Ski Team member Audun Endestadt and I skied 140 miles across the Hayes Range in three days and four hours, winning a $1000 bet, which like gentlemen we declined to collect. With alpine-style attitudes and nordic racing skis and technique (skating and double-poling almost 75% of the distance), we crossed the four largest glaciers of the Hayes Range: Black Rapids, Susitna, West Fork and Yanert. We crossed three passes over 5500 feet and traveled completely self-contained. After the ordeal of the winter Brooks Range traverse which Chuck Comstock and I had suffered three weeks before, this trip, in spite of (or because of) its speed, was a vacation.

ROMAN DIAL

Traverse of the Brooks Range from Kaktovik to Kotzebue. On March 25 with 100-pound loads, Chuck Comstock on Nordic racing skis and I left Rokotvik, Barter Island, Alaska and headed west across sea ice. Our bottle of 80-proof whiskey froze the first night out. We then crossed the North Slope to the base of Mount Chamberlain. A ground blizzard and tight schedule foiled our attempt on that peak. We followed Carnivore Creek south and then crossed a 4500-foot pass over to Franklin Creek. We broke miserable trail to Canning River and then skied 30 miles upstream in one day on the Marsh Fork of the Canning. We skied over a low pass at Porcupine Lake into the Ivishak drainage, where I broke both skis, started a tent fire and tasted death at − 65° F. By splinting both skis with a spare racing ski and aluminum ski pole cut up, we were able to continue. While crossing into the Ribdon River valley, I set off a slab avalanche above me. Other misadventures included perpetual sub-zero temperatures, 20 miles of overflow, a collapsing snow bridge in the dark while postholing in the Ribdon and wet feet at − 20°. We made it to the Pipeline Haul Road after 17 days of skiing, having covered 250 miles and suffering *no* frostbite whatsoever. In July, my wife Peggy and I returned to the Pipeline Haul Road and hiked west up Trembely Creek over Falsoola and Kinnorutin Passes in two days. On the third, I soloed the south ridge of Doonerak in 45 minutes and spent two hours in 80° sunshine on the summit. On my way back to camp, I traversed P 6400, east of Doonerak. Finding no cairn, I assume it is a first ascent. Peggy and I then followed Amawk Creek to the North Fork of the Koyukuk, which we floated in a Sherpa raft to Ernie Creek. We crossed the Ernie Peak Pass and floated the Anaktuvuk River to near Anaktuvuk Pass. It took us another week to walk and float to the Arrigetch from Anaktuvuk. My wife, who was pregnant, hitchhiked a plane ride back to Battles from Takahula Lake. I continued on to the Arrigetch peaks, where I traversed Ariel, climbed the first spire west of Elephant's Tooth and the second spire west. Having made these easy fifth-class climbs in the rain, I felt confident to attempt Wichman Tower under storm conditions. Verglas and rime stopped me 50 feet below the summit ridge. An anchor pulled on my second retreat rappel, but I caught myself with an arm around a rock horn. I left the Arrigetch over Escape Col between Ariel and Xanadu, hiked through the Little Arrigetch and finally reached Twelve Mile Creek on the Noatak River, four weeks and 350 miles after leaving the Haul Road. I paddled to Kotzebue down the Noatak River in a two-man Klepper kayak solo in ten days. In all, I covered 1000 miles in 60 days, making the first east-west traverse within the Brooks Range.

ROMAN DIAL

Chigmit Mountains, Reconnaissance. In late May 1983, Peter Reed and I travelled by float-plane to Lake Iliamna in search of good rock. We had heard from geologists that the nearby Chigmit Mountains possessed large quantities of granite which might be suitable for climbing. We camped on the shore of Knutson Bay in the northeast corner of the lake. From camp we could see the impressive 2000-foot south buttress of Knutson Peak and we left for the face with high hopes. Upon our arrival we were disappointed to find no vertical crack systems that would offer a natural line of ascent or places for protection. The rock itself was indeed granite but of a variety we had never seen before. Unlike the fine-grain granite common in the Sierra, the rock was large-grain made up of massive quartz crystals. The high quartz content of the rock made the composite very brittle, and early attempts in placing bolts proved fruitless. The rock, being covered with lichen, might provide excellent friction climbing but without protection and only after considerable gardening. We were able to salvage the trip by finding a miniature "Lost Arrow" at the west end of the buttress which was relatively clean and produced several pitches of good climbing at 5.7, A2. On the south side of Knutson Bay, we climbed an enjoyable outcropping which provided short free climbs in the 5.4 to 5.9 range.

STEVE DAVIS

Mount Gerdine. Two previous ascents of Gerdine were made from the east, by Paul Crews, Sr. and Jr., Rod Wilson, George Wichman and Lowell Thomas, Jr. in 1963 and by Japanese in 1967. On April 19 Lowell Thomas, Jr. landed Mike Frank, Jim Sprott, Tom Meacham and me on the Hayes Glacier at 6000 feet. We set up camp at 7000 feet on the irregular ridge southwest of Gerdine. The next day we scrambled up this ridge to P 10,270 where the steepening ridge with blue ice and dwindling afternoon convinced us that we did not like this route. We retreated uneventfully to spend the next two days in camp while cold winds blew through the area. On April 23 we set out at 7:30 to traverse the bowl south of Gerdine to the south ridge proper just north of P 10,510. From there we climbed the south ridge over several icy pitches and then traversed along the east side of P 10,700 into the bowl east of the summit. Our route from there duplicated the original summit climb and we reached the summit (3432 meters, 11,258 feet) just after four P.M.

GREGG HIGGINS, *Mountaineering Club of Alaska*

Valley of the Pillars, Wrangellia. After nearly a decade on Valdez waterfalls, Carl Tobin and I stepped up to the big ice of Wrangellia. Carl had known of the ice for years, but after an October traverse through Wrangellia I substantiated the rumors with photos. The most beautiful waterfall in the world I told slide show audiences, flashing a shot of an eight-tiered marvel plunging down a forested escarpment. Excited by the photos, the Alaskan Alpine Club put together a six-man expedition. Club president Jeff Keener, secretary Carl Tobin, and members Eric Breitenberger, Chuck Comstock, Keith Echelmeyer, and I made up the team. In early January Keith flew all of us in with his Cessna 185. After tying down the plane, the six of us skied three miles to the Valley of the Pillars and established Base Camp. The following day Carl, Chuck, and I started up *Broken Dreams,* the beautiful eight tiered waterfall. The climb was 1500 feet long with each tier ranging in length from 75 to 200 feet. Carl said the climb was reminiscent of *Polar Circus.* The eighth and final tier was a free-hanging pillar for at least 60 feet with a big crack and some obvious stress deformation. Moments after Chuck backed off the noisy ice the pillar collapsed! A bit shaken we finished the route on rock to the right. The climb had one bivy on the ascent, complete with wood fire. We rated *Broken Dreams* a water-ice

VI. Meanwhile Eric led *Full Bore* (WI V, 165 feet) across the valley. This single pitch of very big ice is especially impressive. Eric claimed it more difficult than *Rigid Designator,* yet easier than *The Fang* in Colorado. Eric, Jeff and Keith also climbed *Lone Wolf* (WI III, 1500 feet) just upstream from *Broken Dreams.* On January 7 and 8 Carl, Chuck, Eric and I climbed *Star Babies* (WI V +, 1000 feet) which offered four tiers ranging in length from 165 to 300 feet. Carl's lead on the second step was particularly spectacular with huge cauliflower ice bulges reminiscent of Colorado's Bridal Veil Falls. *Star Babies* also yielded one splendid campfire bivy. On January 7 Jeff and Keith climbed *Boys of Summer* (WI IV, 1000 feet) to the right of *Star Babies.* The day before flying out, Carl, Eric and I made the second ascent of *Full Bore* while Keith and Jeff climbed *Asian Lady* (WI II, 165 feet). In total the Alaskan Alpine Club Expedition to the Valley of the Pillars made six first ascents.

ROMAN DIAL

Polar Bear Peak, Northwest Face, Chugach Mountains. During beautiful weather and suprisingly mild temperatures, Charlie Sassara and I climbed Polar Bear Peak (6619 feet) during February 15 to 17. Believed to be only the third ascent of the mountain, this climb produced the first one in winter and the first ascent of its spectacular northwest face. Leaving the Eagle River Vistor Center at dawn, we hiked up the historic Iditarod Trail for six miles before crossing the open river to begin our bushwhack. We followed the drainage into a beautiful cirque where we were surrounded by impressive peaks and pocket glaciers. A nine-hour day left us on top of a steep snow slope below the rock shoulder of the northwest face with 3500 feet to go. We found an ideal bivouac site in a hollow formed by the wind. The following morning we climbed unroped with a full compliment of rock-and-ice hardware up the shoulder, following a series of snow ramps connected by verglased rock. This shoulder proved to be the key to the hanging glacier on the upper face. Once on the glacier, we climbed up to 55° snow to the summit pyramid. A pitch of verglas followed by a challenging chimney led us to the sharp summit four hours after starting. The view from the top was unbelievable with not a cloud seen over all of Alaska. We were able to see the long snow gully on the south side that led to the two prior ascents. After a rappel of the chimney, we down-climbed the rest of the pyramid and enjoyed a quick glissade down the glacier. Down-climbing the shoulder was no problem in our euphoric state. Following a second bivouac we descended the drainage following Heritage Creek to the river. We reached the visitor center in six hours.

STEVE DAVIS

Thompson Ridge Area, Chugach Mountains. On June 12 Jim Miller flew Bob Jacobs, Ole Kanestrom and me to the Thompson Ridge area. We landed on a sandy gravel bar near Ross Green Lake, where a Polish expedition had set up Base Camp. We joined them for a week of climbing in this spectacular wilderness. A Pole, Paweł Kubalski, climbed with us. Later that same day, the four of

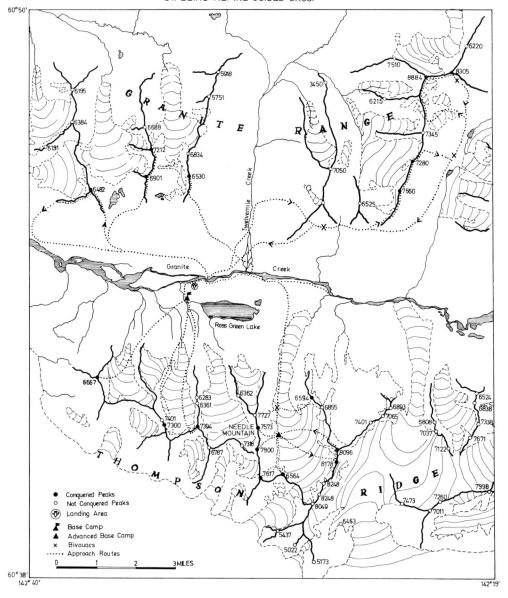

ACTIVITIES OF POLISH EXPEDITION ALASKA`86
and
ST. ELIAS ALPINE GUIDES GROUP

us set out to establish Advance Base on an unnamed glacier which lies along the east face of Needle Mountain. We set up camp at 5000 feet early the next morning after climbing through the badly broken icefall all night. Due to snow conditions, we did all our climbing at night. Most of the couloirs began to avalanche around 9:30 A.M. On June 14 we left camp at midnight to ascend the northwest rib of P 8178. This peak lies on the ridge which is due east of Needle Mountain. We made our way through the crevasses and then through the séracs near the base of the rib. The snow rib was 45°, steepening to 55° or 60° a few hundred feet below the summit. On top we were greeted by a beautiful sunrise and panoramic views of the Bagley Icefield and all the way to Mount Logan to our east. We traversed the ridge from P 8178 to P 8096 to the north and descended its west ridge. On July 15 we ascended Needle Mountain (7573 feet) by the snow couloir on its east face to a col on the ridge just south of the summit spire. Bob Jacobs led the final 30 feet up the spire from which the peak gets its name. On June 16 we climbed the two southernmost of the three 8000-foot spires which lie just south of Needle Mountain. Again we ascended a steep couloir on the east face of the ridge. We returned to camp just before large avalanches wiped out our tracks. Jacobs and Kubalski also climbed P 6564 by its northwest face. Poles Czerwiński, Maczyński, Piekarczyk and Sobolewski had just climbed it from the east two hours earlier. On June 17 we descended to the Polish Base Camp. On the lower glacier it was exciting due to the rapid snow melt. Kubalski was unlucky enough to spend an hour extricating himself from a crevasse. On June 18 we climbed P 6667 by a snow couloir on its east face. Reaching a col just north of the summit, we followed the ridge to the summit. We believe that these were all first ascents except Needle Peak, P 6564 and P 6667, second ascents.

DANNY W. KOST, *Unaffiliated*

Thompson Ridge Area and Granite Ridge. In addition to the mountains mentioned above in Kost's report, the Poles climbed these peaks in the Thompson Ridge area: P 7394 via west ridge by Sławomir Maczyński and Andrzej Sobolewski and June 13; P 7401 via middle summit, which was reached by a ridge from the south, by Staniław Czerwiński and Zdzisław Kosłowski on June 15; P 6594 via south face by Krzysztof Konarski and Dariusz Naszyński on June 16: and P 7617 via east couloir, a snow route up to 50°, by Czerwiński, Maczyński, Andrzej Piekarczyk and Sobolewski on June 18. In the Granite Range, they ascended the following: P 6530 via south ridge by Piekarczyk and American Ole Kanestrom on June 13; P 6901 from the south and P 7212 via south ridge by Kozłowski and Sobolewski on June 26; P 6482 from the south by Naszyński and Piekarczyk on June 26; P 7560 via south face and P 7280 via south ridge by Paweł Kubalski and Maczyński on June 26; and P 8884 (highest peak in the Granite Range) via southwest ridge and P 8305 via west ridge by Kubalski and Maczyński on June 27. All were first ascents. These peaks may be found on US Geological Survey sheets *Bering Glacier,* C-4, C-5, D-4 and D-5.

JÓZEF NYKA, *Editor, Taternik, Poland*

P 9385, University Range, Wrangell Mountains. From August 1 to 8, Bob Jacobs and I led Randy and Kathy Haines, Seth Moshman and Marvin Srulowitz to the Twaharpies Glacier area of the University Range. On August 1 we flew to the Glacier Creek landing strip and hiked up to the tongue of the Twaharpies Glacier. On August 2 and 3 we moved camp to 4300 feet, where an unnamed glacier flows into the Twaharpies Glacier from the southeast. On August 4 we moved up this glacier to 6600 feet, establishing camp below our approach route to the west ridge of P 9385. After a day's snowfall, on August 6, we started up but at 8000 feet the visibility was less than 150 feet and so we turned back. On August 7 Jacobs, Moshman and I started up the glacier again. The glacier was heavily crevassed between 7000 and 7800 feet. From there to the saddle at 8000 feet between P 8205 and P 9385 it was a steep snow-and-ice climb. The saddle drops to 7800 feet at the base of the west ridge, which we followed to the summit. P 9385 is the westernmost peak of the ridge locally known as "Solidarity Ridge." The ridge is five miles due west of the three Twaharpies peaks. We believe we made the first ascent of the peak.

DANNY W. KOST, *Unaffiliated*

P 12,659. In July Fred Beckey, Bill Lahr and I started out to complete a climb Fred, Jim States, Chris Kopczynski and I had attempted in 1985 when we failed in bad weather. Our objective was P 12,659 in the Wrangell-Saint Elias National Park. It lies near Bona, Bear, University Peak and Churchill. The 30-mile-long Barnard Glacier flows past the peak's western end. The peak rises 7000 feet above the glacier. Getting to the area was full of difficulties. After various problems, we were helicoptered from McCarthy to the glacier east of the peak. At four A.M. the next morning we set out for the northeast ridge on frozen snow. Once on top of the ridge, we roped up and began to thread our way along the huge cornices. The exposure on the northwest side was over 3000 feet and the view of the surrounding peaks was breath-taking. The firm snow of early morning started to give way. The ridge presented vertical walls of mush which at first forced us out onto steep, mushy and unstable snow on the south face and finally stopped us. The retreat was no easy matter due to the soft snow. We decided that our second attempt would be on the steep 3500-foot east face. A storm moved in that night and kept us in the tent for the next two days. In the evening of the second day, Bill Lahr and I decided to go for it. Fred Beckey wasn't well and chose not to go. We two departed at eleven P.M. on July 13. We started up a 45° gully directly below the summit. After 500 feet, the gully narrowed to 20 feet and was filled with endlessly flowing snow. We looked for another gully farther north which forced us to drop 150 feet and traverse snow-covered rocks in the semi-darkness. Bill started and was carried off by a wind-slab avalanche. I managed to grab a pile of rope and quickly loop it over a rock horn; I brought him to a halt after a 40-foot slide. The slope got continuously steeper and more exciting, especially since we had no rock gear. After nearly 300 feet, the final pitch to the summit ridge steepened to nearly vertical and the ice became soft. I finished the pitch by digging deep holes for my arms and doing half pull-ups until I reached the crest of the ridge. The final 600 feet up the ridge to the summit were less steep but far more dangerous, due to wind-packed snow. I was nearly buried when a large crevasse bridge collapsed. Twice we heard the snow around us settle with a sickening thud. Finally we reached the tiny summit. On the descent it was Bill's turn to have a crevasse bridge fall out from under him. Moments later, all the snow below me broke loose and slid off the mountain, leaving me on the fracture line. From Base Camp we spent 2½ days enjoying the views of dozens of unclimbed peaks as we passed several of the Barnard's tributary glaciers on the way to the air-lift spot.

GARY SILVER

St. Elias. Alaskans Bob Antonson, Dave Blanchet, Ray Koleser and Todd Miner climbed St. Elias by the south ridge, the route first climbed by the Harvard group in 1946. They believe that this was the 15th ascent of the mountain.

St. Elias Attempt. Günter Zimmermann, Urban Gebhart, Walter Kischlat, Winfried Hartmann and I were flown by Mike Ivers of Gulf Air Taxi on May 29 from Yakutat to the east fork of the Tyndall Glacier. That same day we made Camp I on a little saddle at 4500 feet. We were stormbound for three days. On June 2 we established Camp II at 6600 feet and the next day made Camp III at 9000 feet. On July 4 we reached Haydon Col at 10,000 feet, where we made Camp IV. On July 5 we climbed Haydon Peak (12,945 feet) via its northeast face in beautiful weather. On the 6th we got to 13,500 feet on the south-southeast ridge of St. Elias, but were driven back to Haydon Col by a heavy storm. The next day our tent was destroyed by the storm and we spent two more days and terrible nights in snow and cold in our wrecked tent. When it cleared on June 10, seven feet of snow had fallen. After a day of digging for our equipment, we retreated and were flown out on June 15.

FRITZ RADUN, *Deutscher Alpenverein*

St. Elias Southeast and East Ridges Attempt. On June 13, Steve Bain, Karen Bush, Charlie Carr, Ben McKinley, Chip Morgan and I were on a fork of the Newton Glacier right below the southeast ridge of St. Elias. Our goal was to complete the unclimbed southeast ridge, an extremely technical, long, exposed route. The following morning we wove our way across yawning crevasses to the base of a couloir that led up to the ridge. A large sérac near the couloir gave way, setting off an avalanche that consumed the entire couloir in Volkswagen-sized boulders. We looked for alternatives. Charlie Carr led up three pitches on a loose class-5 rock face that we believed connected with a snow ramp to the ridge. We fixed the route and returned to camp. When we returned the following day, we noticed that our fixed lines had been drenched in avalanche debris. Only 20 minutes after Charlie and I had returned from a high-speed retrieval of the gear, an enormous rock-and-snow avalanche swept the face. Luck was with us that day. We moved camp to just north of the base of the southeast ridge and tried to find a route onto the ridge from this side. Charlie Carr, Chip Morgan and I climbed steep avalanche-prone slopes beneath séracs and over large slanting bergschrunds. Charlie led the last steep pitch on loose snow and rock to a knob on the ridge where we could assess the 2000-foot exposure on both sides of the knife-edged ridge that grew to 5000 feet where the ridge leveled off. Immediately ahead lay loose steep snow that with the slightest loading appeared ready to collapse onto the Newton Glacier. Then came a steep multi-pitch rock section that looked loose and slightly overhanging near the top. These sections were minor in comparison to the steep rock and ice 3000 feet higher. It was obvious it was too late in the year for safe snow conditions. Regrouped for the east ridge, we carried loads and camped just below 11,000 feet. We had a choice of either the sharp, jagged ridge or a long, steep snow face. Charlie Carr led onto the steep face and discovered loose granular sugar snow that would not pack and offered no protection. On our return we found that the face would have involved at least eight pitches of completely unprotected, steep, exposed and avalanche-prone climbing. The next day we tried the jagged ridge. An hour and a half of painstaking step-cutting and stamping put me near the top of the ridge where one slip would have sent all of us tumbling 2000 feet to the Newton Glacier. I put in all my remaining protection, plus both my tools; the snow could not have been more dangerous. Karen Bush led past me onto the ridge and found slightly denser snow. Steve Bain climbed along the ridge and Charlie Carr went past him. They found weak cornices. We agreed that we could not justify the objective hazards and quit. One last note: for most of the climb we had a commanding view of the Abruzzi route. The huge avalanches that swept down all parts of the upper Newton Glacier, some starting from Russell Col itself, others sweeping across the glacier and up the other side, deposited sérac blocks larger than small houses and made this route and its approaches highly dangerous. It would be foolhardy to consider the route, especially in May, June and July.

Peter A. Cooley*

Washington—Cascades

East McMillan Spire, North Buttress, Southern Pickets. From Terror Basin, Rachel Cox and I walked north along the Terror Basin-Azure Lake divide. Where this ridge steepens and merges with the east ridge of McMillan Spire, a horizontal ledge leads to Stetattle Ridge, the divide between McMillan Cirque and Azure Lake. We followed Stetattle Ridge to a col (class 3), made two 165-foot rappels, climbed down ice and snow to benches in the upper McMillan Cirque and traversed west on slabs which were exposed to falling ice. A rock spur led up between icefalls directly to the base of the north buttress of East

---

* Recipient of an American Alpine Club Climbing Fellowship Grant.

McMillan Spire. We began at the toe of the buttress, scrambling east around a large gendarme to a prominent notch. From the notch a fifth-class pitch and 200 feet of third class brought us to a bivouac on a large shelf. From there it was possible to walk down and right to active springs in a large shallow cave. There was no water higher. In the morning we climbed six fourth-class pitches up and left to a large rubble-covered platform on the crest of the buttress, overlooking the huge chimney-and-corner system on the lower east face. We climbed up and right for three pitches to the base of a long open-book. This is the first corner system west of the crest of the buttress, ending in a series of blocky overhangs. Three beautiful pitches of 5.7 to 5.9 on excellent rock led up the corner to grassy ledges immediately below the overhangs. A short horizontal pitch to the left on ledges brought us back to cracks and corners near the crest. Here we made a second bivouac. After a pitch, crack systems to the left and right were blocked by overhangs. We opted for an improbable outside corner leading straight up between the overhangs, which provided a surprisingly moderate and safe 165-foot pitch. After one passes the overhangs at about mid height on the buttress, many lines are possible. We climbed up and left along the crest for several pitches of solid, enjoyable fourth and fifth class. Where a loose and blocky vertical step about 60 feet high blocks the crest, we traversed up and right, emerging on a huge ledge. Above this point the rock deteriorates. Whereas the lower two-thirds is solid gneiss, the upper portion is loose, slabby schist. However, the climbing, mostly third class, is much easier. We climbed seven rope-lengths just west of the crest, then traversed 200 feet right to join the 1977 route for two pitches to the summit. We descended the west ridge and couloir to Terror Basin. Bergschrunds necessitated two 150-foot rappels. (28 pitches, 10 of which are fifth class. V, 5.9.)

PETER KELEMAN, *Fourth Avenue Alpine Club*

Johannesburg, Northeast Face, Winter Ascent, North Cascades. In mid February Josh Lieberman and I took advantage of perfect weather and low snow cover to drive 18 miles up the Cascade River road. We walked the last four miles up the road. Johannesburg was nearby. We traversed out onto the glacier beneath the northeast face to the bottom of the prominent couloir on the left side. This couloir is described by Mark Bebie in *A.A.J.,* 1986. We were drawn upward. Instead of traversing right as Bebie and Stoddard did, we stayed in the couloir. Most of the climbing was third class. Large chockstones occasionally blocked the parallel-sided gully, forming vertical steps. Snow beneath the chockstones was unconsolidated and so these steps entailed climbing on one of the walls on thin ice and rock over the abyss. Once we followed a tunnel beneath a big block. As darkness fell, we dug in under another block. The couloir reaches the top of the face several hundred yards east of the summit. After traversing the horizontal crest toward the summit for some time, we saw the last few hundred feet: jumbled gendarmes and crazy cornices. We decided not to proceed. As it was, we were benighted in the "wrong" couloir as we descended the south side of the east ridge.

PETER KELEMAN, *Fourth Avenue Alpine Club*

Cutthroat Peak, East Face of North Summit, North Cascades. Joe Bajan and I on September 21 did this fine route, which is about 500 feet north of the Chouinard and Burdo routes on the main east face. We followed granite flakes just right of the obvious gully in the middle of the face directly below the north summit. The second pitch ascended a large left-facing open-book for 165 feet. The third pitch went up the right side of the "Black Staircase," which is easily seen from below. The fourth pitch finished the staircase and led up the gully to easier climbing. Eventually we got to the north summit and followed the north ridge to the main summit. (III, 5.9.)

STEVEN C. RISSE

Dorado Needle, West Buttress, 1985. In October 1985, Dan Cauthorn and I found our way to Dorado Needle. Our route starts in a recess to the right of the buttress proper and ascends a wall just left of a chimney for the first pitch. Several more moderate pitches lead to a huge slabby platform. A loose pitch up a gully leads to a chimney on the exposed crest. Ledges, edges, and blocks lead left across the buttress face, then up to the blocky crest. Another lead works along the crest, past a tower (5.7), to the base of the inviting slabs forming the upper pillar. Three excellent pitches up faces and along narrow arêtes lead to gullies which are followed left to the regular route and summit. (III, 5.7.)

WILLIAM PILLING

El Dorado Peak, North Couloir. The north face of El Dorado Peak is a hazardous enigma. In October, Dan Cauthorn and I—carrying plenty of noodles and tuna packed in oil—emerged from the depths of the Cascade forest empire to investigate this hidden facet of the "Queen of the Cascade River." There were no clouds to cause concern. (Still, you never know.) We left our camp below the west face of El Dorado at six A.M. and walked toward the Dorado Needle-El Dorado col until we could climb onto the glacier beneath the north face of Eldorado. The elegant and unmistakable couloir required 6 to 8 pitches of frozen snow and water ice between 55° and vertical, finishing on the knife-edged summit arête. On the summit at one P.M., Cauthorn summed it all up: "Good climb, good climb . . . I think so, don't you?" (III).

WILLIAM PILLING

Mounts Triumph and Despair, Winter Ascents. The winter of 1986 was an unpredictable one in the Cascades. During the last two weeks of February, six feet of new snow were followed by torrential rains and spring-like clearing. On March 1, Mark Bebie, Brian Sullivan and I skied the Thornton Lakes road and an old logging spur leading up Damnation Creek. From the head of the creek, the effect of the previous two weeks of weather was obvious. Avalanche fractures were visible everywhere, and we stumbled across two miles of debris to reach our campsite at Triumph Pass. The next morning we cramponed up the northwest shoulder of Triumph, then climbed a steep snow ramp to the south ridge, placing an occasional snow fluke or picket to combat the exposure. Brian and I admired our corniced and fluted surroundings as Mark struggled up the crux of the route, a glazed chimney of loose rock. One easier pitch of mixed ground brought us to the summit. We stomped out platforms and spent a long lunch gazing at the winter spectacle of the Picket Range. Later that afternoon we moved our camp to an avalanche-choked lake below Mount Despair. On the morning of March 3, Mark and I climbed perfect frozen snow up the southeast face of the peak. The clouds and wind were increasing, so we began a careful descent after just a few minutes on the summit. We rejoined Brian back at camp and started the long trip back to the car. The skiing was terrible, but the pleasure of having visited such wild and remote country made up for it.

LOWELL SKOOG

The Pyramid, North Rib. This rib begins in MacMillan Cirque 2500 feet below the summit of the Pyramid. It starts as a rock buttress, then changes to an elegant snow crest as it merges with the east shoulder of Degenhardt Glacier. On June 27, my brother Carl and I crossed from Terror Basin into the cirque by downclimbing and rappelling the steep glaciers just east of MacMillan Spire. We crossed the glacier below Inspiration Peak and gained the rib about 200 vertical feet above its toe, where a horizontal vein of dark rock cuts across toward some trees. We belayed a rightward traverse for a short lead, then started up. The rock was exceptional, and features that looked imposing from below were easily passed by turning corners or following hidden ramps. Six pitches along the rib, a steep snowfield, then four more leads in a fault just right of the crest brought us to the crux of the route. From here a grassy ramp left of the crest appeared to lead into space. A vertical corner above and a wide crack to its right were running with water. I traversed the wall to the right of the crack with minimal protection, then reached an edge beyond it and climbed carefully up and back left. One more pitch on wet, grassy hummocks led us to the snow crest. We climbed for several hundred feet along a knife-edged ridge that the evening sun lit up like a flame. We bivouacked on a shelf next to the snow. The next morning brought threatening clouds. As we hurried up the glacier, the rain began. It stayed with us to the summit horn, down the rappels to Terror Glacier, and through the soaking brush as we hiked down Goodell Creek the following day. (III or IV, mid class 5.)

LOWELL SKOOG

Mount Shuksan, Lower Curtis Glacier and Southwest Face. On August 24, John Stull and I completed a route up steep ice in a broad gully on the upper right side of the Lower Curtis Glacier. Easier but dangerous séracs on the right side forced us left up two pitches of ice adjoining the rock. From above the second icefall we traversed left and ascended class three-and-four rock for 1500 feet up the right side of the southwest face. Higher on the face we followed a rib of better rock that produced several fifth-class pitches. From the top of the face we followed the Sulphide Glacier to the summit.

ALAN KEARNEY

Half Moon, Lunar Rubble. On July 12 Sue Harrington and I completed a six-pitch route on the northwest face. The climb begins to the right of the two prominent dihedrals below the summit. Flakes, cracks and ledges diagonal from right to left and lead into a right-facing corner higher up. At the top of the corner a large roof is traversed on the right ending on the west ridge below the summit. Most of the rock was good but loose rock and poor protection on the fourth pitch elevated the fear factor. (III, 5.10.)

ALAN KEARNEY

Table Mountain, Death Picnic. Due west of Austin Pass and the Mount Baker Ski Area is a mesa-like peak called Table Mountain. When it is cold, the east and northwest faces offer good one- and two-pitch ice climbs. In December of 1985 I attempted a 250-foot climb on the northwest face with Andy Selters. It began 200 yards southwest of Herman Saddle and involved hollow and vertical ice on the first pitch. The second pitch had a half-inch layer of ice separated from the rock by 8 inches of air. A bold mouse with some skill could have succeeded. We retreated. On December 11, 1986, Mark Houston and I did the climb in two pitches and found the ice better than the last year but still weird. The climb is comparable to a Canadian grade V.

ALAN KEARNEY

Amphitheater Mountain, Sunday Morning Buttress. On July 27 Don Monk and I did a short climb on this buttress located one mile northeast of the summit. It is prominent from Cathedral Pass. The route begins on the left of a 50-foot pillar and continues straight up for three pitches. The middle pitch was the crux. The rock was not as good as it appeared (II, 5.10). We also did the Middle Finger Buttress free. The first pitches are some of the most spectacular in the area (5.10).

GEORGE BELL, JR.

Mount Slesse, Northeast Buttress, First Winter Ascent. During the first eight days of March, Jim Nelson and Kit Lewis made the first winter ascent of the northeast buttress of Mount Slesse. After helicoptering to the base, the pair spent the next seven days on the route. Two days were spent waiting out a storm 250 feet below the summit. It was their fifth attempt of the climb.

Mount Stuart, Northeast Face. On October 18, Charlie Hampson and I climbed a new line to the left of Girth Pillar. From our bivouac atop the Ice Cliff

Couloir, we descended to where we could start traversing toward the Girth Pillar access ramp, which we climbed for one pitch. Here, the approach ramp intersects the pillar, and we headed left up a corner, remaining left of the pillar all the way up the false summit face. With the exception of the third pitch in the corner, which went almost all on aid, we free climbed mixed snow and rock. (IV, 5.9, A2.)

MARK BEBIE

Colonial Peak, New Route in Winter. On February 8 and 9, Marc Twight, John Stoddard, Monte Westlund, and I climbed a direct line on the north face of Colonial Peak. Having seen this face towering 2000 meters above the North Cascades Highway for many years, many climbers speculated about the possibility of a cold-weather route. Instead of using the left-trending gully at the head of the basin that Bill Pilling and I climbed on a previous attempt in December, we paired off and opted for two different lines of ice which led from the basin up to our bivouac at about 5000 feet. Our routes involved five or six pitches of ice. The next morning, we aimed for a 50-foot-high ice curtain in mid-face directly below the summit. Above and to the right of this feature are two prominent ice pillars. We climbed these, interconnecting snowfields and one short mixed chimney to gain the summit. Access to the second pillar was tricky, but Monte found a traverse into it from the left. Marc and I climbed a spectacular direct finish under some huge pillowy cornices. This last pitch was composed of the same scary shallow sugar snow John and I had found on Johannesburg in December. We reached the summit five hours out from our bivouac. Since Monte and John third-classed the route, they did not do the direct finish and summited an hour earlier. We descended the west face and reached the highway by 4:30 P.M.

MARK BEBIE

Travel in the Austera Peak Region and Primus Peak, North Ridge. From the southwest, access to the northeast rampart of Austera Peak is a logistical hassle. On September 7 I climbed Austera Peak, then down-climbed toward the northwest, to the first major notch. Here, I descended the 45° snow-and-ice slope to the North Klawatti Glacier. The bergschrund crossing was easy. I then climbed Primus Peak. Where the North Klawatti Glacier joins the west ridge, I descended a couloir to reach the unnamed glacier north of Primus, which I traversed to the north ridge. The 1000-foot ridge is made up of blocks and towers of good rock, but is somewhat loose. I stayed on the crest unless forced to either side by difficulties. Toward the top, the ridge goes through a section of banded rock common in this region. This provided enjoyable climbing to low fifth class. Time: 1 hour on the ridge. I returned by the same route. It is unlikely that this route of approach has been used before.

MARK BEBIE

Lichtenberg Mountain, Northeast Ridge. With mountain bikes offering quick access, Jens Kuljurgis and I made a one-day excursion of this climb. The route began on the west corner of the ridge, where we encountered an awkward (narrow) body jam in half a lead. From there a short scramble put us on the crest. Two more enjoyable leads cleared the difficulties, leaving only a scramble to the summit. The rock was surprisingly sound, encrusted with typical Northwest lichen in places. (II, 5.7.)

GORDY SKOOG

"Wolf Peak, Howling Ridge." This route is located on the north ridge of the minor summit between Sperry and Vesper peaks. Viktoria Stepitova and I approached the climb via the Headlee Pass trail, then over the pass between Sperry and Vesper into the Copper Lake basin. We followed fourth class gullies to the north (right) up to the col between our summit and Big Four Mountain, where the climb begins. (Alternatively, one could approach directly from Copper Lake basin, ascend above the lake until it is possible to cut north to the start of the route. This is likely the fastest approach.) The peak has a substantial unclimbed north face with perhaps 800 feet of vanishing cracks, brush, and questionable blocks. After inspecting the face, we chose to attempt the obvious curving ridge bordering the face on the west and pointing directly at Big Four Mountain. The route is for the most part quite obvious, following the knife-edge ridge for about 8 to 10 pitches. We passed several towers on their west sides. The climbing is mostly quite moderate (5.6 or 5.7) and enjoyable. The route is solid, protects easily with nuts, and has wonderfully exposed belay stances. Towards the summit some minor brush and several short sections of more difficult climbing (5.8 to 5.9) were encountered. (However, we feel it is likely that these more difficult sections could be avoided by future parties.) Climbing time was about 5 or 6 hours; the descent was an obvious walk-off. (III, 5.8.)

DAN JAFFE

Chianti Spire, East Face. "Let's see, the slide is here somewhere. . . . It's an outer space-like hand crack . . . Looks fantastic! I wonder how steep that direct start is." Once below the spire we changed our plans: ". . . It would be nice to get there directly, but it doesn't make sense; it's all broken and undercut. How about over there? That corner looks as if it might go." I spied this start, so the first pitch was mine. A spectacular traverse left under roofs led to a hand crack in the corner. Jim Nelson started the second pitch up a wide icy crack leading to the top of the right shoulder of Chianti's east face. Five pitches up, I approach the crux—it's wet, and I aid around it. The next pitch is wet too, and our "hand crack" now needs a #4 Friend. We rappel off. Two weeks of hot weather later, we swap the leads, Jim taking the good ones this time. Dry rock finds us quickly free-climbing to our high point and then into the unknown. Very soon we top out, making the fourth ascent of the spire, just a tyrolean away from Burgundy. (May 25 and June 8. III, 5.10 − .)

MARK BEBIE

Liberty Bell Mountain, North Face Direct. After an unsuccessful attempt on the Red Gully last year, the stage was set on August 8 for Jim Yoder, Bob Vaughn and me to push up one of the last unclimbed faces on Liberty Bell. Third-classing up left of the Red Gully brought us to the ramp system that leads left to the north-face route. Our climb loomed above a cave-like bullet-hole, 30 feet in diameter. Exposed climbing with limited protection passed through the bullet-hole, then traversed between two huge roofs. Ramping left to an obvious right-facing corner on the left edge of the slabs brought us to a steeper section. Quality face-climbing linked a line of crumbly corners that characterize the weaknesses of the north face. I was thankful for our moderate stash of pins as I finished a 5.10 corner, overpounded a lost arrow and traversed 40 feet of dicey face up to a large crumbly expanding flake. Atop this touchy flake, we used for anchors the first two bolts. From there, Yoder made a remarkable traverse right, using hooks for protection and climbed up to a tension traverse, which turned out to be the only aid on the route. He finished with a scary 5.10 layback to another one bolt-one pin belay. The day was lengthening as we gathered at this remote oasis centered in the middle of the Great Slab with only blank face in sight for another full pitch. A white streak plummeted down the upper portion of the pitch and became the landmark for the finale. Thus began "Bold Bob" pitch. Armed with his 23-ounce framing hammer, Vaughn journeyed up through 5.10 to a toe-aching stance where he jackhammered a bolt in ten minutes, including breaking and replacing a bit. A crux was encountered 20 feet above. Then smiles and backslapping as 5.5 led to the summit ridge. (IV, 5.10.)

LEE CUNNINGHAM, *Unaffiliated*

Washington Cascades Correction. Three climbs done by Gordy Skoog in the Cascades were incorrectly placed in the Utah section. These were Crescent Mountain, "Mother Lode" and Mount Elijah. The Elijah climb was done solo.

California—Yosemite

Lower Sentinel Falls Ice Climbing, Yosemite. In January 1987, during an unusual cold snap, Ed Sampson and I climbed the lowest 750 feet of the frozen Lower Sentinel Falls. The ice was thin but well bonded to the wall. The route was repeated over the next three days by Jim Bridwell and Paul Tier, and then by Jay Smith and Paul Crawford. Six days after our ascent, major sections of the route fell off.

DICK LEVERSEE, *Pro Leisure Society*

California—Sierra Nevada

Mount Russell, West Face. This route starts just right of the Rowell-Jones route, and left of a route I reported last year (*A.A.J.* 1986), in a left-leaning dihedral. After two pitches, I led up and left, crossing the Rowell-Jones to the base of a small right-facing corner. Delicate laybacking and face climbing take one to a hand-crack that is followed to the summit ridge. (III-IV, 5.10). *Mount Russell, Direct South Face.* This route follows the major crack system in the center of the south face. Third class leads into the amphitheater between the Curved Arête and the south buttress. We started in a hand-crack below a large right-facing dihedral. Higher, a left-facing dihedral is entered (crux). Both of these routes were done by Rich Romano and me in July. (III, 5.10.)

FRED YACKULIC

Mount Russell, Sbruno-Sbruski Route. In August, Scott Ayers and I climbed a six-pitch crack system on the south face, to the right of the south buttress. (III, 5.10.) *(Editor's note*—This route and the preceding one are undoubtedly very close to one another. It is not known which route is further right on the south face. Indeed, the routes may share pitches, or even be the same route.)

PAUL LINAWEAVER

Mount Whitney, Peewee's Big Adventure. Joel Richnak and I climbed this fun route which closely follows the northeast buttress of the peak. We roped up about 100 feet right of the east-face route and climbed up and right on flakes to a large detached flake, then back left to a block. After a short distance in a gully, we exited left and went up a beautiful, exposed face. Several more pitches, generally tending left, led to the Peewee, a giant block (also on the east-buttress route). We climbed through the spectacular roof crack of the Peewee, and several easier pitches took us to the top. (III, 5.8 + .)

MIKE CARVILLE

Mount Sill, East Face, Dead Larry's Pillar, Left Side. In August, Kent Davenport, David Wilson and I climbed a new route on the 1400-foot high east face of this spectacular mountain. Our route ascended the left side of a prominent pillar on the southern half of this massive face. The center of this pillar was climbed by Mike Farrell and me in 1978. At that time it was traditional among Palisade Guides not to report new routes in their alpine *Klettergarten*. I hope a departure from this policy will clear up some of the confusion. Both routes ascend a left-leaning crack through an overhanging section before they split. The new route is very steep and the rock is excellent (III, 5.9, 10 pitches.)

MICHAEL GRABER

Twilight Pillar, Clyde Peak, Winter Ascent. In February, David Wilson and I made the first winter ascent of this classic Grade III summer route. A 5.7 pitch directly off the snowfield provided us with the hardest climbing, since it was diagonal and quite icy. Only after we were into the steep rock of the upper arête did we shed our Koflach outer boots and use the Firé Hivernale alpine rock-climbing shoes we were wearing as inner boots. We rappelled to camp with

Photo by David Wilson

PLATE 54

Michael Graber leading the first pitch on Mount Sill, Sierra Nevada, California.

several hours of daylight left, but decided to save our ski run until morning. A storm moved in, dumped eight inches of fresh powder overnight, and gave us the best of all worlds: clear, dry weather for climbing and fresh powder for the 5000-foot ski descent.

GALEN ROWELL

Disappointment Peak, West Face. In September, Dan Frankl and I lugged hardware over Southfork Pass and around the "back side" of the Palisades to a camp on a terrace below Middle Palisade. Our goal was to find a large rock climb on one of these unclimbed west faces, and Disappointment Peak had more to offer than the loftier Middle Palisade that had first drawn our attention. Our route began on the southwest arête, then traversed left into a crack on the main face where fear and cold fingers forced me into about 20 feet of aid after completing a 5.10 section below. Dan and I alternated easier leads for another thousand feet until reaching a knife-edge ridge leading to the summit. In the morning, a snowstorm prevented us from returning over Southfork Pass, and we were forced to walk all day through the blizzard to the easier Bishop Pass trail, completing yet another summer climb in the "Gentle Wilderness" that seems to catch me unprepared far more often than the Himalaya or Alaska. (IV, 5.10, A2.)

GALEN ROWELL

Consummate Corner, Patricia Bowl. While ski touring in Patricia Bowl, above the 10,000-foot road in Rock Creek Canyon, I spotted a wall of granite crags that were hidden from the road. In July, David Wilson and I hiked into the cirque in just half an hour and found one dihedral that was by far the most appealing line. It lies in a cleft about midway along the southern wall of the cirque, and begins out of a snow couloir. After negotiating the snow, two continuous 5.10 pitches led to easier climbing and the summit plateau of a minor unnamed peak. (III, 5.10 + .) (*Editor's note*—At least two other routes have been done here, both 5.10.)

GALEN ROWELL

Mount Stewart, Dawn Pillar. On June 17, David Wilson and I ascended a new route on Mount Stewart's north face. We began climbing on the steepest section of this face, following jam-cracks up the left side of a small pillar directly underneath the west summit. Nine pitches later we stood on the west summit exhilarated over the fine quality of rock that we encountered. This route is about 100 meters west of that climbed by Hooman Aprin, Jack Roberts and me in 1973. (III, 5.10.)

MICHAEL GRABER

Sequoia National Park. On the Memorial Day weekend, Herb Laeger and I added another classic route, *Aspire,* on the magnificent 1200-foot west face of the Fin, facing Castle Rock Spire. We started 150 feet up and right of a prominent pine growing at the base of the original Silver Lining route on the apron. This new route winds its way up and slightly right for 9 continuous pitches, paralleling Silver Lining most of the way. (IV, 5.9.) Foxtrot Dome is the best looking piece of rock on the Mineral King road between the Lookout Point Cliffs and Atwell Mill. It faces east on a hill about a mile to the north of the road and is easily recognized by the long, slender left-facing corner which winds up the center of the face. Park at the creek and walk up the hill to the base. After an easy pitch, Eddie Joe, Roy Swafford, Barry Fowlie and I found a rusty old bolt at the real start of *Foxtrot Corner* proper. Above this, we found no evidence of anyone. We descended the south side of the dome. (II, 5.10, 3 pitches.) From Courtwright Reservoir, looking north, one's eye is drawn to several elegant domes all in a row on the east of Dusy Creek. The dome farthest to the north is Locke Dome, which is the largest of all the formations in the area (1000 feet), two miles north of the reservoir. Access to the area is via the four-wheel-drive road from the reservoir past Maxon Dome; it takes a couple of hours. In July, Herb Laeger, Harold Seiden and I did the first route, *Best of the West,* on the impressive west face. We chose what appears to be the only reasonable line directly up the center of the face, connecting discontinuous cracks with 11 bolts. The climbing is excellent on beautiful rock. (IV, 5.11 +, 8 pitches.) *Knob Business Being Here* is a short route, a variation of Levity's End, which gets to one pitch above Condor Watch Ledge on Moro Rock. In February Ron Carson and I climbed two spectacularly steep knob pitches, one below and one above Condor Watch Ledge. The first pitch comes up to the right side of the ledge (bolts), and the second takes the bold, extremely steep line of knobs above the very left end of the ledge for 165 feet to belay knobs. (II, 5.10 +.)

DICK LEVERSEE, *Pro Leisure Society*

Watchtower and Castle Rocks, Sequoia National Park, 1984 and 1985. The easily accessible and exposed 8-pitch route, *Watch Out,* is on the central main face of the Watchtower about 30 minutes easy hiking from the Lodgepole Campground. Ron Carson, my wife Eve and I completed this route on July 28, 1984. It has several difficult traverses and requires route-finding capabilities. All natural protection was used and the rock was generally clean and solid, but not throughout. The only aid on this 1000-foot, steep climb was a 10-foot section near the start of the fifth pitch. This section would go free if the crack were cleaned or a large needle-like loose flake were pushed off. If free-climbed, it would probably not be harder than the rest of the route. *Watch Out* (IV, 5.11, A3) is between the Timex route (*A.A.J.,* 1984, page 165) and the nose of the Watchtower. A trail to the top of the Watchtower provides an easy descent to the Generals Highway. On May 26, 1985 Patrick Paul, Ron Carson, my wife Eve and I completed *Silver Lining* (IV, 5.9) on the Fin of Castle Rocks massif. Nine long pitches on some of the most beautiful face climbing in California make this climb a must for the High Sierra climber. The setting is spectacular, the rock excellent and the route has substantial 5.9 on every pitch. Natural protection is supplemented with bolts where needed, but often there are thought-provoking runouts. The route ascends the longest section of the west face of the Fin for over 1100 feet and passes the prominent block on its right side during the seventh pitch. Access to the Fin is via an old WPA trail which ascends the 4000-foot gain from the bridge at Hospital Rock. Three days are recommended for the climb and water is usually available in the gully between the Fin and Castle Rock Spire for a few weeks after Memorial Day. A 165-foot rope is recommended. A rappel route starting at a manzanita bush near the top of the Fin's narrow summit ridge avoids a tedious climb down. Two ropes are needed and three bolts have been placed at each rappel point.

HERB LAEGER, *Unaffiliated*

Tombstone Shadow, Big Baldy Dome, Sequoia National Forest. In May, Roy Swafford, Barry Fowlie and I climbed a four-pitch route which starts in a huge left-facing corner on Big Baldy's south face. Steep but easy climbing up the corner leads to a pitch of precarious climbing up an overhanging, leaning finger-crack and chimney. Easier climbing then led to the summit. The loose blocks which helped the route earn its name are now removed. (III, 5.10.)

E. C. JOE, *Stonemasher Alpine Club*

Nowhere To Run, South Buttress, North Mountain, Kings Canyon National Park. Along the "Motor Nature Trail" and above a Park Service residence rises a prominent pillar of rock. In May, Bill McConachie, Barry Fowlie and I found that the route had five outstanding crack pitches, from fingers to off-width. The crux was the fourth pitch. (III, 5.11.)

E. C. JOE, *Stonemasher Alpine Club*

Artesian Route, Charlito Dome, Kings Canyon National Park. Situated next to and just south of the famous Charlotte Dome is a large southwest-facing slab. A right-facing corner on its upper half and a peculiar spring of water halfway up mark the route. In June, moderate but serious face climbing to the corner and two crack pitches put Dick Leversee and me on the summit of this fun back-country route. (III, 5.9.)

E. C. JOE, *Stonemasher Alpine Club*

Kings Canyon Climbs. "The Matterhunk" is our unofficial name for the huge limestone peak formation a mile south of Boyden Cave on Highway 180 on the south fork of the Kings River. In October Herb Laeger, Eddie Joe and I climbed the dramatic 1500-foot northeast arête from the Boulder Creek trail to the summit, staying as close to the edge as possible the whole way. Descent is via the gully below the north face and back down the trail to Boyden Cave. The climbing is very enjoyable, on good limestone, a rarity in California. (IV, 5.10+, 10 pitches.) In August, Eddie Joe and I hired borros to ferry loads to the junction of Charlotte and Bubbs Creeks below Charlotte Dome. We spent the next 2½ days completing one of the Sierra's only two Grade VI back-country routes. *Crystal Banzai,* on Bubbs Creek Wall. (The Kroger route on Tehipite Dome is the other.) We chose an obvious line of cracks, arches and corners on the longest section of the wall (2300) feet), just left of the center. This line curiously follows a bizarre white crystal band from base to top. The route went 90% free with less than 200 feet of aid and entirely clean. We used bathooks to pass a blank section on the fourth pitch and a total of 15 bolts on the 17 pitches. Start at a big pine 100 yards up and right of a huge, white, left-facing dihedral which marks the beginning of the crystal band. Diagonal up and left, intersecting an obvious ramp, to the "Crystal Palace" (ledge) with its "Dungeon" at the top of the huge white dihedral (3rd pitch). Follow the "Crystal Corner" and arch above up and left to bathooking which leads past four bolts to a small stance (2 bolts). From here we climbed up and slightly right to join the main crack-and-corner system, which followed for five more pitches, ending at "Zero Point Ledge," just above the obvious huge "Seagull Roof." Two more pitches of cracks lead up and slightly left to a good ledge. Above this, climb up and right for 100 feet to the arching right-facing dihedral which is visible from the ground. Here, instead of following the corner system up and right, face-climb left for 20 feet to a large right-facing flake and follow this and the thin crack above for a full pitch to "Dead Tree Ledge." Above, face-climb up and left to gain entry into a huge right-facing corner one pitch below the top. Here, instead of climbing the perfectly blank corner above, face-climb left over the corner to easy knobs which lead to the top. Descent is via Charlotte Creek to the west (toward Charlotte Dome). Recommended rack: tiny nuts to 4″ (2 each), 1 #5 Friend, 1 skyhook, 2 bathooks, 2 Leeper cam hooks, hammocks. (VI, 5.11, A3.) In July, Karl McConachie and I finished a new all-free route on the south face of North Dome, above Zumwalt Meadows, *A Tall Cool One.* We followed the obvious continuous crack system to the right of the original Frost route for 11 pitches to the very top of the dome. This is a serious route involving some climbing on less than perfect rock with 8 of the 11 pitches being 5.10 or harder, ranging from finger to off-width cracks. This route is best done late in the season as the third pitch can be very wet and slimy. Recommended rack: Friends-3 each to 4″, 1 #5 Friend. (V, 5.11, 11 pitches.)

DICK LEVERSEE, *Pro Leisure Society*

"Scarlet Slipstream," Cedar Grove, Kings Canyon National Park. In July, Eric Rhicard, Vaino Kodas and I climbed this 6-pitch climb, four of which are 5.10 and the other two 5.11. The rock is superb and the route follows a prominent red water streak for its entire length. Two 165-foot ropes should be taken to rappel the route, which is primarily protected by 30 bolts, but RURPS, a few

small stoppers and small to medium Friends are useful. To find this easily accessible route, park in the day-hiking parking lot at the end of the road near Zumwaldt Meadows. Cross the Kings River on the foot bridge just east of the parking lot and follow the trail upstream along the south bank for 1½ miles. Look for a reddish streak on a low-angle slab on the south wall of the canyon. Climb the red streak for six pitches, starting on the right side with a series of steps just left of the corner in order to reach the first bolt. Then follow bolts, small cracks and corners to the top. Runouts are moderate.

HERB LAEGER, *Unaffiliated*

North of Eden, North Dome, Kings Canyon National Park. In July, Roy Swafford, Todd Vogeland and I climbed an 11-pitch route on the east buttress of North Dome. The route follows a distinct corner system consisting of wide cracks. The crux reminded us of the "Ear" formation on the Salathe Wall, only much harder. Where cracks end, face climbing left around a headwall leads to bushy ledges and more face climbing to the top (V, 5.10 + .)

E. C. JOE, *Stonemasher Alpine Club*

North to the Bone, North Dome, Kings Canyon National Park. In August, Dick Leversee, Mike Meng and I climbed this 11-pitch route which starts left of the 1968 Herbert-Frost Route in vertical left-facing corners and goes up thin cracks near the arête left of the 1968 route. Two sets of roofs are passed at about mid-height and airy free climbing eventually meets the 1968 route near the summit (V, 5.9, A3.)

E. C. JOE, *Stonemasher Alpine Club*

Mama Told Me Not To Come, Voodoo Dome, The Needles. In October, Steve Brower and I climbed this "indirect-direct" start to the *White Punks on Dope* route. Starting left of the normal start, several bolts protect difficult moves leading to a belay at the edge of a giant arch. Two easier face pitches take one to the dihedral pitch on *White Punks*. We found evidence of a previous ascent which had traversed in from the side on the first pitch, and we used their anchor bolts. Higher, though, we felt compelled to remove two bolts that were placed next to good cracks or knobs. (III, 5.11.)

E. C. JOE, *Stonemasher Alpine Club*

It's No Game, Schaffer Buttress, The Needles. In October, Dick Leversee, Steve Brower and I climbed this four-pitch wall which is located across the Kern River from the Needles, near Schaffer Meadow/Cedar Canyon. The climb starts in a gouged-out area with some solid, but dubious looking brown blocks and cracks. A ledge below a steep headwall is the belay. Thin cracks lead to an overhanging slot and a stance right of the crack. After ascending the right side of a huge flake, a difficult step left leads to steep mantels and cracks heading to the top (III, 5.11.)

E. C. JOE, *Stonemasher Alpine Club*

Bear Creek Spire, P 13,600 and Ruby Lake Wall. In December of 1985, Kevin Ball and I made the first winter ascent of the east ridge of Bear Creek Spire, finding it much as Galen Rowell had described it: long and enjoyable. In February of 1987, I returned with Greg Orton to make probably the first ascent of the north buttress. P 13,600 rises on Wheeler Ridge, east of Rock Creek Canyon just below Tamarack Lakes. In December of 1982, I climbed the snow-and-ice gully right of the summit (5.4 rock, 50° ice) and in May of 1984 returned with Susan Williams to climb the arête left of the gully which rises directly to the summit (5.8). Both are probably new routes. To the north of the main Ruby Wall ascended by Galen Rowell in 1982 and 1983 lies a steep wall hidden from the lake. In October Bill Kerwin and I made the first ascent of "The Wall of Flying Reptiles" via the *Pteradon* (5.10, A1.) We followed the prominent corner system with an ever-widening crack on the left wall for five pitches.

ROBERT J. PARKER, *Unaffiliated*

Crystal Crag, North Arête. On a blustery day in late June Rick Taylor and I climbed this beautiful arête. We reached the base after a short hike from Crystal Lake. The route begins in a prominent dihedral on the prow of the arête. The first pitch was reached by dropping into the moat between the remnant of a giant cornice and the clean rock. A few 5.7 moves in a layback-offwidth crack led to a comfortable belay stance on a large sloping ledge. An easier pitch was climbed to an area of broken rock. A third-class pitch led up from here to a shallow gully on the west side of the arête. The fourth pitch ascended the easy fifth-class flakes in the gully to an area directly below a huge deposit of white quartz. A final short pitch of fourth class went up the "crystal dihedral" directly above and led to a short scramble to the summit. The higher south summit was reached along the classic knife-edged ridge after dropping into the notch between the two summits. (II, 5.7.)

WILLIAM L. KRAUSE

Utah

Gates of Hell, South Side of Provo Canyon, 1985. This climb, done on November 27, 1985 by Thomas Koch and Bill Robins, ascends the major face west of the ice climb, *Stairway to Heaven*. Bush whacking and scree climbing from a parking lot a half mile west of the Bridal Veil parking lot got them to a large alcove below the center of the face. Unprotected climbing over the alcove roof (5.10) led them up two pitches of 5.7 limestone to a longer headwall. The headwall went at 5.10, the crux being a 30-foot layback on a broken, unstable flake. Two more pitches of 5.7 to 5.9 limestone led to a large ledge and the sandstone climbing. They traversed 50 feet west and climbed a large dihedral which splits the upper face for three pitches. The last pitch on this good sandstone wanders up to the capping forest. (IV, 5.10 + , varied climbing on loose, dangerous limestone and good sandstone, 12 pitches.)

BRIAN SMOOT

Notch Peak, North Face. Notch Peak is 60 miles west of Delta, Utah at the south end of the House Range. The 2500-foot-high limestone north face was first climbed by Thomas Koch and Peter Deinen in June. The route ascended right of center to a prominent chimney, mostly on poor rock. The third pitch of a white, chalky limestone was so poor that two pins were used for aid and major blocks were broken in the climbing. The bivouac was two pitches from the top. They descended the northwest ridge, using eight rappels. (V, 5.10 + , A3, 18 pitches.)

BRIAN SMOOT

Zion National Park. The classic route, *Space Shot,* had its first solo ascent in October by Rich Strang, an inspired performance especially in light of its being his first desert wall! Some climbers fail to note the critical importance of hammerless ascents. For example, *Space Shot* suffered considerable damage at the hands of two Colorado climbers despite its being a hammerless route. A new generation of Zion locals have made their presence felt with the establishment of Zion's first significant face-climbing route. In May 19-year-old Leif Bjarnson and Bob Quinn completed *Facetastic,* a high-quality 5.11 route up the apparently blank slab below the south face of Observation Point. Among the other shorter routes established in the past year is *Master Blaster* (5.8, A1), a perfect Friend crack that ascends 45 meters through two body-length roofs similar to inverted steps; it is 100 meters to the left of *Headache.* It was put up in June by Bob McLaughlin and me and repeated shortly afterward by Todd Gordon. Equipment should include at least five 1½ Friends! In September Earl Redfern and I made the first ascent of the main north face of Timbertop Mesa via *Thunderbird Wall* (VI, 5.9, A3). This had originally been attempted fifteen years earlier by Jeff Lowe and Cactus Bryan before the mesa had been climbed by any route; the wall had seen at least three even less successful attempts subsequently. The climb required 7½ days for the sixteen 165-foot leads. We discovered the Lowe-Bryan highpoint on the 12th pitch. We found absolutely no bolts despite having used eleven for aid ourselves up to that point (the lines differed by at least four pitches) and several more to reach the top, including one right above their final piton. A hundred meters from the top, Earl performed the crux, a 5.9 layback up a series of bushes. Rather than descending the 1975 Mormon route, we made six rappels down the buttress 350 meters east of the finish of our ascent to intercept the final section of the Mormon route. This may have been only the third true ascent of this enormous mesa.

RON OLEVSKY

Hell Roaring Canyon, 1984 and 1985. On October 31, 1984 I completed the first ascent of the Witch, one of several Wingate Towers, roughly a quarter of the way up the canyon near its south rim. The route, *Midnight Rider* (III, 5.7, A3), is highly aesthetic and recommendable, consisting mostly of clean A1. A previous attempt on the main tower of the group, the Warlock, by Dave Mondeau and me was thwarted by bad weather, lack of time and a relatively minor rockfall injury. We returned in May, 1985 with Dave Kruse and used an alternative approach, rappelling into the canyon from the rim. This attempt was successful in reaching the summit via a spectacular route that actually climbs through the tower from northwest to southeast, but the rock was so loose that it cannot be recommended.

RON OLEVSKY

Snow Canyon. Many new routes have been established in this state park just northwest of St. George. 1986 saw several first free ascents of note. Todd Gordon eliminated the aid from the second pitch of *Pygmy Alien,* thus freeing the route at 5.9. Chris Pendleton freed the aid on the second pitch of *Trouble No More,* a very aesthetic hand-crack that saw numerous repeats. I freed the first pitch of *Highlander* (5.10d), which was originally soloed with aid; this provided meter for meter the finest quality sandstone I have ever found. Most noteworthy of all was a visit by Rob Robinson, who drove all the way from the AAC Annual Meeting in Denver to free *The Journey From the Future,* an awesome overhanging fist crack near the mouth of the canyon on the east side. The eleventh-hour attempt was successful despite two falls with a lowering to rest. This produced the canyon's hardest route at 5.12b. This is no elevated bouldering problem. Robinson carried four N° 4 Friends and "could have used more."

RON OLEVSKY

Wyoming—Tetons

Teton Climbs. Art & Brent Pinnacle. In September 1984, Renny Jackson and Tom Kimbrough climbed a newly discovered and difficult pinnacle on the south side of Cascade Canyon, on the east side of the main Teewinot-Owen cirque. The route required A1 aid to start on the north side, then ascended a 5.9 jam-crack to and over a ceiling. It was surprising to find such an unclimbed tower so close to Jenny Lake at this late date. *Death Canyon Routes. Aerial Boundaries,* one of the finest rock routes of the many in Death Canyon, was climbed in September 1985 by Greg Miles, Mike Fisher, Jeff Bjornsen, and Tom Vajda. This five-pitch, 5.10b route on the southwest corner of P 10,552 consists of liebacking and underclinging, with an overhanging jam-crack as the crux. The first three pitches take one to the lower Sanz descent ledge, with the final two excellent leads exiting onto the normal Sanz descent ledge. *Lay Back in Death* (III, 5.8), first climbed in July 1983 by Dan Burgette, Paul McLaughlin, and Jim Woodmency, also is a west-facing climb above the Sanz descent trail. It ascends a prominent dihedral involving considerable liebacking, while the first pitch contains a squeeze chimney. *Cascade Canyon*. Four new and difficult rock climbs were completed in the vicinity of Guide's Wall and the lower south walls of Storm Point. In August 1984 Renny Jackson and Larry Dietrich climbed *Blobular Oscillations* (5.9), directly to the right of a prominent dihedral on the right side of Guide's Wall. After a few attempts, *Bat Attack Crack* (5.11a) was climbed by Paul Gagner on July 4, 1985. This severe route follows the left-facing arch immediately to the right of the Chouinard start to Guide's Wall. *Hotdogs* (5.8) was climbed by Paul Gagner and Jim Woodmency in July 1986. The route begins at the start of Bat Attack Crack, making a hand traverse to the right, and then follows a delicate flake above. *Morning Thunder* (5.10) consists of two pitches which surmount an improbable roof below the rock scar formed by the July 1985 landslide in Cascade Canyon. It was first climbed on July 9, 1985, by Paul Gagner and Dan Burgette. *Mount Owen, Northwest Face variation.* A second variation on this large face was made on August 9, 1985, by Renny Jackson and Paul Gagnon. After an approach to the face by a traverse from the vicinity of Gunsight Couloir, the upper portion of the face was taken somewhat more directly than either the first ascent (1965) or the first variation (1982). As a result, greater difficulty was encountered and exit onto Serendipity Arête was made higher, only one pitch from its top. In all some five pitches between 5.7 and 5.9 were climbed. *Teewinot, Direct East Ridge.* The steeper sections of the direct east ridge of Teewinot remained unclimbed until August 9, 1986, when Renny Jackson and I approached the base of the ridge by traversing north from the top of the tree-covered apex of the regular route. Two steep sections were climbed. While the lower half is the more difficult pitch, 5.8, the upper is more prominent and contains beautiful solid cracks in the finest of Teton rock. Staying on the crest of this ridge required traversing over three towers before arriving at the summit. *P 10,080 +.* This unnamed minor peak, rising directly above and west of Grizzly Bear Lake, was climbed for the first time on July 29, 1986 by Tom Kimbrough and me. Protected by substantial cliffs on the east, the route selected was on the west face to the summit ridge which was followed north to the summit block, climbed by its northeast corner. Three pitches, one of F7 difficulty, were involved. It appears that this was the last unclimbed peak in the Teton range. *Grand Teton, Enclosure, Emotional Rescue.* A new, more difficult, and more improbable route on the north face of the Enclosure was climbed on July 26, 1985 by Renny Jackson and Steve Rickert. This outstanding climb of ten pitches on excellent rock (IV, 5.10a, A2) is currently the most difficult route yet completed on the Grand Teton. The climb starts at the upper of the two ledges used for entry into the bottom of the Black Ice Couloir from the west; this is below and well to the left (north) of the beginning of the Lowe route (1969). The first lead on the massive rock wall above ascends a 5.8 crack and chimney, followed by a 5.10 crack ending in a hanging belay. Two pitches zigzag upwards toward the gap in the large ceiling which runs all across the west face of this north buttress of the Enclosure. Passing through the gap involved some 5.9 with 15 feet of A2 in one blank section to a second hanging belay. Two more leads exited onto a 4th-class section which was followed for 200 feet to the right to the final difficult 5.9 section on the extreme north corner. Once above this scary pitch, easy mixed climbing on ice and rock led again back to the right, ultimately around to the uppermost west face, from which the summit was attained. *Grand Teton, West Face of Exum Ridge, variation.* In July 1986 Renny Jackson and Steve Rickert made an important new variation to the original Pownall-Merriam route (1954). The variation involved six pitches, starting in the prominent crack just above the beginning of the 1954 chimney system. Three pitches of 5.7, 5.8, and off-width 5.9 with little or no protection were the key to this variation which ended at the beginning of the "V" pitch of the normal Exum ridge. *Grand Teton, Otterbody Chimneys.* Rising from the upper right corner of Teepe's Glacier is a long very steep chimney system formed between the southwest walls of the Second Tower and the main southeast face of the Grand below the East Ridge Snowfield. Because of the obvious very steep and rotten rock in this part of the mountain, no ascent had been attempted in the normal summer climbing season. Renny Jackson and Dan Burgette took advantage of winter snow and ice to make the first ascent of this chimney system on December 28, 1986 in a single day from the valley. Six pitches of mixed ice and rock were found, including vertical ice sections as well as snow over rotten rock. The rock itself was of 5.7 difficulty. *Cloudveil Dome, South Face, variation.* Paul Duval and Beverly Boynton climbed on July 23, 1986 a new 5.9 variation to the left of the Armed Robbery route. Two pitches were climbed by continuing up the ramp at the start of the hard climbing of Armed Robbery.

LEIGH N. ORTENBURGER

Wyoming—Wind River Range

Stroud Peak, Northwest Face. In August, my wife Tommie and I climbed a 12-pitch route on the northwest face of Stroud Peak. We began at the prominent buttress which extends out from the center of the face and ascended cracks and flakes near the crest. Where the buttress joins the face, there are three parallel corners. We chose the crisp, leftmost corner, which is right-facing. Above the corner the last quarter of the face offers many moderate options to the summit (III, 5.9).

JAMES A. HOWE, *Unaffiliated*

Montana

Mount Cowan, Absaroka Range, 1985. In August 1984 Curt Vogel and Lisa Schassberger climbed the first four pitches of a route on the most prominent buttress of Mount Cowan as seen from Elbow Lake. Due to a lack of time, they could not finish the route. In July 1985, Vogel and I returned and completed the remaining two pitches. The route ascends the obvious crack that splits the lower detached flake on the buttress. The climbing consists of fist- and hand-jamming (5.7 to 5.8) on excellent rock with occasional bits of face climbing. There is one roof.

PAT LANG, *Unaffiliated*

The Needles, Big Belt Mountains. The Needles are located on the eastern side of the Big Belt Mountains and can be reached by a private-access road of Bill Galts. This seldom visited area saw much climbing activity in the summer of 1986. Over a dozen friction and face routes from 5.2 to 5.8 + were done on fairly good granite. Protection is a problem, but tri-cams and small nuts seem to protect most routes. Of the climbs Tom Bozeman, Keith Brunckhorst and I pioneered, *Steppin' Out* (5.7) on Arch Rock and a roof route called *Wings* (5.8 +) on No Name Tower remain the best.

RON BRUNCKHORST, *Unaffiliated*

CANADA

Yukon Territory

Season in the St. Elias Mountains. There were fifteen groups climbing and skiing in the St. Elias Mountains in the summer of 1986. They spent 1451 man-days in the area. I summarize the results of some. Canadians Sandy Briggs, Don Merryman, Richard Eppler and Rob McDonald failed to climb the northwest ridge of Vancouver. Canadians Martha McCallum, Geoff Porter, Michael Hendrick and Roderick McIntosh failed to climb Kennedy by first the north and then the east ridge. Americans Howie and Michael Fitz, John Rake and Randy Walter climbed both Hubbard and Kennedy by their standard routes and skied off. They had only three good days out of 20. Americans Jim Rawding, Greg Leger, Jim Hennessey, Kurt Gravara and Lee Schipper were unsuccessful in their attempt on Steele's east ridge. Americans Steve Young, David Phillips, John Powers, Kyle Mathews, Peter Albert, Roger Kubby and Terry Kennedy failed to climb Logan by the King Trench route as did Canadians Mark Rosen and Blair and Scott Halperin. Canadians Dave Chase, Bill Hoyne, Bruce Hart and Mike Saunders failed on Logan's east ridge, but Canadians Bert Middleburg, Darrel Adzich, Max Lautenbader, Ralph Crawford, Eric Ridington and Keith Favelle did succeed; unfortunately Falvelle was killed on the descent.

LLOYD FREESE, *Kluane National Park*

Mount Logan Glaciology Project. Our party members were M. Demuth, R. Glykherr, B. Sheffield, G. Ferguson and me. Beginning on May 9 on the upper Quintano Sella Glacier, we dug and sampled snow pits at Base Camp, King Trench, King Col, Northwest Col and AINA Peak at 2875, 3350, 4200, 5340 and 5630 meters respectively to study snow chemistry variations with altitude. In particular, we were also interested in detecting Chernobyl reactor and Augustine volcano fallout. (The 285-year-long Northwest-Col core shows a history of atmospheric nuclear-weapons testing and volcanic fallout.) All samples were brought down on skis or hauled out on sleds. On the Northwest Col a camp was established and a 6.4-meter dig made down to the 1980 borehole casing, which we now plan to relog in 1987. A series of air samples was taken for CO_2 measurements, which data will compliment the CO_2 measurements made on the air bubbles contained in the ice core, extending from about 1800 AD to 1950 AD. On June 6 Sheffield and Ferguson climbed to the summit on Mount Logan (5951 meters, 19,524 feet) during a rare spell of good weather. The descent was slowed because it involved the sledding and back-packing of equipment down to King Col for helicopter pickup. Limited (fly-in only) helicopter support to 5300 meters restricted our research work this year. Heliocourier support went only to King Trench. We also installed a bronze plaque on Prospector's Col at 5475 meters to the memory of the late aviator, Philip Upton. The figure shows the results of some of the analyses that are available from this project.

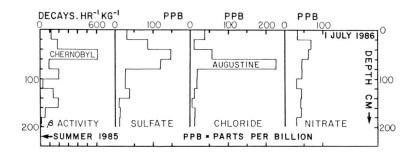

Radioactivity and chemical analysis of snow pit samples from the head of the Donjek Glacier at 3017 meters about 45 kilometers north of Mount Logan. The late March-early April eruption of Augustine volcano in southwest Alaska is recognized by the high chloride and sulfate peaks. The eruptive gases were known to have been high in hydrogen chloride and this result confirms the fact. Nitric acid, represented by most of the nitrate ion present, shows a weak (spring) response but this is not associated with any specific event. Following closely after the volcanic signature is a radioactive peak which is considered to be from the late April Chernobyl reactor explosion in the USSR. The radioactive cloud was known to have reached western Canada on 9 May 1986. A similar snow pit on Mount Logan at 5340 meters was sampled in the same way and analysed for the same species but there were no signals from either events that show any significance. This suggests that both radioactive and volcanic acid clouds were largely confined to the lower troposphere, at least in northwestern Canada.

GERALD HOLDSWORTH, *Arctic Institute of North America*

Mount Logan, First Winter Ascent. On March 16, six Alaskans, Todd Frankiewicz, Willy Hersman, Steve Koslow, George Rooney, Vernon Tejas and I, reached the summit of Mount Logan via the King Trench to become the first climbers successfully to climb the second highest peak in North America in the winter. We helicoptered to the western end of King Trench at 9600 feet, where a Base Camp snow cave was excavated. We used no tents on this expedition, and though the process of erecting a combination ice block-snow trench shelter was a three- to four-hour ordeal, the warmth and wind protection afforded by these structures was instrumental in our success. Camp I was established on March 1 at 11,500 feet just below the constriction of the King Trench Glacier. Camp II was placed at the col beneath King Peak at 13,600 feet on March 4. After ascending the headwall on March 8, we set up Camp III at 15,000 feet. Camp IV was established on March 11 at 17,000 feet, just below the pass that drops onto the great plateau. On March 13, we crossed the plateau to its eastern end and excavated Camp V at 16,700 feet, still three miles from the summit of Logan. The first summit attempt was on March 15. Sunrise temperatures were −35°F with clear skies overhead. Soon after departure, a ground blizzard developed, driving the temperature down and forcing a return to camp after we had gained only 800 feet in two hours. March 16 was clear and cold (−30°F) with practically no wind. We gained the summit in six hours and had a spectacular view of the St. Elias Range with the greatest glaciated terrain outside of the polar regions. Frankiewicz, Hersman and Rooney flew out from Base Camp on March 23, while the other three of us skied 120 miles to the Alaska Highway via the Ogilvie, Logan and Kaskawulsh Glaciers and then down Slims River.

JOHN BAUMAN, *Mountaineering Club of Alaska*

British Columbia

Mount Fairweather from Canada. For years I had been fascinated by Mount Fairweather. Sitting astride the Canadian-Alaskan border, it is the highest peak in British Columbia. The idea of climbing the peak by a Canadian route vaguely developed in my mind. Bradford Washburn's article in the *A.A.J., 1981* reignited my desire for the climb, but it ruled out an all-Canadian route. The steep northeast wall of the summit pyramid which forms the only Canadian portion of the mountain is overhung by a 300-foot-thick glacial icecap. Our desire to avoid ending our climbing careers prematurely on a death route for the sake of Canadian nationalism dictated that we would go for the summit along the west ridge after a Canadian approach. From the head of the Ferris Glacier a ridge led to the Grand Plateau, which we could traverse to ascend the west ridge. On June 14, Fred Thiessen, Ellen Woodd, Robert Brusse, Gordon Frank, Eric White and I left Seattle for Juneau and Gustavus, on the edge of Glacier Bay. From there we were taken by float plane to the head of Tarr Inlet and dropped off on a sandy beach opposite the Margerie and Grand Pacific Glaciers. After carrying our supplies into Canada, we were ferried by Canadian helicopter to the head of the

Ferris Glacier and the base of our ridge at 4700 feet. It was immediately obvious that we could not climb the ridge directly. The first 2000 feet were of nearly vertical metamorphosed shale. For the next three or four days we ferried loads up the glacier steeply skirting the south side of our ridge. From Camp I at 7200 feet we forged a route directly to the ridge crest at 8100 feet through steep ice and snow mixed with rotten rock. The knife-edged crest was spectacular with crisscrossing cornices and precipices of over 2000 feet to the glacier on either side. The narrow ridge led to a final steep headwall that topped on the Grand Plateau at 9600 feet. We should like to name our ridge after Andrew Morrison Taylor, a Canadian. Andy Taylor was one of those who made the epic first ascent of Mount Logan and was of the party that climbed Fairweather for the first time. After six days, we were on the edge of the Grand Plateau waiting for the notoriously bad weather we had been experiencing to improve. Fortunately, after 24 hours, high winds cleared the higher altitudes. This was the start of a five-day fine spell. We donned our skis and traversed the Grand Plateau north of Quincy Adams and Fairweather to camp at 10,500 feet below the west peak of Fairweather. The next day we ascended directly to the col between the west and main summits on skis. As the morning wind died, we ascended the west ridge, reaching the summit at 4:30 P.M. on July 25. This was the second Canadian ascent of Fairweather and by a mainly Canadian route. It was also the first ascent of Fairweather by a Canadian woman.

GRANT MCCORMACK, *Alpine Club of Canada*

Canadian Coast Range

Mount Waddington Area, New Routes. Between July 20 and August 2, six of us from Seattle camped at the Combatant-Waddington col, climbing four new routes. On our first day, Dan Cauthorn and Steve Mascioli climbed the central buttress of Combatant (III 5.8). Two days later, John Stoddard and I did a right-trending couloir leading up to the Angel Glacier on Mount Waddington's north face. We gained the main couloir via a short icy couloir which avoided exposure to ice cliffs above. The next morning Dan and Steve followed our tracks. While we four were returning from our ascent of Waddington, Dan McNerthney and his brother Pat climbed the central rock buttress immediately to the right of the Flavelle-Lane ice route (V, 5.10). After this week of activity we welcomed a storm, but we were eager to get out of the tents after five days. Pat and I repeated part of the traverse that Serl and friends had done the year before. Steve and Dan Cauthorn repeated the northeast spur of Asperity, and John and Dan McNerthney climbed a new route on the left side of the Skywalk pillar on Mount Combatant, "Walk on the Wild Side" (III, 5.11; 8 pitches).

MARK BEBIE

Canadian Rockies

Little Snowdome, North Face, Columbia Icefields. Ward Robinson and I climbed an interesting route in April on the north face of Little Snowdome. It can be seen on the approach to "Slipstream." The face is about 2500 feet high. We climbed the central couloir. There is rock climbing up to 5.8 and some very enjoyable mixed ground. From the valley below, the top of the route looks formidable but in actuality this section consists of a devious chimney pitch which exits onto the ridge through a rock tunnel. We took seven hours and wore crampons throughout. I suspect that the route would not be as safe or enjoyable in summer.

IAN BULT, *Alpine Club of Canada*

GREENLAND

Petermanns Bjerg, Fourth Ascent, Kejser Franz Josephs Fjord, 1985. Iaian Smart, P. Sellars, P. Todd, R. Zeyen and I flew to Mestersvig on July 26, 1985, where we picked up two inflatable boats belonging to Wally Herbert, left from his circum-Greenland expedition. We attempted to leave Nyhaven on the 28th and made only 200 meters of progress due to heavy pack ice. We finally cleared the harbor the next day but were held up at Rann Ø for two further days by a band of pack ice across the inner Kong Oscars Fjord. We finally found a passage at high water between the ice and the south shore. We reached Advance Base at Nanortilik on August 2. After a brief halt, we continued through the night to the head of Kejser Franz Josephs Fjord to make Base Camp at Knaeckedal, completing a voyage of 140 miles. We got to the snout of the Gregory Glacier with two relays on the 6th and to the foot of Petermanns Bjerg on the 8th to camp at 5000 feet. With the weather still holding, we left the same day for the summit by two routes. Zeyen and Todd made the second ascent of the northeast ridge while the rest of us ascended the shattered east-southeast ridge to meet at eight P.M. on the summit (2940 meters, 9646 feet). On August 10, from a camp lower down the Gregory, we ascended a virgin peak (c. 2500 meters; 73°08' N, 28°29' W; provisionally named Luxemburger Spids). On the return journey, Zeyan made a solo ascent of Gog (c. 2600 meters; reportedly first ascended by Odell) and found a cairn 500 meters below the true summit. We regained Mestersvig on August 20, having visited Blomster Dal and Noah Bugt and having made the first ascent of the summit (1739 feet) at the west end of Sofia Sund. An attempt was made on the highest summit of the Syltoppen in the Staunings Alper, but appalling bad rock prevented a complete ascent.

MALCOLM SLESSER, *Scottish Mountaineering Club*

Ingolffjeld, North Face Attempt, East Greenland. Our expedition was composed of Slovene Peter Podgornik, Italians Ferruccio Svaluto Moreolo, Pierantonio Zago, Sergio De Longhi and me as leader. We hoped to climb for the first time the north face of Ingolffjeld, near Kangertigtiatsiaq Fjord. After leaving Tasiilaq, on June 18 we ascended the unexplored Angakkoq Glacier to Base Camp at the foot of the north face of Ingolffjeld. For 12 days it stormed. On June

29 we finally could glimpse the snow-laden face. Notwithstanding the snow, on June 30 Podgornik, Moreolo and I started up a couloir of 60° to 80° ice. After 23 hours we had climbed 1030 meters up the wall to the crest where we rested for four hours. A radio report announced the arrival of more bad weather. We immediately descended with 23 rappels of 60 meters and a 50-meter traverse. We did not continue from our high point to the summit.

GIANNI PAIS BECHER, *Club Alpino Italiano*

Milne Island, East Greenland. Our expedition consisted of John Shrewsbury, leader, Mike Garrett, Margaret Graham, Anne and Henry Wheatcroft, Chris Whitford and me. Milne Island is a remote, and as far as we could ascertain, nearly unexplored island within Scoresby Sound. Approximately 40 miles wide and 70 miles long, it has an icecap reaching 2000 meters. We were flown in from Iceland. During our 18-day stay we undertook two six-day backpacking trips. On the first we crossed the Charcot Glacier to the south and climbed two new peaks, P 1320 and P 1510 as well as Bays Fjelde (1028 meters) and P 960, which had summit cairns. The second trip was north along the coast. We did climb a snow summit of 1120 meters. From Base Camp, which was on the east coast, we climbed P 388 and P 1247.

MALCOLM SALES, *Royal Geographical Society*

NORTH POLE

Two Expeditions to the North Pole. In 1978 Japanese Naomi Uemura reached the North Pole alone with a dog team. He was resupplied by air. He was airlifted back to his base. That same year other Japanese led by Kaneshige Ikeda also sledged to the North Pole. In 1986 five men and a woman made the journey with dog teams but without resupply. At the same time Frenchman Dr. Jean-Louis Etienne hauled his sled alone to the Pole but he was resupplied five times by air. Americans Will Steger, Paul Schurke, Ann Bancroft, Geoff Carroll and Bob Mantell, Canadians Brent Poddy and Richard Weber and New Zealander Bob McKerrow started from Ellesmere Island with 49 dogs on March 8. The heavy loads and rough pressure ice forced them to relay early in the journey. They were visited twice by aircraft, which brought them no supplies. On April 2 McKerrow had to be evacuated, having suffered broken ribs from a careening sled. On April 16 Mantell was airlifted out because of frozen feet. Dogs were also flown out and only 21 of them made the final journey. The six remaining members were flown back from the Pole on May 1. On March 9 Etienne set out, pulling his sled, from Ward Hunt Island, just north of Ellesmere Island and slightly east of where the others had left the day before. Amazingly, the two parties met briefly on April 8. He reached the North Pole on May 11 but because of bad weather had to wait for four days to be picked up by plane. Articles in the *National Geographic* of September 1986 describe both expeditions.

SOUTH AMERICA

Peak-Route Sketches, A.A.J., 1986. The excellent peak-route sketches of Aconcagua and Pumori in *A.A.J., 1986* were done by Dee Molenaar. Unfortunately the credit lines were cut off. Also the dotted line for the French route on the Aconcagua sketch was omitted.

Venezuela

Pico Bolívar, West-Northwest Rib, Sierra Nevada de Mérida, 1985. In a 13-day round trip from Britain, Jan Solvov and I were able to make the first complete ascent of the west-northwest rib of Pico Bolívar (5007 meters, 16,427 feet), the country's highest peak. The rock was disappointingly poor except for the summit ridge. However, the snow and ice, together with the weather, proved excellent. We bivouacked twice and reached the summit on December 29, 1985. We descended the Ruta Weiss on the south face. On New Year's Day I followed the main Toro-León crest, a seven-kilometer classic ridge traverse with continuously exposed scrambling and some more difficult pitches on excellent granite.

LINDSAY GRIFFIN, *Alpine Climbing Group*

Pico Bonnpland, Northeast Face and Ascents in Southern Venezuela. Although the northeast wall of Pico Bonnpland (4882 meters, 16,017 feet) is only 1000 feet high, it offers difficulties of the 4th and 5th grade. Dora Ocanto and I made the climb by new route in early March. In a South American region wholly unrelated to the Andes, the remarkable peaks locally called *tepuyes* represent a new, interesting field. Climbers from Caracas have been particularly active in this area and have opened new routes on the north ridge and the west face of Cerro Autana (difficulties up to 5.9 and 5.11). Other climbs in the same district have been those of the *tepuyes* of Marahuaca, Aratitiope and Salto Angel.

JOSÉ BETANCOURT, *Club de Andinismo Universitario, Mérida, Venezuela*

Ecuador

Frailes Group, Altar, 1985. The two showy peaks of Fraile Central and Fraile Oriental (both c. 17,000 feet) had been climbed for the first and only time in 1974 and 1978, respectively. On December 6, 26 and 30, 1985, Fraile Central was ascended by parties belonging to the clubs of Cumbres Andinas, Intiñán and Ascensionismo San Gabriel. Fraile Oriental was climbed again on December 27 by four members of Cumbres Andinas and on December 31, by F. Almeida and C. Román.

RAMIRO NAVARRETE, *Club de Ascensionismo San Gabriel, Quito, Ecuador*

Antisana Norte. One of the finest peaks in Ecuador, Antisana Norte (c. 18,400 feet) was ascended for the first and only time on November 1972. Now, six climbers from Ambato placed a base camp near the Laguna (lake) del Volcán and a high one on the north glacier of Antisana. Four of the group reached the main summit (5705 meters, 18,717 feet), while Carlos Vascónez and I managed to reach that of Antisana Norte, overcoming along the way a number of ice towers on the west ridge on November 4, 1984.

OSVALDO MORALES, *Ambato*

Peru—Cordillera Blanca

Notable Ascents in the Cordillera Blanca. A number of excellent ascents were made in 1986 in the Cordillera Blanca. The Italian pair Paola Gigliotti and Massimo Marchini climbed San Juan from the Quebrada Cayesh on June 1 and Milpocraju via a variant 200 meters to the left of the 1985 English route. Slovenes (Yugoslavs) Danilo Tić and Milan Romih on May 11 made a new route on the east face of Quitaraju with a 800-meter rise of 55° to 60° snow and ice, which they climbed in only three hours. They made a new route on the north face of Chopicalqui on May 25 between the 1982 route of Eric Dossin and the 1981 Rolland-Sigayret-Roberts route. They also climbed Huandoy Este by the northeast face and north ridge; they later traversed Huandoy Norte and Este. They ascended by the normal routes Caraz I, Huascarán Sur, Artesonraju, Ranrapalca and Chinchey. Spanish Catalans José Luis Sasot and Carles Vallés climbed Huandoy Este by the northeast face and north ridge, Huascarán Norte by the 1974 Italian route on the northwest ridge, the southwest face of Alpamayo and the northeast face of Quitaraju. The northeast face of Huandoy Este was climbed on July 25 by Spaniards Lorenzo Ortas, José Murciano and Javier Oliván, on July 30 by Spaniard Burrueco and me (Peruvian) and on August 4 by Spaniards Miguel Serrano, José Javier Quiñones and Swiss Bertrand Gachoud. Oliván and Burrueco then climbed Alpamayo and Quitaraju. On July 29 Ortas and Murciano left the moraine camp of Pisco, climbed the couloir to the col between Huandoy Norte and Este; on the 30th they climbed the northeast face of Huandoy Norte to within 100 meters of the summit, where they bivouacked again before reaching the summit the next morning. In July Spaniard Xabier Ansa soloed the west ridge of Huascarán Sur in a single day. The climb was repeated by Murciano and Miguel Ausin in August. Spaniards Antonio Urbieto, Lorenzo Buil and Marcos Mairal climbed the east face of Huascarán Norte with two bivouacs in July. I soloed Chopicalqui in seven hours on June 12.

WALTER SILVERIO, *Asociación de Guías de Montaña del Perú*

Nevado Santa Cruz, South Face and Other Climbs, 1984 and 1985. Marco Suárez and I climbed on August 4, 1984 the south face of Santa Cruz (6241 meters, 20,476 feet). We followed the left side of the wall until we reached the southwest ridge at around 19,700 feet, thence over the ridge to the summit. We rappelled down the center of the south face, or Jaeger route. A bivouac at 18,400 feet was necessary. On July 6, 1985, I climbed alone the west buttress of Huascarán Sur. After an attempt on Chacraraju Sur by its south face, I went to climb the south face of Artesonraju, which I did in three days from Carás. Since the level of Lago Parón has greatly decreased, boats or rafts are no longer necessary; a trail runs along its north side.

RAMIRO NAVARRETE, *Club de Ascensionismo San Gabriel,*
Quito, Ecuador

Pisco Este, East Ridge, 1985. Italian brothers, Luca and Michele Dalla Palma, on June 12, 1985 completed a new route, the east ridge, on Pisco Este. In one day they climbed some 2500 vertical feet from the east col with ice up to 85° and rock of UIAA grade VI.

Rinrijirca, Southeast Face, and Other Peaks. Our expedition was composed of British climbers Martin Hair, David Hood, Roger Payne and me from New Zealand. We set up our first Base Camp on May 17 in the Santa Cruz valley at the end of Taullicocha at 4250 meters. Payne and Hair made a new route on the southeast face of Rinrijirca (5810 meters, 19,062 feet). On May 19 they bivouacked at the glacier's edge at 4810 meters. They ascended the southeast face and a couloir on May 20, emerging onto the east ridge at 5500 meters to ascend the north slopes. They descended via the Rinrijirca-Taulliraju col. Two attempts on the east ridge failed because of bad snow conditions. We all climbed Alpamayo by the southwest face, Payne soloed Kitaraju by its north face and Payne and I climbed Huascarán by the normal route. Attempts on Taulliraju's north and south faces failed. We also climbed Rasac in the Cordillera Huayhuash as reported in that section.

JULIE-ANN CLYMA, *Alpine Club*

Carás II, Southeast Face. Our expedition established two separate Base Camps in early July. [The Cayesh portion of the group of Jerry Gore and Terry Moore is covered elsewhere.] From the Laguna Parón Base Camp, Julian Fisher, Andy Warfield and I made the ascent of the unclimbed southeast face of Nevado Carás II. We reached the east ridge some 300 meters from the summit but did not continue because of cloud, fatigue and the lack of time and bivouac gear. The line taken followed the rightmost of three obvious couloirs running the height of the face. We reached it by a complicated and awkward approach through an icefall. The route was almost entirely on snow and ice of 45° to 75°. The crux pitch was at about half-height, being 80 feet of nearly vertical hollow ice and rock. We descended with 14 abseils down the line of ascent. The ascent and descent took three days from July 9 to 11.

MARK SHELDRAKE, *The Lemmings, England*

Huascarán Norte, North Face. After acclimatization climbs on Artesonraju and Alpamayo, Kurt Saurer and I on May 19 left the lake in the Llanganuco and walked up to the north face. We spent a bad night in a snowstorm without a tent. The next day we climbed the glacier with a difficult bergschrund and an icefield. Two pitches of steep rock were climbed with crampons on to the beginning of a big vertical icefall. We had a bad bivouac because of drifting snow. We climbed the difficult icefall on May 21 and came to the less steep part of the wall to reach our third bivouac with wet sleeping bags now weighing seven kilos. We crossed the Spanish route and traversed more to the left. Three pitches of difficult rock climbing led us to the very dangerous north ridge, which was covered with very steep powder snow. We bivouacked again before climbing over the summit of Huascarán Norte for a fifth bivouac near the Garganta.

DANIEL ANKER, *Schweizer Alpen Club*

Huascarán, Anqosh Face, 1985, Correction. The route described in the article in the *American Alpine Journal,* 1986 on pages 81 to 86 was actually a second ascent of the route. It was first climbed on July 13 and 14, 1985 solo by the late Benoît Grison of France. He bivouacked at 5000 and 6400 meters. Obviously Carlos Buhler and Sharon Wood found no tracks of the ascent made only about ten days before theirs.

Yana Raju de Cotush and Other Peaks. Our party set out to make five possible first ascents in the Quebrada Shahuanca by going up and over the Wamashpunta, as a short cut. The first ascent of Yana Raju de Cotush (5185 meters, 17,010 feet) was made on July 14 by Michael Bizeau, Evelio Echevarría and myself. The next few days we waited out storms, only to descend and leave behind four beautiful summits, Nevado Shahuanca being the main prize. The following week we went to the Quebrada Ulta for the unclimbed soutwest ridge of Contrahierbas, which contains many first-ascent points. Due to constant avalanches and deadly cornices we turned back and down the newly completed road that goes over the Shilla Pass. At Base Camp we discovered our cache of food stolen, so take care, as eyes are always on climbers wherever they go! Two weeks later Evelio and I did the first ascents of Huirucancha (4995 meters, 16,390 feet) and Huachucancha (4970 meters, 16,306 feet), the two most prominent rock peaks in the Quebrada Conde. Across this quebrada the follow-ing day I soloed Sucu Jirca (or "Grey Peak," 5130 meters, 16,831 feet) by the northeast face and discovered a large cairn on the summit. As there were no records, no military plates and no time to inspect, I concluded the cairn might possibly be Indian ruins.

ALEX ECHEVARRÍA

Cayesh and Chacraraju Ascents and Tragedy. From May 30 to June 2 Czechoslovaks Břetislav Husička and Petr Hapala made an alpine-style new route of extreme difficulty on the right side of the west face of Cayesh. The

PLATE 55

Photo by Matthew Wells

**North Face of HUASCARÁN
NORTE. —— = Swiss 1986 route;
– – – = Spanish 1983 route.**

climb was on ice and mixed terrain. They were to the left of the yellow ropes left by the Italians. They then made a direct route on the north face of Chacraraju which emerged on the north ridge. This was doubtless the finest route done this year in the Cordillera Blanca. On much of it, it was impossible to belay. On the descent of the 1984 south-face route, Husička was swept to his death by an avalanche coming from the summit cornices.

PHILIPPE BEAUD, *Club Alpin Français*

Traverse from San Juan to the North Col of Cayesh. Italians Paola Gigliotti and Massimo Marchini made an interesting traverse in June from the summit of San Juan, over the top of Maparaju to bivouac in the col between Maparaju and Milpocraju. On the second day they climbed Milpocraju by its west face, at least in part by the British route of 1985. They then continued along under the west face of Cayesh to the north col of Cayesh.

Peru—Cordillera Huayhuash

Rasac, West Face, Left Buttress. On July 17 Guus Lambregts and I approached the west face of Rasac from our Base Camp at Jahuacocha. From the second lake at 4620 meters in the Quebrada Rasac we climbed easy rocks and reached the north rim of the glacier, which we followed to the right. During an earlier attempt, we had to return from our bivouac under the face because of bad weather, which lasted for three days. There are three buttresses on the face. On July 18 we climbed the left buttress on the left side, on the right of a huge sérac wall. It is probably a new route. We reached the summit of Rasac at five P.M. We descended the east face in the full moon, rappelling, and reached Jahuacocha at three A.M. On July 23 we tried to climb the east face of Tsacra Grande from the col between Tsacra Chico Oeste and Tsacra Grande. We had to give up 150 meters below the summit because of dangerous snow.

ROLAND BEKENDAM, *Koninklijke Nederlandse Alpen Vereniging*

Rasac, South Face. Our United Kingdom-New Zealand expedition, Julie-Ann Clyma, Martin Hair, David Hood and I, left the Cordillera Blanca to establish Base Camp on June 8 in the Cordillera Huayhuash on Jahuacocha at 5050 meters. Hair and I decided to try the south face of Rasac and so we set out on June 10 up the valley below Rasac's west face and over the col. On the descent a small step of honeycombed ice gave way, resulting in a blow to my mouth with the ice hammer. An L-shaped laceration in my cheek, a knocked-out tooth and broken sun glasses were patched up and although it was painful, I could carry on. We found a good bivouac spot at 4900 meters below the face. We decided to attempt a new direct line on the left of the face, left of the 1985 New Zealand and the 1977 British routes. We broke trail for 300 meters in soft snow to start up a shallow couloir. The main obstacle appeared to be two bands of icicles which crossed the face, the lower about two-thirds of the way up the route. A

PLATE 56

Photo by H. Adams Carter

RASAC'S South Face. British route, with bottom part hidden on the left; New Zealand on the right.

PLATE 57

Photo by H. Adams Carter

West Face of RASAC on the left and the South Face in the shadow. British route is marked.

few reasonable pitches soon led to what constituted the bulk of the route: sustained steep climbing on good ice where it was rarely possible to stand on balance even after cutting a step. Darkness came before we could finish one of the hardest pitches of the day, a crest of nearly vertical, collapsing snow with marginal aid moves on featureless rock. We looked for a bivouac on some of the easiest angled ice of the day: 60° to 65°. After an uncomfortable night, the main problem that day was the icicle barrier. After trying one blind alley, we climbed vertical and overhanging ice to reasonable terrain. Darkness fell during two short pitches above the barrier and we resigned ourselves to chopping another ledge from the 65° slope. Technical difficulties continued on the third day but the way ahead seemed certain. After a blind alley in the flutings, we arrived at a flat patch below a huge but easily avoidable cornice. Although it was only mid afternoon, we bivouacked early. In the cool of the morning of June 14, we easily reached the summit. Looking for the normal east-face route for the descent, we mistakenly went down in the wrong direction, heading for what had appeared to be old tracks. Nonetheless, we made a safe descent of the unappealing and dangerous icefall which descends northeast from the summit and in doing so completed a traverse of the mountain by two previously unclimbed routes.

ROGER PAYNE, *Alpine Club*

Sarapo Southwest Face. Our expedition consisted of Peruvian Alberto Callupe, Swiss Louis Deuber, Austrian Richard Franzl, German Hans Zebrowski and me. After trekking in the region, we established our Base Camp below Sarapo Qocha. Our objective was Sarapo's southwest face. We placed a camp in the glacial basin below the face at 5100 meters. The approach from Base Camp was on the right side of the icefall where we were least endangered by falling ice. We placed 100 meters of rope. We set out on the face on July 20 and got to the summit on the morning of July 22 after two bivouacs and 20 hours of climbing. The face averaged between 55° and 60° with the steepest pitch at 80°. We believe this to be the second ascent of the face, which was first climbed by Casimiro Ferrari and other Italians in 1979.

ČESTIMÍR LUKEŠ, *Czech living in Switzerland*

Southern Peru

Salcantay, Southwest Face to the East Peak. The southwest face of Salcantay is some 5000 feet high and had before this year not been climbed, despite several previous attempts. Our team climbed a line on the right side of the face. It was of mixed nature in the first half and all snow and ice in the upper half. The whole face is subject to avalanche danger from unstable séracs and cornices. This is particularly true in the first half. The second half became difficult due to snowfall during the ascent which produced spindrift slides. If a heavy fall of snow had occurred, this would have become a dangerous place indeed. The overall grading is of alpine ED. The route includes rock pitches of alpine IV and

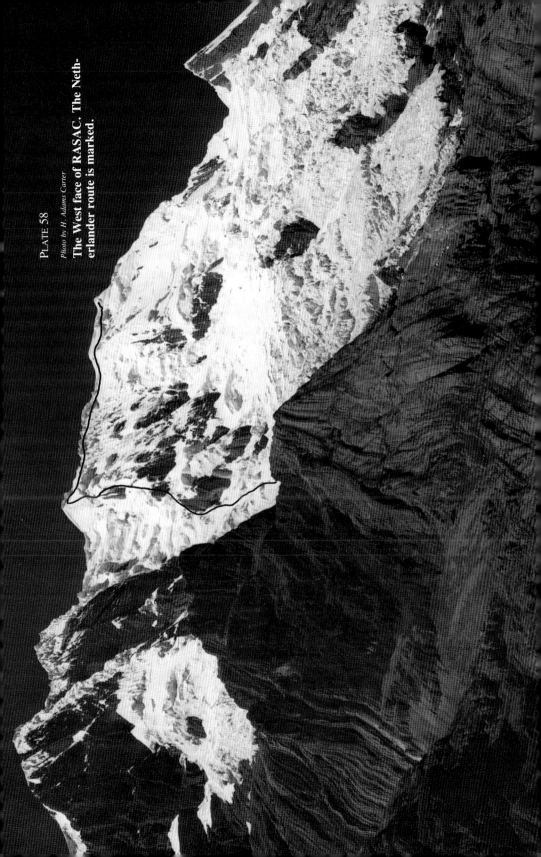

PLATE 58

Photo by H. Adams Carter

The West face of RASAC. The Netherlander route is marked.

V (all short), some tricky mixed climbing and ice up to Scottish grade V, although most of the ice climbing is of grade III. We climbed in two separate parties, staying relatively close together. Peter Leeming, Duncan Francis and I were the first group and Paul Harris and Keith Milne the second. The ascent took place between August 4 and 7. We bivouacked three times on the ascent, once below the central hanging glacier, once on it and once above. We reached the east peak, which is about 6140 meters (20,145 feet) but did not traverse to the main summit, which lay a half mile to the west. The descent took two days down the east ridge.

MARK LOWE, *North London Mountaineering Club*

Huayna Ausangate, Kiru II and Payachata, Colque Cruz Group, 1985. Our expedition consisting of Bruno Anselmi, Italo Bazzani, Graziano Lampa, Livio Lanari, Dr. Giulio Zagaglia and me as leader climbed on the northern side of the Colque Cruz group. We left Mallma on July 30, 1985 with pack animals, passed through Yanacancha and established Base Camp the next day at 4900 meters on the north side of the Colque Cruz group on a plateau locally called Oquecocha. On August 2 we were forced back off Kiru by bad weather. On August 3 Bazzani and Lanari made a new route on Huayna Ausangate or Vizcachani as it is known locally (5720 meters, 18,767 feet), climbing on extremely steep ice via the north face. They had started from a camp at 5200 meters in the valley known locally as Muyuc-Ccocha. On August 5 the whole expedition made the first ascent of Kiru II (5500 meters, 18,209 feet) by its north face. [Kiru II lay south of Base Camp and east of Huayna Ausangate, apparently just north of the main chain.] We carried a camp to 5000 meters in a valley locally known as Jarihuanaco east of Base Camp and north of Colque Cruz I. On August 10 we all climbed Payachata, locally called Cadarache (5420 meters, 17,782 feet) by the west slope. We were the first Italians to make the ascent.

MARIO COTICHELLI, *Club Alpino Italiano*

Bolivia

North and South of Pelechuco, Cordillera Apolobamba, 1985 and 1986. The tortuous road from Ulla Ulla to Pelechuco roughly divides the Cordillera Apolobamba into a northern half that extends from Bolivia into Peru and a southern half that lies entirely within Bolivian borders. In June of 1985, my son Bill and I finally arrived at Pelechuco. Our objective was to climb the peaks rimming the valley between Kantantica and Soral Este. (See the map opposite p. 38 of *A.A.J.*, 1960.) During the following days we struggled for 20 kilometers with huge loads up an old Aymaran trail paralleling the Río Sanches-Cucho and finally set up Base Camp five kilometers from the west end of the valley. The next day we climbed north up steep scree around the south side of the third peak east-southeast of Soral Este. We continued north along the east side of the north ridge for one kilometer, climbed onto the lower section of the ridge and

PLATE 59

Photo by Mark Lowe

**Southwest Face of SALCANTAY.
The route diagonaled up from left to
right past the right end of the hanging glacier to the east peak.**

continued south up crumbly, class 5.4 rock to the 5100-meter summit for a first ascent. While we were climbing, Indians ransacked our camp of food and various articles, forcing us to revisit Pelechuco to replenish our supplies. We then established a high camp (4850 meters) at the terminus of the glacier fed by the northeast face of P 5610 and the northeast face of P 5560. The next day we ascended the glacier to the col between the peaks and continued up the 65° south face of P 5610 through deep, dry, soft, avalanching snow to the broad top for a second ascent and likely new route. The following day we ascended P 5560, which lies about one kilometer west of Kantantica. We again ambled to near the top of the glacier above camp and proceeded to climb the tumbling ice on the 65° west side of the north ridge. We gained the ridge and followed it to the summit for a first ascent. We dubbed the peak Kantantica Oeste. Our next goal was Soral Oeste, located atop the icefield at the head of the valley. We took two days, one in a snowstorm, to find our way through an icefall below the south face of Soral Este and finally set up a high camp at 5200 meters below the south face of the west ridge of Soral Oeste. (We later discovered that a very simple rock-scrambling route to the icefield exists along the northernmost end of the northeast face of Azucarani.) In a thunderstorm, we climbed the east side of the south-face snow fin of Soral Oeste up 60° soft snow with many hidden crevasses to complete a new route. Three days later we climbed a 4800-meter rock tower lying below the south face of Soral Este. From our camp in the valley we ascended the tower by its southeast ridge in six leads of solid, enjoyable, 5.6 rock climbing.

Bill and I, accompanied by my daughter, Barb, returned to the southern half of the Cordillera Apolobamba during July, 1986. We headed east across the 4400-meter altiplano about five kilometers north of the road fork to Ulla Ulla and Pelechuco. (See map on page 105 of the *Jahrbuch des Deutschen Alpenvereins, 1985.*) We hiked past Lago Khello and two more lakes into a high valley leading to the southeast. This valley led to Base Camp 300 meters above the terminus of a large glacier at 4880 meters, eight kilometers west of Nevado de Cololo, 40 kilometers from where we left the road. On July 8, Bill and I climbed southwest up scree and snow to a snow-and-rock ridge for three kilometers (class three) leading to the top of the 5400-meter peak. A large man-made pillar adorned the top. On July 9, we all climbed an easy snow peak by its northwest ridge to its finlike summit four kilometers south of Cololo for a first ascent. Bill and I left camp on July 11 to climb a 5580-meter volcano-shaped peak four kilometers south-southwest of Cololo and 1.5 kilometers northeast of the aforementioned peak. We belayed, using pickets up the icy 60° northwest face to the long, flat, huge-corniced top, believing this also to be a first ascent. Bill and I next left camp on July 13 and made a contour across the icefield south of Cololo for seven kilometers. We descended into a huge moat and then scrambled up scree into a col between a sharp rock peak, the second summit southwest of Cololo and a more gentle summit lying to the southwest. A class-three scramble up the northeast ridge led to the top of this 5490-meter peak and a first ascent. After placing a cache, we next set up High Camp at 5300 meters near the southwest shoulder of Cololo. This camp was easily gained by ascending a non-obvious, yet simple rock cleaver on the east side of the icefall, north of Base Camp. Two days later, Bill and I ascended soft snow up the shoulder of Cololo onto the glaciated, broken south face and zigzagged upwards for six picket-belayed leads to the summit pyramid. High winds and heavy snowfall turned us back at 1600 hours. We then endured a three-day storm in our tent on the icefield. On July 21, Bill and I set out for a last attempt on Cololo in extremely cold but clear weather which contributed to superficial frostbite of Bill's right big toe. We reached the summit pyramid a little before noon. Bill kicked steps up the 70° west side of the southeast arête for 70 meters and then cut through a three-meter cornice onto the arête for another lead. The exposure to the east was a sheer 700 meters. One more lead to the top of the 5915-meter peak brought us the third ascent amidst a gusty snowstorm (grade III +). We returned to camp at 10:30 P.M. after descending in a whiteout with intermittent snowfall. We later returned to Base Camp and found our cache had been stolen. After a long 12-hour slog out to the road and a miserable two-day ride we were back in La Paz.

JAMES PETROSKE

Ancohuma, Illampu, Haucaña, Cordillera Real. Our expedition of 19 Austrians left La Paz on July 25 for Millipaya. From there we went by truck to Mina Ancohuma. The next morning we traversed for two hours to Base Camp at 4500 meters below the Nevados de Millipaya. This is the best way to reach the Illampu-Ancohuma massif from the northwest. Our first camp was on the glacier between Ancohuma and Illampu at 5100 meters and our second at 5800 meters below the west ridge of Ancohuma (6430 meters, 21,095 feet). This was climbed on July 30 by Walter Groher, Reinhard Streif, Horst Geringer, Richard Tweraser, Erhard Kirchmayr, Peter Lengauer and Heinz Helminger, on July 31 by Ossi Pletschko, Ernst Gritzner, Alfred Gaugg and Fritz Neumeister, and on August 1 by Rudolf Wurzer, Rudolf Schönauer, Joschi Auer, Erwin Aberl and me. Manfred Brunner became altitude sick and was brought down by me from the highest camp. On August 3 Streif and Groher climbed Illampu (6362 meters, 20,872 feet) by a new route on the southwest face left of the German route, which they joined on the upper part. On August 7 Lengauer, Helminger, Pletschko, Tweraser and I climbed P 5960 (19,554 feet), P 5970 (19,587 feet) and Pirámide (5906 meters, 19,377 feet), northwest of Haucaña. Two days later, Wurzer and Schönauer climbed the same mountains. Lengauer and Helminger found a new route on Haucaña (6206 meters, 20,360 feet) from the southwest. Brunner and Aberl climbed a nameless 5400-meter peak northwest of Pico Schulze. After returning to La Paz, Groher, Melminger and Lengauer climbed Huayna Potosí via the south face and were back in La Paz after only 12 hours.

SEPP FRIEDHUBER, *Naturfreunde Oberösterreich, Austria*

Casa de Guías, Huaraz. The Asociación de Guías (guides) del Perú has managed to have its own home built in Huaraz, which has been named the Casa de Guías. President of the association is Celio Villón and address of the Casa is Centro Comercial 28-G, Huaraz, Peru. The 23 guides that belong to the association were trained by Swiss professional guides and state that they are able to lead climbers to any peak in the cordilleras Blanca and Huayhuash. Fees are US $30 a day for 1 guide to 3 clients, or $40 a day for 1 to 6 clients. The building, at present being finished, will have a cafeteria and facilities to lodge clients. Future plans also contemplate a small museum and a library.

EVELIO ECHEVARRÍA

Huayna Potosí, First All-Woman Ascent. The Unión Panamericana de Montañismo and the Federación de Andinismo de Chile jointly sponsored a South American all-woman expedition to the Cordillera Real of Bolivia. Twelve climbers with a distinguished record participated and were led by Magaly Campos, of Chile. An attempt on Chearoco had to be abandoned at 19,400 feet when a collapsing sérac injured one member, who had to be evacuated. As a consolation prize, Huayna Potosí (6088 meters, 19,975 feet) was climbed on August 3 by its normal route in only one day from La Paz and back by five members of the expedition (Carina Vaca, Argentina, Narda Wurth, Chile, Vicky Reaño, Colombia, Luisa Gallardo, Ecuador, and myself, Venezuela.

ROSA PABÓN, *Club Universitario de Andinismo, Mérida, Venezuela*

Nevado Apachita Cuno, First Ascent, and other Climbs, 1983. From July 10 to 28, 1983, a party of ten, sent by the Club Andino Córdoba, was active in the area of Chachacomani. We placed a Base Camp in Hichucota valley. Several of us ascended first Janco Anco (c. 5300 meters, 17,389 feet) and Huila Llojeta (5244 meters, 17,207 feet) in order to become acclimatized. On July 13, Janco Huyo (5512 meters, 18,084 feet) was climbed via its southeast ridge by M. Badra, J. Gudiño and M. Schneider, while the rather difficult southeast face and glacier was climbed by F. Marocchi, G. Raynié, A. Vargas and me. The two women that were part of our party, María Bustos and Amalia Agued, unsuccessfully attempted the northwest glacier of Cerro Negruni (5400 meters, 17,717 feet). We then transferred our Base Camp over the Mallo pass to the Escondido Lake basin, from which the two women, Schneider and M. Aprile ascended Jiska Pata (5430 meters, 17,815 feet) while Marocchi, Raynié, Vargas and I climbed Janco Laya (5545 meters, 18,190 feet) by its northwest glacier (both on July 19). The first ascent of the fine rock tower of Torre Aimara (c. 4800 meters, 15,748 feet) was performed the 21st by Aprile, Raynié, Schneider and Vargas. We again transferred our Base Camp, this time into the Chachacomani valley. At no time did we have any outside help. We made attempts on several peaks of the Chachacomani group but we only succeeded in accomplishing the first ascent of Nevado Apachita Cuno (c. 5600 meters, 18,375 feet) by its northwest glacier (Aprile, Badra, Raynié and Schneider, July 27).

ALBERTO TARDITTI, *Club Andino Córdoba, Argentina*

Zongo Pass Area Ski Descents; Cunatincuta (Chekhapa) and Ayllayco. In early July, Don Pattison and Jimmy Katz attempted to nordic ski 19,996-foot Huayna Potosí, but encountered exceptionally windy and sun-crusted conditions and did not reach the summit. During the climb, they noticed a lower peak across the valley which appeared to offer better snow conditions: 17,445-foot Ayllayco. A few days later, they made what they consider to be the first nordic ski descent of this peak. (It has also been skied on alpine equipment.) The angle was a moderate, but interesting 40°-45° and the snow conditions were firm on the northwest face. In mid July, I joined the two skiiers in Bolivia. After some fascinating touristing on the shores of Lake Titicaca, we struck into the Zongo Pass region again. This time we hiked five or six miles to Cunatincuta (also called Chekhapa), 18,400 feet according to Alain Mesili's guidebook to the Cordillera Real, and made what we suspect was the first ski descent (none are listed in Mesili's book). I was on alpine skis, my partners on nordic gear (Rossignol skis and Merrell boots). We reached the top in perfect weather, but waited several hours until two P.M. for the sun to warm the northwest face enough to melt some of the surface ice. On the steepest section (45°), the snow had softened to corn, but on lower-angled slopes soft ice prevailed. The snow (and skiing) occupied the upper 2500 feet of the mountain. Though we are unaware of any previous nordic skiing in Bolivia, the Cordillera Real seems more suited to such skiing than Peru's Cordillera Blanca. Had the mountains not been subjected to an exceptionally dry spell before our arrival, adequate snow would likely have been encountered on most peaks. Huayna Potosí would be a superb nordic descent because of its moderate angle and lengthy slope. We hired expensive taxis from an agency to get to the mountains, but one could probably do better by flagging down taxis in the street and bargaining for their services.

JOHN HARLIN

Illampu, East Face. On July 9 two Spaniards from the Canary Islands, César Tejador and Antonio Ramos reached the summit of Illampu (6362 meters, 20,873 feet) by a new route on the left side of the east face, left of the buttress climbed in 1975 by A. Mesili. The first part was on rock of UIAA Grade V and the middle and upper sections were 60° ice. They descended to the left of the new route via previously unclimbed and dangerous terrain. They bivouacked at about 6000 meters.

JÓZEF NYKA, *Editor, Taternik, Poland*

Sajama. On June 1 Dr. Cleve Armstrong, Robin McIntosh, Karen Ann Young, Richard Markham and I reached the summit of Sajama (6542 meters,

21,463 feet) via the west rib. After making extensive research, we believe that ours was the first American ascent of this route; the only other documented ascent of this route was that of Germans in 1975.

JENNIFER J. SEARS, *Colorado Mountain Club*

Chile—Northeast Andes

Ojos del Salado, Cerro "Radioactivo" and Cerro "Ojitos," While in the area in the first two weeks of March, our expedition made the ascent of Cerro "Radioactivo," shown on the maps as P 5750 (18,865 feet), about six kilometers southwest of the new and quite comfortable Hospedería Murray at Barrancas Blancas. This climb was made by a multinational group consisting of Chileans Gino Casassa, Marie Claude Bastres, Rodrigo Mújica, Americans James B. Scott, Burton A. Falk, Blaine A. Gibson, Charles J. Grashow and British John H. Rogers on March 8 for a second recorded ascent. They simply followed the ridge for four hours from the last place one can drive a jeep. The first recorded ascent was made in 1969. The climbers, whose names and details of the climb were found in a plastic bag in a cairn, gave the peak its name. Cerro "Ojitos," a peak or prominent shoulder northwest of Ojos del Salado and southwest of the Refugio Andino, was climbed by Casassa, Mújica, Scott, Falk, Gibson, Rogers and Peruvian James Dirks on March 10. A barometric altimeter reading on the summit gave an elevation of 19,200 feet (5852 meters). No cairn was found on the summit and so one was built in which the name of the peak and those of the climbers were left. The Ojos del Salado was climbed on March 12 in 12 hours by the same group without Dirks and with American John Kurnick from the new Refugio Tejos on the north side. They ascended to the crater rim and then to the north or "technical" summit, described by Captain René Gajardo in *A.A.J.*, 1957. The summit register has between 100 and 200 names of climbers who have reached this point since its first ascent.

RICK JALI

Argentina—Northern Andes

Macón, Rumibola and Llanaleria, Ancient and Modern Ascents. The three peaks named belong to the high desert of Salta province. Cerro Macón or Icomán (5490 meters, 18,012 feet) located along the way of the Antofagasta-Salta railroad, was ascended by Cristián Vitry and several members of the Club Amigos de la Montaña. The group located at 16,400 feet some pre-Columbian enclosures, which contained pieces of wood and pottery. The same Vitry, plus Antonio Zuleta, climbed Cerro Rumibola (5420 meters, 17,782 feet) on whose higher slopes they found again remains of ancient enclosures and even some petroglyphs. Two weeks later, Vitry, Zuleta and a woman, Talía Lino, of the Club Andino Córdoba, ascended Cerro Llanaleri (5300 meters, 17,389 feet), a possible first ascent. Both Rumibola and Llanaleri are situated near the town of La Poma.

EVELIO ECHEVARRÍA

Argentina—Central Andes

Aconcagua and Cordón de la Plata Traverses. In ten days, between February 17 and 27, the Mendoza guide Gabriel Cabrera traversed Aconcagua by climbing the Pirámide buttress (southwest ridge), south summit ridge and main summit. He descended the Glacier de los Polacos and then traversed along the base of the north side of Aconcagua to reach Plaza de Mulas and Puente del Inca. The same climber undertook in September a winter traverse. After bivouacking on the summit of Cerro de la Plata (5850 meters, 19,193 feet) he descended to the ridge of peaks that connects Plata with the Tres Mogotes group. He then accomplished a high-altitude traverse over twelve peaks over 16,500 feet, including several unclimbed lesser points. He then returned to Punta de Vacas by way of the Tupungato river valley.

LUIS A. PARRA, *Club Andinista Mendoza*

Aconcagua, North Face. Two members of an Italian expedition, Claudio Schranz and Mauro Ferrari, climbed Aconcagua via the Polish Glacier from the Berlin shelter on January 25. Schranz remained at the shelter and on January 27 made a new route on the north face. He said that the new route was not difficult. It was more a question of route-finding among the pinnacles and gullies.

Aconcagua, Clean-Up Operation. The operation "Aseo del Aconcagua" was undertaken by 18 members of the Club Universitario de Andinismo, Mendoza, seven of whom were women and all under 24. Their objective was to clean up the normal route on Aconcagua, from Confluencia to the very summit, which was reached, and cleaned, by three of the volunteers. Most of the rubbish collected in the operation was from expeditions from Western Europe which have a long and well established tradition of conservation and national parks. The behavior of these foreign visitors has made inevitable the imposition of fees destined for the collection of rubbish on Aconcagua.

LUIS A. PARRA, *Club Andinista Mendoza*

Cerro Cajón Perdido. Attempts. More than 20 climbers, which included Italians from Venice and Argentinians from the town of General Alvear, joined forces for a campaign among the little known peaks of the southern part of the province. They climbed Cerro Alvear (4534 meters, 14,878 feet), the south face of Risco Plateado (4920 meters, 16,142 feet) and explored the unclimbed east face of Sosneado (5189 meters, 17,025 feet). Their main objective, Cerro Cajón Perdido (4660 meters, 15,291 feet), a fine rock cathedral, repulsed all attempts. In one the climbers reached some 150 feet below the final rock tower, but had to retreat on account of the steepness of the unstable rock. Leaders were Francesco Santon, Italian, and Guillermo Rodríguez, Argentinian.

LUIS A. PARRA, *Club Andinista Mendoza*

Vallecito-Rincón Traverse and Other Mendoza Climbs. A Randis and M. Sánchez, of the Club Mendoza de Regatas, traversed the almost two-mile ridge connecting Vallecitos and Rincón peaks, both over 17,000 feet. It took them 14 hours to traverse all obstacles, which included the first ascent of five lesser points or peaklets (December 1985). The south-face wall of Pico Franke (5000 meters, 16,404 feet) was climbed for the first time on December 6, 1986 by J. Giaquinta, M. Sánchez and J. Santamaría, a route very exposed to rockfall.

Luis A. Parra, *Club Andinista Mendoza*

Argentine—Chilean Patagonia

Crossing of the Northern Patagonian Icecap and Cerro Largo, 1985. In November and December of 1985 American Bonnie Schwahn and Chileans Gino Casassa and I were on the Northern Patagonian Icecap (Hielo Continental Norte). We made the crossing of the icecap in 17 hours round-trip. It was the first east-to-west traverse, the first on cross-country skis and the first crossing in one day. We started on November 29, 1985 from our small tent on the eastern side of the Soler and Nef Glaciers. We arrived at midday at the snow line below the San Quintin Glacier on the Pacific side. After a short rest, we began the return and after 17 hours and a 58-kilometer trip were back at our tent that night. Two days after the crossing, on December 1, 1985, we climbed "Pico Naranja" (2700 meters, 8858 feet), one of the summits of Cerro Largo. We climbed on skis and made a telemark descent.

Rodrigo Mújica, *Chilean Section of the Club Alpino Italiano*

Volcán Lautaro, West Face. An official expedition of the Federación de Andinismo de Chile reached the Continental Icecap by way of Fiordo Exmouth and headed for Volcán Lautaro (3380 meters, 11,089 feet), previously ascended by Argentinians and British parties. On February 10, the five members of this expedition reached the summit, having ascended the west side, a new route (G. Chauriye, C. Gálvez, P. Jara, R. Labbé and M. Munjín).

Evelio Echevarría

Cerro "Aguilera" Attempt. A Chilean-British expedition jointly led by F. Medina and M. Hickman and comprising nine other climbers and scientists entered the Patagonian Icecap through the Fiordo Andrew and marched toward Cerro "Aguilera" (unofficial name, 2400 meters, 7874 feet). Attempts could get no higher than 4000 feet, but in the course of this expedition it was verified that the mountain was a volcano (November 1985 through January 1986).

Evelio Echevarría

San Lorenzo Sur and Cerro Hermosa Este. My husband Gino Buscaini and I approached the San Lorenzo group from the Estancia El Rincón and went in three days with loads via Lago del Volcán, Río San Lorenzo and Río "Paso

PLATE 60

Photo by Paul Fatti

SAN LORENZO. The South African route ascended the buttress left of the center to the east ridge left of the summit.

Clandestino" to the southwest San Lorenzo Glacier. We first made two attempts on the principal summit of San Lorenzo (3706 meters, 12,159 feet). We got to 2850 meters on December 10, 1985 on the east ridge but had to turn back because of dangerous conditions caused by too hot weather! On December 22 we attempted the San Lorenzo route of Padre De Agostini after crossing to the east of Cerro Hermoso, descending to the Río de Oro and ascending the Río Tranquilo. We got to 2700 meters where wind and snowfall turned us back. Because of lack of food, we could not make another attempt. When we returned, we found that four South Africans were trying the east ridge. We understand that they were successful. On December 29, 1985 we climbed the south face and east ridge of Cerro Hermoso Este (c. 2400 meters, 7874 feet). The route was the most elegant and most logical. In the recent warm summers the glaciers and ice faces have changed considerably. The difficulties were only two 75° rope-lengths of ice. On January 15 we climbed San Lorenzo Sur (3385 meters, 11,105 feet) by the south face and west ridge. The climb was all snow and ice. We climbed a couloir close to the rocks on the right, working our way through two sérac bands to arrive on the ridge at 2800 meters. We worked our way along the west ridge at times past ice walls and mushroom formations to reach the small round plateau at the summit. We descended the same route.

SILVIA METZELTIN BUSCAINI, *Club Alpino Italiano*

San Lorenzo, East Face. On January 15 Erwin Müller, Russell Dodding, Hans-Peter Bakker and I reached the summit of San Lorenzo (3706 meters, 12,159 meters), the first party ever to climb the mountain from the Argentine side. We had made an unsuccessful attempt in 1980. The ascent was made via the 2200-meter-high east ridge and involved steep ice climbing with a 5-meter vertical rock band just below the summit. From the roadhead at Estancia El Rincón, close to the Chilean border, a 15-kilometer hike led to a beech grove sheltered behind a moraine ridge and Base Camp. It took four hours to cross the difficult terrain over the moraine and glacier to the col at the base of the east ridge, where we dug a snow cave for Advance Base. The next task was to establish our box tent as high as possible on the ridge. We set off on December 27, 1985 at the beginning of a good weather spell. After 32 hours of continuous climbing, mostly on steep ice, we eventually came across a bergschrund at 3000 meters, forming an ideal sheltered campsite, well situated for tackling the final 700 meters to the top. We retreated to Base Camp to recover and pick up supplies. Bad weather kept us at Base Camp for another week and then, on our first attempt to get back on the mountain, a snowstorm forced us to retreat. Finally, on January 8, we were back on the ridge. After another exhausting climb, right through the night, we arrived at the bergschrund camp on the following afternoon to find our box-tent half buried under the snow but still intact. For the next three days we were kept prisoners while the storm raged outside. Eventually, on January 13, the storm broke. The climbing was steep and sustained. Although we made steady progress, we were still far from the summit when night overtook us. There was nowhere to bivouac on the steep ice and we continued to climb by torchlight. Early morning saw us tied to ice screws on a tiny stance, preparing a meal on a precariously balanced stove and waiting for daylight. Eventually the sun appeared and we continued upwards. By lunch time we reached the base of the rock band and prepared to tackle the 50-meter sheer cliff of hazardous rock and ice-filled cracks. The first attempt by Dodding ended at an impassable section, and he was lowered to the stance from a piton at the high point. I took over the lead and, following a different line, inched my way up the icy rock. Two-and-a-half hours later, I was at the top of the band with the summit in sight. It was another few hours before the other three joined me and in the fading light we made our way to the summit ridge. Just below the final rock pillar on the ridge we found a site for our bivouac tents. Eventually, in the early hours of the morning, we crawled into sleeping bags, having been on the go for 46 hours. Fortunately the good weather held and the next morning we awoke late to find the summit little more than a rope-length away. That afternoon we negotiated the final obstacle, the rock pillar, and made our way to the summit of San Lorenzo. It took us the whole of the following day to descend to the bergschrund camp. After a rest day there, we finally arrived at Base Camp on the evening of January 19.

L. PAUL FATTI, *Mountain Club of South Africa*

San Lorenzo. On December 10, 1986 my husband Gino Buscaini, Argentine Cristina Agued and I reached the summit of San Lorenzo by the easy route of the first ascent made by Padre De Agostini. We believe that ours was the fifth ascent. San Lorenzo was also climbed by the Italian Casimiro Ferrari and three others on January 18, 1987 by the east ridge, previously climbed by South Africans. They found UIAA difficulties of V to V + on the upper rock buttress. This year's weather was typically "Patagonian," which made us retreat from a number of our objectives.

SILVIA METZELTIN BUSCAINI, *Club Alpino Italiano*

Patagonia, Southern Summer Season of 1986-7. The weather this season was not as good as last year and so few ascents have been made up to now, late February, 1987. On December 7, Slovenes Franc Knez, Silvo Karo and Johan Jeglič finished a new route on the southeast face of Torre Egger. They rated it VII, A3. They fixed rope on the lower 500 meters of the 900-meter face. Afterwards the same three climbed the Mocho (near the Cerro Torre), which I believe had previously been climbed only once, by Australians. There was only one ascent of Cerro Torre, made on January 9, 1987 by Italians including Paolo Vitoli by the Maestri bolt route. Fitz Roy was climbed by seven different groups, Spanish, Austrian, Swiss, Italian, Argentine and South Tirolean. Spaniards A. Trabado and M. Vidal climbed to the summit twice, once by the Californian route and once by the Argentine one. South Tiroleans Reinhard Patschneider and Fritz Kurt climbed the Argentine route on December 20 in 25 hours round-trip. A few days before Christmas, Argentine Sebastián de la Cruz made his third ascent of Fitz Roy, accompanied by Jorge Tarditti. They ascended the Californian route and descended the Argentine route, which de la Cruz had pioneered last year. Another scene of much activity was the Aguja Poincenot. Italians completed the east face. [See below.—*Editor*.] Other Italians made a new difficult route on the west buttress. Spaniards Fernando Cobo and Máximo Murcia did a new route on the south face. The "normal" Whillans route was climbed by Austrians Hans Bärnthaler and E. Lidl and by Swiss Peter Lüthi and Edi Caviezel. On January 18, 1987 Lüthi and Argentine Paul Cottescu ascended Saint Exupery. [Italians Grassi, Rossi and Pe made climbs listed below—*Editor*.] Teen-agers from Bariloche, M. Joss and D. Rodríguez, in January climbed Gorra Blanca and Guillaumet.

VOJSLAV ARKO, *Club Andino Bariloche, Argentina*

Fitz Roy, First Winter Ascent. Gabriel Ruiz, Eduardo Brenner and I made the first winter ascent of Fitz Roy, climbing it by the Supercouloir. Starting from the Piedra del Fraile, we spent the night of July 25 in a tent 100 meters below the couloir. We entered the couloir at six A.M. on July 26 and climbed unroped to save time. There was powder snow covering blue ice. At eleven A.M. we reached the famous great block some 1000 meters above the beginning of the couloir. That is where the difficult climbing begins. The first bivouac was three pitches below the towers of the ridge. To save weight, we took no sleeping bags, only bivouac sacks. The second day of climbing, July 27, we set out at six o'clock in the moonlight. There were strong winds and it was snowing. At five P.M. we got to the easy part of the ridge, but the bad weather prevented our getting to the summit until 8:30 P.M. That night we descended to the col. Because of west winds, we bivouacked on the east side. On July 28 we made 12 rappels to the block and then climbed down, reaching the tent that night. The next day we had to plow for 13 hours through deep new snow back to the Piedra del Fraile; it had taken us five on the approach. Two of us suffered frostbitten hands and one required some amputation.

SEBASTIÁN DE LA CRUZ, *Club Andino Bariloche*

Fitz Roy, Nearly Complete Ascent of the North Face, Tehuelche Route. More details are now available about the new Italian route on the north face of Fitz Roy, mentioned on page 203 of *A.A.J.*, 1986. This lay between the 1984 Polish route and the French route of 1979 done by Afanassieff. The climbers were Carlo Barbolini, Massimo Boni, Mauro Petronio, Angelo Pozzi, Mauro Rontini and Marco Sterni. They climbed the first third of the 6000-foot-high face on December 29 and 30, 1985, but they were plagued by bad weather and winds up to 100 mph and turned back. On January 17, 1986, after seven days on the face, they got to their high point, 50 meters below the summit, where they joined the Afanassieff route. They took another long day to make the descent.

PLATE 61

Photo by Angelo Pozzi

Tehuelche Route on FITZ ROY.

There were 46 rope-lengths. It went 90% free with mostly UIAA difficulty of VI+ and 25 meters of VII as well as direct aid of A1 and A2.

Cerro Norte. Italians Casimiro Ferrari and G. Maresi made the second ascent of Cerro Norte (2950 meters, 9679 feet) by a new route, the east-northeast buttress on December 31, 1985 and January 1, 1986. The first part was rock which led to a snow plateau. The final part was ice up to 70°. The final move to reach the summit involved ice of 120°.

Fitz Roy, Cerro Torre and Aguja Guillaumet. Several ascents in late 1985 and early 1986 were not reported in *A.A.J.*, 1986. Frenchman Yves Astier soloed the American route on Fitz Roy in 12 hours on December 29, 1985. With J. M. Boucansaud he climbed the Maestri bolt route on Cerro Torre on January 14 and 15. Austrian Thomas Bubendorfer made a remarkably rapid climb of the American route on Fitz Roy solo in 7½ hours from the col in mid January. Reaching the summit on February 10, Americans Michael Bearzi and Eric Winkleman climbed Cerro Torre in three days via the Ferrari west-face route. A full account and beautiful pictures of this climb appear in *Rock and Ice* of July-August 1986. The summit of Aguja Guillaumet was also visited in early January 1986 by three Argentine groups: Jorge Sonntag, Máximo Schneider and Oscar Pandolfi; G. Anguilar and Sebastián Sturla; and Daniel Puy and Sebastián Letemenia. The Argentines Sebastián de la Cruz and Gabriel Ruiz climbed Guillaumet on February 8.

Aguja Poincenot, Southeast Buttress. Our expedition was composed of Graziano Bianchi, leader, Andriano Carnati, Alessio Bortoli, Massimo Colombo, Corrado Brustia, Mario Vismara, Bruno Vagletti and me. The base of the southeast buttress of the Aguja Poincenot was reached up the Río Blanco Glacier, which, depending on conditions, presents varying difficulties and great objective dangers. It was necessary to fix rope in sections of the icefall, but the real problem was séracs on the Piedras Blancas Glacier which for a distance of 700 meters discharged without any predictable schedule down over the lower part of the route leading to the base of the buttress. The 200-meter shield at the base of the buttress varied in difficulty depending on the snow. The next 500 meters were of vertical or overhanging rock with no place to stop. The final 300 meters were of steep rock with difficult and discontinuous passages. Our new route ended where it joined the 1962 Anglo-Irish route. The final section on that route gained another 300 meters. We established Base Camp at 780 meters on November 25 and an intermediate camp at the tongue of the glacier at 1550 meters on November 29. We placed Camp I on December 12 a little below the face at 1780 meters, where we dug three snow grottos: two to shelter the tents and one for a kitchen. The first climbing on the wall took place from December 7 to 11. We were storm-bound in Camp I from December 11 to 13. Climbing was resumed on December 14, interrupted by stormy weather on Christmas day.

PLATE 62

Photo by Aristide Galbusera

AGUJA POINCENOT.

Plate 63·

Photo by Aristide Galbusera

Climbing on Poincenot.

On December 26 Bortoli, Carnati and Colombo reached the summit. A year before, in the Southern winter of 1985-6, we had climbed 600 meters of the wall.

ARISTIDE GALBUSERA, *Club Alpino Italiano*

Aguja Guillaumet. After climbing Aconcagua by both the normal and the French south-face routes and five attempts on Fitz Roy driven back by bad weather, our Basque expedition reached one summit. In unstable weather in February, J. C. Tamayo climbed Aguja Guillaumet via the northeast ridge from a camp on the Paso Superior.

ALBERTO POSADA, *Federación Vasca de Montaña*

El Mocho, Aguja del S and Cerro Adela Sur. Giancarlo Grassi, M. Rossi and R. Pe climbed in the Fitz Roy region in November and December of 1986. They climbed the "Todo o Nada" couloir on the southeast face of El Mocho on November 18. The face has two prominent pillars which encase a deep ice couloir which is continuously steep and in places vertical. This may be the most difficult ice climb yet done in Patagonia. The left pillar had been climbed by Jim Bridwell. The same three Italians on December 6 and 7 made a new route, the right pillar which they called "Bizcochuelo." The 15-pitch climb was on extremely difficult rock with passages of up to UIAA VII + . On November 30 the same three climbed the Aguja del S ("S Needle") in the Saint Exupéry group from the Torre Glacier. This difficult climb on the northwest face rose 1300 meters, of which 700 meters were in a 40° to 50° couloir, 400 meters on cracks, 100 easy meters and 140 meters on the final rock pyramid. The last climb was done by Grassi and Rossi on December 9 and 10. The pair ascended Cerro Adela Sur (c. 2900 meters, 9515 feet) by its northeast face. From the Adela Glacier they climbed through crevasses up two vertical slopes. After bypassing a rock band on the right, they continued up extremely steep, up to vertical, ice to emerge on the summit ridge just right of the top. (This information was kindly furnished by Giancarlo Grassi and Luciano Ghigo.)

Pier Giorgio Correction. On page 206 of *A.A.J*, 1986 it states incorrectly that the *west* face of Pier Giorgio was climbed. It should have stated the *north* face.

Cerro Castillo, 1987. On January 26, 1987 my husband Gino Buscaini and I climbed an 800-meter-high, snow-and-ice couloir which had an angle of 55° in the upper part of the west face of Cerro Castillo (Coyhaiquel; 2670 meters) in Chile. We climbed the whole couloir to the col (2570 meters) on the summit ridge. Unfortunately we could not continue on to the summit because of a snow storm. We found no signs of previous climbers but this is the logical route to the summit of this lovely peak.

SILVIA METZELTIN BUSCAINI, *Club Alpino Italiano*

Central Tower of Paine, West Face. Fabrizio Defrancesco, Fabio Stedile and I arrived at Base Camp on October 14. After several unsuccessful attempts, stopped by bad weather, we finally completed on November 2 the first ascent of the west face of the Central Tower of Paine. The route followed a crack which starts at the bottom of the wall and ends at the top. In this wonderful red-colored rock in a dreamy landscape, you may still find many possibilities for new routes. We were climbing on eight days, bivouacked four times on the wall and climbed 800 vertical meters. There was continuous UIAA difficulty of VIII, A3.

MARIO MANICA, *Club Alpino Italiano*

Central Tower of Paine, East Face. Ermano Salvaterra, Mauricio Giarolli and Elio Orlandi made a difficult new route on the east face of the Central Tower of Paine. They spent ten days on the climb with eight bivouacs. They rated it at UIAA grade VII, A3.

Torre Norte del Paine, Solo, 1985. Italian Elio Orlandi climbed the North Paine Tower solo on December 29, 1985. He was accompanied to Base Camp by Nora Rigotti. On December 28 he approached the western foot of the three towers, where he bivouacked. On the 29th he rapidly climbed the couloir between the north and central towers, getting to the top of the Brecha Bich at 1:30 P.M. He was attracted to the south face of the north tower and set off immediately. He had overcome the difficult pitches of the long crest by 7:30 and reached the summit at 9:30 P.M. He descended until one A.M., when he bivouacked on a ledge, and on the 30th he continued down to his bivouac tent on the moraine. The onset of bad weather drove him back to Base Camp on the 31st and ended his climbing in the region.

ANTARCTICA

Framnes Mountains, MacRobertson Land. I was working in a scientific capacity in the Framnes Mountains near the Australian station of Mawson in the winter of 1984 and the summers of 1984-5 and 1985-6. The three main ranges of Henderson, Masson and David are visited regularly and the easier peaks have mostly been climbed. The fourth range, the Casey Range, has rarely been visited. In January 1984, while working there, I made a north-to-south traverse of the range. In the Framnes Mountains very few summits require technical skill. The attraction is the remoteness of the locality and extreme isolation. I have drawn up a list of major peaks and tried to indicate what I believe are first ascents. *Henderson Range:* Henderson (970 meters) by P. Law, L. Bechenaise, Shaw, February 1955, Goldsworthy Ridge (960 meters) unknown; *Masson Range:* Rumdoodle Peak (721 meters) unknown, Ward (1030 meters) by W. Williams, M. Conde, January 1985, Ferguson Peak (900 meters) by J. Trealor, Conde, Williams, January 1985, Burnett (1050 meters) by Williams P.

Crossthwait, December 1984; *David Range:* Fang Peak (900 meters) unknown, Elliot (1300 meters) unknown, Coates (1280 meters) by J. Bennett, G. Mantin, R. Lachal, A. Varana, January 1966, Hordern (1510 meters) first ascent unknown, traverse over east peak and 10-meter-lower west peak by W. Williams, Crossthwait, December 1984.

WARWICK WILLIAMS, *Australia*

Vinson Massif, Sentinel Range. On November 24, our group reached the summit of the Vinson Massif. We were Pete Ackerman, Bob Failing, John Otter, Bill Martin, Mike Meyer, Dave Tollakson and I. The ascent commenced following our November 17 landing aboard our privately chartered Twin Otter aircraft piloted by Giles Kershaw. Due to poor weather, we were delayed four days in reaching the mountain following our initial Antarctic refueling stop at the Chilean Marsh Air Base on the Peninsula's King George Island. One further refueling at the Chilean Air Base at Cavajal on the Peninsula's Adelaide Island was also required before the final 3½-hour flight to Base Camp. From Base Camp at about 7500 feet we followed the original 1966 American route, establishing three intermediate camps before the final seven-hour summit push. Significant stormy weather did not materialize during our ascent, although one breezy day with accompanying poor visibility forced an aborted summit attempt on November 23. The lowest air temperature noted during our seven-day ascent was − 36° F recorded at Base Camp, although summit weather, amid ultimately clear and slightly windy conditions, was probably much colder. Within two weeks following our descent, three other groups, one led by Adventure Network's Martyn Williams for Mountain Travel and others including Reinhold Messner and Hector MacKenzie were also successful in reaching the summit. It was Messner's seventh continental summit. By our reckoning, 53 persons have now summited the Vinson Massif.

PAUL PFAU

Vinson Massif. On November 27, Reinhold Messner, Wolfgang Tomaseth and I reached the highest point of Antarctica 26 hours after Giles Kershaw had landed us below the peak. The weather was wonderful and the climb, during which we slept at what is normally Camp II, was a real pleasure. Reinhold Messner thus became the second person, after Canadian Pat Morrow, to reach the highest summits of all the continents, considering Carstensz Pyramid the highest point in Australasia rather than insignificant Kosciusko, which is the highest in Australia.

OSWALD OELZ, *Schweizer Alpen Club*

The Highest Summits of the Continents. In trying to calculate which are the highest summits of each of the continents, one must first figure whether *Australia* should be taken as a continent by itself or whether the islands of the Pacific should be included in *Australasia*. The highest summit of Australia is Kosciusko (2230 meters, 7318 feet). The highest point in Australasia is Carstensz Pyramid (given both as 5030 meters, 16,503 feet and 4884 meters, 16,023 feet) on the island of New Guinea. If the islands are excluded, clearly Dick Bass was the first to climb all the highest points. If the islands are included, Canadian Pat Morrow was the first. He made the following ascents: McKinley, June 9, 1977; Aconcagua, February 9, 1981; Everest, October 7, 1982; Elbrus, July 25, 1983 and July, 1986; Kilimanjaro, August 17, 1983; Vinson Massif, November 19, 1985; and Carstensz Pyramid, May 7, 1986. Reinhold Messner is the second to complete the list which has Australasia in it: Carstensz Pyramid, 1971; Aconcagua, 1974, McKinley, 1976; Kilimanjaro, 1978; Everest, 1978; Elbrus, 1983; Vinson Massif, November, 1986.

EUROPE

Czechoslovakian Exchange. A climbing exchange should show you more than just new climbers and new crags. It is equally important to live a new lifestyle. In a Socialist country there is no shortage of rules to keep you in line every step; as if there weren't enough to worry about on those frightening sandstone towers. Alan Bartlett, Charles Fisher and David Knox arrived a week before I did. They were well entertained by our principal hosts: Vladimír Weigner, Petr Brzák and Standa Vanék. Sightseeing in Prague and climbing on local limestone cliffs were punctuated with rain. When I arrived on September 3, the terror started immediately at Adrspach-Teplice. We just were not used to 20- to 40-foot runouts on sandstone covered with ball bearings. Watching the Czechs run up those towers in their authentic bedroom slippers didn't do much for the ego, until you realized that all shoes work the same on this funky rock. The Czechs climbed beautifully where we struggled to follow in marginal style. But the routes were steep, strenuous and committing. Our little group doubled in size with the arrival of Todd and Holly Skinner, Beth Wald and Dan Michael, who were on their way to the Soviet Union for the World Speed Climbing Championships. They brought with them to the Teplice Film Festival the film, *On the Rocks,* which was a tremendous success. Just a word about the Czech climbing culture: I refer of course to the pub or *pohovinstnu,* which we translated as "nasty, smoky, overcrowded, loud pub." The Czechs have a saying: "As you drink, so shall you climb!" But it is not everywhere that you get to meet the man who has climbed K2 twice. Their climbing serves a real purpose: it is the one chance to express themselves in a society where free speech is a rare luxury. We moved on to Turnov and the climbing in the nearby Česky Raj ("Czech Paradise"). The climbing on the sandstone towers was unique because we could actually use real gear. And we used it liberally. We also saw a 16-year-old hardman throw a dynamic up and out a good sized roof, first try, no sweat, hang-by-a-hand and howl. Leaving Turnov, our little group saw a drastic reduction. Fisher headed home to teach his NOLS course and Knox left to keep his business on track. Skinner and company went off to East Germany and the USSR, leaving just Alan Bartlett and me. We went to the Elbsandsteingebirge and climbed for one day and watched it rain for three. A memorable climb was a Bernd Arnold route, called "Big Wall." Obviously there is more than one conception of big wall. This had its first bolt 70 feet up a 5.9 corner! The next stop was the High Tatras. After a 10-hour overnight train ride, we hauled ourselves up a three-hour slog to a beautiful hut at the head of a lovely valley surrounded by horrendous rock. We each did one route that day. Alan summed it up by declaring it "the *worst* route in the Universe." The next morning he headed back for the sandstone towers, while I stayed on the granite to find something worthwhile, which I did. With my friend Roman Kamler, I did the *best* route of my life, a five-pitch finger crack at 7500 feet. Roman put it all in perspective when he said, "Paul, now we are friends for the life. We have done together the climb." Agreed! We later did another fantastic climb, Sračka Wall, which was the first free ascent of a Bernd Arnold route, protected entirely by ancient fixed pins. The Czechs will be coming to the United States this summer. If you get the chance, climb with them.

PAUL KALLMES

ASIA

Bhutan

Kankar Pünzum Attempt. Our expedition consisted of Albert Fellinger, Dr. Wolfgang Trost, Gerhard Berger, Toni Ponholzer, Helmut Ortner, Sebastian Ruckensteiner and me as leader. We left Bumtang on July 28 and took ten days, two of them inactively, on the approach. Base Camp and Advance Base were at 5000 and 5400 meters. We tried the same route as the Japanese in 1985 on the south ridge. We placed Camp I at 6300 meters at the foot of the ice dome, a prominent summit in the ice ridge. We continued along the sawtooth ice ridge without gaining altitude to the place where the summit ridge shoots sharply up. There, at 6600 meters, we gave up on August 26. There were only two days out of the 21 we were on the mountain without snowfall. Daily snowfall was up to 50cms. We would have had to traverse off the summit ridge left in many places. The avalanche danger there would have been great.

SEPP MAYERL, *Österreichischer Alpenverein*

Masa Gang, 1985. More information has been received on the first ascent of Masa Gang or Masang Kang than was reported on page 211 of *A.A.J.*, 1986. The Kyoto University Alpine Club was led by Ryohei Hori. The main group of the expedition left Thimpu on August 30,1985 and on September 13 got to Base Camp at 5025 meters on a yak pasture called Dreteng three kilometers southeast of the Toma La. Advance Base was established on September 16 two kilometers west at 5400 meters. From there the route up the mountain went south. On

PLATE 64

Photo by Sepp Mayerl

KANKAR PÜNZUM from the South.

September 23 they set up Camp I at 6075 meters below the foresummit. There was steep snow-and-ice climbing before they set up Camp II on the top of the foresummit at 6417 meters on October 8. Camp III was established on October 12 between the foresummit and the main summit. They measured altitudes which seem to differ from those previously given and believe the summit was about 6800 meters (22,310 feet). On October 13, 1985 the summit was reached by Goro Hitomi, Toshihiro Tsukihara, Kotaro Yokoyama and Shigeki Nakayama, on October 14 by Dr. Kozo Matsubayashi, Hironori Ito, Shinya Takeda and Masanaru Takai and on October 15 by Yasuhiko Kamizono, Hironori Ito, Koichi Nanno and Tadao Okada.

Nepal

Kangchenjunga Attempt. An Australian expedition of five tried to climb Kangchenjunga by the normal route on the southwest face. Leader Michael Groom reached the expedition's highest point alone on May 13 in a bid to see how high he could get above Camp IV, where two others gave up the summit push which the three were making. Groom got to 8400 meters and turned back when the wind came up and it clouded over. He rejoined Shane Chemello and James van Gelder at Camp IV at 7600 meters. Thus ended the first Australian attempt on Kangchenjunga.

MICHAEL J. CHENEY, *Himalayan Club,* and ELIZABETH HAWLEY

Kangchenjunga. Our expedition climbed Kangchenjunga by the southwest face, the normal route. We left Kathmandu on August 22 and got to Ramze, the last camp before the glacier, in 12 days. There, we lost our fifth Sherpa, Lhakpa Nuru, who mysteriously disappeared, never to be seen again. We then had the usual porter problems and bad weather, which made us take nine days to get the rest of the way to Base Camp, which should have taken us two; we and the Sherpas had to ferry to Base Camp, which we placed at 5000 meters on September 15. We established Camps I, II and III at 6100 meters on the intermediate ridge, at 6700 meters and at 7200 meters on the upper "plateau" on September 22, 25 and 27. On October 6 we returned to Camp III. By then, all camps were stocked and 1200 meters of rope had been fixed. Heavy snowfall prevented our establishing Camp IV and forced us back to Base Camp. Finally on October 16 we placed Camp IV at 7800 meters, having had to dig out Camp II and replace Camp III, which was destroyed by avalanches that fell from Yalung Kang. The next day a summit attempt in bad weather failed when one member had superficial frostbite. The constant bad weather changed on the 20th, but it was cold and windy. We started a last try on October 21, getting to Camp IV on the 23rd. At two A.M. on October 24 Josep Parmañé, Ang Rita Sherpa and I set out. At 8400 meters the intense cold forced me back. My companions reached the summit at one P.M. and were back in Camp IV at five P.M. This was Ang Rita's fourth 8000er. He has climbed Dhaulagiri four times, Everest three times, Cho

Oyu and Kangchenjunga each once. Our Catalán expedition was composed of Josep Permañé, Ramón Estiu, Francesc Casas, Joan Cardona, Xabier Erro, Santi Carrillo, Salvador Coll, Kim Bover, Dr. Jordi Terrades and me as leader.

JOAN HUGAS, *Girona, Spain*

Nepal Peak Attempt. Our French-Nepalese expedition had six French members, M. and Mme Ansart, S. Lazizi, Dr. F. Tanery, my wife and me, and three Nepalese, Chewang Rinzee Sherpa, Lhakpa Sherpa and Jambia Sherpa. We hoped to climb the virgin south face of Nepal Peak (6910 meters, 22,670 feet). At the end of September we established Base Camp at 5000 meters at Pengpema and Advance Base at 5200 meters at the base of the south face. Despite snowfall, Camp I was set at 5700 meters in a small cwm at the right side of Nepal Gap. Snow conditions and weather were very poor. There were frequent avalanches on the south face. We chose a safe and direct route to the south ridge up a steep 300-meter-high gully. My tent was destroyed by the wind at our 6200-meter Camp II on the ridge. Lazizi, Chewang, Lhakpa and Jambia made three summit attempts. The first two were stopped by lack of visibility. The third on October 16 was conducted in better weather, but it was windy and cold. We had to stop at 6600 meters where our route met a very steep part of the ridge covered with brittle ice. We lacked equipment for this section. When I reached Advance Base, I had eight fingers and a foot badly frozen.

DOMINIQUE HEMBISE, *Club Alpin Français*

Kumbhakarna (Jannu) Attempt and Tragedy. A three-man Australian expedition was led by Terry Tremble. All three reached 7550 meters on October 31 in their alpine-style push on the south ridge from Base Camp. This was the fourth day of ascent. That night it was planned to set out at midnight for the summit, but Keith Eggerton became ill and as his health deteriorated, it grew clear to the other two that they must get him down. His symptoms were those of high-altitude sickness, although he was believed to have acclimatized well to altitude. He collapsed and died at 7400 meters on November 1. The other two continued the descent and left the mountain.

MICHAEL J. CHENEY, *Himalayan Club*, and ELIZABETH HAWLEY

Makalu Attempt. Our 4-man attempt on the regular route on Makalu failed. On May 20 Chris Dube and John Bouchard left; Chris had early signs of cerebral edema. Rick Wilcox and I started up on a third assault, but he got severe diarrhea and vomiting at Camp III at 7040 meters. He staggered off down. That left me with three Sherpas. We went up to Camp IV at 7440 meters. After a day of high winds, I set off with the Sherpas on May 26. We could see the top from 7530 meters. We had a nasty surprise. It was all steep rock for the last 380 meters with no snow couloir which used to lead to the east summit ridge. The Sherpas did not want to go any further. I went alone to 8100 meters and then turned back at the foot of the rock.

NED GILLETTE

Makalu Attempt. A French expedition of ten was led by Raymond Renaud to Makalu's northwest side. Sherpas Sirdar Lhakpa Norbu and Pasang Dawa reached the expedition's high point of 8300 meters on October 13 and were turned back by strong, cold winds. The winds continued for the next several days and the expedition was abandoned. A Gurung wood-cutter and kitchen helper died during the expedition.

MICHAEL J. CHENEY, *Himalayan Club,* and ELIZABETH HAWLEY

Makalu Ascent and Tragedy. On September 10, Marcel Rüedi and I flew from Kathmandu to 2800 meters in the Barun valley. Three days later we got to Base Camp at 5400 meters below Makalu. We, with four other Swiss and Austrians, were members of a six-man and three-woman Polish expedition led by Krzysztof Pankiewicz. On September 17, Krzysztof Wielicki, Rüedi and I climbed the Kukuczka ridge to 6900 meters where we bivouacked. The next day Rüedi and Wielicki reached the Makalu Col before we all returned to Base Camp. On the 21st the same two left Base Camp and climbed to 6900 meters. The day after, they got to Makalu Col and on the 23rd to 7900 meters on the normal route. Wielicki thus describes the climb: "We began at 7:45 climbing toward the top. I led all the way. The first 100 meters were very difficult in the deep snow, until we joined the tracks of Ducroz and De Marchi. When we reached the snowfield below the summit at about 8200 meters, we had to decide which route to choose. I took a new variant because the French couloir and the Kukuczka ridge seemed too long and I feared deep snow. I climbed directly for the summit by a rock-and-snow couloir. It was 45° to 50°. I left 20 meters of fixed rope on the rocky part. The snow was very deep and soft. Marcel was 40 to 50 meters behind me. The couloir joined the last 15 meters of the Kukuczka ridge, which was very windy and steep. After that, I had 60 meters of snow to the summit, which I reached at 3:45. I descended fast to the top of the couloir where I met Marcel. He looked well. I gave him all the liter of tea and chocolate. I told him, 'I'm going down to the tent and will prepare hot drinks for us.' He answered, 'O.K. I'm going to the top.' I didn't see him again as the couloir was hidden. It was four P.M. When I reached the tent at seven o'clock, it was nearly dark. I prepared drinks, but Marcel didn't come. It was a horrible night. Our only headlamp had been damaged on Makalu Col. I thought he would come after midnight when the moon rose. I don't remember the night too well. I feared he had fallen on the steep traverse or in the couloir. He had no ice axe. Sunrise came at six o'clock and I waited until 9:15 when I decided to go down to Makalu Col for help, thinking that Messner and company were climbing up. In the tent I left a full thermos of hot water mixed with chocolate, the gas stove and all the down equipment. On Makalu Col, before eleven A.M., I met Messner,

Kammerlander, Mutschlechner and four Sherpas, who had come up from Camp I. Kammerlander took binoculars and said, 'I see Marcel. He is at 8000 meters coming to Camp III.' After a meal they all seven went up to their Camp III. I remained on Makalu Col. I can't understand why Marcel suddenly lost his strength. At four P.M. two Sherpas came down with the tragic news that Marcel had died. When they reached their Camp III, which was 100 meters below ours, Reinhold sent two Sherpas up with medicine. Marcel was sitting 30 meters below our tent, but it was too late. He had died. The Sherpas said that our tent wasn't open. I couldn't go back to Marcel that same day and went down to Base Camp. I had known Marcel only a few days, but I felt he was an old friend. I can't forget him and his optimistic face. Maybe it was my fault, but I couldn't tell him, 'Stop! Come back!' He was for me one of the biggest Himalayan tigers. It is difficult to tell what I felt and what I feel. I lost Marcel!" Messner, Kammerlander and Mutschlechner found that Rüedi had bivouacked at 8100 meters after reaching the summit. Marcel Rüedi, along with Erhard Loretan, was the most successful high mountain Swiss climber. Makalu was his tenth 8000er. Although he had pulmonary edema on Dhaulagiri in 1980 when he climbed his first 8000er, after that he was incredibly strong at high altitudes. The success of his lightning-fast ascents of K2, Shisha Pangma and Cho Oyu misled this amateur climber, who had to be careful of his spare time, and so he climbed his last 8000er "too fast, too high!" He was doubtless a victim of pulmonary and cerebral edema. [The Poles continued with their efforts until October 21. On October 15 Wanda Rutkiewicz and companions got to Camp III, but the wind was so strong that they had to give up the attempt.—*Editor*.]

OSWALD OELZ, *Schweizer Alpen Club*

Makalu and Lhotse, the Last of Messner's 8000ers. Our expedition was composed of Reinhold Messner, Hans Kammerlander, Friedl Mutschlechner, Giuseppe Enzio, Fernando Bernascone, Wolfgang Tomaset, Denis Ducroz, Giuliano De Marchi, Sabine Stehle, Brigitte Oberhollenzer and me as leader. De Marchi and Enzio did not go on to Lhotse. We were flown to Tumlingtar on August 18 and on August 29 got to Base Camp at 5400 meters at the place called French Base Camp. On September 3 we placed Camp I at 6800 meters at the foot of the couloir that leads to the Makalu La. We followed the normal (French) route. On September 9, Camp II was set up on the col at 7400 meters and the next day Messner, Kammerlander and Mutschlechner established Camp III at 7800 meters. On September 11 they started for the summit, but Mutschlechner had kidney pains and all gave up at 8000 meters. The next week was stormy and snowy. On September 23 De Marchi and Ducroz left Camp III and nearly reached the summit, stopped 30 meters below it by an impossible cornice. The two had climbed the French route up to the shouder left of the summit. Very late, they reached their highest point and returned in the dark to Camp III. On the 24th the Pole Krzysztof Wielicki and the Swiss Marcel Rüedi, members of a Polish expedition, went to the summit. Wielicki got to the top between three and four

P.M. and Rüedi much later. The next morning Wielicki descended, having waited all night in Camp III for Rüedi. In Camp II he met Messner, Kammerlander and Mutschlechner, who were climbing directly from Camp I to Camp III. They saw Rüedi descending very slowly. When they got to Camp III, they saw him 100 meters from camp, dead, seated in the snow. He had left Zürich only two weeks before. Messner and his companions left Camp III at six A.M. and following the tracks of Rüedi and Wielicki, reached the summit of Makalu at 11:30, going up the ridge that divides the west from the north face. This much more direct variant is more difficult and has a very steep section around 8000 meters. They found the place where Rüedi had bivouacked at 8100 meters. They returned to Base Camp the next day. A snowstorm on September 28 prevented any further ascents. We returned on foot to Sedoa and were heli-coptered to Lukla. On October 10 we were at Everest Base Camp. We had an agreement with Eiselin's expedition for access through the Khumbu Icefall. The bad weather kept them from success on their Everest attempts. On October 14 Messner, Kammerlander, Mutschlechner and Thomaset left Base Camp with Sherpas for Camp II at 6400 meters. The next day the climbers were kept tent-bound by wind until noon. Mutschlechner had to descend with a toothache. The other three and the Sherpas climbed to Camp III at 7450 meters. Despite a strong wind on October 16, Messner and Kammerlander set out and climbed the final couloir not without difficulty, but there the wind actually helped them, shoving them upwards; in an hour they ascended 250 meters. They were on the summit of Lhotse at 1:45. Thus, Messner completed his ascents of all 8000ers. The pair descended that night to Camp II and the next day to Base Camp.

RENATO MORO, *Club Alpino Italiano*

Makalu Attempt. An expedition led by Cesare Cesa Bianchi and composed of Cristina Moneta and Stefano De Benedetti established Base Camp at 4700 meters on September 14. They used the camps we left set up for them from our expedition. Because of bad weather, they placed a camp at 6200 meters and got to the 6800-meter camp on October 1. On October 10 the three reached camp at 7400 meters. Only Cesa Bianchi continued on to Camp III but without hope of the summit because of the terrible snow conditions.

RENATO MORO, *Club Alpino Italiano*

Makalu Winter Attempt. The two-man team of Noboru Yamada and Yasuhira Saito took one look at the south face of Makalu and decided it was impossible for only two to scale such a steep route in winter when there is little snow cover. They turned to the southeast ridge. Their alpine-style ascent came to a halt at 7500 meters when they twice reached that point from a bivouac at 7400 meters. The wind and low clouds prevented their seeing where they were going. They reached their high point on December 9 and 11. They waited a week in Base Camp for the weather to improve. It did not and with their food running out, they quit.

ELIZABETH HAWLEY

Kangchungtse, Northwest Ridge Attempt and Tragedy. The seven climbers were Wally Berg, Bruce Hunter, Jerry Longbons, Edwin Terrell, Ken Madden, Dr. Gary Ruggera and I. We began the long approach from Hille on March 18 with our Nepalese staff of eight and 70 porters. By the time we arrived at Makalu Base Camp at 16,100 feet on March 31, most of us had suffered one type of intestinal disorder or another. Advance Base at 18,100 feet was established on April 4 and Camp I at 19,560 feet on April 9. On April 11, after carrying to the site of Camp II at 21,400 feet, Edwin Terrell returned to Camp I looking more exhausted than was expected of him. Dr. Ruggera monitored him closely and at midnight, after hearing faint rales in his chest for the first time, mobilized the camp to escort him down to Advance Base in the night. With the help of Madden, Longbons and Ruggera, Terrell arrived at Advance Base six hours later. In the afternoon he suddenly became worse and a second tedious descent toward Makalu Base began. By nightfall, Ruggera, kitchen boy Kamie and I had managed to descend another 1000 feet with Terrell when we were forced to bivouac, sending Kamie ahead to Base Camp for more help. He had been carried another half-mile the next morning when he died of pulmonary edema, perhaps complicated by a virus contracted during the approach. Our high point of 22,000 feet was reached by Longbons and Ruggera on April 20 and the attempt was abandoned on April 21.

GLENN FORTNER

Kangchungtse. A nine-man Korean expedition climbed Kangchungtse (Makalu II) by its northwest ridge, the same route as the Japanese in 1976. Leader Lee Dong-Yeon, Park Tae-Gyu and Shim Jae-Young reached the summit on September 27. They were only the second expedition to succeed on the northwest-ridge route. They found some old Japanese rope on the ridge.

MICHAEL J. CHENEY, *Himalayan Club,* and ELIZABETH HAWLEY

Kangchungtse (Makalu II) Attempt. A 7-man Israeli team was led by Doron Erel. They got to 7400 meters at Makalu La via the normal route on October 13 a month after they had started. Strong winds drove them down and the climbers were too tired to mount another push for the summit. Three of the four who had gone to Makalu La had mild frostbite. The four who got to the high point were leader Erel, Dan Bolotin, Itzhak Siegler and Tony Zamir.

MICHAEL J. CHENEY, *Himalayan Club,* and ELIZABETH HAWLEY

Chamlang. A joint Korean-Nepalese expedition of five was led by Woo Jong-Duk. After establishing four camps and bivouacking, Woo, Bae Hyo-Soon and Huh Gung-Yeal, Ang Dawa Wangchuk Sherpa and Azuwa Sherpa got to the summit on October 10. They climbed the south ridge.

MICHAEL J. CHENEY, *Himalayan Club,* and ELIZABETH HAWLEY

Chamlang, West Ridge. We got to Base Camp on September 22 with 13 Japanese and three Sherpa members. The approach was difficult in the unpopulated area and because of rain. The unclimbed west ridge looked deceptively easy. On September 26 we established Camp I at 5600 meters despite rockfall danger. On October 3 we placed Camp II at 6100 meters on a ridge covered with sugar snow. Above Camp II the route was particularly difficult on the knife-edged ridge because of unconsolidated granular snow. We fixed 4000 meters of rope. On October 11 we established Camp III at 6500 meters as our final camp. On October 16 Osamu Kushimi and Wangar Sherpa started out at five A.M. and climbed a steep snow corner. After seven hours they reached the summit (7319 meters, 24,012 feet). Four members supported them to 7000 meters.

AKIO SHINYA, *Japan Dairy College*

Mera, Southwest Buttress. Our expedition, consisting of George Davidson, Mal Duff, Lesley Shipway, Ian Tattersall and me as leader, reached Base Camp on March 20, having trekked to Lukla and crossed the Hinku valley via the Zatre Wala Pass. Over the next three days we moved equipment up to Advance Base on the banks of the Dudh Kund. Duff and Tattersall remained at this camp to reconnoiter the final approach and were joined by Shipway and me for the attempt on March 26. However, we two descended the next day because Shipway, who was suffering from bronchitis, was going very slowly and the approach was seriously threatened by séracs from the eastern and western icefalls. Duff and Tattersall made good progress through the western icefall before making a rising traverse to reach the crest of the southwest buttress. They followed the buttress crest except for occasional excursions onto the flanks to avoid overhangs. They reached the summit (6654 meters, 21,830 feet) on March 30. The route was graded E.D. inf. because of the seriousness of the approach, hard ice and bad rock with poor protection.

RAY DELANEY, *England*

Ama Dablam Attempt. Iain Allen, and Ian Howell of Kenya, Alastair Stevenson of Australia, Americans Bruce Kleppinger and I attempted Ama Dablam's south ridge in April. Stevenson and I established Base Camp at 15,000 feet on March 31 and Advanced Base at 16,500 feet on April 4. The others arrived on April 7. On April 8 Stevenson and I occupied Camp I at 19,000 feet, to be joined there by Allen and Howell on April 10 and Kleppinger on April 11. The latter was suffering from an unspecified Patagonian parasite and never went above Camp I. The rest of us occupied Camp II on April 15, which is only 500 feet higher than Camp I, but to reach it requires more than a dozen pitches of tricky and exposed traversing. Altitude is gained more quickly above Camp II, and the four of us occupied Camp III at 20,500 feet on April 19. This was the first camp that showed no sign of previous expeditions. Up until now each camp had sported pre-carved tent-sites with the inevitable bits of trash, and the route had been made painfully obvious by residual fixed ropes rendered untrustworthy by the effects of ultra-violet light and ice- and rockfall. Above Camp III, the only glacier camp, the ice became very shallow, hollow and brittle, and would not accept any protection. After a second attempt to climb the upper ice slopes, and in the face of deteriorating weather, on April 20 we opted for descent, reaching Advanced Base the following day.

SKIP HORNER

Ama Dablam West Face. Our expedition was composed of Swiss Ruedi Homberger, Christian Jäggi, Willi Kuhn and Franco Giorgetta and Czecho-slovaks Josef Rybička, Michal Brunner, Jiří Havel, Miroslav Mžourek, Karel Jerhot, Günter Koch and me as leader. It was my idea to climb the line on the west face attempted in 1979 by Peter Hillary. After a couple of days of recon-naissance, from October 9 to 11, I climbed the route solo, with bivouacs at 5300 and 6500 meters. I reached the summit (6812 meters, 22,350 feet) at 11:10 P.M. on October 11 and bivouacked there. On the next two days I made a very exciting descent via the southwest ridge to 6400 meters and then down the south face. Without such equipment as a rope and pitons, it was very difficult. The ascent was of UIAA difficulty IV + (80°) and the descent IV (70°). A week later, Homberger and Jäggi also climbed the west face. They followed my route to a point where they could traverse right to the top of the comparatively flat section of the southwest ridge, which they followed to the top. They reached the summit on October 18.

MIROSLAV ŠMID, *Czechoslovakia*

Ama Dablam. This Swiss expedition climbed Ama Dablam by the normal south-ridge route. All six members reached the summit. On October 22 leader Pierre-Antoine Hiroz, the only French member Pierre Dutrievoz and Yves Rau-sis went to the top. Four days later the other three did so too. They were the leader's sister Marie Hiroz, Guy Formaz and Stéphane Borgeaud. The first group had two camps above Base and the second had three.

MICHAEL J. CHENEY, *Himalayan Club,* and ELIZABETH HAWLEY

Ama Dablam, Winter Attempt. Roger Massardier, the leader of this French expedition, broke both his legs very early in the climb while on moraine just above Base Camp and so there were only three members with no climbing Sherpas attempting an unclimbed route on the south face directly to the summit. This would have been to the right of the Yugoslavian route of last autumn. They regret that they did not make a fast alpine-style ascent, for the weather in early December was excellent, but by the time they were looking for the site of Camp II, the winds were very strong. The wind twice broke their tent at Camp I, and on December 13 they gave up. Their highest point was 6100 meters, reached on December 10 by Bruno Guibert and Bruno Rebelle.

MICHAEL J. CHENEY, *Himalayan Club,* and ELIZABETH HAWLEY

PLATE 65

Photo by Miroslav Šmíd

AMA DABLAM'S West Face.
— = Šmíd's ascent;
· · · = Šmíd's descent;
– – – = Jäggi and Homberger's
variant

Thamserku Attempt. A Spanish expedition was led by José Luis Fernández. The three other members, José Manuel González, Srta Azucena López and Miguel Angel Rodríguez, got to 6300 meters on the new route they were attempting, the west face, on October 27. They descended the next morning because their stove at their highest bivouac was broken. They could not climb again because of their fixed date to leave Nepal.

MICHAEL J. CHENEY, *Himalayan Club,* and ELIZABETH HAWLEY

Kangtega Attempt and Ama Dablam Ascent. German Hans Eitel led a group of ten from Germany, Austria, the United States and the South Tirol. Eight first attempted Kangtega by its southeast face while two went directly to Ama Dablam. Six and a Sherpa reached a high point of 6000 meters on Kangtega on April 8 and then withdrew from the mountain two days later when dangerous avalanching continued. They then went to Ama Dablam, where the other two had already pitched two camps, to try the west face. The Kangtega party did little climbing there. The summit was reached in nine hours on April 15 by South Tiroleans Alois Brugger and Kurt Walde who began their summit push from Camp II at the bottom of the west face early that morning. They climbed the central couloir, a new route to the right of the 1985 Japanese route. They descended the normal south-ridge route and were back in Base Camp on the morning of the 16th.

MICHAEL J. CHENEY, *Himalayan Club,* and ELIZABETH HAWLEY

Kangtega and Lobuje East Ascents and Nuptse Attempt. English-woman Alison Hargreaves, Americans Henry Kendall, Marc Twight, Tom Frost and I were active in the Khumbu region near Everest during the pre-monsoon season, climbing two new routes and attempting a third. All were done pure alpine-style. Kendall and I climbed a new route on Lobuje East (6119 meters, 20,075 feet), following a steep snow-and-ice gully on the left side of the east face. Hargreaves and Twight repeated it shortly afterward. Hargreaves, Twight, Frost and I moved on to Kangtega (6779 meters, 22,241 feet). In a ten-day round trip from Base Camp, we climbed a difficult new route on the right side of the northwest ridge, encountering very technical ice and mixed climbing on the ice tongue right of the ridge proper. On May 1, Frost and I reached the slightly lower northwest peak, while Hargreaves and Twight continued on to the main peak via a steep final ice face. We descended the northeast couloir, first climbed by the Japanese in 1979. After moving Base Camp to 5200 meters on the Lhotse Nup Glacier, Twight and I attempted the southeast buttress of Nuptse. We followed the prominent buttress between the original British route and the Cassin-Messner ramp. After 1300 meters of very technical climbing on the buttress, the angle of the route recedes to more moderate snow and ice until the final 400 meters, when it reverts to rock for a difficult finish at very high altitude. Bad weather delayed our start until May 19. Encountering very difficult climbing (5.10, A4) during a single eight-day push, we reached a high point of 6700

PLATE 66

Photo by Jeff Lowe

**NUPTSE'S Southeast Buttress. Part
climbed is solid line; projected route
is dashed.**

meters on May 26. However, bad weather had moved in and with the possibility of an extended wait with little food, we retreated, reaching Base Camp on May 27. The route is one of the finest I have been on and has just the combination of features I am looking for: steep, technical mixed ground, and altitude. Above all, it's a safe line. There is nothing hanging over you, so you can just relax and enjoy the outrageous climbing.

JEFF LOWE

Lobuje West Winter Ascent, 1987. Seldom-attempted Lobuje West was scaled so quickly by a Korean expedition's advance party that when the team leader Lee Hee-Bong and other climbers arrived at their base, they learned that the mountain had already been climbed and all tents and other gear brought down. In this first winter attempt and first Korean attempt on Lobuje West, five men, Deputy Leader Park Jae-Hong, Choi Sang-Hyun, Dim Hang-Il, Rinji Sherpa and Mingma Nuru Sherpa, had gained the summit on January 30, only the third day after they had pitched Base Camp.

ELIZABETH HAWLEY

Nuptse, Southeast Buttress Winter Attempt. Americans Jeff Lowe and Marc Twight did not get quite as high on their buttress in the winter as they had last spring. This winter they abandoned their climb after reaching 6700 meters on December 31. They reported they had "insufficient strength." Lack of strength was due to gastro-intestinal illness. This winter attempt, like last spring's, was done without fixed camps, fixed rope or Sherpas.

MICHAEL J. CHENEY, *Himalayan Club,* and ELIZABETH HAWLEY

Lhotse Shar Attempt. We were Beda Fuster, Werner Steininger and I as leader. We got to Base Camp on September 21 at 5350 meters on the moraine between Lhotse Shar and Imjatse (Island Peak). We carried loads up the rocky spur to 5750 meters for three days and established Advance Base on September 24. On the 25th Fuster and I reconnoitered to 6100 meters, left a dump there and fixed rope over the first step, but the weather went bad. A second attempt from October 2 to 5 failed after rope had been fixed over the second step and the night spent at Camp I at 6750 meters, but again bad weather drove us back. After a third attempt failed in bad weather, Fuster and I went back up and on the second day, October 19, got to Camp I which was badly damaged by avalanche snow. On the third day we climbed to 7250 meters and established Camp II in clear but very windy weather. On October 21, I was sick and stayed in Camp II. Fuster set out at 4:30 A.M. alone for the summit. At eleven A.M. he reached the snow dome at 8050 meters but the wind gusts were too strong for him to continue over the narrow ridge to the summit slopes. He had to turn back 350 meters below the summit. After one more night in Camp II, we descended to Base Camp.

TONI SPIRIG, *Schweizer Alpen Club*

Lhotse Shar Tragedy. The ten-man Spanish team's attempt on the south face of Lhotse Shar ended abruptly when on October 30 Pedro Alonso fell 2400 meters to the bottom of the face from ten meters below the site for Camp IV at 7400 meters. He and the expedition's doctor Javier Sánchez intended to occupy Camp IV and go for the summit from there with one more camp or bivouac at 8000 meters. On October 28 Manuel Aparicio and Ramón Rodríquez had reached the site for Camp IV and dumped loads there. After the fall, Dr. Sánchez descended to search for him and had to bivouac. He was severely frostbitten in nine fingers. Neither Sánchez nor the other members were able to find the body. The climb was abandoned after Alonso's death.

MICHAEL J. CHENEY, *Himalayan Club*, and ELIZABETH HAWLEY

Lhotse Shar Attempt. Scots Mal Duff and Sandy Allan hoped to make a two-man, alpine-style ascent of the south face of Lhotse Shar in early May. This quick ascent was never achieved. They were climbing on the southeast face for acclimatization when, on May 9 at 7000 meters, Duff was hit on the head by a falling sérac and only just managed to descend safely to Base Camp. He left for medical treatment. The climb appeared over until Miss Alison Hargreaves, who had just scaled Kangtega with Jeff Lowe's American expedition, joined Allan in another bid on Lhotse Shar by the southeast face. They had been on the mountain together a very few days when they were forced at 6500 meters to abandon the effort because of slab avalanches. The highest point reached on the mountain was 7000 meters on May 9.

MICHAEL J. CHENEY, *Himalayan Club*, and ELIZABETH HAWLEY

Lhotse. A four-man Japanese expedition, led by Masaaki Fukushima, climbed Lhotse by the normal route. They had three climbing Sherpas. On May 4 leader Fukushima, Toshihide Haruki and Sherpas Nima Temba and Nima Dorje reached the summit. They used artificial oxygen while sleeping in Camps III and IV and while climbing to the summit.

MICHAEL J. CHENEY, *Himalayan Club*, and ELIZABETH HAWLEY

Japanese Everest Attempt. A Japanese expedition failed to climb Everest. The leader, Haruyuki Endo, who had successfully scaled Everest in October 1983, came again to the mountain with the hope of getting Miss Takeo Nagao to the summit as the first woman atop Everest without the use of artificial oxygen. But no one got to the top this time. They climbed on the normal South Col route. When it was time for the final push, Takeo Nagao was ill and had to return to Camp III on the Lhotse Face. Endo, Tadanori Matsunaga and Pemba Tshering Sherpa managed to reach 8600 meters on May 10 before extremely cold winds finally drove them back. The four-person expedition had no strength left to mount another summit attempt.

MICHAEL J. CHENEY, *Himalayan Club*, and ELIZABETH HAWLEY

Polish-Austrian Everest Attempt. Poles Tadeusz Karolczak and Aleksander Lwow and Austrian Helmut Putz originally wanted to climb the south pillar of Everest, but the Japanese set unacceptable conditions for making the Khumbu Icefall accessible to them. (They also apparently had permission for the west ridge.) The Japanese finally agreed that this small team could go up the route after May 1. After climbing on the west ridge up to 7100 meters, the three descended to Base Camp on April 30. Putz had a problem with an old back injury and stopped climbing. The two Poles started up the normal route through the Western Cwm and reached 7800 meters on the Geneva Spur on May 13. They descended, intending to go for the west ridge. But now Karolczak became ill. Lwow, now entirely alone since the Japanese had gone home, went up the icefall to 6700 meters in the Cwm on May 24, but he was halted there by a two-day heavy snowfall. He descended to Base Camp through a greatly changed icefall on May 27 and the climb was finished.

MICHAEL J. CHENEY, *Himalayan Club,* and ELIZABETH HAWLEY

Everest Attempt. Xavier Murillo, Pierre and Annie Beghin and I were helicoptered to Namche Bazar on September 21. We were at Base Camp on the 24th. The weather was beautiful. The rest of the international expedition led by Swiss Fredy Graf had made the route through the icefall and was trying for the summit. I left alone for 7400 meters on September 26. I rested there until 1:30 A.M. before leaving for the South Col, which I reached at four A.M. I spent two hours resting and drinking. I caught up to three Swiss making their summit bid at 8500 meters at eleven o'clock. At twelve noon we were at 8600 meters. The wind was very strong and it was snowing. The Swiss descended and I kept on for 50 meters more. I then descended to 7400 meters to sleep. I was back in Base Camp the next day. Then it was bad weather for the whole month of October. I stayed on till October 24. [He must be the first person to have reached 8600 meters on this route without having slept on the South Col.—*Editor.*]

ERIC ESCOFfiER, *Club Alpin Français*

Everest Attempt and Tragedy. I led an international group of 25 to try the normal route on Mount Everest. Aside from our climbing objectives, we had three physicians who carried out high-altitude medical research. Because the weather was so good at the beginning, we got to Base Camp before September 1, when we could start to set up high camps. The fine weather continued so that by September 9 we had already established Camp III on the Lhotse Face at 7400 meters. Then the weather turned sour. It was hard work to fix rope and break trail to the South Col. On September 25 at 4:30 P.M., French guide Serge Koenig, Chuldim Dorje Sherpa and I reached the south summit from Camp IV on the South Col. There was deep new snow and above it was double-corniced. We had to turn back. Two days later, three Swiss, Dr. Simon Burkhard, Raymond Monnerat and Peter Weber were stopped by bad weather at 8600 meters. They spent a stormy night on the South Col, hoping for good enough weather to make another attempt but had to start down the next morning. Dr. Burkhard was killed on the Lhotse Face in an avalanche as they descended. On October 4, Gayalu Sherpa was buried under falling sérracs in the Khumbu Icefall. Although there were further carries to the South Col, we had to abandon the expedition on October 14.

FREDY GRAF, *Schweizer Alpen Club*

Everest Winter Attempt. The six-man Korean expedition which attempted the South Col route on Everest was led by On In-Hwan. They set up Base Camp, Camps I, II, III and IV at 5300, 5500, 6500, 7400 and 8000 meters during December. Neo Young-Ho and four Sherpas reached the South Col twice, on December 17 and 22. There they were pinned down by fierce winds. They called off the expedition on December 24.

KAMAL K. GUHA, *Editor, Himavanta, India*

Everest Winter Attempt by Koreans, 1987. Another South Korean expedition, led by Park Young-Bae, was attempting a winter ascent of the British route on the southwest face of Mount Everest. On January 30, 1987, Tsuttin Dorje Sherpa fell to his death while carrying a load up the face. The climb was given up. The expedition reached a high point of 8300 meters on January 25 and again was as high on some of the subsequent days.

ELIZABETH HAWLEY

A New Map of Mount Everest. For nearly 50 years I have dreamt of making a very detailed map of the Mount Everest area, using all the most modern tools of photogrammetry. As time went by, aerial cameras, lenses and aircraft continually improved and so it was lucky that my responsibilities as Director of Boston's Museum of Science kept me from undertaking this project until after my retirement in 1980. It has turned out to be an eight-year project, beginning in 1980 to 1983 when Barbara and I made three trips to China and Nepal to secure permission for the high-altitude flights over the Nepalese-Chinese border. This work has been financed jointly by the Museum of Science and the National Geographic Society. When completed, the first edition of the map will be published in the National Geographic Magazine, probably in 1988. I have directed the project from the start, ably assisted by my wife Barbara, Dr. Barry Bishop of the National Geographic and Werner Altherr, Vice President of Swissair Photo Surveys Ltd. and now, in the reproduction phase, by Dr. John Garver, Chief Cartographer of the National Geographic and Francis Jeanrichard, Director of the Swiss Federal Institute of Topography. This work is also being coordinated with His Majesty's Government of Nepal under the chief of its Survey Department, Arjun B. Basnyat. Overall ground control has been developed from the British, Chinese and Austrian maps of the area, evaluated and adjusted by West German vertical photography taken from the US Space Shuttle in December 1983, flying at an altitude of 243 km (152 miles) under perfect weather conditions. The area was rephotographed by our team on December 20, 1984 from an altitude of 12,000 meters (39,400 feet) with a Swissair Wild RC-10 aerial camera from a Learjet 35 of Swedair/Stockholm. Contouring of the 380-square-mile area on a scale of 1:10,000 has been completed by Swissair Photo in Zürich. Relief-shading, cliff-drawing, nomenclature and all cartographic artwork preparatory to printing are now being done at the laboratories of the Swiss Federal Institute of Topography (Landestopographie) in Wabern. Printing will be done by the National Geographic in the USA. This National Geographic map will be on a scale of 1:50,000 with 50-meter contours. The ten 1:10,000 sheets covering the same area will be available on special request for research purposes. They promise to be a remarkably detailed base for future work in the geology and glaciology of this complex and remote region. They will also yield a wealth of information for mountaineers. An extremely large-scale map of Everest above 7000 meters is now being prepared in Zürich as a research project of the Science Museum. The whole area goes southward from the terminus of the Rongbuk Glacier to Pheriche and eastward from Pumori to the center of the Kangchung Basin. For all of us involved, this has been a unique and exciting experience in international science and camaraderie: the US Space Shuttle, a US Learjet, owned by Swedair and flown by a Swedish aircrew, a Swiss camera, aerial photographer and laboratory expert, West German space photography, computer analysis of control by Zürich's ETH, photogrammetry by Swissair—and close collaboration from the start between Boston's Museum of Science, the National Geographic, Swissair Photo Surveys, the Landestopographie, His Majesty's Government of Nepal and the People's Republic of China.

BRADFORD WASHBURN

Pumori East-Ridge Attempt. This two-man Japanese expedition came to an abrupt end on October 6 when the leader, Mikio Mitsuhata, was searching for the site of Camp II at 6000 meters. He was struck by a snow avalanche and fell 40 meters, fracturing his left leg. The east-ridge route, which they were trying, they think would have been a new route.

MICHAEL J. CHENEY, *Himalayan Club,* and ELIZABETH HAWLEY

Pumori, South Face. Base Camp was established on October 7 on the eastern flanks of Kala Pattar. On October 10 we pitched a tent at 5500 meters on Kala Pattar where Rick Allen and I acclimatized. The U.S. members, Morris Kittleman and Dave Saiget, arrived at Base on the 11th and decided to spend several days acclimatizing. On the 14th we two Scots began to climb the south face and bivouacked at 5600 meters. The following day took us up mixed ground where we were forced to abseil into the main couloir. We climbed this for several difficult pitches and bivouacked at 5850 meters. We ascended the

PLATE 67

Photo by Sandy Allan

South Face of PUMORI.

rest of the couloir on the 16th and bivouacked in a cave at 6100 meters. We moved together over the next two days, bivouacking at 6600 and 7000 meters. On the morning of the 19th at ten A.M. we stood on the summit. We descended the southwest ridge for several hundred meters and then climbed down the large couloir on the west face, arriving at a safe site on the Changri Shar at ten P.M. at 5400 meters. The next day we returned to Base Camp. The Americans later made an attempt but retreated from 6000 meters because of high winds. We believe this was a previously unclimbed route.

SANDY ALLAN, *Scottish Mountaineering Club*

Pumori Southwest-Ridge Attempt. One member became seriously ill from high altitude and never reached Base Camp. The other four, New Zealanders John Roberts, leader, and Kevin Conaglen, Australian Stephen Macdonald and American Keith Swenson all reached their high point, 6550 meters, between October 24 and 26. They then abandoned the climb because they were exhausted. Viewing the climb with hindsight, they feel they should have done a rapid alpine-style ascent instead of fixing 900 meters of rope on their route.

MICHAEL J. CHENEY, *Himalayan Club,* and ELIZABETH HAWLEY

Pumori, South Face. The members of the expedition were Edin Alikalfić, Mario Bago, Janez Benkovič, Željko Gobec, Branko Pusak and I as leader. We established Base Camp and Advance Base at 4620 and 5240 meters on October 6 and 10. In spite of bad weather in the next four days, we climbed up the face to 5740 meters on the 14th and up to the crest of the southwest ridge at 6250 meters on the 15th. On October 16 Benkovič climbed to the summit and the same day returned to Advance Base. Two days later Alikalfić reached the top followed the next day by Pusak. Pusak and Bago cleaned the face the next day and Base Camp was evacuated on October 21. The route is to the left of the 1979 Jeff Lowe route and in the last part follows the southwest ridge. A tent was pitched at 6100 meters. We fixed 450 meters of rope. The lower part of the slope averages 45° and the upper part 50° to 60° with places up to 80°.

DARKO BERLJAK, *Mountaineering Association of Zagreb, Yugoslavia*

Pumori Winter Ascent via East Face. A Japanese expedition climbed a new route on the east face of Pumori. Hiroshi Aota and Yoshiki Sasahara made a quick alpine-style ascent that took them to the summit on the third day, December 3. The leader Kazuyuki Takahashi caught cold on a trekking peak before the climb and did not even go to Base Camp.

MICHAEL J. CHENEY, *Himalayan Club,* and ELIZABETH HAWLEY

Pumori Winter Ascent. On November 25 Michael Dimitri and I made Base Camp at Gorak Shep in order to climb Pumori. On December 1, we climbed directly from Kala Patar to 6000 meters on the southwest ridge, but Dimitri had an intestinal illness and so we descended the next day. The weather was windless and mild and snow conditions were excellent. On the 3rd we watched two Japanese reach the summit after a three-day climb of the east face. Michael was still sick and so the next day I climbed to 6000 meters on the east face, meeting the Japanese on their descent. Leaving camp at seven A.M. on December 5, I reached the summit at 11:15 and was back in Gorak Shep at 3:30 P.M. I believe I followed the 1985 Catalán route. After a rest day, I climbed back to 6000 meters on the southwest ridge to retrieve our gear and also to remove the abandoned food and gear left by the post-monsoon expeditions.

TODD BIBLER

Gyachungkang, South Face. Our expedition of ten French and three Nepalese military men climbed Gyachungkang's previously unclimbed south face. The peak itself had been climbed only once, by Japanese in 1964. We approached from Jiri in two weeks and set up Base Camp on April 22 at 5020 meters on the moraine of the true right bank of the Ngojumba Glacier. To figure a route through the icefalls defending access to the south face took ten days of effort and reconnaissance. On April 28 we set up Camp I at 5800 meters on a snowy spur after we had climbed a rocky ridge that let us bypass the first icefall. On April 30 we placed Camp II at 6200 meters after winding in a complex route through the glacier where we were often exposed to falling ice. There the ascent of the south face really began. An 800-meter-high ice slope, which in places was very steep, led to Camp III, installed on May 4 and 5 at 7200 meters on a platform hacked into a narrow snow ridge. The dry, cold weather at the end of April gave way to unstable weather. Preparing the route was difficult, especially in the rock barrier between 7300 and 7500 meters, where we climbed a series of chimneys. On May 11, R. Flamatti and Pierre-Alain Royer set out for the summit but were driven back by storm at 7850 meters, suffering frost-bitten hands and feet. On May 12, Eric Gramont and Frédéric Maurel succeeded in climbing an overhanging dihedral just below the easier snowy summit slopes and reached the summit (7952 meters, 26,089 feet). On May 13, Gérald Trésallet and I and on May 15, Alain Estève and Hubert Giot got to the top.

JEAN-CLAUDE MARMIER, *Lieutenant Colonel,*
Ecole Militaire de Haute Montagne

Gyachungkang, South Face Attempt. Our expedition was composed of Basques Antxon Zamabide, F. Garatea, Martín Zebaleta, Kike de Pablo and me and Americans Hooman Aprin, Ron Matous, Dr. Robin Houston, Edward Farrar and Michael Ruckhouse. In Kathmandu we found out that the route we had hoped to climb had been done by the French in the spring. On September 26 Matous, Aprin, de Pablo and I set up Base Camp at 5100 meters in the same spot as that used for the south face of Cho Oyu. On October 1 after we tried to pass across the icefall that gives access to the Nup La, we set up Camp I more to the west at 5700 meters, near the ridge that leads to Ngojumba Kang. The weather was bad and it snowed every day until October 15. Matous fell sick, while Aprin, de Pablo and I waited for 12 days before making the route in deep snow through the second icefall. On October 19 we set up Camp II at 6250 meters and on the 20th broke trail to the bergschrund at the foot of the southwest spur of Gyachungkang at 6500 meters. As we descended to rest at Base Camp, we found at Camp I the rest of the expedition, which had arrived at Base Camp on October 14. On October 26 we attacked the face: Aprin, de Pablo and I on one rope and Zabaleta and Matous on the other. The last two descended from 6700 meters. We three bivouacked at 6800 and 7100 meters but descended on October 28 after fighting all night not to be blown away by a furious wind.

JOSÉ LUIS ZULOAGA, *Orhi Mendi, Federación Vasca Montaña, Spain*

Cho Oyu, Southwest Buttress. A noteworthy accomplishment was a new route on Cho Oyu climbed by Polish climbers from Zakopane led by Ryszard Gajewski. Base Camp was established on April 5 at 5300 meters. They hoped to prepare the Messner variation for descent and established two camps on this route up to 6800 meters. Unfortunately they were turned back by the American expedition which informed against them in Kathmandu. They then moved to their Advance Base to 6000 meters at the foot of the nearly 2000-meters-high southwest buttress and concentrated their efforts on the new route. This ascends the prominent buttress 1.5 kilometers to the right of the Messner route. It is on ice and snow with a 150- to 200-meter-high rock face at 7000 meters, which they climbed directly with UIAA grade III. Three camps were established above Advance Base at 6600, 7100 and 7600 meters. The steeper sections were fixed with 500 meters of rope to facilitate the descent. The new route joins the old Tichy route at 7750 meters. It is not very difficult and relatively safe. In the future it may well become the "normal" route from the southwest. On April 29, starting from Camp III at 7600 meters, Gajewski and Maciej Pawlikowski climbed to the summit. On May 1 Piotr Konopka completed a solo ascent. On May 3 Marek Danielak and Andrzej Osika stood on the highest point. During the descent Danielak fell seriously ill but the rapid efforts of Dr. Lech Korniszewski saved his life. For Pawlikowski this was his second ascent of Cho Oyu, each time by a new route; he was also on the winter ascent of the southeast face.

JÓZEF NYKA, *Editor, Taternik, Poland*

Cho Oyu. An international expedition was led by the Swiss Stefan Wörner. They followed close after the Poles on the new route up the southwest face of Cho Oyu. The expedition had originally been given a permit to attempt Cho Oyu via its east ridge from the south face of Ngojumba Kang, but their attempt was stopped at 6400 meters in a very dangerous chaos of séracs and crevasses. Wörner states that the east-ridge approach to Cho Oyu appears as difficult as a traverse from Lhotse Shar to Lhotse's main summit. [This route was attempted by British in 1984 and Poles and Americans in 1985. Americans Mark Richey and Rick Wilcox got to about 7950 meters.—*Editor.*] They then turned to the southwest face. Seven members reached the summit, a route which is more direct, shorter and safer than the Tichy route. On May 3 Austrian Peter Habeler and the late Swiss Marcel Rüedi left a bivouac at 6000 meters and climbed to another bivouac at 7600 meters. After being held stormbound there for a day, they reached the summit on May 5. On May 9 American Jan Smith and German Rüdiger Schleypen got to the top, followed by three soloists: German Jörg Daum on May 10, Deputy leader Yugoslav Bogdan Brakas on May 11 and Austrian Manfred Lorenz on May 16. None used oxygen and all climbed semi-alpine-style.

MICHAEL J. CHENEY, *Himalayan Club,* and ELIZABETH HAWLEY

Cho Oyu. Cowboys on Cho Oyu consisted of Americans Michael Bacon, Alan Jennings, Charlie Schertz, Ed Yoshida and me as leader, Michael Clarke, who is an Englishman who has acquired American citizenship, British David Hambly and Canadian David McClung. We flew to Lukla on March 21, but our baggage came overland through Jiri. We spent ten days acclimatizing in the Khumbu while waiting for our baggage to arrive. We took the standard approach to Base Camp through Thame, Marlung and Lunak. The weather was poor with heavy snows. One yak died in the deep drifts; we compensated the owner. On April 7 we established Base Camp at 5200 meters at Kangchung, wrongly marked on the Schneider map as Dzasampa; Dzasampa is located further up the Nangpa Glacier at the base of the icefall. During the next ten days, we used a dozen porters to help transport baggage to the site of Camp I with temporary camps at Dzasampa and at a place above the icefall. On April 17 we all occupied Camp I on the moraine of the Gyabrag Glacier at 5920 meters. This camp served as Advance Base. On April 20 Schertz and I occupied Camp II at 6350 meters on the northwest ridge. On April 23 Hambly and Bacon occupied Camp III at 6720 meters on the ridge at the base of the icefall. We all returned to Base Camp for our only rest period. On May 7 a four-man party tried to establish Camp IV at 7500 meters. High winds and intense cold turned us back a few yards above Camp III. On May 10 we again attempted to establish our high camp and make a summit attempt. Using lines we had previously fixed in the icefall, which had ice up to 80°, we broke new ground and reached the base of the first rock band on the western face of Cho Oyu. Bacon and Schertz dropped their loads and Hambly and I established Camp IV 100 meters higher at 7500 meters. The next morning we left at 6:30 and started through the first rock band. We bore to the right, joined the west ridge at 7800 meters and progressed up the ridge, a series of moderate ice pitches, to the flat snow area below the second rock band. We took a direct line through this, exiting on the right side into the broad, long summit area. We reached the summit at 2:30 P.M. on May 11. During the half-hour we stayed on the summit, we took photos and displayed the flags of Nepal, the United States and Great Britain. The thermometer read − 20° C and the wind was estimated at 30 kph with gusts up to 60 kph. At the summit was a metal flag pole with a metal Chinese flag attached. The true summit should not be confused with the lower false summit, which is closer to the second rock band. On the false summit is a pole with odd bits of prayer flags. Comparison of summit photos seems to indicate that it was there that Jan Smith got. No other summit attempts were made. Supplementary oxygen and high-altitude porters were not used.

JAMES FRUSH

Cho Oyu. Our team consisted of Etsuro Hino, Tateo Yamashita, Miss Taeko Noda, Takayushi Kawada, Mrs. Mutsuko Okuma, Tsuyoshi Murakai, Miss Masae Okamoto and me as leader. We pitched three camps on the south face of Ngozumba Kang, hoping to climb Cho Oyu by the east ridge. On September 29 Hino, Miss Noda and Miss Okamoto were at Camp III at 7500 meters, but we gave up the route because of deep snow. From October 5 to 9 we moved over the Nangpa La to Base Camp on the normal route. We set up Camps I, II, III, and IV at 5600, 6300, 6750 and 7200 meters on October 10, 11, 12, and 13. Because of strong wind we stayed at Camp IV on October 14 and 15. On October 16 Hino climbed to the summit.

NOBUO SHIRAISHI, *Kitakyushi Alpine Club, Japan*

Cho Oyu Tragedy. The expedition to Cho Oyu which I led was composed of three Swiss: Pierre-Alain Steiner, Christian Dupré and me. After having arrived on October 8 at Base Camp at 5300 meters near the Nangpa La, we climbed to 6300 meters for acclimatization. We left on October 19 for an Advance Base at the foot of the west face at 6000 meters. That same day we started up a new route on the face and joined the Polish route at 7300 meters. The wind was so strong that we stopped for several hours. On the morning of the 20th the wind was the same and we decided to descend to wait for several days. Unfortunately, while descending, Steiner fell some 600 meters, which put an end to his life and the expedition.

ERHARD LORETAN, *Club Alpin Suisse*

Gaurishankar Attempt. After two weeks of bureaucracy in Kathmandu, Iñaki Alvarez, Koldo Tapia, Txema Cámara and I were finally able to take the bus to Charikot, arriving there on September 11. The approach was very difficult because of the monsoon rains, the stream crossings, the bamboo forests and the leeches. [Other reports say they also had difficulties with the local police. — *Editor.*] We got to Base Camp at 4800 meters on September 16, the 5400-meter col on the 17th and Advance Base at 4300 meters on the glacier on the 18th. The route to be attempted was on the southwest face left of the Roskelley route. On September 20 and 21 we bivouacked at 5500 and 6000 meters and climbed to 6100 meters on the 22nd. The weather was continuously bad with avalanches sweeping the face. We descended to Base Camp. Despite the weather we did climb two virgin peaks: Tsirigma Ikuspegi (5430 meters, 17,815

PLATE 68

Photo by Thomas Oeser

West Ridge of DORJE LHAPKA is on the right center. Camp I was at the right edge of the photo; Camp II was on horizontal part of the ridge.

feet) and P 4830 (15,847 feet). In the first week of October, we tried another attack, getting to our supply depot. On October 6 we left the mountain.

JAIME ALONSO, *Alpino Tabira Mendizale Taldea, Spain*

Dorje Lhakpa. Our joint expedition was composed of Germans Klaus Stark, leader, Mathias Rau, Helmut Müller, Dr. Bernd Meyer and me and Nepalese Ang Pasang and Pemba Tarke. We used a new approach from the south through the Balephi Khola. Three Japanese expeditions had climbed Dorje Lhakpa before, all by the west ridge. Their approach was by the Langtang valley and their Base Camps were on the Langshisa Glacier. Our Base Camp at 4500 meters was on the moraine of a glacier coming from the southwest face. Camp I at 5500 meters was at the foot of the west ridge, about five hours from Base Camp. Camp II at 6000 meters was just beyond a horizontal section of the ridge. Meyer, Müller, Rau and Stark established Camp II on November 5. The next day they set out for the summit but got to only 6700 meters, as the distance was too great. On November 7 Meyer and Müller tried it again, setting out earlier. Meyer reached the summit (6966 meters, 22,845 feet) at three P.M. and Müller at 7:30. Meyer got down to Camp II at eight P.M. but Müller was forced to spend the night at 6700 meters and reached Camp II the next day.

THOMAS OESER, *Deutscher Alpenverein*

Langsisha Ri. Simon Cox, John Goulstone, Steve Upton, Kirsten Sorenson and I left Kathmandu on March 29 and after seven anxious days and one heavy snowstorm reached Base Camp at 4500 meters at the edge of the Langsisha Glacier. From there we carried equipment and food up the south face to the site of Camp I at 5700 meters. We moved up to Camp I on April 12. The route between these two camps was relatively straightforward but somewhat danger-ous because the mountain was holding a lot of snow. The route to Camp I ascended 1000 meters of snow slope to gain a small col and another 200 meters to a large plateau below the final 725-meter face. The face above the plateau is spectacular. Four hundred meters of steep snow gully brought us to the final summit icefield. It was from 45° to 60° and in perfect condition. Nine pitches of superb climbing on good ice led to the summit (6427 meters, 21,086 feet). We had left Camp I at three A.M. and got to the summit at midday on April 14, being considerably slowed by deep snow in the gully. After spending two hours on the top, enjoying the views, especially into Tibet and across the Dorje Lhakpa group, we descended. Five 50-meter abseils brought us to the top of the snow gully and then an unroped descent took us back to the plateau. Kirsten Sorenson had remained at Camp I as she had intended, while the rest of us went to the summit.

MARTIN HUNTER, *New Zealand Alpine Club*

Langtang Lirung. Our expedition climbed Langtang Lirung by the southeast ridge, previously ascended by Japanese in 1980 and 1981. We were Fukashi

Suzuki, Takashi Miyazaki, Toshiyuki Fukui, Toshiaki Jinnai, Takayoshi Taga, Takashi Takeuchi, Tomoharu Tada, Dr. Naoto Toma and I as leader. On March 23 we reached Base Camp beside the Langtang Glacier at 4200 meters. Camp I was placed at 4800 meters on March 28. The route to Camp II ascended a gully and was placed in the col at the foot of the southeast ridge at 5600 meters on April 5 after four days of storm. The most difficult part of the climb was between Camps II and III on the ridge, where we fixed rope and wire ladders on steep rock and ice. Camps III and IV were established at 6100 and 6500 meters on April 19 and 29. On May 3 Fukui, Taga, Tada and Takeuchi reached the summit (7234 meters, 23,734 feet).

KENRYO NUMA, *Himalayan Alpine Club of Ohtani, Japan*

Langtang Lirung Southwest Ridge. The eight-man expedition which I led established Base Camp at 4250 meters on September 18 below the previously unclimbed southwest ridge. We placed Camps I, II and III at 5100, 5500 and 6000 meters on September 22 and 27 and October 1. Our progress was slowed by bad weather. On October 4 we tried to get to Camp IV but could get to only 6500 meters. On October 8, Yoon Kye-Jung, Song Suk-Hee, Sin Chang-Jin, Jon Weon-Sik, Ang Rinzing Sherpa and I left Camp III for the summit at four A.M. but did not reach until ten P.M. a snow wall of 80°, where we bivouacked. The next day we climbed the wall and got to the last pitch of the southwest ridge, where at 7000 meters we set up Camp IV. On October 10 we six left Camp IV at six A.M. and got to the summit at ten.

YOON DEONG-JUNG, *South Korea*

Langtang Lirung Attempt. A Spanish expedition of five led by Miguel Angel Puertas attempted to climb Langtang Lirung by its southeast ridge, successfully ascended by Japanese in the spring of 1986. Strong winds prevented the climb. The highest point reached was 6300 meters, gained by Javier Valero on October 13.

MICHAEL J. CHENEY, *Himalayan Club,* and ELIZABETH HAWLEY

Ganesh I Attempt. Our expedition consisted of Micheline Matile, Christian Meier, André Kohler, Michel and Marie-Rose Geissbuhler, Laurent and Christine Paillard, Patricia Mercier and me. We placed Base Camp on April 20 at 3800 meters on the Song Jung Glacier, southeast of Ganesh I. We had three high camps at 4500, 5100 and 5600 meters on the southeast ridge, established on April 23, May 1 and 2. We had hoped to climb the south ridge higher up. Two members got to 5800 meters on May 3, but we had to abandon the climb on May 6 because of bad weather, heavy snowfall and wind. Above 5700 meters there was a 600-meter-high steep slope with dangerous snow.

OLIVIER MATILE, *Club Alpin Suisse*

Ganesh II Attempt. A six-man Korean expedition led by Park Jong-Tae hoped to climb Ganesh II by its west ridge from the south face of Ganesh IV, the same route attempted unsuccessfully by Swiss in the autumn of 1984. The high point of 6600 meters was reached on May 10 by deputy leader Park Chung-Sang and Choi Ok-Rim. The climb was then abandoned. By now Park had injured his leg, one of their two climbing Sherpas had broken his leg and two other members were out of action from injuries received from falling séracs. For most of their climbing period, the weather was bad with low clouds obscuring the route and frequent snowfall.

MICHAEL J. CHENEY, *Himalayan Club,* and ELIZABETH HAWLEY

Manaslu Attempt and Tragedy. A 16-person German-Austrian expedition led by Michael Dacher hoped to climb Manaslu by the normal northeast-face route. On May 3, three members established Camp IV at 7400 meters. Then disaster struck and Camp IV was never reached again. A party of five had set out that day from Camp III, but two of them realized they could not make it all the way to Camp IV and turned back. One of these two, German Wilhelm Klaiber, apparently fell while descending the fixed ropes going back to Camp III. No one saw him fall. He simply disappeared and was never seen again. During that night there was heavy snowfall. The three in Camp III, Germans Fred Bässler and Arthur Wirthensohn and Austrian Dieter Oberbichler, the deputy leader, descended on May 4. Oberbichler now fell; again no one saw him fall, but the other two suddenly came upon his body as they were moving down. He must have shot past them, for he had been behind them. Oberbichler was already dead; the two tried to bring his body down with them, but while doing so, Bässler broke his ankle and got mild frostbite and Wirthensohn got badly frostbitten fingers on both hands. A final summit push was attempted with six members moving up from Base Camp on May 9, but they got no higher than Camp III because of heavy snowfall. The climb was abandoned on May 11.

MICHAEL J. CHENEY, *Himalayan Club,* and ELIZABETH HAWLEY

Manaslu Northeast-Face Attempt. A Colombian expedition of nine was led by Carlos Eduardo Gómez. They attempted the normal route. The maximum altitude reached was 7250 meters, where Camp IV was established. It was reached by Manuel Arturo Barrios and Juan Pablo Ruiz on October 31 and again by Barrios and Marcelo Arbeláez the next day. On November 2 it was decided to abandon the climb because of strong winds and cold. Two members had already been mildly frostbitten and it was feared that more serious frostbite might be in store if they continued.

MICHAEL J. CHENEY, *Himalayan Club,* and ELIZABETH HAWLEY

Manaslu Southeast-Face Attempt. A 10-man expedition from Macedonia, Yugoslavia was led by Jovan Poposki. They attempted the southeast face, the route of the Poles in the autumn of 1984. Frequent heavy snowfall in September and the first half of October and then fierce winds in the latter half of October meant defeat. The highest point of 7400 meters was reached on October 29 by Dimitar Ilievski, Solbodan Jovanoski and Borce Jovcevski.

MICHAEL J. CHENEY, *Himalayan Club,* and ELIZABETH HAWLEY

Manaslu Northeast Face. A light-weight expedition of six Poles and two Mexicans was led by Jerzy Kukuczka. They established Base Camp on September 8 at 4400 meters. From September 17 to October 26 in very bad weather they climbed the difficult and complicated east ridge to the lower plateau. They then changed their route. From November 5 to 10 they made the first ascent of the northeast face from the Manaslu Glacier in pure alpine-style. The three men bivouacked at 5500, 6300, 7300, 7600 and 8000 meters. There were several pitches of hard, mixed climbing between 7300 and 7500 meters and on the slopes of the virgin eastern summit (7992 meters). On November 9, they reached the summit plateau where they made their fifth bivouac. The next day Carlos Carsolio, who was suffering from frostbite, stayed at the bivouac while Kukuczka and Artur Hajzer went to the summit. It was frigidly cold. "Though the effort was enormous, I shivered the whole time," said Kukuczka. Poor weather and complicated terrain made it necessary to take 62 days to reach the summit. This is the first 8000er to be climbed in November. It was Kukuczka's 12th 8000er.

JÓSEF NYKA, *Editor, Taternik, Poland*

Himalchuli North Tragedy. Germans Dr. Wolfgang Weinzierl and Peter Wauer and South Tirolean Günther Einsendle set out for Camp I on October 15, hoping to pitch Camp II on the southwest ridge at 6500 meters. The only survivor, Siegfried Reiter, does not know where they actually pitched Camp II, where they obviously were struck by one of the avalanches that came down the mountain during and following a bad snowstorm from the night of the 15th to the morning of the 17th. Reiter was in Camp I during the storm.

MICHAEL J. CHENEY, *Himalayan Club,* and ELIZABETH HAWLEY

Himalchuli. Our expedition was composed of Hizuru Nakamura, Noriyuki Muraguti, Hiroyuki Suzuki, Kiyoshi Furuno, Itarou Isakawa, Sigeki Imoto and me as leader. We climbed Himal Chuli by the south ridge and the southwest face, a new route. We established Base Camp, Camps I, II, III, IV and V at 4950, 5550, 5920, 6370, 6950 and 7250 meters on September 6, 16, 20, 25, October 7 and 13. The summit (7893 meters, 25,895 feet) was reached on October 26 by Nakamura, Furuno, Imoto and Nima Dorje Sherpa.

SADAO OKADA, *Nikon University Alpine Club, Japan*

Himalchuli Winter Attempt and Tragedy. A Polish expedition led by Józef Stepien hoped to climb the main peak of Himalchuli by its southwest ridge. Although there were seven members, only two were really high climbers. Deputy leader Wiesław Panejko and Jacek Klincewicz got to 6200 meters on December 29. The next day Klincewicz unaccountably lost his footing and plunged some 1000 meters to his death. The expedition was given up.

ELIZABETH HAWLEY

Bhrikuti Attempt. An expedition of nine French, a Nepali, a Sherpa and a Tamang were climbing on the Japanese route of the spring of 1982, the west ridge. On April 30, Jean-Yves Ferrand, Pierre Gaillot and Bruno Kriner got to 6250 meters but Ferrand fell into a crevasse. Too much time was consumed getting the injured man out for the other two to continue the one-hour climb to the summit that day. Their tight schedule required them to leave the mountain immediately.

MICHAEL J. CHENEY, *Himalayan Club,* and ELIZABETH HAWLEY

Tilitso Tragedy. A 16-member German expedition led by Hans Huhn had hoped to climb Tilitso. During the approach to Base Camp, a huge snow avalanche on the west side of the Mesokanta La caught ten climbers. Rudolf Springmann and Hermann Ebert were killed. The survivors decided not to continue on to Base Camp and the expedition was abandoned.

MICHAEL J. CHENEY, *Himalayan Club,* and ELIZABETH HAWLEY

Annapurna, South Face Attempt. [The Bulgarian expedition failed to climb Annapurna's south face by the Polish route in the winter, as described briefly in *A.A.J.*, 1986 on p. 293.] Their ambitious plan for climbing both Annapurna and Dhaulagiri in the spring soon fell through. Frequent heavy snowfall meant lengthy periods of unfavorable climbing conditions. The team, now reduced to nine Bulgarians including their Base Camp-bound leader, Boian Atanasov, and three Sherpas reoccupied Base Camp at 4300 meters only on March 25. Camps I, II, III and IV were established at 5400, 6100, 6500 and 6850 meters on April 5, 17, 19 and 23. New ropes were fixed. Their high point was 7550 meters, to which deputy leader Ivan Valtchev and Vesseldev Tschaushev climbed on May 9. During that day's ascent, Valtchev counted ten places where the ropes had been seriously damaged by falling stones. He therefore called off the entire effort.

MICHAEL J. CHENEY, *Himalayan Club,* and ELIZABETH HAWLEY

Annapurna Attempt. A five-man Italian expedition led by Giacomo Stefani had hoped to climb a new route on Annapurna, the northwest buttress and north face. Early on they decided against the route because it was all exposed rock rather than snow-covered for which they were equipped. They followed the

1950 French route but got no higher than 6200 meters, the site for Camp III, which Pierino Maccarinelli, Severangelo Battaini and Alberto Stefani reached on April 25. After that, snow conditions became dangerous. The climbers were hit but uninjured by a slab avalanche on May 1. With no signs of improving weather, they abandoned the climb on May 4.

MICHAEL J. CHENEY, *Himalayan Club*, and ELIZABETH HAWLEY

Annapurna. After our ascent of Nanga Parbat, Fausto De Stefani, Almo Giambisi and I headed for Nepal, to climb the normal route on the north side of Annapurna. Well acclimatized from Nanga Parbat, we quickly established Camp I at 5000 meters and made a carry to 5500 meters. Then the weather turned bad and the avalanche danger was great. As we waited in Base Camp, a large French expedition appeared, including the legendary Maurice Herzog, who had made the first ascent of an 8000er by the very route we were trying. After another week of waiting, we decided on a rapid ascent from Camp I. We set out from a 5500-meter bivouac and climbed in a single day to 7000 meters, where we bivouacked. The next day, September 21, we ascended to the summit and descended to bivouac again at 7000 meters. We were back in Base Camp in two more days. Our joy lasted very little time since the very strong French climber, Benoît Grison, fell on the unclimbed northwest ridge and died.

SERGIO MARTINI, Club *Alpino Italiano*

Annapurna Northwest Ridge Attempt and Tragedy. Our expedition was composed of Jean-Paul Vion, Georges Payot, Godefroy Perroux, François Marsigny, Benoît Grison, Jacques Latarjet and me as leader. Our expedition was the excuse for Maurice Herzog's return to his Base Camp of 1950; despite his age and amputations of hands and feet, he came back on foot to the foot of the north face of Annapurna. We headed for the unclimbed northwest ridge up a 600-meter couloir. After arriving at the normal Base Camp at 4000 meters on September 13, we left on the 17th for Camp I at 5000 meters on the main north-face glacier. On September 21 we placed Camp II at the foot of the couloir which joins the northwest ridge at 6000 meters. Rope was fixed the whole length of the couloir. On September 23, Grison ascended to fix the upper third. He fell to his death probably as he descended. We gave up the expedition after getting this terrible news. We had hoped to place Camp III at the top of the couloir, Camp IV at 7500 and go for the summit from there, possibly with a bivouac.

JÉRÔME GREGGORY, *Club Alpine Français*

Annapurna, Attempt by the Northwest Spur of "Nameless Peak." Between Annapurna I and Varah Shikhar (Fang) lies a peak which must be over 7700 meters, which has been called the "Nameless Peak." A distinct spur descends to the valley of the Miristhi Khola. Dr. Hervé Bouvard, Patrick Gabarrou, Pemba Norbu Sherpa and I hoped to climb this spur and then carry on up the west ridge to the summit of Annapurna. We established Base Camp, Camps I, II and III at 4000, 4600, 5500 and 6700 meters on September 16, 18, 20 and 22. Base Camp was at the bottom of the northwest spur of Annapurna, in the same place as that of Messner in 1984 when he ascended the northwest face. Our route this year was to the left of our 1984 attempt and ascended the left side of the spur. It lay partially to the right of Messner's route, which we followed more or less from Base Camp to Camp II. From Camp I to II, at Camp II and somewhat above, the route is very exposed to avalanches. Camp III was placed at the same place as our 1984 Camp IV. We climbed above Camp III until we rejoined the Messner route at about 7000 meters. We suggest that the still unclimbed "Nameless Peak" be called "Namaste."

HENRI SIGAYRET, *Groupe de Haute Montagne*

Annapurna via Khangsar Kang (Roc Noir) Attempt. Eight French and three Nepalese climbers were led by Marc Batard. They hoped to climb over Singu Chuli (Fluted Peak) and Tarke Kang (Glacier Dome) to reach the east ridge of Khangsar Kang and thence the east ridge of Annapurna. They took much time on the route above Base Camp southwest of Singu Chuli (6501 meters, 21,330 feet), which they climbed by a new route, the south ridge. Not until November 7 did Batard, Kami Rinji Sherpa and Kami Tenzi Sherpa climb Tarke Kang (7193 meters, 23,600 feet) where they found such bad snow conditions that they gave up the climb. The other French climbers were Louis Audoubert, Bernard Douay, Terry Faure, Michel Frisque, Marc Gratalon, Michel Metzger and Anne Genevey.

MICHAEL J. CHENEY, *Himalayan Club,* and ELIZABETH HAWLEY

Annapurna Winter Ascent: Kukuczka's 13th 8000er, 1987. Jerzy Kukuczka and his fellow Pole Artur Hajzer got to the summit of Annapurna on February 3, 1987 on the first winter ascent of the peak and the first Polish ascent. Wanda Rutkiewicz and Krzysztof Wielicki, the other summit pair, were unfortunately unsuccessful, getting only to 6800 meters. Their expedition was basically on the 1950 French route on the north face. No Sherpas went above Base Camp. They used no artificial oxygen at any time.

ELIZABETH HAWLEY

Annapurna II Attempt. Our expedition to the west ridge of Annapurna II was composed of Lucy Smith and me, co-leaders, Sue Giller, George Vansickle, Julie Brugger, John Trainor, Devin McGowan, Polly Fabian and Craig Sea-sholes. We met with many frustrations. Deep winter snows and high winds seemed to be the rule this spring. This long route (6 miles and 14,000 feet gain from Base Camp) begins by following the northwest buttress of Annapurna IV to the west ridge. Once on the west ridge, it traverses nearly 1½ miles at 24,000 feet to a final 2000-foot summit day. The mountain has now been attempted 28 times, successfully only four times: 1960 British-Nepalese-Indian and 1969 Yugoslav via the west ridge, 1973 Japanese via the north face and 1983 Australian via the south face. The 1973 Japanese ascent has been reported incorrectly as being on the northeast ridge. We encountered six feet of snow at 12,400 feet and thus were forced to place Base Camp 3000 feet short of our intended site. We fought through deep, and sometimes unstable, snow to 20,000 feet where we topped out on the Dome. This sits on the Himalayan crest separating Mustang from the Indian plains; predictably there were high winds. Camps were established as follows: Base Camp, Camps I, II, III, IV and V at 12,400, 15,500, 17,200, 19,300, 21,200 and 22,200 feet on March 24, 28, April 7, 18, 24 and May 3. After a month and a half of effort we abandoned the climb. Vansickle and Trainor reached a height of 24,000 feet on the west ridge. We requested permission from the ministry via radio and through our liaison officer to climb Annapurna IV when it became clear that we could not reach the summit of Annapurna II. Our request was denied five days later. Historically, expeditions have climbed both peaks or at least Annapurna IV when turned back from Annapurna II. The two peaks are best described as separate high points of the same mountain. The Ministry of Tourism now gives permission for them separately and imposes severe penalties for illegal ascents. In addition, expeditions to Annapurna II via the west ridge may find themselves sharing the route with an Annapurna IV expedition, as we did with the Nepalese Police team. A Spanish Basque expedition of six also was climbing the route with us due to a misunderstanding during the permit process.

SHARI KEARNEY

Annapurna II Attempt. An expedition of six Spanish Basques led by Jesús Bereciartua tried to climb Annapurna II up the north face and along the west ridge from Annapurna IV. They set up Camps I, II and III at 4800, 5500 and 6300 meters on March 28, April 8 and 13. On April 30 Francisco Javier Maiz and Francisco Javier San Sebastián reached 7000 meters but then the expedition was given up because of bad weather.

MICHAEL J. CHENEY, *Himalayan Club,* and ELIZABETH HAWLEY

Gangapurna. Our expedition was made up of two women, Nam Nan-Hee and Jeoung Young-Hee, both of whom went to the summit, and six men, Kim Ki-Chul, leader, Uhm Gae-Sung, Shim Gun-Shik, Nam Young-Hyun, Min Kyeong-Young and me. We climbed the east ridge from the south, roughly the Polish route in the autumn of 1985. We got to Base Camp at the source of the Modi Khola at 4200 meters on March 26. It was a long way to Camp I and so we had an intermediate dump. We traversed the lower slopes of Annapurna III to avoid avalanches and established Camp I at 4800 meters under a cliff just below the Gangapurna Icefall. Bad weather then held us up. We climbed a rock buttress to the right of the icefall, fixing some rope. We went up a sharp snow ridge and placed Camp II at 5600 meters on April 8. After climbing the knife-edge, we got to the normal Gangapurna route, which ascended crevassed snow to the col. We placed Camp III at 6300 meters on April 14 just below the col. Blue ice and snow ice at 60° were climbed to reach the col. Camp IV at 6800 meters was an hour above the col. On April 18, Uhm, Nam and Ang Kami Sherpa started at 4:30 A.M. but returned because of the wind; they set out again at 7:45 and got to the summit (7455 meters, 24,457 feet) at 1:45 P.M. On April 20 Jeong, I and Godre Magar also went to the summit.

SEOK CHAE-UHN, *Korean Alpine Club*

Gangapurna and Annapurna III Attempts. A six-man Korean team led by Kim Jung hoped to ascend Gangapurna's north face, traverse Annapurna III's northeast ridge and descend Annapurna III's north ridge. Neither summit was reached and no traverse was made. The expedition split into two teams and attacked the two peaks simultaneously, but after several weeks of heavy snow-fall and unexpected demands on equipment such as fixed rope, it was decided to give up the Annapurna III bid and try for Gangapurna and descend via Annapurna III if possible. This strategy also failed as the members were very tired and the Sherpas were no longer interested in the climb. The highest points reached were 5300 meters on September 21 by Han Ik-Heui and Dawa Norbu Sherpa on Annapurna III and 7150 meters on September 27 by Cho Chung-Ho and sirdar Ang Kami Sherpa on Gangapurna. They were on the north face of Annapurna III and the northwest ridge of Gangapurna.

MICHAEL J. CHENEY, *Himalayan Club*, and ELIZABETH HAWLEY

Annapurna III Attempt and Tragedy. An Italian expedition led by Maurizio Maggi was called off immediately after the death of Massimo Caslino, who was struck by a falling sérac on September 26. He fell about 350 meters and his body was found the next morning. The team's highest point was 6500 meters, the proposed site for their third and last camp. This was reached on September 25 by Battista Scanebessi. They were on the southwest ridge, a route not previously attempted.

MICHAEL J. CHENEY, *Himalayan Club*, and ELIZABETH HAWLEY

Annapurna IV. A 24-person Nepalese Police expedition led by Mrs. Bas-undhara Lama climbed Annapurna IV by its normal route, the northwest ridge. The climbing leader was Inspector Gupta Bahadur Rana. Much of the route-making had been done by the much smaller Basque and American expeditions. The summit was reached on May 2 by Sub-Inspector Kamal Bhandari, Head-Constable Ngwang Yonden Sherpa, Constables Indra Bahadur Ghale, Nuru Sherpa, Pasang Tshering Sherpa and Phurba Tshering Sherpa.

MICHAEL J. CHENEY, *Himalayan Club*, and ELIZABETH HAWLEY

Annapurna IV. We climbed the normal route, the north face and northwest ridge of Annapurna IV. From our 4800-meter Base Camp we placed three camps 5200, 5800 and 6360 meters. We two guides, Jean Frank Charlet and I, seven clients and Sherpas Mingma and Sundare were, after three weeks of fine weather, just a day from the summit when we were struck by a storm that obliged us to descend. The day after, again with lovely weather, Sundare, Charlet, Patrick Bouchet and I started back up and got to Camp III on the second day. Three of us reached the summit on November 7. Charlet had to turn back an hour from the summit, fearing frostbitten feet. The first part of the route is more difficult; we placed 500 meters of rope. If much snow fell there, one would risk being trapped high up because of avalanche danger. The route follows a very aesthetic spur which descends at right angles to the face. The second part is along the long ridge, easy *if* the snow is hard. This part is often wind-swept and subject to windslabs.

MICHEL VINCENT, *Club Alpin Français*

Varaha Shikhar (Fang) Attempt. Six Koreans led by Kim Jong-Duk hoped to climb a new route, the east face, on Varaha Shikhar. The highest point reached was 5450 meters, where Choi Young-Dae, Kim Sung-Mo and Ang Kami Sherpa pitched Camp II on September 15. Several days of heavy snowfall buried or avalanched away a substantial part of the expedition's fixed rope and climbing hardware. With this loss of gear, the expedition was given up.

MICHAEL J. CHENEY, *Himalayan Club,* and ELIZABETH HAWLEY

Annapurna Dakshin Attempt. The first Yugoslavian women's Himalayan expedition hoped to climb the southwest ridge of Annapurna Dakshin (Annapurna South; 7219 meters, 23,683 feet), the 1982 Japanese route. Marija Frantar, leader, Nives Boršič, Maja Dolenc, Irena Komprej, Ana Mažar, Danica Mlinar, Mira Uršič, Sanja Vranac and I got to Base Camp at 4000 meters on April 16. It was 800 meters too low because the porters refused to carry higher. On April 18 we established Advance Base at 4800 meters. We then followed a big couloir leading to a snow plateau. From there on we did not follow the original route but used a couloir further left, which we considered safer. Camp I at 5700 meters was placed on April 24. We then climbed 2½ kilometers along the ridge, going up and down on some hard ice-and-rock climbing. Camp II was set up at 5800 meters on May 9. From there we climbed to 6100 meters, where we decided to abandon the attempt. The ridge was narrow and long. We had very bad weather with much lightning. Of the 45 days we were on the mountain, only four were without snowfall. The bad weather came at least by nine or ten o'clock.

VLASTA KUNAVER, *Planinska Zveza Slovenije, Yugoslavia*

Dhaulagiri. We climbed Dhaulagiri by the normal northeast ridge. We got to Base Camp at 4650 meters on April 5. There were many crevasses in the glacier going to Camp I at 5700 meters, which we established on April 10.

Camps II and III were set up at 6600 and 7150 meters on April 20 and 22. We fixed 800 meters of rope between Camps II and III. On May 3, five of us set out from Camp III with a tent which we left at the site of Camp IV at 7500 meters. Sepp Hirtreiter and I got to the summit at noon. Heinz Schauer, Dr. Kurt Dehn and Ang Phurba Sherpa could not make the last 50 meters to the top because of a severe thunder storm. Five of us bivouacked without sleeping bags in a two-man tent at Camp IV. On May 5, Walter Larcher, Willi Odenthal and Dr. Lutz Pflegung climbed to the summit from Camp IV. Larcher is Austrian and the others German.

GÜNTHER HÄRTER, *Deutscher Alpenverein*

Dhaulagiri Attempt. Slovene climbers, Stane Belak and Marjan Kregar, were anxious to complete the route unsuccessfully attempted by them and two others in the autumn. Actually these two Yugoslavs in the pre-monsoon season of 1986 did not climb the east face but crossed over at about 6500 meters to the normal northeast-ridge route. Their high point was 7650 meters, which they reached on May 9. They abandoned their effort on May 30 when it was apparent that constant heavy snowfall made the climb impossible for a two-man, semi-alpine ascent.

MICHAEL J. CHENEY, *Himalayan Club,* and ELIZABETH HAWLEY

Dhaulagiri Attempt and Tragedy. An Austrian expedition led by Edi Lindenthaler and composed of Josef Inhöger, Erich Unterberger, Hans and Hansjörg Linderthaler, Franz Müllender, Hans Gapp and Martin Hornegger had hoped to climb the northwest ridge of Dhaulagiri. After reaching their 4700-meter Base Camp on September 17, Müllender felt the altitude enough to descend to the 3700-meter Italian Base Camp. He reascended on the 20th as he was feeling better, while the others pushed forward to the northwest col. The next morning, Müllender was worse again and was taken back down to the Italian Base Camp. There he appeared better, but during the evening his condition worsened and he died at about eight P.M. from pulmonary edema. [We are grateful to Robert Renzler for this report.]

Dhaulagiri South Face Attempt. Our 16-member team had 12 Poles, two Canadians and a Pole from both France and Australia. Our objective was the 4000-meter-high south face of Dhaulagiri. We established Base Camp at 3800 meters on September 16 and Advance Base at 4300 meters three days later. On September 21, Camp I was set on the lower part of the prominent buttress just to the left of the center of the face. The first part of the buttress forms a 1200-meter-high rock wall. We placed Camp II on its upper part at 5800 meters on October 4. The rock was of continuous difficulty up to UIAA Grade VI-. Part of it was so friable that a bolt hole could be made with a few blows. Above the rock wall the route ascended a 60° to 70° ice rib with passages of 85°. Camps III and IV were set up at 6100 and 7100 meters on October 20 and 26. We fixed

3200 meters of rope. The upper part of the buttress, climbed by Maciej Pawlikowski and me, had mixed pitches of UIAA V. Camp V at 7500 meters was
established on October 30 by Maciej Berbeka and Mikołaj Czyżewski. The
wind tore their tent apart that night. The next morning Berbeka climbed alone
over easy snow to reach the southwest ridge, joining the Japanese route of 1978.
Although the way to the summit was now without difficulties, the weather was
bad and time had run out. We gave up and descended the same route. Base Camp
was cleared on November 2.

EUGENIUSZ CHROBAK, *Klub Wysokogórski Kraków, Poland*

Dhaulagiri Attempt. Five French climbers led by James Merel climbed only
to 6100 meters on Dhaulagiri's normal northeast-ridge route. They had frequent
heavy snowfall. All five members and one Sherpa reached the high point on
October 5 and then abandoned the climb since they felt they had no chance to
reach the summit.

MICHAEL J. CHENEY, *Himalayan Club*, and ELIZABETH HAWLEY

Dhaulagiri Winter Attempt by Spaniards. The Koreans agreed to share the
normal northeast-ridge route with the Spanish Catalans. The highest point
reached by this expedition was 7000 meters, where leader Enric Lucas and Joan
Carlos Griso bivouacked on December 22. The next day they descended because Griso was developing high-altitude sickness. They had had bad weather
and now a bad spell returned. By the time the weather turned fine, their food was
running out and they decided on December 26 to quit.

MICHAEL J. CHENEY, *Himalayan Club*, and ELIZABETH HAWLEY

Dhaulagiri Winter Attempt by Koreans. A Korean expedition led by Cho
Jung-Sol ended its attempt on the normal northeast ridge on December 25 at
8025 meters, only 42 vertical meters below the summit. Strong wind and cold
forced the summit-attack team back. They were Chung Sang-Kiun and sirdar
Ang Dorje, both of whom got frostbitten toes and fingers. Another member,
Kim Jin-Goun, had a seriously frostbitten toe from earlier climbing and so with
two members and one Sherpa out of action, the climb was called off.

MICHAEL J. CHENEY, *Himalayan Club*, and ELIZABETH HAWLEY

Dhaulagiri II, Ascent and Tragedy. A four-man Korean expedition to the
south face and east ridge of Dhaulagiri II was led by Lee Don-Yong. They
established an Advance Base at 4900 meters and Camps I, II and III at 5400,
5800 and 6900 meters. Camp IV was destroyed by a snow avalanche almost
immediately after it was set up and it was not re-established. On May 12 Kim
Sung-Kyu and Sherpas Dorje and Dakipa reached the summit (7751 meters,
25,429 feet) in a nearly 12-hour climb from Camp III at 6900 meters. During the

descent to Camp III Kim disappeared and was never seen again. No one knows what happened to him, but it is believed that he probably fell from the difficult, steep ice section at 7300 meters. This was the first Korean ascent of Dhaulagiri II. Cho Myung-Ho and Kim Ki-Tae also participated.

MICHAEL J. CHENEY, *Himalayan Club,* and ELIZABETH HAWLEY

Tukche. A huge Royal Nepalese Army expedition led by Lieutenant Colonel Bhagrinath Narsingh Rana had 71 members of whom 50 went above Base Camp. They climbed the northwest face, possibly a new route, and placed one camp above Base Camp. On October 22, Nir Bahadur Rayamajhi, Surya Gurung and Phurtenzing Sherpa reached the summit. Seven more climbed to the top on October 23 and another seven on October 25.

MICHAEL J. CHENEY, *Himalayan Club,* and ELIZABETH HAWLEY

Tripura Tumba (Hanging Glacier Peak). On September 12 Katashi Tokimoto, Shunsuke Kobayakawa, Hiroaki Ioka and I as leader set out from Jumla with 50 porters. We went up the Jagdura valley north of Hurikot village. The approach was difficult. At times we had to retrace our steps because we could not get up the valley on one side or the other. We sometimes had to cross the river with a rubber boat. Base Camp at 4500 meters was placed on September 24 at the head of the Hanging Glacier valley on the north side of Tripura Tumba. We started to make the route on the 26th and placed Camp I at 5500 meters on the northwest ridge on September 29. On October 6 we reached the 5700-meter col but could not find a campsite. The northwest ridge above the col was knife-edged mixed snow and rock. On October 14 we established Camp II at 6300 meters, cutting into the steep snow slope. On the 15th we extended fixed ropes for 400 meters but were storm-bound the next day. On October 17 Tokimoto, Sirdar Ang Phuri Lama and I set out at six A.M. and reached the summit (6563 meters, 21,500 feet) at 10:15 A.M. in windy but fine weather. This was the first ascent of the peak.

NORIYUKI HATA, *Okayama University Alpine Club, Japan*

India—Kumaon

Suli Top, Eastern Kumaon. An Indian expedition led by Rama Kant Mahadik successfully climbed Suli Top (6300 meters, 20,670 feet). They ascended an icefall which had three steps to reach the north col. After a four-day storm they completed this first ascent on July 3 via the north ridge.

India—Garhwal

Nandakhat and Bauljuri. After an approach march complicated by heavy rains which had washed out a bridge over the Pindari River, Dr. Deepak Kulkarni, Milind Pathak, Dr. Suhas Mate, Dr. Deepak Rokade, Vishwas Kunte, Anil Chavas, Vishwas Dixit, Ulhas Kelkar, Shyam Jambotkar and I as leader on August 8 arrived at Base Camp at 13,800 feet. We had to take ten days to establish Camp I due to heavy rain and murky weather. We set this camp on a grassy field to the south of Traill's Pass. High-altitude porter Sanghi and I occupied Camp II on August 23 at 18,100 feet on a rocky ridge north of Camp I. We opened the route to Camp III at 19,300 feet, just below the ice wall of the east face. Phatak and I with high-altitude porters Sanghi and Tashi occupied Camp III on August 28. Finally, the challenge was in front of us: the 2200-foot-high ice face. On August 30 I called the others at four A.M. After a half-hour's walk we were at the base of the wall. We attacked the face. At eleven A.M. we were 700 feet below the top. Higher, we had an extremely steep pitch which took us to a snow plateau just below the summit. The next 50 feet were in knee-deep snow. Then the route was between a pyramidal formation and the rectangular summit. The summit was a 250-foot knife-edged ridge. The four of us stepped on the highest point (6611 meters, 21,690 feet) at 2:40 P.M. The descent to Camp III was difficult and took nine hours. We had to rappel down the wall. We returned to Camp III at 9:50 in the dark. On September 5 we placed Camp I for Bauljuri at 16,020 feet. Camp II was occupied on September 7 by all ten members and six high-altitude porters. On September 8 the summit (5922 meters, 19,430 feet) was reached at 7:40 A.M. by all, except for Dr. Jambotkar who was suffering from a headache.

PRAJPATI BODHANE, *Holiday Hikers Club, Bombay, India*

Trisul Attempt from the West. Our members were Santiago Alvarez, Juan José Iglesias, Baldomero Rodríguez and I. Until the end of August when we arrived at Base Camp it rained a great deal. We approached up the Nandakini valley in five days from Ghat with ten porters. We placed Base Camp at 4300 meters and Camp I three days later at 5100 meters. Camp II was placed at 5950 meters two days after that. We had to give up at about 6350 meters because our superlight equipment made the climb too hazardous. The west face of Trisul is very interesting and offers many routes of great difficulty.

GONZALO SUÁREZ, *Gijón, Spain*

Kamet and Abi Gamin. An eight-member expedition from Bombay was led by Shrikant Oka. It left the roadhead at Malari on May 16 and set up Base Camp at 4725 meters at Vasudhara Tal. They were in close contact with the Army team, particularly for weather and aerial survey reports. Sanjay Barole and Anil Kumar left Camp VI on June 11 and reached the summit (7756 meters, 25,447 feet) at eight A.M. At the same time a 45-man team from the Regiment of Artillery was led by Major H.S. Mann. Nine members climbed Abi Gamin (7355 meters, 24,130 feet) in two groups on June 13 and 15. Four, including three who had earlier scaled Abi Gamin, got to the summit of Kamet on June 19. That same day, eight other members climbed Abi Gamin, making a total of 17 atop that peak. In the post-monsoon period, another Army expedition was back. The 32-man team was led by Lieutenant Colonel S.S. Patwal and the deputy was

Major Mann. They set up Base Camp at Vasudhara Tal on September 9. Camp V was established on Meade's Col on October 2. A number of the members reached the summit on October 3 at 3:10 P.M. That same day four other climbers ascended Abi Gamin. There were two more Indian expeditions in the area. On August 28 a group led by N. Purohit climbed Abi Gamin. Members of a 9-man expedition led by Ujjwal Ganguly, Dibya Kanti Mukherjee and Lhakpa Tsering, climbed Abi Gamin on September 19 and Atanu Chatterjee, Subhas Das and Sherpa Kei Kami climbed Kamet on September 20.

KAMAL K. GUHA, *Editor, Himavanta, India*

Gangotri Region, Indian Ascents. An expedition to Sri Kailas (6932 meters, 22,745 feet) was led by Bijoy Datta. Sachin Karati, Dawle Majkindo and high-altitude porters Tej Bahadur and Man Bahadur left Camp VI at 6150 meters and gained the summit via the west col on June 11. P 6166 (20,229 feet) on the Sweta Glacier was climbed in June by an 11-member team led by Shyamal Dey. On June 6 Indranil Banerjee, Dr. Susante Bhattacharye, Sandip Dey and a high-altitude porter Manjit Rai climbed virgin peak Yanbuke (5953 meters, 19,530 feet). In early September this climb was repeated by members of an expedition of the Ordnance Factory Trekkers in Ishapore. Bhartekunta (6578 meters, 21,580 feet) and Baby Shivling were climbed in June by an expedition led by C. S. Pandy. In early September a group led by Srikanta Mitra climbed Jogin I (6465 meters, 21,210 feet). A team led by Major H. C. Lohumi climbed Gangotri I (6672 meters, 21,890 feet) and Gangotri II (6590 meters, 21,620 feet) in June. Gangotri III (6577 meters, 21,578 feet) was ascended by climbers led by Miss Gangotri Soneji.

KAMAL K. GUHA, *Editor, Himavanta, India*

Satopanth Tragedy. Indians hoped to climb Satopanth from the north. Dr. Minoo Mehta, Nandu Paghe and a high-altitude porter were buried in an avalanche on May 21 when they were resting in their tents at Camp II at 6000 meters. Leader Bharat Manghre and another porter, Nar Bahadur, who were pitching another tent, had a miraculous escape, but they were storm-bound there for five days. During the descent from that camp, Manghre expired and only Nar Bahadur reached Gangotri on May 29. A rescue party from the Nehru Mountaineering Institute and helicopters were pressed into service, but the bodies could not be found.

KAMAL K. GUHA, *Editor, Himavanta, India*

Satopanth, South Face. The members of our expedition were Marek Głogorowski, Tomasz Kopyś, Andrzej Mierzejewski, Krysztof Pilawski, Aleksander Rygier, Michał Takarewski, Dr Ryszard Urbanik, Ziemowit Wirski and I as leader. We established Base Camp at Nandaban at 4300 meters on May 26. Advance Base was placed on May 26 on the Swachand Glacier below

PLATE 70

Photo by Aleksander Rygier

South Face of SATOPANTH.

the south face of Satopanth at 5000 meters, On June 9 Kopyś and I started on the summit climb up the south face and took three days to complete the climb at six P.M. on June 12. We descended the north-face route, getting back to Base Camp on June 13. Our route led through couloirs and ice-and-snow bands. We went up the middle of the summit cone and emerged to the right on the ridge below the summit. Our bivouacs on the ascent were at 6200 and 6800 meters. The face is about 1500 meters or 5000 feet high. The snow conditions were difficult with soft, loose snow and the rock was rotten and stratified the wrong way.

RYSZARD KOŁAKOWSKI, *Klub Wysokogórski Warszawa, Poland*

Satopanth. One of the three Altitude Extrême expeditions climbed Satopanth by the normal route with bad weather and difficult snow conditions. Two members were carried away by a snow avalanche but were able to escape without injury. After starting on July 27, seven Frenchmen, guide Dominique Marquis, Louis Brigaudeau, Dominique Louandre, Yves Mantoux, Régis Page, Daniel Glorian and Gérard Gastineau, and two French women, Elizabeth Sans and Dominique Chelle, reached the summit on August 18.

CLAUDE JACCOUX, *Expéditions Altitude Extrême, France*

Gangotri I Ascent and Tragedy. A Polish women's expedition consisted of Ewa Kalinowska, leader, Dr. Danuta Kasiura, Jolanta Patysnowska, me and one male member, Marek Bumblis. We climbed Gangotri I (6672 meters, 21,890 feet) by a new route, from the southwest. Base Camp and Advance Base were established at 4500 and 5000 meters. A 500-meter rock rib was fixed with rope. On the glacier above the rock rib, we set up four camps, the last at 6200 meters beneath the southwest col. A steep snow-and-ice slope led to the col and from there to the top of the mountain. The summit was reached on October 12 by Kalinowska, Patysnowska, Bumblis and me. Tragically, during the descent Ewa Kalinowska was killed on October 15.

ANNA BRUZDOWICZ-DUDEK, *Klub Wysokogórski, Poland*

Satopanth. The Klub Wysokogórski Rzeszów organized an expedition to the Gangotri region led by Jerzy Wala. They climbed Satopanth by the normal north ridge. Above Advance Base at 5100 meters, they established Camps I and II at 5800 and 6300 meters. From October 19 to 22 the ascent was made by Jacek Czyż, Andrzej Makaran and Wiesław Szczepanik. On October 23 Marek Rzasa and Swiss Kurt Graf tried to repeat the ascent but failed at 6800 meters.

JÓZEF NYKA, *Editor, Taternik, Poland*

Kedar Dome. A 15-member Polish expedition led by Marek Grochowski hoped to climb two routes on Kedar Dome. Base Camp was established at Topoban on September 20. On the 25th Andrzej Jakubowski, Zbigniew

Mikołajczyk, Marek Oreńczuk and Waldemar Zmurko reached the summit by the normal route. Much snow fell and avalanches twice buried Advance Base. From October 1 to 8 the same team attempted the left buttress of the east face of Kedar Dome, but continuous snowfall made them retreat not far from the summit. This face remains one of the great rock problems in the Gangotri area.

ZBIGNIEW KOWALEWSKI, *Klub Wysokogórski Warszawa, Poland*

Shivling Tragedy and Ascent of Southwest Ridge. After a three-day walk Australians Graeme Hill, Jon Muir, my sister Belgian Véronique Koch and I got to Base Camp on April 24. There was a lot of snow after the heaviest winter snowfall in ten years. We established Advance Base by May 5. While Jon fixed rope on the first 250 meters of our new route, the rest of us started up the normal west-ridge route on May 10 but descended after a day because of headaches. Our liaison officer Dr. Mohmed Vahanvati, an eye surgeon, was climbing with us. On May 13, he and Hill went back up. On the only rope we had fixed on the way up to our previous bivouac, the doctor died while jümaring, apparently from exhaustion and panic. Graeme's attempts to revive him were unfortunately unsuccessful. Graeme and I went down valley to report, a ten-day trip with bad weather and much new snow. A party of ten from the Nehru Institute of Mountaineering in Uttarkashi followed in our steps and evacuated the body. We were back in Base Camp on May 24. We then spent three days fixing rope on mixed ground on the face up to the southwest ridge. It was hard to get to the bottom of the face. Wherever we went, we had to tunnel along in trenches of deep snow. My husband Jon Muir had to dig around for a few days to recover gear buried in a bergschrund under six meters of snow avalanched from the face. Once we had the face fixed, Jon, Hill and I got up its 650 meters to the previously unclimbed southwest ridge, where we established our first camp. This was the last unclimbed ridge leading to Shivling's west summit. From there we fixed rope towards the buttress, spending three nights before moving up the ridge to spend another night on a small platform. A few pitches above Bivouac II, the climbing was only on rock. We climbed the shoulder to the very bottom of the prow. We then traversed one pitch to a snow ledge, where we spent four nights, cleaning the route behind us and fixing the prow to the summit ridge. The crux of the climb, led by Jon in eight hours over a period of two days, is the pitch above the ledge. Two more pitches took us to the summit ridge. There were six pitches along it. We got to the summit on June 15 and spent the night there. The next day we descended one pitch on the ridge before making seven abseils to the col between the two summits. From the col there were two more abseils down the sérac at the top of the west summit. We were back in Advance Base seven hours after leaving the summit.

BRIGITTE MUIR, *Australia*

Shivling, Northeast Face. Paolo Bernascone, Fabrizio Manoni and I as leader got to Base Camp on June 3. From June 4 to 12 we reconnoitered the normal route and our objective, the unclimbed northeast face. After three rest days, we set out at eight in the evening of June 15 with four days' food and equipment to take advantage of the lower temperatures that made safer the great amounts of unstable snow on the face. We were slowed by more difficulties than we had foreseen, by the bad conditions and by several events. The loss of our stove kept us from drinking for the last three days and the loss of climbing gear forced us to climb much free without protection. Falling ice on the next-to-last day of the ascent injured my arm. We made the ascent in eight days and the descent in one. Since the face had no ledges, our bivouacs had to be on shelves carved out of the ice. The first 150-meter-high rock band was of UIAA V, VI and Al. The 350 meters of mixed climbing to 5500 meters had 85° ice and rock of V to VI. Higher, rising to 6000 meters, was an ice slope of 65° at the beginning and 70° to 75° in the second half. Finally mixed climbing led through a 85° to 90° couloir to the base of the 200-meter wall. Above that, 100 meters along the east ridge took us to the summit cap and the summit (6543 meters, 21,467 feet).

ENRICO ROSSO, *Club Alpino Italiano*

Shivling. A British Royal Air Force expedition made the second ascent of the southeast ridge of Shivling. The expedition, of which I was the leader, 22 strong and both climbers and trekkers, spent four weeks based on the Gangotri Glacier. The summit climbers were Nev Taylor, Nick Sharpe, Al McLeod, Andy Watkins, Jim Morning and Bill Batson. After finding a way through the cliffs guarding the southern flank of the mountain, we established a two-tent camp at the foot of the ridge at 5100 meters. The main obstacle on the lower part of the route, a huge gendarme, was turned on the right. The ridge became increasingly steep for 1000 meters on sound granite. A bivouac was made at 5600 meters and a second where the ridge abuts a steep, holdless headwall. A traverse left along a rising fault line provided a sensationally exposed pitch with good holds. This ended on the edge of the 50° snowfield that led to the main (northwest) summit of Shivling. The first pair reached the top on September 5, leaving ropes in place on the crux for the other four to follow the next day. They abseiled down the same route.

C. MICHAEL DAVIDSON, *Squadron Leader, Royal Air Force*

Thalay Sagar Attempt. Kitty Calhoun and I started up the north face of Thalay Sagar on September 18 with seven days' food, one rope and a portaledge. We hoped to climb the face's central couloir. Climbing on the lower apron was slowed by thin 60° to 75° ice; it was difficult to find anchors on thin ice or in slabby rock. Where the ice was thin, it required delicate hooking. After four days we had entered the couloir and gotten to nearly 21,000 feet, but the perfect weather changed to become unstable. Within a minute after snow began to fall, spindrift avalanches would funnel down the couloir, most strong enough to knock the leader off run-out pitches. Above was the crux ice of the climb, three or four pitches of steep waterfall-ice. For eight storm days we lived off one-and-a-half day's worth of food and fuel and when it finally cleared on the ninth day, it was bitterly cold and we were too weak to continue. Throughout the climb we found no hope of chopping any sort of comfortable bivouac ledge; in our portaledge we endured almost constant avalanches during the storm days. Slowed by the difficulty of finding anchors, we took two days on the descent.

ANDREW SELTERS, *American Alpine Institute*

Meru, South Ridge Attempt. On July 10 we placed out Base Camp at 4850 meters on the moraine of the Kirti Bamak (glacier) below the foot of the south ridge of Meru. Our objective had been the east face of Thalay Sagar, but the first 1000 meters were so threatened by avalanches and of such bad rock that we changed and attempted the south ridge of Meru. After nine days of alpine-style climbing (UIAA grades III to VI +) Luca Grazzini, Paolo Camplani and I got to a 5700-meter high point on the ridge. Because of the monsoon weather and a lack of food, we turned back, still nearly 1000 meters from the summit. The upper snowfield did not appear to be too difficult.

DONATELLO AMORE, *Club Alpino Italiano*

Meru North. Our light-weight Indo-Swedish expedition was composed of Swedes Ake Nilsson and Birger Andren and Indians Charu Sharma, Dr. Tejvir Singh Khurana and me. Andren had to leave shortly after reaching Base Camp due to high blood pressure. Base Camp was established on August 28 and Advance Base was at 5000 meters. After three load carries, we four set off to climb the 800-meter face and then the final snow slope. We used no porters above Advance Base and made the climb in a single continuous push. We made the first two bivouacs at 5500 and 5750 meters. Though we found fixed rope from previous expeditions, it could not be trusted as it was frayed by rockfall. The rock in the lower parts was poorer than above. The third bivouac was on snow at 5950 meters. Higher, the snow was poor and, due to sinking in, progress was slow. We made a forced fourth bivouac 200 meters below the summit without sleeping bags. We reached the summit (6460 meters, 21,162 feet) the next day, September 7. We were back in Base Camp on the 9th. We made studies on the interrelationship between retinal hemorrhages and high-altitude sickness. This was the fourth ascent of Meru North and the first Indian and Swedish ones. After this ascent, Dr. Khurana climbed Kedar Dome with Ajeet Bajaj. They left Base Camp at Tapovan on September 17 and set up Advance Base at 4900 meters on northwest ridge, the normal route. On the 19th they reached the summit (6831 meters, 22,410 feet). Though the climb is only an easy snow plod, it was a quick two-man ascent.

MANDIP SINGH SOIN, *Himalayan Club*

Meru North Tragedy. In the post-monsoon season, a three-man Japanese expedition led by Sohei Suzuki had a tragic end to their second attempt on Meru

**SHIVLING. The route is on the
left skyline.**

North. They had chosen a line of mixed snow and rock to the left of the original route on the northeast face. An avalanche buried the three climbers at 5600 meters. Two years ago they had attempted the same route but had to abandon the attempt as one of them accidentally dropped the bag containing the gas cartridges.

MANDIP SINGH SOIN, *Himalayan Club*

Chirbas. A 15-man Calcutta expedition led by Indra Nath Mukherjee made the first ascent of Chirbas (6529 meters, 21,420 feet). The trek began from Bhairon Ghati on May 26. The weather was unfavorable during the approach march along Nelang and Gulli Gad. Base Camp was set up at 13,000 feet at Sirkata on May 30. Emergency and intermediate camps at 15,600 and 15,800 feet were set up on the left bank of Gulli Gad. Thereafter the weather improved. After Advance Base was established at 16,500 feet, temporary camps were set up at 17,500 and 18,500 feet. The summit camp at 19,000 feet was pitched on the Chirbas-Kalidhang Col. From there Goutam Dutta and high-altitude porter Sher Singh gained the virgin summit via the west ridge on June 8.

KAMAL K. GUHA, *Editor, Himavanta, India*

Chandra Parbat. Our team established Base Camp at Vasuki Tal at 16,075 feet on September 17 and Advance Base at 16,800 feet after crossing the Sundar Bamak on September 19. Bikash Chandra Sayal, Miss Ila Mondal and I established Camp I at 18,700 feet on the Suralaya Bamak on the 22nd. Camp II was placed at 19,690 feet on the 24th. I decided to move south to gain the south ridge of Chandra Parbat which seemed safer. With high-altitude porter Badar Singh, I established Camp III at 20,670 feet on September 25 after climbing continuously for 8½ hours in heavy snowfall. The next morning we left for the summit with knee-deep snow. A 150-foot rope was fixed on the last pitch. At 11:10 we were on the summit (6778 meters, 22,073 feet).

KIRON MUKHERJEE, *Howrah District Mountaineers*

Jogin I and III Ascents; P 6529 Attempt. A 19-man expedition of the London Metropolitan Police and Scotland Yard was led by Superintendent John Peck; the climbing leader was Lew Hardy. On September 6, 8, and 10, Jogin I (6465 meters, 21,210 feet) was climbed by ten members, including Superintendent J.M. Das, who, with the liaison officer, formed the Indian members of the party. Das, R. Parry and J. Price climbed Jogin III (6116 meters, 20,066 feet) by the southeast ridge, a new route. These three also climbed P 5215, east of Jogin III. The attempt of P 6529 was given up at 6100 meters because of soft snow and difficult terrain. Two members suffered frostbite.

MANDIP SINGH SOIN, *Himalayan Club*

Bandarpunch Group. An Indian expedition was composed of Dr. S.B.L. Sharma, Ram Chander Bhardwaj, Ashok Kumar Gupta, Chandra Sekhar,

Amarjit Singh, Baljit Singh and Sudhir Upadhyay. All reached the top of Kala Nag (6387 meters, 20,956 feet) in mid June. The ascent by the 60-year-old leader Sharma is commendable. In early October an expedition led by S.K. Ghosh climbed Bandarpunch II (6302 meters, 20,675 feet).

KAMAL K. GUHA, *Editor, Himavanta, India*

India—Himachal Pradesh

Himachal Pradesh, Indian Ascents. A team from Dum Dum was led by Pabitra Bhusan Sanyal. The summit of CB53 (6095 meters, 19,995 feet) was gained on September 8 by Soumitra Ganguly, Chandan Lohia and high-altitude porter Maniram. This was the first Indian ascent of this peak. An 11-member team was led by Jishnu Dutta Goswami. Details are awaited but apparently they were successful on Menthosa (6443 meters, 21,140 feet) and Phabrang (6172 meters, 20,250 feet). A six-member ladies' team from New Delhi consisted of Rani Puri, Bharati Dubey, Vasanti, Nzeen Katrak, Vimla Negi and Anita Rekhi. Beyond Batal they set up two transit camps, Base Camp and three more camps. Katrak had pneumonia at Camp I and had to be brought down. Despite this and porter problems, Vasanti, Rekhi and a high-altitude porter reached the summit of Central (6213 meters, 20,620 feet) at the end of September. Kulu Pumori (6533 meters, 21,500 feet) was climbed by five members of an expedition led by Mahendra Sharma in September. A team led by Nisth Chakraborty climbed Chau Chau King Nilda, also known as Guan Nelda (6303 meters, 20,680 feet), in the autumn. Devachan (6187 meters, 20,300 feet) was climbed in September by an expedition led by Sunil Das.

KAMAL K. GUHA, *Editor, Himavanta, India*

KR6. Japanese climbers Shoichi Hasegawa and Atuhisa Kasugadani left Patisio to make their Base Camp on August 1 north of KR2 at 4650 meters. They went over a col in the northwest ridge of KR2 and descended to the Chandra River, where they put Advance Base. They ascended the glacier northeast of KR6 to place Camp I at 5200 meters. On August 9 they reconnoitered to 5550 meters. On August 10, with porters Labato Lama, Lhato Chando and Tikam Ram, they headed for the summit. From 5600 meters they had 40° to 50° ice along the ridge. In all they fixed some 750 meters of rope. The last 200 meters before the summit (6187 meters, 20,300 feet) were particularly steep.

Karcha Parbat. Base Camp of the expedition I led was set up on the true right bank of the Karcha Nala at 14,550 feet beneath the southwest face of Karcha Parbat on August 11. Advance Base was placed at 16,000 feet on August 15. Camp I was established on the west ridge at 17,500 feet on August 19 and Camp II at 18,800 feet on August 22. On August 23, Samarendra Nath Dar, Rabindra Nath Pal, Chayan Chacraborty and high-altitude porters Yograj Thakur and Alam Chand at 5:45 A.M. set out for the summit (6270 meters, 20,570 feet), which they reached at 10:50 A.M. Karcha Parbat had not been attempted since the Irish first ascent of 1977. We followed the Irish route with variations. Ours was the first Indian ascent.

JIBAN KRISHNA PAUL, *Diganta, Calcutta, India*

P 6036 and P 6150, Miyar Nala, 1985. Scots from Edinburgh University, Peter Smith, leader, Fraser Alexander, Ulric Jessop, Teresa Lee, Alister Matthewson and Jonathan Whittaker, climbed these two peaks alpine-style in early September 1985. They climbed P 6036 (19,803 feet) by the north ridge and P 6150 (20,177 feet) by the south ridge and east face. These are both probably first ascents.

JÓZEF NYKA, *Editor, Taternik, Poland*

India—Kashmir-Jammu

Climbs in Kashmir-Jammu. Nun (7135 meters, 23,400 feet) was climbed in July by six of the ten Spaniards who attempted it, including José María Jayme and Santiago Amibas. They were followed to the summit on October 1 and 3 by nine Japanese led by Eizo Yoneyama. They climbed the north ridge. Nearby Pinnacle Peak (6930 meters, 22,737 feet) was climbed in October by Poles led by Marek Jozefiak. Hattal (6220 meters, 20,407 feet) was climbed in August by Japanese led by Akira Terada. Japanese led by Yuesto Endo ascended Brammah I (6416 meters, 21,050 feet) during August or September.

P 6230, Kishtwar Himal. Bob Reid and I made the first ascent of P 6230, previously known to some as "Kishtwar Weisshorn." We climbed the southwest face of this pyramidal mountain. We approached from the Dharlang Nala with six excellent porters from Dangel and established Base Camp on August 27 at 4250 meters. After crossing a ridge west of the face, we placed Advance Base on August 29 at 4725 meters near the snout of the glacier below and west of the face. In good weather we set out, taking only two 9mm ropes and three days' food. Straightforward ice climbing led to a terrace, from which steeper climbing that culminated in awkward crevasses and a short undercut ice wall led to a bivouac below and left of a stable sérac at 5500 meters. The following day several hours of snow climbing took us to a 300-meter-long, 40° to 55° summit icefield. We got to the summit (6230 meters, 20,440 feet) at 1:30 P.M. on August 31 after climbing for 7½ hours from the bivouac. Due to a shortage of ice screws for rappels, the route was down-climbed and the bivouac was reached in the dark. We descended the rest of the route the next day.

EDWARD FARMER, *England*

Sickle Moon, South Face and Southeast Ridge, Brammah Massif, Kishtwar. Our expedition consisted of Corinne Pesenti, Véronique LaPlante, Félix Brunod, Claude Vard, Bernard Teiller, Hervé Spuytte and me as leader. From the roadhead at Putimahal just above Palmar, we ascended the Nanth Nala through Sondar to Base Camp on the Brammah Glacier near the foot of the south face of Sickle Moon. Base Camp was established at 4084 meters on July 17. The next day we reconnoitered the icefall which would give access to the col at the foot of the southeast ridge. Camp I was at 4700 meters. We climbed in the icefall and then on the south face, fixing 200 meters of rope in the icefall and on the 50° to 60° ice slopes. Camp II was established at 5400 meters on July 24. After several days of bad weather, we returned to Camp II. It took two more days to get to the col at the foot of the southeast ridge at 5820 meters on July 29. On July 31 the seven members of the team all started up the ridge and bivouacked at 6230 meters. The following day, the slope was still steep, 60° to 70°, and we often had to traverse below the crest of the ridge, which was impassable. The bypassing of the 6415-meter foresummit took time as the rock was rotten. That evening we bivouacked at 6350 meters on the plateau below the summit. On August 2 we left camp at 8:30 A.M. and all seven reached the top (6574 meters, 21,568 feet) at noon. The two women made the first female ascent of the peak. It took three days to return to Base Camp. From 6350 to 5820 meters we rappelled down a great couloir to the left of the ridge to get to the col.

JEAN-FRANÇOIS GRANDIDIER, *Club Alpin Français*

P 6150, Durung Drung Glacier. The 12-man Tokyo High School Teacher Expedition was under my leadership. We placed Base Camp on the Pensi La near the tongue of the Durung Drung Glacier. Advance Base was placed up the glacier on the 7th at 4400 meters, west of Z3. Camps I and II were established on August 9 and 11 at 5350 and 5500 meters on the ridge which runs south from Z3 on the eastern side of the glacier. On August 16 Akira Mitsui and Tetsufumi Nagashino climbed along the north ridge of P 6150 (20,177 feet) to the summit. This is the next peak to the north of Doda (6550 meters), for which we had permission. The summit climbers discovered that they were not on Doda when they saw the higher peak after getting to the summit of P 6150.

KIYOTERU TAKAHASHI, *Japan*

India—Eastern Karakoram

Rimo I Attempt, Eastern Karakoram. The Indo-International Rimo-Shyok Expedition had three goals. Our plan was to approach Rimo I via the Depsang Plain, an 18,000-foot plateau which rolls off into Tibet and which no foreigner had traversed since Eric Shipton in 1946. We would then attempt the virgin Rimo I (7385 meters, 24,230 feet) by a route on the east side and finally raft down the Shyok River, which has headwaters in the Rimo area. The peak had seen only one previous attempt and the river had never been run. Our team was composed of 12 members: Indians Colonel Prem Chand, leader, Rajiv Sharma, Magan Bissa, J.P. Singh, Errol De Souza and Sashank, Australians Roddy McKenzie, Terry Ryan and Brett Ryan, Englishman Dave Read, New Zealander Peter Hillary and me from the United States. Although permission for our approach through a restricted area inside the Inner Line had been approved months earlier, we were still delayed for over three weeks while Indian bureaucracy sorted itself out and gave final approval. During this delay we watched the short Karakoram summer fade into autumn. The approach along the old Central Asian trade route was still recognizable from Shipton's writings in *Mountains of Tartary,* although it is now littered with military debris and swarms of Indian military personnel, who for the most part seem to resent and distrust the presence of foreigners. As we ascended the South Rimo Glacier and established Base Camp at 16,600 feet on August 30, we thought we had left the army behind. We were wrong. Mail was censored and radio messages never sent to the outside world. They even sent a platoon up to Base Camp to monitor our activities. From Base Camp, the furthest point our ponies could reach, we still had 12 kilometers of glacial travel to reach the mountain. Advance Base was occupied on September 4 at 17,700 feet on the glacier, but the weather deteriorated and caused frequent delays for the rest of the expedition. On September 8, we occupied Camp I at 18,700 feet. The route from here ascended a snow-and-ice gully up the south face, but due to frequent storms and much fixing of rope in the hope of getting as many members as high as possible, we did not occupy Camp II at 21,300 feet until October 4. On October 6, we turned back from 22,500 feet due to deep snow, serious avalanche and crevasse conditions and stormy weather. By this time, the Indians had all vacated the mountain and our river descent had been cancelled because the river had dried up and frozen! Our leader Prem Chand had inexplicably begun to walk out from Base Camp, leaving the expedition under the leadership of Bissa. The day before the six foreign members got back to Base Camp, having cleaned the mountain and the three higher camps, Bissa and the others evacuated Base Camp, taking all the ponies, porters and most of the supplies. We were forced to leave 200 kilograms of our own gear at Base Camp and each carry 35 kilograms for the next several days as we tried to catch up to the main party, only one day ahead of us. We subsisted on porridge and noodles left over from the mountain. On the second day of the walk-out, a local army garrison confiscated all of our film, including a movie we had made to satisfy our major sponsor, Grindleys Bank of India. As of this writing, the condition and whereabouts of the film is still unknown. On October 16, we were relieved to arrive back in Leh, feeling like escapees from a prisoner-of-war camp.

SKIP HORNER

Saser Kangri Attempt. Our Franco-Indian expedition jointly led by K.C. Mehra and me was never really able to make an attempt on Saser Kangri. The reason doubtless was the undeclared war in the Siachen region between India and Pakistan. We French were not informed of this, or that we were permitted to try the mountain only on its western side, until we reached Leh. We could not approach the more reasonable eastern side as we had planned. We went to

Panamik and from there carried on two reconnaissances to the Phukpoche and Panamik Glaciers. The routes from the west are such that no expedition could reasonably expect to reach the summit: a difficult gorge, a closed cirque, a 2000-meter-high face continually swept by ice avalanches that fall from the edge of the plateau and finally a 6-kilometer ridge above 7000 meters which leads to the summit. Blocked as we were by the military, we had no choice but to give up.

BERNARD PUJO, *Club Alpin Français*

Saser Kangri III. I was the leader of the 25-man Indo-Tibetan Border Police expedition. We left Leh on April 16 and approached up the Shyok valley along the old "Silk Route" toward Sinkiang. The Shyok had to be forded 17 times before we got on April 26 to Base Camp at 15,300 feet at the snout of the North Shukpa Kanchang Glacier. We approached the peak up that glacier. We established Camps I, II, III, IV and V at 16,300, 17,000, 18,700, 20,000 and 21,700 feet. We had to climb steep ice and rock, especially above Camp III and fixed 2000 meters of rope. We were lucky that on May 15 the weather was untypically fine when we got the chance to make the first summit climb. Dawa Tsering, Rubgias, Suddi Man, Magan Singh, Sharap Shalden and Tsering Sherpa left Camp V at four A.M. and reached the summit (7495 meters, 24,590 feet) at 11:45 A.M. A second summit party, Phurba Sherpa, Bihari Lal, Neem Dorjee, Tejwar Singh, Tsering Somla and Sher Singh, climbed to the summit the next day. A third summit attempt had to be called off when R.S. Negi suddenly developed pulmony edema while climbing to Camp IV and had to be evacuated, first by being carried down and then by helicopter. After the completion of the climb, we rafted down the turbulent, icy-cold Shyok to get back to habitation.

S.P. CHAMOLI, *Indo-Tibetan Border Police*

Sia Kangri. We have returned from traversing the entire Siachen Glacier and an ascent of Sia Kangri (7422 meters, 24,350 feet). There was a war going on, right in the heart of the mountains of central Asia, a war mostly unknown to the outside world. An international team of Americans, Canadians, a Briton and Indians was pinned down by Pakistani heavy artillery at 17,000 feet below the Sia La. On June 20 my co-leader, Major Cherian, our liaison officer Major Sethi and I decided to cancel the ascent of Sia Kangri by our American team. The Indians continued. There was shelling of the south face at 22,500 feet on June 22 while the climbers were on their way up. The Pakistani forces at Conway Saddle (20,670 feet) were only 600 yards away from the Indians. Indians Shafi, Paljor, Amar, Angchuck, Des Raj and Cham Charma did reach the summit of Sia Kangri. Jerry Corr, Jim Caruthers, Walt Hotchkiss, Dr. Paul Kustra and Briton Mark Jennings got to Indira Col and Turkestan La.

LEO LE BON

Pakistan

K2, South-Southwest Ridge Attempt and Tragedy. Our expedition reached Base Camp on May 31 and took its place in line on the moraine of the Godwin Austen Glacier. We found ourselves among nine expeditions on the south side and four expeditions on the unclimbed south-southwest ridge. This concentration of climbers was initially dismaying, but the collection of Who's Who in Himalayan climbing, past and present, provided an interesting backdrop to our attempt, as we spent many days in Base Camp in foul weather. Our group consisted of eight climbers from the Pacific Northwest, Base-Camp manager Chelsea Monike and liaison officer Major Mobshir Hussain Tarar, who, as senior army officer in the Base Camp, provided counsel to other expeditions' liaison officers as climbers shuffled from one route to another. On June 3 we set up Camp I at the head of the De Filippi Glacier. From June 6 to 9, John Smolich, leader, Brian Hukari, Kerry Ryan and I fixed 1000 meters of line on the Negrotto Face to the saddle at 6300 meters. Andy Politz and Jon Sassler occupied Camp II on the saddle the next day. Bad weather drove us all to Base Camp on the 11th. On June 18 we started again to build up Camp II and while the rest of us ferried loads, Politz and Ryan helped the Italians fix line to Camp III at 6800 meters. Camp III was reached on June 20. That evening Murray Rice, Politz, Ryan and Dassler stayed in Camp II, Hukari and I descended all the way to Base Camp and Smolich and Al Pennington remained in Camp I, planning to do another carry the next morning. On June 21 at 5:30 A.M. a boulder fell from the south-southwest ridge just above Camp II and started an avalanche on the Negrotto Face. Smolich and Pennington had left Camp I about 20 minutes before and were caught in it as they started up the face. Hukari and I found Pennington's body near the surface three hours later. We carried him to the Gilkey Memorial the next morning and held a service attended by the international community. We found no trace of Smolich. The slab depth at the starting zone was two or three feet, but at the base it was 15 to 20 feet. It scoured the slope to blue ice. We abandoned the route and the expedition as our permit was specifically for the south-southwest ridge. Ours was the only expedition on the south side that did not start on, or send one or more members to, the Abruzzi Ridge. Probably as a result, we were the only expedition on the south side not to reach the summit. The Polish expedition on our route took over our fixed line to Camp III and our tents, rope and food in Camp II. They completed the previously unclimbed route in early August. Considering the small windows of good weather which they had, most certainly our work on the lower half of the route was instrumental in their success, and so we share their feeling of victory on what Renato Casarotto had referred to as the most difficult route in all the Himalaya and Karakoram.

STEVE BOYER

K2 Tragedy. The Italian climber Renato Casarotto was trying to climb solo the long, then still unclimbed south-southwest ridge of K2 with a slight deviation to the right in the upper part. A first attempt ended at 8200 meters about

PLATES 71 and 72

Photos by Steve Boyer

Slope below Negrotto Col on K2 before and after the avalanche.

June 23. A second try reached a similar height about July 5. In his third attempt, in mid July, he reached a little higher, about 8300 meters but decided to withdraw in view of the weather, playing safe as usual. He descended the whole length of the ridge to the foot of the mountain and the De Filippi Glacier where on July 16 he was watched by Kurt Diemberger as he fell into a crevasse only about an hour's walk from Base Camp. The crevasse was about 40 meters deep. He managed to get out his radio from his rucksack and call his wife who was at Base Camp and had been told by Diemberger to turn the radio on. He whispered, "Goretta, I am dying in a crevasse near Base Camp." She organized a search party from the Italian, British and German expeditions nearby, including their doctors. Very soon they found him in the bottom of the crevasse, still alive. After lifting him to the surface, all efforts of the doctors were useless and he died soon afterwards. Following the wishes of his wife, his body was placed back to rest in the crevasse. This is a great loss for Italian mountaineering and a cruel blow for Goretta Casarotto, who has always accompanied him in far-away expeditions and given him priceless moral and practical support on all his solo climbs. She accompanied him in 1985 when together they reached the summit of Gasherbrum II.

XAVIER EGUSKITZA, *Pyrenaica, Bilbao, Spain*

K2. After a period of acclimatization, two Basques, Mari Abrego and Josema Casimiro, officially members of Renato Casarotto's expedition but climbing independently, made a swift, illegal ascent of the Abruzzi Ridge of K2 in a five-day alpine-style push. In a period of good weather, they moved up each day, carrying their tent and all necessary food, fuel and gear. They went up to Advance Base, Camps I, II, III and IV at 5250, 6050, 6750, 7400 and 8150 meters from June 18 to 22. In still excellent weather on June 23 they climbed the "Bottleneck and got to the summit just after the Barrards, Michel Parmentier and Wanda Rutkiewicz. They took five days to make the descent in bad weather, arriving at Base Camp on June 27. They were accompanied part of the way down by Wanda Rutkiewicz.

GREGORIO ARIZ, *Club Anaitasuna, Spain*

K2, Women's Ascents and Tragedy. French climbers Michel Parmentier, Maurice and Liliane Barrard were joined by Pole Wanda Rutkiewicz. Both women had already climbed two 8000ers. Apparently the expedition was not a happy one from the beginning. Maurice Barrard lost the expedition's funds, passports and airline tickets in Rawalpindi. They reached Base Camp at the end of May. According to other climbers on the mountain there was little harmony among them from the start. In early June they got to 7000 meters and descended to wait out nine days of storm. They set out again on June 18 but progress up the mountain was slow. Above the fixed ropes and Camp III, Liliane Barrard was having considerable difficulty. They moved unroped. She took three or four hours before she would move up over a sérac. On June 22 all four bivouacked in a two-man tent without sleeping bags at 8300 meters. On the 23rd they left for the summit in lovely weather. Wanda Rutkiewicz became the first woman to reach the summit of K2 when she went ahead of the others who rested for an hour a half-hour below the top before going on to the the summit. When they got back to their bivouac tent at 8300 meters, the Barrards insisted on spending a second cold night there. On the morning of June 24 Parmentier started ahead to melt water at 7900-meter Camp III. Rutkiewicz followed. She looked back to see the Barrards descending slowly, apparently exhausted. They were never seen again. The two spent the night at Camp III and Rutkiewicz descended to Camp II with Basques Mari Abrego and Josema Casimiro, who had reached the summit on the same day as they had. She waited for Parmentier for two days before she descended. Meanwhile Parmentier was waiting for the Barrards. He finally left when it began to storm. He had to be directed down the route by Benoît Chamoux, who told him on the radio just where to go. He was uninjured, but Wanda Rutkiewicz had frost-bitten hands and feet. Austrians found Liliane Barrard's body at the foot of the south face on July 19.

Broad Peak and K2. An Italian group, "Quota 8000," which has a six-year program to climb all fourteen 8000ers, had K2 and Broad Peak for its goal in 1986. The team consisted of Italians Agostino Da Polenza, leader, Marino Giacometti, Gianni Calcagno, Soro Dorotei, Martino Moretti, Tullio Vidoni, Frenchman Benoît Chamoux and me* from Czechoslovakia. On June 4 we placed Base Camp below K2 at 5100 meters. We placed Camp I at 5700 meters and Camp II on the Negrotto Col at 6300 meters on K2. After bad weather we turned to Broad Peak. On June 16 we placed Camp I at 6300 meters on the normal route on Broad Peak but returned to Base. On June 18 Dorotei, Giacometti, Moretti and I spent the night at Camp I and the next day camped at 7100 meters. On June 20 the three Italians got to the summit, but I had to stop on the 8030-meter foresummit because my movie camera froze. Chamoux left Base Camp on the evening of June 19 and, taking advantage of our tracks, reached the summit also on the 20th. He was back in Base Camp 24 hours after he started. I spent a day at 7100 meters and on June 22 climbed to the summit of Broad Peak solo. After the death of the two Americans on the south-southwest ridge of K2, we decided to climb the Abruzzi Ridge. Bad weather held us up at 7800 meters. Calcagno, Vidoni, Moretti, Dorotei and I set out again on July 3. We bivouacked at 6700 and 7800 meters and got to the summit of K2 on July 5. Chamoux left Base Camp at ten A.M. and Advance Base at six P.M. on July 4 and again using our tracks, got to the top at 4:30 P.M. on July 5. We all descended together. On July 6 Austrian Kurt Diemberger and Englishwoman Julie Tullis, who were our film team, got to the "Bottleneck" at 8200 meters.

JOSEF RAKONCAJ, *Československy Horolezecky Svaz*

---

* Rakoncaj is the first person to have climbed K2 twice, each time by a different route, having also climbed K2 from the north in 1983.

Broad Peak and K2. This expedition was a semi-commercial undertaking. Most of its members had little more in common than the DM 12,000 (about $6300) each had to pay into the expedition treasury. From West Germany came the leader, Dr. Karl Maria Herrligkoffer, Base Camp Manager Doris Kustermann, Heinrich Koch, Toni Freudig, Manfred Heinrich, Joachim Labisch, Markus Precht and scientist Dr. Irene Simon-Schnass; from Poland, Jerzy Kukuczka and Tadeusz Piotrowski; from Austria, Peter Wörgötter and Johann Hirschbichler; from Switzerland, Beda Fuster, Diego Wellig and Rolf Zemp; I have dual Swiss-USA citzenship. I was to produce a documentary film for West German television. After various problems on the approach, we established the Broad Peak Base Camp at 4900 meters near the start of the original first-ascent route. After a day at Base, they began to build up a line of three camps in expedition-style, while the K2 team moved out on July 7 to set up its Base Camp on the Godwin Austen moraine at 5100 meters near the start of a rib in the south face of K2, well to the left of the route attempted previously by Doug Scott. The Poles were determined to follow this rib and move up to the left of dangerous séracs in the center of the face in the hope of reaching the great Sickle Couloir and the summit slopes beyond the Bottle Neck. The three Swiss and Freudig gave the Poles initial support as far as Camp I, and Freudig carried to Camp II, but the Swiss indicated a strong dislike of the line, considering it a death-trap in case of a heavy snowfall. They asked Herrligkoffer, who had been helicoptered in from Payu to the Broad Peak Base on July 13 in celebration of his 70th birthday, for permission to attempt the normal Abruzzi Ridge on K2. This request was turned down. Fuster, Zemp and Wellig turned to Broad Peak, departing from K2 Base at three A.M. on June 19. They moved past Broad Peak Base and made a carry to Camp II at 6300 meters. They were joined there by Wörgötter and Prechtl, and on June 20 all five moved up to Camp III at 7400 meters. June 21, a beautiful day, saw the three Swiss, the Austrian and the German on top. The next day they were followed by Koch and Labisch, but these two went only to the 60-foot lower foresummit. The same foresummit was attained on July 6 by Freudig, Heinrich and our favorite Balti porter "Little Karim," who had carried a hang-glider to the top of Gasherbrum II for Boivin the year before. Dr. Herrligkoffer's health had declined at an alarming rate. On June 26 he and Doris Kustermann were picked up by helicopter and evacuated to Skardu. Wellig departed for home. Fuster and Zemp decided to disregard our leader's veto and to climb K2 by the Abruzzi Ridge. The two left K2 Base Camp shortly after midnight on July 2. Breaking trail in knee-deep snow, they reached their first bivouac site at 6700 meters late in the afternoon. A strong wind kept them awake for most of the night and continued into the next day. At noon they started up again, using some of the fixed ropes of previous parties. A second bivouac was on a narrow ledge under a large rock which protected them from avalanches and falling rocks. On the third day they moved up the Black Pyramid, where they were joined by members of the QUOTA 8000 expedition who had followed their tracks. The third bivouac was at 7600 meters below the shoulder. At four P.M. on July 5 they all stood on the summit of K2 on a magnificent, almost windless day: four Italians, a Czechoslovakian, a French-man and two Swiss. It had taken Fuster and Zemp 3½ days from Base to top and it took another 1½ to descend. Weeks later, during a debriefing session at the Ministry of Tourism in Islamabad, the Swiss were asked to pay another Rs. 45,000 for having climbed K2 by a route other than the one specified in our official permit. Since none of us had that much money, the Ministry threatened Fuster and Zemp with a four-year ban. The successful new route of Kukuczka and Piotrowski and the tragic death of Piotrowski are covered elsewhere in this *Journal*.

NORMAN DYHRENFURTH

K2, Abruzzi Ridge. Our expedition had 19 members. An advance party of four accompanied 290 porters and got to Base Camp on June 20. The main party reached Base Camp on June 23. We set up Advance Base at 5300 meters on June 25. We established Camps I, II and III at 6200, 6800 and 7350 meters on June 27, July 3 and 8. We tried to occupy Camp IV at about 8000 meters, but bad weather drove us back. A five-man summit team started on July 16 but with bad weather our attack failed. On July 30 Jang Bong-Wan, Kim Chang-Sun and Jang Byong-Ho left Base Camp and on August 2 set up Camp IV at 8000 meters. On August 3 they left Camp IV for the summit, while seven other climbers stayed in their tents. Each Korean had one cylinder of oxygen, used on the ascent but not the descent. They reached the summit at 4:16 P.M. An hour later two Poles and a Czech also got to the summit. Wojciech Wróż slipped, fell and was killed at 8200 meters on the descent. Possibly he rappelled off the end of a fixed rope. On August 4 our team descended to Advance Base.

KIM BYUNG-JOON, *Korean Alpine Federation*

Broad Peak, Gasherbrum II and Southeast Face of K2. Our expedition consisted of Viktor Grošelj, leader, Bogdan Biščak, Rado Fabjan, Žare Gugej, Tomaš Jamnik, Dušan Jelinčič, Silvo Karo, Pavle Kozjek, Ničo Kregar, Matevš Lenarčič, Mojmir Štangelj, Andrej and Marija Štremfelj and me. We estab-lished our first Base Camp at 4900 meters at the foot of Broad Peak on July 8 and Camps I and II at 6200 and 7000 meters on July 11 and 16. The next day four of us climbed to 7500 meters but abandoned the attempt due to bad weather and deep snow. We established Camp III at 7500 meters on July 26 and on the 28th Grošelj and Biščak reached the summit of Broad Peak. The next day Fabjan, Jamnik, Andrej and Marija Štremfelj got to the top. The latter was the first Yugoslavian woman to climb an 8000er. That same day, I soloed to the top from Base Camp in 19 hours. Kozjek reached the top solo on July 30. The last party, Jelinčič, Karo, Lenarčič and Štangelj, succeeded on August 4. Quickly after the success on Broad Peak, Biščak, Grošelj, Kozjek and Andrej Štremfelj launched an alpine-style climb on Gasherbrum II. They made the round-trip from a differ-ent Base Camp in 32 hours. From a bivouac on the plateau, they reached the summit in 14 hours on August 4. I made a reconnaissance ascent of the southeast face of K2 from 5300 to 8000 meters. Starting on the afternoon of August 3, I reached the shoulder of K2 the next day in 17 hours. The route followed in some parts the one the British tried in 1983 and finished on the shoulder, where it joined the Abruzzi Ridge (UIAA VI−, and V+, 75°). After reaching the Abruzzi Ridge, I climbed another 100 meters but because of strong wind and snowfall I descended via the Abruzzi.

Tomo Česen, *Planinska Zveza Slovenije, Yugoslavia*

K2, Northwest Ridge Attempt. Our expedition consisted of Alan Rouse, leader, John Barry, Alan and Adrian Burgess, Phil Burke, Brian Hall, John Porter and Dave Wilkinson, with Jim Hargreaves, Base-Camp manager, Dr. Bev Holt and Jim Curran, film maker. With 200 porters, we arrived at K2 Base Camp on May 23. We retained 10 porters to help ferry gear onto the Savoia Glacier, where Advance Base was established at the foot of the west face of K2, the Base Camp site used by Japanese and British west-face expeditions. From there we established Camp I at 6100 meters in the hanging valley that separates the northwest and west ridges. Above is a 700-meter mixed face which was fixed-roped in roughly the 1982 Polish line to Camp II at 6800 meters. Above the snow slopes, old Polish ropes led leftwards through mixed ground into diagonal gully-and-ramp systems. Porter and Rouse had fixed new rope up to 7400 meters by the third week of June. However, continued bad weather was slowing progress, with only the odd spell of fine. Brian Hall returned home with a damaged knee and John Porter left to return to work on July 1. By July 8 Adrian and Alan Burgess reached the high point and Adrian managed one more rope-length before the weather once more showed signs of breaking. The inevitable decision was reached that with too few active climbers to continue a fixed-rope ascent and not enough good weather to risk an alpine-style push on technically difficult ground, the northwest ridge had to be abandoned, Wilkinson, Barry, Burke, Rouse and the Burgess twins made a short foray on the Abruzzi Ridge before being turned back by bad weather. The same day, July 16, Renato Casarotto had his fatal crevasse fall. The whole team tried unsuccessfully to rescue him, and for many, this, the sixth death on K2 that summer, was the turning point. By the 20th, only Rouse and I were left. What happened later is well documented elsewhere in this *Journal*.

James Curran, *England*

Broad Peak. Numerous ascents of Broad Peak by the normal route are now being made every year. Some are given in separate reports. See accounts by Josef Rakoncaj, Norman Dyhrenfurth, Gregorio Ariz and Tomo Česen. Swiss led by Frank Tschirky and Germans and Austrians under the leadership of Franz Piffl joined forces. On July 7 Austrians Fritz Schreimoser and Sebastian Oelzel got to the summit. The foresummit, which is 17 meters lower than the main summit, was reached that same day by German Peter Brill, Austrian Henriette

Eberwein and Swiss Bruno Sprecher and on July 8 by German Max Wallner and Swiss Daniel Schaer and Alain Fenart. On August 16 Germans Michael Dacher, Siegfried and Gabriele Hupfauer and Karl Fassnacht climbed the peak. Fassnacht was badly frostbitten on the descent and had to be evacuated by helicopter from Base Camp. This was Dacher's eighth 8000er and Sigi Hupfauer's fifth. Frau Hupfauer was the sixth woman to climb Broad Peak. Also on August 16 an Australian Army party led by Major Patrick A. Cullinan put eight men on the summit. They were Cullinan, Major Brian Agnew, Captains Zacharias Zaharias, Peter Lambert, Terry McCullagh, and James Van Gelder, and Messrs. Michael Rheinberger and Jonathon Chester. After descending from K2, Wanda Rutkiewicz made an unsuccessful solo attempt. Coming from their climb of Chogolisa, Scots Liam Elliott, Hamish Irvine and Ulric Jessop climbed high on Broad Peak. On the summit ridge, Elliott fell through on overhanging cornice and was killed. The attempt was given up.

Broad Peak, 1985. In *A.A.J.,* 1986 on page 277, a portion of the account written by Sadao Tambe was omitted, telling of the second part of the expedition when six of their members climbed to the summit of Broad Peak. On August 12 one group bivouacked at 7850 meters and Jyoshi Wada, Munehiko Yamamoto and Tetsuya Toyama got to the summit while Masushi Takita had to quit shortly below the top. That same day, after bivouacking at 7580 meters, Shin Kashu, Tsuneo Shigehiro and Riichi Nishizutsumi reached the summit and Yoichi Yabukawa had to stop right below it. They had previously climbed Masherbrum.

Gashebrum I (Hidden Peak) and Tragedy. Every expedition set up its Base Camp on the Gasherbrum Glacier on the western side of the peak because the southern approaches from the Abruzzi Glacier were banned by the military in view of the Indo-Pakistani conflict on the nearby Siachen Glacier. Swiss led by Paul Tschanz made an attempt from the Gasherbrum La in June. They got to within 20 meters of the summit before giving up in high winds. Three Japanese men and a woman under the leadership of Osamu Shimizu started an ascent, following a line to the left of the Messner route. In cooperation with a French group, they set up Camp III at 7000 meters. Then, on August 2, the leader and Kiyoshi Wakutsu reached the summit after a very long climb from Camp III. The French, led by Alain Cokkinos, had been preparing the route to the same Camp III. They set up a Camp IV at 7400 meters. Dr. Christine Janin, Antoine Barthélémy and German Joswig Reinmar got to the top on August 3. Christine Janin is the second woman to climb Hidden Peak. This was her second 8000er; she climbed Gasherbrum II in 1981. A Swiss commercial expedition of six, organized by Stefan Wörner, climbed the north spur via the Gasherbrum La. The summit was reached on August 18 by German Gerhard Schmatz, German Andreas Bührer, and Austrians Manfred Lorenz and Karl Köllemann. During the descent, Bührer slipped at 7000 meters and fell to his death. It was Schmatz's third 8000er and Lorenz's second.

XAVIER EGUSKITZA, *Pyrenaica, Bilbao, Spain*

Gasherbrum I, Northwest Face, Correction. On page 271 of *A.A.J.*, 1986, two different routes on the northwest face of Gasherbrum I (Hidden Peak) were given. When one compares the descriptions and the route sketches, it becomes clear that Di Federico solo and Chamoux and Escoffier climbed the same route. Contrary to what the Frenchmen thought they did not follow Messner's and Habeler's route of 1975 but climbed a new route, which Di Federico repeated a short time later.

BERNARD DOMENECH, *Club Alpin Français*

Gasherbrum II. Among the many groups attempting Gasherbrum II, the French commercial expedition, led by Bernard Muller and Laurence de la Ferrière, made an early ascent on June 6. During May and early June, the weather was unusually cold and only three people managed to reach the summit: Eric Guillory, Robert Caminati and Guy Chardini, all French. Meanwhile the organizers were engaged in the evacuation of two other clients who suffered severely frozen feet at the bottom of the summit pyramid. It is believed that they eventually had their feet amputated.

XAVIER EGUSKITZA, *Pyrenaica, Bilbao, Spain*

Gasherbrum II. This mountain is now frequently ascended. Some climbs are noted elsewhere in this journal. See reports by the French and Yugoslavs. Spaniards Juan del Olmo and Roberto Vásquez reached the summit on July 9. Tragically the expedition leader, Carlos Rábago, died on July 12 at 7000 meters of high-altitude sickness. Pakistanis Mohammad Sher Khan, Mohammad Fakharul-Haq, Abdul Jabbar Bhatti and Mirza Mohammad Atta-ul-Haq got to the top on August 3. This was Sher Khan's third ascent of Gasherbrum II. On August 16 the summit was reached by Germans Dieter Siegers, Jürgen Altgelt, Karl Zöll, Volker Stallbohm and Swiss Martin Fischer. All climbed the normal route. Unsuccessful expeditions were Italians led by Mario Pietro Rossi, Basques led by Eugenio Gerrotxategui and two German groups led by Georg Welsch and Siegfried Hupfauer.

Gasherbrum IV Attempt. A British expedition consisted of David Lampard, leader, his wife Rhoda, Andrew Atkinson, Alan Phizacklea, Alan Scott, Alan Shand, Christine Watkins and Bob Wightman, They first attempted the west ridge but gave up at 6600 meters because of avalanche danger. They then moved to the south ridge, where they rapidly got to 7300 meters. Lampard and Phizacklea were set for a summit try when the weather deteriorated. An injury to other members of the party made them decide to give up the attempt.

Chogolisa, Northeast Ridge, and Broad Peak. Our original group, Mari Agrego, Josema Casimiro and I had hoped to climb together, but for reasons with the permissions, the first two had to join Renato and Goretta Casarotto; they climbed K2 as reported elsewhere. I joined another Spanish expedition led by

PLATE 73

Photo by H. Adams Carter

CHOGOLISA. Spanish route diagonaled up from the left on the ridge in front of the shadow.

Sebastián Alvaro, composed of Antonio Pérez, Ramón Portilla, Félix de Pablo, Guillermo de la Torre, Juanjo Sansebastián and José Carlos Tamayo. We established Base Camp on June 10 on the Upper Baltoro Glacier at 4900 meters. We ascended a glacier that is below Chogolisa's northeast ridge, which divides the north from the east face. With some bad weather, we placed Camp I at 5500 meters on June 14. We reached the northeast ridge, climbing some 50° to 60° slopes between ice séracs. We continued along the ridge crest at 40° to 50° to a hollow at 6300 meters, where we placed Camp II on June 20. Flatter slopes on a plateau took us to the foot of séracs at 6950 meters, where we installed Camp III on June 21. On June 22 Tamayo and de Pablo got to the summit and on the 23rd Portilla and I reached the top. On the summit we found a small doll dressed as a Japanese child, evidence of the only other ascent to this northeast summit by a Japanese expedition 28 years before. The other four ascents of Chogolisa have been to the southwest summit. Ours was the sixth ascent of Chogolisa if you count both summits and the first up the northeast ridge. De la Torre descended by hang-glider on June 23. On July 6 Sansebastián and Portilla reached the summit of Broad Peak in a two-day alpine-style ascent.

GREGORIO ARIZ, *Club Anaitasuna, Spain*

Chogolisa Traverse. From September 10 to 15 our expedition, Liam Elliot, Hamish Irvine, Ulric Jessop, Simon Lamb and I as leader, made the first complete traverse of Chogolisa's twin summits (7665 meters or 25,148 feet; 7654 meters or 25,112 feet). The southwest summit was reached at 8:30 A.M. on August 14 after we had spent two days ascending the 1500-meter-high northwest face of the southwest ridge, at the head of the Vigne Glacier, and another day in high winds climbing the southwest ridge itself. Also on the 14th we traversed the summits' connection arête in nearly perfect conditions to the slightly lower northeast top (Bride Peak). All five members then made a rapid descent to 7000 meters. Weather conditions were mixed throughout but were perfect on the summits' day with good visibility as it had to be! Technically the route was not trying, but large cornices abound on Chogolisa's ridges, which in places were very delicate. The southwest summit is a razor-edge whilst the northeast summit is a rocky surmount 20 meters high and very exposed. Sadly, later in the summer, Liam Elliot was killed on Broad Peak, falling with a huge cornice from 7900 meters on the summit ridge down the east face.

ANDREW R. FANSHAWE, *Alpine Climbing Group*

Trango Towers. Five expeditions climbed on the Trango Towers this season. Three parties attempted a new route on the east face of the Nameless Tower: Pole Wojciech Kurtyka with three Japanese, the American group described in this journal and Frenchmen led by Michel Piola. Germans Helmut Münchenbach, Christoph Krah and Peter Popal attempted a 5900-meter tower adjacent to the Great Trango Tower. They failed 300 meters from the top. Italians includ-

PLATE 74

Photo by Wojciech Kurtyka

NAMELESS TOWER'S Southeast Face, Trango Towers.

ing Renzo Vettori, Oscar Piazza and Arnaldo Pinter tried to repeat the Nor-
wegian route on the Great Trango Tower. All were beaten back by bad weather.

Nameless Tower Attempt, Trango Towers. There were four of us, three
Japanese, Noboru Yamada, Kasuhiro Saito and Kenji Yoshida, and I from
Poland. Still today I don't understand what happened on the Trango Towers. On
the 19th day after establishing Base Camp, my dear Japanese friends unexpectedly and to my total bewilderment called off our attempt on June 23 at a
third-height of the southeast face of the Nameless Tower. The weather was
splendid, we had more food than we could eat and the tower was enthralling. We
arrived at Base Camp at 4000 meters on the Dunge Glacier on June 4. On June
8 we carried 100 kilograms of food and equipment to the base of the tower at
5200 meters. The approach was dangerously exposed to snow avalanches slid-
ing off the surrounding slabs and séracs. We recommend a night approach to the
east side of the tower. On June 9 and 10, assisted by Yamada, I climbed and
fixed with rope five pitches up to UIAA Grade VI, A2. That brought us to the
big snow band. On June 20 we carried the remaining gear from the Base Camp
to the snow band, a total of 150 kilograms. After a bivouac there, on June 21 we
started on the final push. The climb developed obstinately. During the first two
days, Yoshida and Saito climbed three pitches. Saito took a fall, painfully hitting his knee. The next morning it was my turn. I tackled a very fine pitch and
just as I was scanning the excellent and promising rock above, the astounding
call for retreat came from below. I was furious, but helpless. At midnight we
were back on the Dunge Glacier. Surprisingly, after returning to Base Camp,
our relations took a new course. They became more warm-hearted. We slowly
came to understand each other. The tension between us vanished. I came back
to the plains with two loves greater than before: Trango and the Japanese.
Defeats are good.

WOJCIECH KURTYKA, *Klub Wysokogórski, Kraków, Poland*

Nameless Tower Attempt, Trango Towers. On July 1 Tom Hargis, Randy
Leavitt and I established Base Camp at the foot of the Nameless Tower in the
Trango group, on the Dunge Glacier. Our objective was the southeast face of
Nameless Tower. From Base Camp we followed a long and dangerous couloir
to the lower tower, where we found 600 feet of fixed rope and some food, left
by Wojciech Kurtyka and his Japanese friends' attempt on the same route. On
July 6 we went up on the route and hauled some 350 pounds of gear to about
18,500 feet. Fatigue from our ascent of Gasherbrum IV, and high clouds, called
for retreat. Several days of freezing rain ensued. On July 16 we went up again,
climbing appalling snow above the fixed rope, to the base of the main tower.
Gigantic blocks bombarded the face. We climbed four pitches up to A4, and
spent two nights on the wall in porta-ledges, reaching about 19,000 feet. At one
point, Randy was almost killed when a tower of ice, lodged in the dihedral he
was climbing, collapsed and narrowly missed him. In view of the back-breaking

logistics of hauling heavy loads, the broken nature of the rock, and constant rockfall, we chose to retreat. Eighty days in the Karakoram may have also dampened our resolve.

GREG CHILD

Hushe Karakoram Expedition. We spent two months in the Central Karakoram, exploring, climbing and geologising around the Masherbrum, Gondogoro, Chogolisa, Charakusa and Aling glacier systems, approaching from the Hushe valley. A late winter left snow in Hushe village until early April; conditions higher were somewhat bleaker. We had Base Camp on the Gondogoro Glacier during late April and May. British Dick Renshaw, Jon Tinker, Mark Miller, Simon Yates and I and Australian Craig Kentwell all climbed Gondogoro Peak (c. 5700 meters) on May 7 to 10. Miller and Yates climbed "Blob Peak" (c. 5800 meters) south of Masherbrum from May 14 to 16. Meanwhile, Renshaw and Tinker attempted a complicated mixed route on the east face of the lowermost peak of the three that make up the Biarchedi massif, east of Masherbrum. They climbed 2500 feet up the face before retreating. Kentwell and I went to the head of the Gondogoro Glacier and climbed to the main col connecting northwards to the upper Vigne Glacier between Chogolisa and Biarchedi, south of Mitre Peak. We studied the geology of the Aling Glacier to the Chongking Col which connects to the Liliwa and Baltoro Glaciers, the Masherbrum south Glacier and the Charakusa Glacier leading to K7. Renshaw, Tinker, Miller and Yates made three attempts on Trinity Peak from the Chogolisa Glacier but were defeated by weather and deep snows. The expedition left Skardu in mid May but Miller, Yates and Tinker travelled up to Hunza for another unsuccessful attempt to climb the granite spire of Bublumiting on the Ultar massif above Baltit.

MICHAEL SEARLE, *England*

Latok II Attempt. [This peak is the same one attempted by an American expedition in 1978 and British in 1982 by the same route. It had been called Latok I previous to an Italian expedition, which interchanged Latok I and II. The Norwegians call it Latok II. We are not sure which is now officially given by the Pakistanis.—*Editor.*] After leaving Dassu on June 22, Dr. Magnar Osnes, Øyvind Vlada and Olav Båsen and I arrived at Base Camp on the Choktoi Glacier at 4500 meters on June 28. We believed Latok's north ridge was ideal for an alpine-style climb. It is a superb line with difficult climbing and few objective dangers. The ridge is 2500 meters high and little is easier than 5.8. We planned considerable time for acclimatization and spent 12 days around and above Base Camp before the ascent. On June 30 Båsen and Vlada climbed a 5600-meter peak near Base Camp; the south face gave 300 meters of rock climbing up to 5.10. We all made the first ascent of a P 5860 with 350 meters of ice climbing along the north ridge. After two of us fixed rope 300 meters up the north ridge of Latok on July 8, all of us established Camp I at the foot of the

PLATE 75

Photo by Fred Husøy

LATOK II's North Ridge.

PLATE 77

Difficult rock above Camp II on Latok II.

PLATE 76

Photos by Fred Husey

Low on LATOK II's North Ridge, looking toward Baintha Brakk.

ridge at 4700 meters on July 10. We moved up the next day to Camp II at 5100 meters. After a day of bad weather, on July 13 we moved to Camp III at the top of the rock pillar at 5350 meters. Up to Camp III it was climbing on good rock with difficulties up to 5.10, A2. On July 14 we fixed rope to Camp IV at 5650 meters and moved up there the next day, fixing 300 more meters of rope. On the 16th we moved up to Camp V at 6050 meters. From Camps III to V it was mostly ice climbing. The mixed climbing to Camp VI at 6400 meters was difficult and we occupied the camp only on July 18. Snow began to fall, piling up 2½ meters in eight days. We made one foray up 100 meters. On July 27 two of us climbed 150 meters, but again it began to snow. On the 28th, still in bad weather, we gave up the attempt. We had been on half rations for the last eight days.

FRED HUSØY, *Norsk Tindeklub*

Braldu Brakk Attempt. French climbers led by Claude Nizon unsuccessfully attempted to climb Braldu Brakk. Details are missing.

Rakaposhi, Northwest Ridge. Our expedition made the second ascent of the northwest ridge, partly by a new route, and the sixth ascent of the peak. We were Dries Nijsen, leader, Ton van den Boogaard, Rudolf de Koning, Mathieu van Rijswick and I. We reached Base Camp at 3700 meters on July 15 and Camp I at 4800 meters on July 18. From there we climbed a shorter route to the right of the 1964 attempt to get to the ridge at 6000 meters, where it joined the Polish route of 1979. Because of heavy snowfall, it was not until July 30 that Camp II was placed at 5500 meters. Camp III was established on August 3 at 6350 at the end of the difficulties. Up to there we had fixed 800 meters of rope. Then our luck changed. The weather went bad. Camp I was destroyed by an ice avalanche. Camp II disappeared under heavy snow. Nijsen got cerebral edema. It was not until August 14 that we reached Camp III again. Van Rijswick lost his pack and I suffered from continuous nausea. Van de Boogaard and de Koning moved under the summit pyramid as the Poles had to the southwest ridge and on August 17 reached the summit (7788 meters, 25,550 feet).

ROBERT ECKHARDT, *Koninklijke Nederlandse Alpen Vereniging*

P 19,200 Between Bualtar and Barpu Glaciers. Our expedition was composed of Colonel Richard H. Hardie, Captain John James F. Farquharson, Lieutenant Peter Robson, Lance Corporal Anthony Williams, Troopers Stephen Williams, Simon Prince and Ulrich Romf and me as leader. Our objective was an unnamed peak of 19,200 feet (5852 meters) in the Rakaposhi Range of the Karakoram. [The mountain climbed lies 16 miles due west of Rakaposhi. It is just south of a peak which is shown on *Baltit* NJ 43-14 Series U502 of the US Army Map Service as being 19,625 feet (5982 meters) high. On many other maps, however, the altitude of the latter peak is given as 5669 meters (18,600 feet). The peak climbed may therefore be somewhat lower than 19,200 feet.—*Editor.*] All British members reached the summit via the northwest ridge. Base Camp was established at 14,000 feet on July 3 just below the snout of the Koro Glacier. The route to Camp I bypassed the glacier by contouring across snowfields on the northwest side of the glacier. Camp I was placed on July 6 at 16,000 feet on the bend of the Koro Glacier. Camp II, a snowcave at 18,200 feet, was placed above two icefalls on July 8. We put in 600 feet of fixed rope in the upper icefall. From there we climbed 200 feet to the north col and then followed the northwest ridge, steep in places, to the top. The summit was reached on July 13 by Hardie and Prince, on July 14 by Farquharson, S. and A. Williams and on July 15 by Robson, Romf and me.

ALISTAIR M. ROXBURGH, *Lieutenant, Queens Dragoon Guards*

Diran Attempt and Tragedy. Seven Japanese led by Y. Yaezu had hoped to climb Diran (7257 meters, 23,810 feet) by its north ridge. On July 20 R. Iida disappeared between the 5000-meter col on the north ridge and 5400-meter Camp III. The expedition was called off.

Yakshin Gardin Sar. Iñaki Aldaya, Alfredo Zabalza, Tomás Miguel and I left Pasu on June 6. We reached Base Camp in six days with 13 very good porters. We used the same Base Camp and the same route as the 1984 Austrian party. The first attempt ended at 6400 meters due to lack of food, bad weather and fatigue. We reached the summit (7530 meters, 24,705 feet) on July 9 on the second try from camp at 6500 meters after three bivouacs. We needed two more for descent in bad weather. The main problems were the snow and the difficulty. We used the fixed rope of previous parties. We suffered serious frostbite and several of us have lost toes and fingers.

ALEJANDRO ARRANZ, *Spain*

Shani, Naltar Valley. Guy Muhlemann and I, members of our Scots expedition, on August 14 reached the summit of Shani (5800 meters, 19,029 feet), near Gilgit, in the Karakoram. Base Camp was situated at 3750 meters below the east side of the mountain. The route climbed a glacier below the north face to reach the west ridge. It would be a suitable descent for anyone contemplating an ascent of any of the excellent and difficult lines on the south or north sides of the mountain. On August 19 Dairena Gaffney, Sally Macintyre and we two climbed Sentinel Peak (5260 meters, 17,257 feet) at the head of the Naltar valley.

ROGER D. EVERETT, *Alpine Climbing Group*

Chiring Attempt and Tragedy. A Japanese expedition led by T. Shigetani established Base Camp at 4460 meters on the Chiring Glacier on June 3. Camps I and II were placed at 5050 and 5560 meters. On June 25 H. Kanda was killed when he fell into a crevasse below Camp I. The expedition was abandoned. Chiring is 7090 meters or 23,262 feet.

Shimshal Valley Climbs and Tragedy. Six Irish Mountaineers, Margaret Magennis, Dawson Stelfox, John Armstrong, Willie Brown-Kerr, Jenny Clark and I, visited the Malangutti Glacier in the Shimshal valley in July to attempt peaks up to 6000 meters, which require no permit. We established Base Camp on July 6 at 3200 meters and Advance Base three days later at 4100 meters in the Madhil valley, a subsidiary of the Malangutti. An attempt by Stelfox, Brown-Kerr and me on July 12 on the north ridge of unclimbed Shifkitin Sar (c. 5800 meters) was repulsed by dangerous snow conditions above the subsidiary 5300-meter peak. All members but Armstrong, who was suffering from altitude sickness, easily ascended a 5200-meter peak to the north of the col previously visited by Venables and Renshaw in 1984. Magennis, Stelfox and I continued via friable rock scrambling to a second 5200-meter peak on the same ridge, returning to the col by the same route. Further climbing was ended by bad weather. A mid-Wales expedition arrived at Base Camp as we left. Two of their members fell on the descent after a successful ascent of Ardver Sar (c. 6400 meters). Dave Robbins died and Chris Clark lay for ten days with two broken ribs while the team summoned a rescue helicopter. The delay occurred because "trekking" parties are not required to lodge a $4000 deposit in Islamabad for such a situation and the authorities refuse to send out a helicopter until they see your dollars.

PAULA TURLEY,* *Dalraida Climbing Club, Ireland*

Lupghar Sar East Attempt. We went from the Shimshal River to the Momhil Glacier, hoping to try the east ridge of Lupghar East (7200 meters), but there were dangerous hanging glaciers on the ridge. We decided to try the climb by the col between Lupghar Sar East and Dut Sar (6858 meters). We reached Base Camp on the Momhil Glacier at 4200 meters on July 5. Camp I was placed on July 10 on a little glacier on the north side of the east ridge. On July 17 we made camp below the couloir. On August 1 we tried to climb the final 150-meter-high snow wall below the col but failed. The climb was abandoned. We were Miss Ihoko Sasaki, Miss Miyuki Tanaka, Yoshio Maruyama, Osamu Kagaya and I as leader.

HIDEO ODASHIMA, *Akita Climbers Club, Japan*

P 6931 and P 6572, Batura Glacier. [P 6931 lies at the head of the Batura Glacier four kilometers northeast of Kampire Dior. The Italians give it an altitude of 7016 meters, derived from a Chinese glaciological survey, but the official altitude is 6931 meters or 22,740 feet—*Editor.*] Our 14-man expedition of which I was the leader began the long approach march from Passu with 178 porters on July 3. We got over the first part of a tedious icefall on the Batura Glacier on July 10 and placed Base Camp there at 4450 meters. Without wasting time, we began to reconnoiter the south side of P 6931. On July 11 we set up

---

* Recipient of a Vera Watson-Alison Chadwick Onyszkiewicz award.

Camp I at 4950 meters beyond a second icefall. After a snowfall, Camp II was set up on July 15 at 5400 meters above a third icefall, which was bypassed on the right. This was at the foot of the south face. Domenico Alessandri, Antonio Tansella, Fernando Di Fabrizio and Lucio De Sanctis on July 17 moved up the face to establish Camp IIIa. Alessandri and Tansella got to 6100 meters and descended to 5900 meters to camp, but bad weather put an end to the attempt. A second try started on July 27. Alessandri, Antonio Capassi and Domenico Mancinelli set out from Camp II on July 29, climbing up the south face toward the west ridge. The snow began to get soft, the slope steepened and there were sections of blue ice covered with loose snow. They gained the ridge at 6500 meters but found the knife-edged ridge badly corniced and with rock towers and bare ice. They gave up only 400 meters from the summit. Tansella and Giulio Sampietro decided to take a quick look at the north side of the mountain. Carrying a light camp, they bypassed the fourth icefall by climbing a steep couloir on the foot of the west ridge and placed Camp IIIb on the glacier at 6000 meters northwest of the summit. On August 1 they crossed the glacier in a northerly direction and climbed to a 6150-meter col in the ridge which runs west from the north ridge of P 6931 and then rises beyond the col to a beautiful snow peak of 6572 meters (21,561 feet). The two climbers continued up the snow-and-ice east ridge of P 6572, overcoming some 65° pitches and were on top at 10:45 A.M. Informed by radio, Capassi, Mancinelli and Alessandri left Base Camp and bivouacked halfway up the fourth icefall and climbed to Camp IIIb the next day. On August 3, these three plus Tansella set out. At 7:30 they reached the crest of the north ridge, overcoming bare ice, unconsolidated snow and mixed terrain with some 60° pitches. After a halt at a 6700-meter col, they continued along the long ridge and got to the summit of P 6931 at 10:30 A.M. They left the top at one o'clock. At four o'clock at 6600 meters a huge mass of rock broke off 40 meters above them. Mancinelli was struck and his left femur was broken. Luckily he was well anchored. Unable to establish radio contact with Base Camp, Tansella descended to Camp II. Alessandri and Capassi immobilized Mancinelli's leg as best they could and evacuated him to 6300 meters, where they had to bivouac. With heroic efforts by all members, Mancinelli was evacuated to 5500 meters, where he was picked up by helicopter. [This account had to be somewhat condensed.]

LUIGI BARBUSCIA, *Club Alpino Italiano*

Batura I and Haramosh Attempts. There were two unsuccessful Polish expeditions, one to Batura I led by Jerzy Tillak and the other Haramosh led by Jacek Bruzdowiez. Details are not known.

Maidon Sar, Batura Group, 1985. From Karimabad, Kike de Pablos and I first ascended with two porters the Ultar Gorge, hoping to explore possible routes on Ultar and Bojohaghur Duan Asir. After three days of exploring very complicated terrain of rock needles, waterfalls and séracs, we descended to

Karimabad, convinced there were too many falling stones, séracs and avalanches. We did climb a minor 5900-meter (19,350-foot) peak on the ridge that descends to the southwest from Bojohaghur Duan Asir. We then went to Pasu and ascended the Batura Glacier to the junction with the Rupur Glacier. The north faces of the Batura chain offer faces of 3000 to 4000 meters with no alpine-style possibilities. We again descended to Pasu from where, with three porters, we ascended to camp at 4000 meters on the Pasu Glacier. In four days we climbed by its east ridge Maidon Sar (6600 meters, 21,654 feet), which lies on the ridge between the Pasu and Batura Glaciers. (It is the second peak to the east of Pasu Peak. A shepherd told us what the peak is called.) We bivouacked once at 5100 meters and twice at 5900 meters and reached the summit on August 13, 1985. We next made an attempt on the east ridge of Shispare (7611 meters, 24,971 feet), which we reached by a spur on the north. We had to withdraw because of bad weather after bivouacs at 4300 and 5500 meters. We finally explored from the village of Gulmit the approaches to Shispare from the southeast from the Ghulkin Glacier and also the Baltbar valley, which leads to the southwest face of Lupghar Sar. Its western summit (7010 meters, 22,999 feet) is unclimbed and offers a magnificent route on its southwest spur.

JOSÉ LUIS ZULOAGA, *Bizkaiko Expedizioa, Spain*

Sangemar Mar, Southwest Face Attempt. Our Belgian expedition to Sangemar Mar ("The Shining Mountain") had as members, Jean-Claude LeGros, Marcel Charlier, Bertrand Borrey, Marc Debaecke, Vincent Dewaele, Albert Decremer, André Menu, Jean-Claude Coppenole, Jean-Jacques Clayeman, Jean-Phillippe Perikel, Guido Klinkenberg, Sorella Acosta, Madeleine Loret, Evelyne Felix and me as leader. From the village of Aliabad we had a three-day approach along the Hasanabad Glacier and then the Muchichul Glacier. Hiring porters in Aliabad was easy. We got to Base Camp on July 7 at the abandoned village of Gaimeling at 3600 meters. We quickly established Advance Base on July 9 at the foot of the glacier at 4450 meters. Camp I was placed on a narrow ridge at 5000 meters on July 12, Camps II and III on a snow plateau at 5500 and 5800 meters on July 14 and 17. This took us to the foot of the principal difficulties. From the moment we started real climbing, we realized that the snow conditions were far from good. The monsoon was coming; the temperature was too high, the snow was soft and the avalanches incessant. On July 18 we were forced back to Base, where we were trapped for ten days. On the night of July 24 a fall of enormous rocks caused great damage in Base Camp, luckily injuring only one person. Finally good weather returned. After finding Camps I, II and III completely destroyed, we set up Camp IV at 6000 meters. We set out for a try on the summit (7050 meters, 23,130 feet) on July 28 but the bad snow and the numerous avalanches obliged us to turn back. On a scree slope above Advance Base, one of us fell breaking four ribs. He was helicoptered to Gilgit.

JACQUES COLLAER, *Club Alpin Belge*

Ultar II Attempts. Our expedition consisted of Japanese Masahiko Fujimori, Masaaki Mori, Satoru Miyashita, Kazuo Kishi, Shigeo Furuhata, Ken Takahashi, Kiyohiko Sugimoto and me as leader, Pakistanis Tufail, deputy leader, Raja and Mansoor, and American George Smith. First we tried the north face from the Ghulkin Glacier. We left Gulmit on May 30, went via Gulkin and placed Base Camp at 3150 meters on May 31. From 3350 to 4050 meters there was an icefall, where we fixed rope. We had a relay camp at 3900 meters in the icefall, established on June 7. On June 10 two members and I occupied Camp I on the plateau above the icefall. A large avalanche attacked our tent and we lost equipment and food, rope, boots, ladders, etc. We decided to withdraw from this route. On June 18 we went to Gulmit and moved to Kalimabad by tractor and jeep. Again we approached from Kalimabad with 30 porters the south face of Ultar II, which is 7388 meters (24,240 feet) high. We placed Base Camp at 4120 meters on June 21. Two days later we established Camp I at 4875 meters. We climbed over a 5060-meter peak to gain the plateau at 4875 meters. We made a higher camp on June 26. We tried two routes on the rock face from there but the route was too dangerous because of falling stones and ice. We stopped climbing on July 2 after having reached 5500 meters.

TOSHIO NARITA, *Mitokoshu, Japan*

Nanga Parbat, Diamir Face. Our original objective was a new route on Nanga Parbat, the route attempted by Mummery on the Diamir Face. Persistent bad weather and observation of the numerous avalanches on the lower part of the face made us decide to climb the normal route on the Diamir Face. However, above Camp IV in the Bazhin Basin, we climbed to the summit by the variant followed by the Basques Zuloaga and Kike de Pablo in 1983. From Camp IV the route goes horizontally south to a point just below the summit to climb directly up snow slopes oriented west. We were Dr. Juan Caridad, Rafael Vidaurre, Julio Muñoz, Moisés García and I as leader. Camp I was at 4950 meters at the foot of a rock spur to the right of the Kinshofer Icefield, protected from avalanches. Camp II at 6200 meters was on an ice ridge below rocks and very airy. Camp III was finally placed at 6650 meters on an ice platform, moved down slightly from a rock-and-ice spur. Camp IV was at 7250 meters in the Bazhin Basin. The first summit attempt on August 5 was made by Italians Giambisi, De Stefani and Martini and by me, but after four hours we were driven back by weather and bad snow conditions. We returned to Base Camp. On August 11 members of all three expeditions set out again. We were at Camp IV on the 14th. On August 15 García, Vidaurre and I and Italians De Stefani and Martini got to the summit at three P.M. after twelve hours of climbing. Visibility was poor; it was windy and cold. One Italian and four of the Benelux climbers who had started with us did not get to the top, although on the 16th three of the Benelux expedition made it.

MIGUEL GÓMEZ, *Valencia, Spain*

Nanga Parbat. Our Benelux expedition had as members Belgians Jan Vanhees, Lut Vivijs and Pascale Noel (the latter two are ladies), Luxemburger Eugène Berger and me from the Netherlands. In mid-June Vanhees, Vivijs and I traveled to the Swat valley, hoping to climb Falakser (5918 meters) above the village of Kalam. It proved very difficult, mainly because of the aggressive attitude of the local people. To avoid trouble, we had to ask permission and police protection at Madyan. Although we reached 5250 meters on the north ridge, the route by which the mountain had previously been climbed, the snow conditions were bad and the ridge badly corniced. On June 20 we returned to Kalam. On July 4 we started the approach march to Nanga Parbat. On July 7 we got to Base Camp at 4150 meters at the far end of the Diamir valley. From July 13 to 15 we climbed to 5000 meters on the Mazeno ridge. From July 17 to 21 we made a second acclimatization trip on Ganalo Peak but were stopped at 5750 meters by bad weather. On July 28, after bad weather, we installed Camp I on Nanga Parbat. On July 29 we climbed the Löw couloir to Camp II. After more bad weather, on August 2, 3 and 4 we went to Camps I, II and III, lay over in III in bad weather on the 5th, and continued to Camp IV on August 6, still in bad weather. We descended to Base Camp. On August 11 we started up again and were back in Camp IV at 7200 meters on August 14. On August 15 eleven climbers (Italians and Spanish were also active on the mountain) headed for the summit. The three of us and one Italian returned because of cold and sickness, but Berger kept on with Spaniards Miguel Gómez, Rafael Vidaurre and Moisés García and Italians Fausto De Stefani and Sergio Martini. Berger had to turn back from near the summit but the Italians and Spaniards reached the top. Vanhees, Vivijs and I decided to make another attempt. We left Camp IV at 10:30 P.M. on August 15 under a bright moon and in fine weather. After twelve hours of continuous climbing we reached the summit at 10:30 A.M. on August 16. The next day we got back to Base Camp.

HANS LANTERS, *Koninklijke Nederlandse Alpen Vereniging*

Nanga Parbat. After a four-day approach, on June 20 Italians Sergio Martini, Fausto De Stefani, Almo Giambisi and Carlo Claus got to Base Camp at 4200 meters at the foot of the Diamir Face. Despite bad weather, they established Camps I and II at 4950 and 6000 meters. They prepared the route along with a Spanish expedition. The Diamir route is steep up to 7000 meters, where they placed Camp IV in the first days of August before bad weather drove them down. On August 13 all but Claus, who was 60 years old and had not acclimatized well, were back in Camp IV. An attempt on the 14th failed in deep snow. They were joined by Spaniards Gómez, Vidaurre and García at the high camp. All six set out on August 15. Giambisi had to turn back early in the cold and he did not escape frostbite. The other five reached the summit of Nanga Parbat. [Strangely enough, Italian accounts do not mention the Benelux expedition, which was on the mountain at the same time.]

Nanga Parbat and Rakaposhi Attempts. A Japanese expedition led by Seishi Wada failed to climb the Rupal Face of Nanga Parbat. They had previously failed on Rakaposhi. Details are missing.

Nanga Parbat Attempt. A seven-member Polish party, led by Kazimierz Malczyk, set up Base Camp on August 4 below the 1962 Diamir Face route. A week later Camp III had been established at 6900 meters. Unfortunately, on August 13 the weather changed for the worse. They tried five times to reach Camp III again but could not. During 49 days on the mountain, only nine could be used for climbing.

ZBIGNIEW KOWALEWSKI, *Klub Wysokogórski, Warsaw*

Mazeno Peak Attempt on Northwest Face. José Luis Zuloaga, Kike de Pablo and I attempted a new route on Mazeno Peak (7120 meters, 23,360 feet) on the Diamir side of Nanga Parbat. We climbed alpine-style from July 29 to August 6. We failed to climb the final 200 meters because of very bad weather. The difficult rock-and-ice route rose from 4300 meters. The descent was made with thirty-six 60-meter rappels.

ALBERTO POSADA, *Federación Vasca de Montaña, Spain*

Tirich Mir Attempts. This season's unusually poor weather and associated dangerous conditions in northwest Pakistan also affected Tirich Mir (7708 meters, 25,290 feet), where our expedition of Steve Callen, leader, Mike Aughey, Dave Harries, Steve Hart, our only New Zealander, Dave Wilson, Mike Woolridge, Hilary Young and I were attempting the west ridge. Porter rates were high. The three-day approach from Shagrom now has a standard rate of 530 rupees per porter. However, their generous nature and hospitality more than compensated and we were impressed by their honesty and reliability under adverse conditions. Base Camp was reached on August 11 in heavy snow and from the 14th to the 24th, during the only period of settled weather, everybody established food and equipment dumps at 6600 meters, having camped at 5400, 5950 and 6300 meters. Some then climbed Dirgol Zom (6778 meters, 22,238 feet) by both the north face and the east ridge. The west ridge of Tirich Mir was inspected to 6800 meters. On August 30, after a short spell of poor weather, Woolridge and I left Base Camp, followed a day later by Harries and Hart. We reached our Camp IV site near the dumps after three days. A sudden, prolonged and heavy snowfall buried our tents overnight and we moved them to the safest place, protected by a small overhanging sérac barrier. In the subsequent days, we were unable to reach our food and gear. We were avalanched three times and were finally able to make an arduous three-day descent to Base, which we reached on September 8. On September 14, while some members began the walk out, Harries and I started reascending in improving weather. It took five days to reach Camp IV. Unable to find equipment or food under five or six meters of compact avalanche debris, we were beginning to move up for a quick attempt when bad weather struck again. After two days of snow and tem-peratures of − 30° C, a break allowed another tiring descent to a completely deserted Base Camp. We made the four-day walk out to Shagrom, which we reached, rather hungry, on September 26. Two expeditions were given permis-sion for Tirich Mir prior to us. The jeep road from Chitral is particularly hair-raising and the Italian Gervasutti Memorial Expedition, led by Franco Ribetti, failed to reach the roadhead when their jeep went off the road, killing the liaison officer and Dr. Alessandro Nacamuli. The West German team, led by Siegfried Ludwig, abandoned their efforts a little below our Camp I due to the conditions.

LINDSAY GRIFFIN, *Alpine Climbing Group*

China

Gyala Peri. In 1985 the Himalayan Association of Japan sent two men to reconnoiter Gyala Peri, which lies just north of the great bend of the Yalu-Tsangpo (Brahmaputra). In 1986 an expedition of six returned with Kazuo Tobita as their leader. The approach was difficult with constant rain and danger-ous river crossings. They set up Base Camp at 3200 meters on September 16. Their route was the west face and then the south ridge. Climbing began on September 22. Advance Base was placed at 4200 meters at the foot of the west face on September 25. Camps I and II were established on October 3 and 11 at 5000 and 5650 meters. They gained the south ridge at 6000 meters and placed Camps III and IV on it at 6300 and 6750 meters on October 19 and 21. Two unsuccessful summit tries were made on October 29 and 30. On October 31 Yoshio Ogata, Yasuhiro Hashimoto and Hirotaka Imamura got to the summit (7151 meters, 23,461 feet). Further details and photographs appear in *Iwa To Yuki* Annual 1986 and N° 120 of February, 1987.

Kula Kangri (Künla Kangri*). The Kobe University Scientific and Moun-taineering Expedition to Tibet consisted of 25 Japanese, i.e. 12 climbers, eight scientists, three TV cameramen, a newspaper reporter and myself as leader, and 17 Chinese, i.e. five climbers who helped with high-altitude transport, four scientists from the Academia Sinica and others (liaison officer, interpreters, drivers). In all we were 42 members. We arrived at Base Camp at 4400 meters north of the mountain on March 17. Advance Base was at 5300 meters and Camp I at 5700 meters just below the west ridge. We climbed a steep ice wall up to Camp II at 6200 meters on the ridge and Camp III was at 6800 meters. A 70-meter-high rock wall rises in the upper part of the ridge. Fortunately we could traverse south to a small snow couloir. Camp IV at 7100 meters was dug out of the snow slope. On April 21 C. Itani, J. Sakamoto, H. Ozaki and

---

* According to the Swiss authority, Professor Augusto Gansser, the name of the peak is Künla Kangri. However, local people near Base Camp pronounced it Kula Kangri. The col where we had Camp I was used as the shortest route to Bhutan. We found there a prayer flag and the skeleton of a yak.—*K.H.*

PLATE 78
Photo by Kazumasa Hirai
KULA KANGRI.

E. Ohtani reached the summit (7554 meters, 24,784 feet) at 4:15 P.M. The next day T. Morinaga and H. Hasegawa also climbed to the top. The scientists left Base Camp on April 15 to work towards Chengdu. They were the first foreigners to work first around Base Camp and then on their 2800-kilometer trip back to Chengdu. They did research in entomology, botany, geology, geomorphology, political sociology, cultural anthropology, etc.

KAZUMASA HIRAI, *Kobe University, Japan*

Karjiang, Kula Kangri Group. This peak lies just northeast of Kula Kangri. Under the leadership of Nobuhiro Shingo, six climbers of the Himalayan Association of Japan traveled from Lhasa to Monda. They headed up the glacier on September 9. At first they tried to reach the higher south summit (7221 meters) but it was too difficult and so they turned to the central summit, which was slightly lower (7216 meters, 23,675 feet). On October 13 they set up Camp III at 7000 meters. On October 14 leader Shingo, Kenji Tomoda and Hiroshi Iwasaki climbed to the summit. There was some overhanging rock near the top and the wind was very strong. On October 16 Tsutomu Miyazaki and Akinori Hosaka also reached the top. More details appear in *Iwa To Yuki,* N° 120 of February 1987.

Anye Maqen Attempt. Late August found our group of eight American climbers, Karl Gerdes, Jerry Tinling, Tony Watkin, John Byrne, Bruce Mc-Cubbery, Jay McCubbery, Rich Henke, and me winding our way toward Anye Maqen through the high pasture lands of the Tibetan plateau. We spent much of our time exchanging pleasantries with the nomadic Tibetan families we passed, drinking a hard white liquor in their huge Yak hair tents where the customs included checking all guns at the door as you entered. Base Camp was established at 4175 meters, on the wrong side of a river that in the late afternoon became almost unfordable due to glacial melt. This led to some adventurous crossings and bareback yak riding, with Bruce taking the only real dunking. With time short, we quickly established a high camp below the ridge first climbed by Galen Rowell and party several years ago. (*A.A.J.,* 1982, pages 88-92.) Six of us then reached a wind-swept ridge at 5500 meters and spent a long night holding down the tents against a storm that lasted well into the next day. Late in the afternoon Karl Gerdes, Rich Henke, and I crossed a short corniced arête to establish a bivouac in a crevasse just below the face leading to the summit plateau. Morning dawned clear, but by noon Rich and Karl were pinned down by a lightning storm at 5800 meters, and retreated. This was to be our high point, as storms continued for the next two days. One last rodeo-ride river crossing, and we began the long trip home.

BROCK A. WAGSTAFF

Yulong Shan Attempt. Imposing as it may appear from the Yunnan town of Lijiang, Yulong Shan (Jade Dragon Peak) presents no special technical challenge to explain its 50-year virginity and rebuff of four attempts. Only the weather guards it. So far, that has been enough. In April Mick Deiro, Dan Batwinas, Andy Fried, Russ Faure-Brac, Andrew Palmer, Kenny Moser and I as leader threaded the pony carts, roto-tiller-mobiles, bicycles and "honey wagons" for three days from Kunming to Lijiang. A two-hour truck ride from Lijiang brought us to the Base Camp established by the American team in October 1985. Racing on an absurdly tight climbing schedule, we set up Base Camp, carried packs up a forested cow trail to the snowline and established Advance Base, all on the first day. Though crippling bronchial diseases struck one member after another, the supply carrying continued. Good weather allowed rapid progress. University of Chicago anthropologist Chas McKann, studying the Naxi culture near Lijiang, joined our effort. With Glacier Camp established, Deiro and Batwinas made a powerful push to the long summit ridge and established Ridge Camp. Several days later they made a make-or-break try, attempting to cover the entire distance from Glacier Camp in a day. Fighting ill health and deteriorating weather, they got to within 500 vertical feet of the summit before pitching a small tent on the ridge. Though the next day was clear and the summit less than two hours away, they were so spent that they felt their only choice was to return. Fried and Faure-Brac tried next, hauling heavy loads to Ridge Camp. A major weather change came in. Snowstorms scoured the ridge and visibility dropped to 100 feet. With our tight climbing schedule coming to an end, Palmer, McKann and I left Glacier Camp the next day for Ridge Camp. Spindrift avalanches raked the route, drenching us in icy showers. Visibility dropped to 50 feet. We found Fried and Faure-Brac wisely bivouacked at Ridge Camp. While they rappelled and hiked back to Glacier Camp, we took up residence at Ridge Camp. We awoke to the same howling snowstorm and minimal visibility. On this, our last climbing day, we turned back.

ERIC S. PERLMAN

Ningchin Kangsha. Ningchin Kangsha, which used to be given by G.O. Dyhrenfurth as Nodzin Kangsan with an altitude of 7252 meters, lies southwest of Lhasa on the highway from Lhasa to Kathmandu, two kilometers from the Lalo La. It was climbed by a Tibetan Mountaineering Association team. They had Base Camp and Camps I and II at 5000, 6100 and 6900 meters. Twelve members, including three experienced Tibetan climbers, Sang Zhu, Pemba and Jia Bu, reached the summit (7191 meters, 23,593 feet) on April 28. It took them only 20 days to climb the mountain from the time they unloaded supplies alongside the highway. This peak was attempted in 1985 by a Japanese party form Oita Prefecture, but they were stopped at 6600 meters on the southwest ridge.

SADAO TAMBE, *A.A.C.* and *Himalayan Association of Japan*

Nianqintanggula. A 12-person expedition from Tohoku University in Japan was led by Mario Kuzunushi. They left Lhasa on March 25 and traveled about 100 kilometers on the highway and another four off of it to place Base Camp at

4800 meters at Panyuto. Advance Base was established on April 5 at 5300 meters near the frozen lake, Panitsuo. Nianqintanggula has a row of subsidiary peaks to its southeast of 7111, 7117 and 7046 meters. From Advance Base, P 6053 on the south side of the first was climbed for acclimatization. The party ascended the south glacier after crossing the frozen lake and on April 8 established Camp I at 5700 meters on a branch glacier. On the 17th Camp II was first placed at 6230 meters where the route reaches the west ridge and then on the 20th moved up to the west-ridge col at 6270 meters. The weather deteriorated in the second half of April. On May 3 a temporary Camp III was set up on the west ridge at 6600 meters and that was moved up three days later to 6800 meters. Rope was fixed to the base of the summit rock wall to 7000 meters. On May 8 Hiroshi Naganuma, Yusake Maruyama and Michiharo Wada overcame the UIAA IV + rock to reach the summit (7162 meters, 23,495 feet according to the Japanese although an altitude of 7088 meters, 23,584 feet has been given us by the Chinese). [It is not clear to the Editor where this peak is located.]

Everest North Face Attempt. Our expedition consisted of Todd Bibler, Carlos Buhler, Dana Coffield, Mark Jennings, Douglas Kelley, Andrew Lapkass, Michael Lehner, Sandy Stewart, Ann Whitehouse, Brinton Young and me as leader. We reached 7775 meters in our attempt to make the second ascent of the great couloir on the north face of Everest. Bad weather, avalanche danger and exhaustion delayed and then ended our attempt to place Camp VI and to try for the summit. We got to Base Camp at 5200 meters at the foot of the Rongbuk Glacier by jeep and truck on March 19. Camp I at 5675 meters was established a week later and Camps II and III at 6000 and 6150 meters on the main Rongbuk north of the north face by late March. The route from the foot of the face to Camp IV at 7150 meters was obstructed by a bergschrund at the start and made more difficult by 2000 feet of blue ice. Spring conditions differed considerably from the styrofoam-like snow in the fall of 1984 when the Australians made the first direct ascent of the couloir. We spent much time fixing 18 ropes before occupying Camp IV on April 19 and another three weeks putting up Camp V at 7775 meters. After five attempts to establish Camp VI, our permitted time expired and the team turned back, reaching Base Camp on May 24 and Lhasa two days later.

JOSEPH E. MURPHY

Everest Attempt. Our expedition hoped to climb Everest by the North Col route without high-altitude porters or artificial oxygen. We were six climbers: Luis Bernardo, Pedro Nicolás, Salvador Rivas, Angel Sánchez, Carlos Soria and I as leader; Dr. Mariano Arrazola, scientist Eduardo M. de Pisón and photographer Tote Trenas. We established Base Camp, Camps I, II, III, and IV at 5150, 6100, 6500, 7050 (on the North Col) and 7600 meters on March 22, 31, April 1, 19 and May 9 respectively. The wind was strong and continuous, making progress difficult near the North Col and nearly impossible above Camp

IV. The wind destroyed tents in various camps and in Camp IV blew away several loads which had been tied down on a platform. Rivas had to quit as he could not acclimatize. We kept on trying to get higher until June 2. Several climbers spent a month and a half above 6500 meters and even 18 days above 7000 meters. We were well acclimatized and hoped to make the summit until the end, but we were prevented by the wind. We made a film and carried out geomorphological and geological studies.

JERÓNIMO LÓPEZ, *Federación Española de Montañismo*

Everest Tragedy, North-Col Route. A Chilean expedition was composed of Claudio Lucero, leader, Rodrigo Jordan, Andrés Marambio, Pedro Bralić, Marcelo Gifferos, Fernando and Cristián Garcia-Huidobro, Pablo Straub and Victor Hugo Trujillo. They were attempting the traditional North-Col route. Tragedy struck on August 16 when the corniced lip of a crevasse on the North Col gave way, triggering an avalanche. Trujillo was buried and died.

XAVIER EGUSKITZA, *Pyrenaica, Bilbao, Spain*

Everest Attempt. During the post-monsoon season, a large climbing and filming party attempted the north ridge of Qomolongma (Everest) via the traditional Rongbuk-East Rongbuk-North Col route. Our objectives were to climb and film the route. We were also to search for traces of Mallory and Irvine. The party reached the Rongbuk Base Camp in two groups; half the team travelled across China and Tibet via Chengdu and Lhasa, while the other half, with the bulk of the supplies, reached Rongbuk via Kathmandu and the Friendship Highway. Climbing above Base Camp began in the last week of August. The East Rongbuk approach has traditionally been accomplished in three stages above Base Camp. Recent expeditions, however, have reduced this part of the route to two stages, with a single camp between Base and the established Advance Base site at 21,500 feet below the North Col. Advance Base was established on September 21, and the Col (23,200 feet) was reached a day later. At this point the good weather of late summer began to deteriorate, and the next two months gave us a cycle of increasingly unstable weather. September was marked by intermittent storms with significant snowfall, and in October the storms increased, temperatures dropped, and by the third week the high winds characteristic of winter had set in. Climbing was possible during periods of good weather which became shorter and less frequent as the season wore on. The unstable weather increased the instability of the snow on the slopes below the Col, making much greater the avalanche danger which is always present on that section of the route, and further reducing the number of climbing days available to us. Camp V at 25,500 feet was established on September 28 during a break in the weather, and this remained our high point a month later when, on October 23, I made the decision to abandon the attempt. The team left Base Camp on October 29. On October 17, Dawa Nuru Sherpa, of Thame, was struck by a small slab avalanche at about 22,000 feet while descending from the North Col to Advance Base. He was swept a short distance and died of injuries sustained in the fall. Rescuers reached the body approximately 40 minutes after the accident occurred, and carried his body down to Ronguk for cremation, which was done three days later in the ruins of the nunnery under the direction of lamas from the monastery. While we were prevented by the weather from reaching the summit, we substantially accomplished our filming objectives, producing footage for a U.S. film featuring the efforts of the women members of the team (Mutual of Omaha's *Spirit of Adventure,* shown as an ABC sports special on February 15, 1987) and footage for an historical film on the early attempts on Everest (Arcturus Motion Pictures; co-produced by BBC — to be shown in the autumn of 1987). Exploration of the early routes on the mountain was hampered by the heavy snow cover and, ultimately, our inability to reach the upper portion of the north face. The expedition team included: David Breashears (deputy leader), Ken Bailey, George Bell, Mary Kay Brewster, Catherine Cullinane, Donna de Varona, Sue Giller, Eric Green, Tom Holzel, Al Read, Steve Shea, David Swanson, Mike Weis, Jed Williamson, Mike Yager (Americans); Dave Cheesmond, Roger Vernon (Canadians); Alistair MacDonald, Audrey Salkeld (Britons); Sirdar Nawang Yongden and fifteen Sherpas (Nepalese); and me as leader. During our time on the mountain we benefited from close cooperation with the British Northeast Ridge team (Brummie Stokes, leader) with whom we shared the Base, East Rongbuk and Advance Base Camp areas. In Kathmandu, Lhasa, Beijing and on Everest, members of the team represented UNICEF, His Majesty's Government of Nepal and the governments of the Tibetan Autonomous Region and the People's Republic of China, through participation in the "First Earth Run"; a worldwide UNICEF project for children celebrating the International Year of Peace.

ANDREW C. HARVARD

Everest, Northeast-Ridge Attempt. Base Camp at 17,000 feet was reached on August 7 after a seven-hour drive from Xigar along the Friendship Highway and a subsequent dirt track which winds its way past the Rongbuk Monastery. Two weeks were needed before an interim camp at 19,000 feet was established and the yak drivers arrived to start ferrying our three tons of food and equipment up the mountain. Twenty-one yaks were engaged for this movement, which was completed in 21 days. The yak herders were very reliable and unlike other expeditions, we never had a single item stolen or lost. Mo Anthoine, Joe Brown, Paddy Freaney and Bill Barker set up Advance Base at 21,500 feet on the site of two previous northeast-ridge expeditions. We were appalled at the mess we found there and spent two days cleaning it up. Despite poor weather, Camp I at 23,200 feet was established a week ahead of schedule. The long traverse over suspect avalanche-prone ground up to the Ruphu La was avoided by ascending the right edge of a rock buttress some 1525 feet high. This removed two sides of a large triangle and saved many hours of load-carrying. Avalanches and high winds along the ridge forced the team twice to beat a hasty retreat to Base Camp before a snow hole could be placed for Camp II just below the first buttress at 24,000 feet. Two weeks, interspersed with bad weather, were needed to stock the camp and fix ropes to the top of the second buttress. A bold bid to cross the Pinnacles was made by Harry Taylor and Trevor Pilling. Hoping that the weather would improve on October 16, they pushed on up the ridge with 50-pound loads and set up Camp III at 26,200 feet, close to the first steep slope of the Pinnacles. Violent winds hammered the ridge as the pair dug a snow hole to sleep in. The next day the wind grew to hurricane strength, creating a $-70°$ F wind-chill factor. Progress over the Pinnacles was impossible. They turned back and struggled to safety, forced at times onto all fours by the wind. After a Sherpa with the American expedition was killed whilst descending from the North Col, I decided to abandon the attempt. We were hit by no less than four fierce storms which deposited eight feet of fresh snow, making the climbing too dangerous towards the end. Despite this bad weather, morale and team spirit remained high throughout.

BRUMMIE STOKES, *England*

Everest, The Hornbein Couloir Direct from Tibet. Swiss Erhard Loretan, Nicole Niquille, Jean Troillet, as well as my wife Annie and I from France, arrived on July 17 by jeep and truck from the Nepalese-Tibetan border. Troillet wanted to solo the central pillar between the Hornbein and the Great Couloirs. We put two tents on the Central Rongbuk Glacier at 5800 meters, two hours from the bottom of the north face. After that, we acclimatized on small peaks around Everest, but we did not go onto the north face. At the beginning of August, Loretan injured himself jumping with his parapente (parachute). His ankle was very bad and we were afraid it was broken, but after two weeks he could walk again. Bad weather with snow and clouds went on to the end of August. My wife had to go back to France at the beginning of the month and Niquille left for Switzerland at the end. On August 29 it was clear and cold, perhaps the famous "break" during the monsoon. Troillet decided to join Loretan and me to have a better chance for the summit. We left Advance Base at 5800 meters before midnight to try a route similar to the 1980 Japanese route. Our loads were very light; no tent, no climbing equipment, no rope, one light sleeping bag each, one stove and a half pound of food apiece. During the night and the morning of the 30th, we climbed the broad, 50° couloir, taking turns breaking trail. Happily, the deep snow was stable. After 12 hours we reached 7800 meters. We dug a cave to rest during the afternoon. Just before dark we started for the summit via the Hornbein Couloir. At 8000 meters I was so sleepy that I decided to go back to the snow cave to have another try in the daylight. But I could not find it! I sat in the snow to bivouac without any equipment; we had left the sleeping bags at the cave. There was no wind and so I passed the night without frostbite. Meanwhile Loretan and Troillet climbed the Hornbein Couloir and at 2:30 P.M. on August 31 they reached the summit. I think this may have been the quickest ascent of Everest. Three hours later they reached the cave

PLATE 79

Photo by Pierre Beghin

MOUNT EVEREST from the North.

where I was. And two hours after that they arrived at Advance Base! They glissaded on their backs, with their ice-axes to control their speed. In the night I did make another attempt, but having had little to drink and little sleep, I had to stop at 8300 meters; I began to fall asleep and lose my balance and returned to the cave. The next morning in two hours I reached my skis at the foot of the north face. One half hour later a huge powder-snow avalanche swept the whole couloir. On September 5 we returned to lower Base Camp where the jeep was waiting for us.

PIERRE BEGHIN, *Groupe de Haute Montagne*

Everest Solo Attempt. With my support team of Ruth DeCew, Ed Webster and Kristina Kearney, I arrived at Base Camp at 17,000 feet on July 1. Advance Base Camp was established on July 8 at 20,400 feet on the East Rongbuk Glacier. Between July 12 and August 24 it snowed on the mountain on most days. I first climbed to 23,000 feet on the North Col on August 12 and then followed that by two summit attempts, the last on September 7. I then set up a new Advance Base Camp on the Main Rongbuk Glacier at 19,000 feet. I left there at 9:30 P.M. on September 17 and climbed the Japanese Couloir. In the morning I approached the Hornbein Couloir but abandoned the attempt at 25,300 feet because of the snow conditions.

ROGER MARSHALL, *Unaffiliated*

Everest Hang Gliding. We arrived in Base Camp on September 8, but because of confusion with the Chinese and the yak drivers, we didn't establish Advance Base at 5500 meters until September 16. On the 19th, Camp I was placed at 6000 meters. We began fixing ropes on the west ridge on the 21st, generally following the 1983 Bob Craig route except at the start, where we went on the left side of the crest. On September 24 we put Camp II at 6600 meters just below a prominent rock on the crest. On October 3 we began hauling hang gliders. It took over a week to get a glider to Camp III on the crest of the west shoulder at 7170 meters. On October 5 leader Steve McKinney made a trial flight from 6200 meters down to Camp I, using pre-takeoff oxygen and skis. The pilots were in position on October 11, but high winds prevented attempts from the shoulder. On October 16 we dismantled Camp III and pulled the glider down. Other members included climbers Kim Carpenter, Heidi Benson, Pete Athens, Catherine Freer, Craig Colonica and me and pilots Bob Carter and Larry Tudor.

ANDREW POLITZ

Changtse. A large joint Japanese-Chinese expedition was made up of 17 Japanese, 19 Chinese climbers, five Chinese supporters and three Chinese press members. The Japanese leader was T. Horiuchi. They arrived at Base Camp at 5050 meters on April 23 and placed Advance Base at the confluence of the

Changtse and East Rongbuk Glaciers on April 30. After ascending the Changtse Glacier they climbed the east ridge. After placing a temporary camp at 6200 meters, they established Camp I at 6930 meters on May 8. On May 10 sixteen climbers reached the east ridge at 7100 meters and continued on to the summit (7553 meters, 24,780 feet). The eight Japanese included S. Matsubara, Y. Miyamoto, T. Furuhata, K. Shimakata, Masamitsu Yamada and Makoto Yamada and the eight Chinese included the Tibetan woman Gunsang. A second summit party on May 11 was composed of eight Chinese. The Japanese who were to have been with them had to withdraw to evacuate a climber suffering from high-altitude sickness.

Cho Aui. Cho Aui lies on the Tibetan-Nepalese frontier west of Cho Oyu. The leader of this ten-man Himalayan Association of Japan expedition was Hiroshi Yajima. After approaching via Xigar, they got to Base Camp near the Gyabrag Glacier at 5800 meters on September 21. Camp I was established on the glacier at 6100 meters on September 25. From there they carried out reconnaissance and prepared the route. Beyond the icefall there was a difficult ice face, which took them onto the northwest ridge. They fixed rope to the ridge crest and placed Camp II on the ridge at 6700 meters on the 29th. After a rest at Base Camp, they were back in Camp II. Yukitoshi Endo, Yoshihiro Shikoda, Katsushi Emura and Katso Matsuki left for the summit on October 11, but they had to bivouac at 7200 meters. On October 12 at noon they got to the summit (7350 meters, 24,115 feet). Leader Yajima, Mitsuyoshi Onodera, Osamu Sato, Keiji Ishikawa, Toshio Yamada and Omohaka Okobu reached the top at two P.M. on October 14.

Shisha Pangma. Two groups of Trekking International were on Shisha Pangma, the first composed of Italians and Spaniards led by Alberto Re, the other made up of French, Japanese and Austrians guided by Claude Jaccoux. The weather was terrible and there was much snow. It was not possible to get the yaks to 5400 meters and it was hard work to carry the loads. The first group could not climb above 7000 meters though they pitched three camps. The second group had better weather at the end of August and the beginning of September. On September 10, French climbers Eric Escoffier and Xavier Murillo and Japanese Takashi Ozaki got to the top separately. After more bad weather, Frenchman Michel Vincent on September 19 and Austrians Michael Leuprecht and Josef Oberauer on September 20 reached the summit.

RENATO MORO, *Club Alpino Italiano*

K2, North Ridge Attempt. Our expedition, sponsored by the American Alpine Club, undertook an ascent of the north ridge of K2. The expedition consisted of two parties, a support team of eighteen "porters" and a climbing team of eight climbers: Lance Owens, leader, George Lowe, Alex Lowe, David Cheesmond, Gregg Cronn, Steven Swenson, Catherine Freer, and Choc Quinn.

PLATE 80

Photo by George Lowe

K2 from the North.

The support team, accompanied by two climbers, Quinn and A. Lowe, departed the United States on April 18. They established Base Camp at Shipton's "Sughet Jungal" on May 15. From May 16 until June 3 loads were carried the 29 kilometers from Base Camp to Advance Base at 4975 meters, two kilometers from the foot of the north ridge. Considerable effort was spent cleaning up debris left by the Italian expedition at Base Camp and on the glacier. A lovely camp on the glacier seemed to have been almost intentionally trashed, much to our disgust. On June 3 the remaining six members of the climbing team arrived at Base Camp, and immediately began carrying remaining loads to Advanced Base. The support team departed from the mountain on June 10. On June 13 Camp I was established at 5700 meters beneath a prominent overhanging sérac in the center of the slope to the right of the north ridge. The slope avalanched with every storm, and an occasional larger slide would shower over the overhanging lip of the sérac above the camp, partially burying the two tents below with spindrift. On June 19 Camp II was established on the site of the prior Japanese and Italian camp, at 6600 meters. On June 20 the route was pushed to 7200 meters. This day, we saw members of the British expedition around the corner at about 6800 meters on the west ridge, our only brief contact with anyone else on the mountain. Throughout early June weather had been good, but after the third week of June, a series of storms continually interrupted our progress. The slopes below Camps I and II were avalanche-prone and were avoided for two days after every storm. On July 6, Swenson, G. Lowe and A. Lowe established Camp III at 7600 meters on the site of the Italian camp. Due to storms and high avalanche danger, no further progress was made until July 30, when G. Lowe and A. Lowe broke trail through unconsolidated, waist-deep snow from Camps III to IV at 7950 meters on the north ridge. Exhausted by the effort, they were forced to return to Camp II for a rest day. All members of the expedition carried to Camp III on August 2, and on August 3, A. Lowe, G. Lowe, and Swenson occupied Camp IV for a summit attempt the next morning. At two A.M. on August 4, the summit team awoke to find G. Lowe had developed pulmonary edema, probably a result of his extreme efforts breaking trail in deep snows to Camp IV. Refusing aid, he immediately descended alone to Camp III where oxygen was obtained and his further descent assisted by Freer. A. Lowe and Swenson continued with a summit attempt, but turned back at 8100 meters due to slow progress in poor snow conditions. By that afternoon, another storm had moved in and the entire climbing team had safely descended to Advance Base. On August 12, Freer, Swenson, and Cheesmond departed from Advance Base for another summit bid, again reaching Camp IV when weather deteriorated and forced a final retreat. The entire expedition had departed from Base Camp by August 24. Having chosen not to take a shortwave radio, our expedition had no communication with the outside world between May and late-August. Not until we returned to Kashgar did we learn of the difficulties on the Baltoro, and realize our luck in avoiding any roughly comparable difficulties during our summer on the mountain.

LANCE S. OWENS

P 7167, Kunlun Mountains. Our expedition traveled from Urumqi via Kashgar to the western end of the Kunlun Mountains. Base Camp was some 60 kilometers east of Tansuihai at 5270 meters on the Litang River. This was established on July 20. From there it was still some 25 kilometers to the summit of P 7167. The most difficult part was carrying loads across the Doctor and Zhongfeng Glaciers. Camps I, II and III were placed at 5515, 6160 and 6670 meters on August 3, 10 and 12. Camp III was a snow cave. We climbed up the glacier on the south side to hit the east ridge where we had Camp III. We followed the east ridge to its junction with the south ridge. We fixed rope and prepared the route above Camp III for two days. At nine A.M. on August 16 Shinji Kobayashi, Shuya Nakashima, Tetsuya Baba, Yukimasa Numano and Masanori Sato left for the summit (7167 meters, 23,514 feet). On August 17, the second group, Kunio Obata, Takeshi Murata, Yukiko Kukuzawa, Mitsuhiro Sugawara, Dr. Shigeru Masuyama and I, also successfully reached the summit.

KEIJIRO HAYASAKA, *Tokyo University of Agriculture Alpine Club*

Tuomur or Pik Pobedy Attempt, Tien Shan. We hoped to climb Tuomur, which the Soviets call Pik Pobedy, from the Chinese side. Our Japanese women's expedition was made up of Dr. Shiori Hashimoto, Yuko Kuramatu, Mayuri Yasuhara, Nobuko Yanagisawa, Kiyoko Ishikawa, Yoko Nakamura, Fumie Kimura, Norkio Otuka, Kazuko Bizen and me as leader. There were many glaciers and so finding the right approach was difficult. We placed Base Camp at 3900 meters on July 27. Camps I and II were established at 4800 and 5400 meters on August 1 and 5. On August 13 we had a very big avalanche at 6200 meters. Three of us were carried down 500 meters, but we were unhurt. On the 16th during the night, another avalanche swept three tents away at Camp II at 5400 meters. I was carried into a crevasse and suffered a broken leg. The expedition was given up.

JUNKO TABEI, *Japanese Alpine Club*

Kongur Attempt. Nancey Goforth, Kathy Nilson, Pat Dillingham, Joan Provencher, Nancy FitzSimmons-Bloom, Deb Pranian, Suzanne Hopkins, Carole Petiet and I* traveled to Xinjiang to attempt Kongur (7719 meters, 25,325 feet) during June and July. We were the first American women's expedition granted a permit to climb in China. We hoped to repeat the southwest rib climb, by which the 1981 British expedition made the first and only ascent of Kongur. We arrived at Base Camp at 14,800 feet on June 16. After several days of acclimatization, we began skiing loads up the Corridor Glacier. We used no high-altitude porters. Our liaison officer, Me Me Ti, and interpreter, Su Keren, stayed at Base Camp. Advance Base was established on the Koksel Glacier at 17,000 feet on June 27 and occupied on July 1. By the time Camp I at 19,200

---

* Recipient of a Vera Watson-Alison Chadwick Onyszkiewicz grant.

feet was made, only four of us were able to proceed; the others had a variety of serious respiratory infections. The weather also began to deteriorate with daily snowfall. Camp II at 21,000 feet was established on July 10. FitzSimmons-Bloom, Dillingham, Petiet and I continued to carry loads to Camp II. While we moved up to Camp II for our summit push on July 14, we reluctantly decided to retreat due to bad weather and avalanche conditions. We could not have completed the route in the time remaining.

KATHLEEN GIEL

Mustagh Ata. Our expedition consisting of Ann Smith, Bob Allison, Bob East, Dr. Kent Davidson, Mary Ann Davidson and me arrived at Base Camp at 15,400 feet on July 24. During the next ten days we established five high camps. On August 4 Ann Smith and I made it to the summit from our 21,200-foot High Camp. We had four fairly good days out of 18 on the mountain. Three other teams arrived at Base Camp after us: 19 Italians, 8 Japanese and 4 from Hong Kong. Another American team led by Phil Ershler was scheduled to arrive after we left.

JACK ALLSUP

Mustagh Ata, Approached from Pakistan. From Islamabad on July 25 we headed by bus for the 4960-meter-high Kunjerab Pass on the Pakistani-Chinese frontier. This road has been open to tourists only since May. We got to the Chinese border town of Parali on the 27th and continued with two trucks to the Subashi plateau at 3800 meters. On July 29 we were transported to Base Camp at 4600 meters by 25 camels. Of the 15 climbers on the west side of Mustagh Ata, ten used skis. Camps I and II were placed at 5450 and 6080 meters on July 30 and August 1. The most difficult part of the route was from 5800 to 6600 meters, where we placed Camp III; this was because of crevasses. Two days of storm were followed by stocking of Camp III from August 4 to 7. It then stormed for five days. On August 13 we set out again. On August 15 Beppe Zandonella, Rolando Menardi, Filippo Sala, Libero Pelotti and Giulio Maggi climbed to the summit from Camp III. Camp IV was placed at 7080 meters. On August 17 Daniele Consolini, Natalina Furini, Alberto Foglio, Ettore Nanni and Roberta Faldella reached the top. Eliana Palazzi, Rossalio Patuelli, Luciano Pasquali and I, who were without skis, failed to reach the summit.

ARTURO BERGAMASCHI, *Club Alpino Italiano*

USSR

Pamir Mountains. The yearly Soviet International Mountaineering Camps have become more and more popular. Last summer climbers from 18 countries participated, 45 climbers from Switzerland, 42 from the USA and 34 from Bulgaria. High quality routes and a general rise in climbing standards typified the activity. A number of teams climbed Pik Kommunizma. Perhaps the most notable foreign ascent was of the 2500-meter-high south face of Pik Kommunizma by five Bulgarians between July 27 to August 2.

JÓZEF NYKA, *Editor, Taternik, Poland*

Pik Kommunizma, Pamirs. With successes on the 7000-meter peaks in the Pamirs now becoming commonplace, I have only two reasons to report our experiences. The first is to emphasize how accommodating the Soviets have been in assisting foreign mountaineers. For example, we had helicopter drops of food and gear at two high locations on Pik Kommunizma. The second is to point out that one has plenty of company on the peaks: about 350 climbers from 19 nations in three different Base Camps. According to our Soviet hosts this year had the worst weather since 1968. Nevertheless, from our Base Camp, 43 out of 80 climbers achieved the summit of Pik Kommunizma. There was one fatality, a Colorado man from high-altitude pulmonary edema. Our party consisted of John Ellsworth, Terry Moore, Mike Renta and me. Arriving at the main Base Camp of Achik-Tash at 3750 meters, we did an afternoon climb of Pik Petrovsky (4820 meters, 15,814 feet). Two days later we flew by helicopter to the Fortambek Base Camp at 4000 meters, where we joined 76 other international climbers plus 15 Soviets. For conditioning, we made an overnight climb of White Rock Peak (5100 meters, 16,733 feet). Moore, Ellsworth and I continued on to the summit of Pik Umarov (5224 meters, 17,139 feet). Two days later, on July 21, we turned our attention to the Burevestnik Rib route of Pik Kommunizma. Following the Soviet style of acclimatization, we first climbed to Camp I at 5100 meters and the next day to Camp II at 6000 meters. On the 25th we left much of our gear and food and returned to Fortambek for rest. On July 28 we ascended to Camp II. During the night, Ellsworth developed stomach problems and had to withdraw. Renta, Moore and I continued across the 12-kilometer Pamir Ice Plateau to Camp III at 6100 meters. On July 31 we reached Camp V at 6900 meters and on August 1 set out for the summit of Pik Kommunizma, traversing over Dushanbe Peak (6900 meters, 22,638 feet) on the way. Moore and I reached the top but Renta was forced by exhaustion to turn back 60 meters short of the summit.

ROBERT ROCKWELL

Piks Kommunizma, Korzhenovskoi and Lenin. "Team Alaska" led by Gary Bocarde and Susan Havens consisted further of Keith Fleischman, Willie Hersman, Margarite Kaniniski, Al Pack, Pete Panarese, Mardie Prentke, Steve Taylor and me. On July 19 we were flown by helicopter from the Achik-Tash Camp at 3620 meters to the Moskvin Base Camp below Pik Kommunizma at 4500 meters. A week of storms prevented our planned acclimatization climbs. As the clouds lifted, on July 26 eight of us made the arduous carry over mixed ice, rock and snow to the lower Borodkin Ridge to Camp I at 5240 meters. The next day Bocarde, Havens, Pack, Panarese and I occupied Camp I. The next two days were spent carrying loads over the top of 6270-meter Kirov Peak and dropping to Camp II at 5970 meters on the great ice plateau. Sadly, crossing Kirov, we passed the evacuation of American Steve Manfredo, then unconscious from high-altitude pulmonary edema. He would expire the next day after being carried to below 5000 meters by a Soviet rescue team. A rest day at Camp II preceded our move to Camp III at 6640 meters. Pack turned back at 6300 meters with possible symptoms of high-altitude cerebral edema. We climbed to crowded Camp IV at 7020 meters on the crest of Pik Dushanbe. On August 2 we climbed unroped to the summit of Pik Kommunizma (7483 meters, 24,550 feet) in clear, calm weather. Later that day five more Americans led by Eric Simonson stood atop the Soviet Union's highest peak. Since all the others had to leave, Bocarde, Havens and I made a rapid ascent of majestic Pik Korzhenevkoi (7105 meters, 23,310 feet). Well acclimatized from Kommunizma, we climbed from a valley at 4300 meters in successive days to 5430 and 6320 meters. The third day we were tentbound. Despite the whiteout, six Russians attempted the summit unroped. Two hours later, one of them was blown off a cornice, sustaining fatal injuries in a 300-meter fall. Luckily, the weather cleared on the second night. On August 9 we three ascended the remaining 700 meters along the airy Zatelan ridge to the summit. It was then back to Achik-Tash for an attempt on the last Pamir 7000er, Pik Lenin (7134 meters, 23,406 feet). The excellent weather continued as we left the alpine meadows at 3600 meters for camps at 4410, 5230 and 6420 meters on Lenin's normal route. On the summit day Bocarde was soon halted by a GI problem and descended with Havens. I climbed to the summit alone and met my partners that evening at 6120 meters. At our farewell party, my favorite encounter was with a Russian photographer on his 20th season in the Pamirs. He asked me if William Putnam was still president of the American Alpine Club and proudly displayed an aging parka given him in 1974 by young John Roskelley. It was with great pleasure that I found such American legacies alive and well in the Soviet Pamirs.

ANDREW L. EVANS

Pik Kommunizma. Our team was composed of Ken Bures, Al Bernsconi, Chuck Betcher, Dan Aguillar, Dave Grier, Al Chambard, Ken Asvitt, LaVerne Woods, Dan Holle, Tim Gage, Gunter Bergner, Burt Falk, Jim Scott, and me as leader. We ascended the mountain from the Fortambek Glacier. This route is highlighted by thousands of feet of Soviet fixed lines that become abraded by the end of the climbing season, and 12 kilometers of trekking at 20,000 feet across the Pamir Ice Plateau. On the plus side, the route is very interesting rock and ice climbing with less objective hazard and fewer climbers than the more popular route from the Moskvin Glacier. The Soviets also provide an airdrop on the plateau for teams that climb from the Fortambek side. We had poor weather for the first part of the trip which hindered our acclimatization schedule. When it cleared, we had to hussle to make the summit by the deadline imposed by the Soviets. The summit was reached in shirt-sleeves weather on August 2, our last possible day, by Holle, Bergner, Betcher, Chambard, and me.

ERIC SIMONSON

Pik Kommunizma. Our 11-member team was composed of Scott Fisher, leader, Wes Krause, Stacey Allison, George Schunk, Brad Udall, Steve Man-fredo, Mike Carr, Liz Nichol, Maggie Fox, George Kahrl, and me. Leaving Moscow at midnight, we arrived at the Achik-Tash Base on July 12 after 7 hours of flying and a 4-hour bus ride. After two days at Achik-Tash, acclimatizing, being issued the unique Soviet mountain rations, meeting with the International climbing directors, and overcoming jet lag, we were helicoptered in two loads to the Moskvin Base. Turning our attention to the Borodkin route, we established Camp I (17,000 feet) on July 17, Camp II (19,800 feet) on July 19 on the Pamir Ice Plateau, and sat out an unusual week-long storm before moving to Camp III (21,600 feet) on July 26, and Camp IV (23,100 feet) near the summit of Dushanbe Peak on July 27. The next day Fisher, Krause, Allison, Schunk and I reached the 7,483-meter (24,550-foot) summit; it is worth noting that Stacey Allison may be the first American woman to have climbed Pik Kommunizma. Tragically, Steve Manfredo died two days later on July 30 at 15,500 feet from complications related to the pulmonary edema he contracted at Camp IV the night of July 27.

Mark Udall

Ak-Su,Turkestan Range, Kirgiz SSR. Our group of 16 climbers from the Alpine Club of the Natural Science Faculty of Charles University of Prag spent 15 exciting days at the beginning of July in the Ak-Su region on the northern slopes of the Turkestan Range. (Ak-Su means "white water" in the Kirgiz language.) We flew to Oach and then traveled by bus via Leninabad and Isfana. The climbing base at 2800 meters was reached by truck. The region surprised us with its rich vegetation, fantastic rock-climbing possibilites and unbelievable beauty. The upper Ak-Su valley is a fascinating amphitheater with 1000-meter perpendicular walls of hard, solid, excellent granite. The Soviets have climbed there only for the past three years and so most of the faces have only one or two routes. The most thrilling is a wall of Ak-Su Skalnoye ("Rocky Ak-Su") which rises from 3500 to 5200 meters above a moraine-covered glacier. Pik Alekandra Bloka (5229 meters) is an astonishing mountain resembling Fitz Roy by its shape, dimensions and sheerness, but fortunately not by its climate. The other big walls are on Admiralitek, Petrogradek and Bolshoy Iskander. During our stay, we, the first foreigners there, climbed Maliy, Bolshoy Iskander, Aktiubek, Aleksandre Bloka and the highest mountain in the region, Ak-Su Glavnoye (5355 meters 17,569 feet). Although we had not been given permission for new routes on the big walls, a strong team of Čermák, Hlaváček, Kamler, Reif and Polák tried a new one in the middle of the 1700-meter-high wall of Ak-Su Skalnoye. They reached about two thirds of the way up when Kamler was hit by a falling rock and badly injured his hip. Rappelling down 27 pitches was hard and took two days. We had great respect for the injured man as well as for his partners. The accident saved us from problems we would otherwise have had from the authorities for this unallowed ascent. Except for Kamler's injury, our doctor had to cure frequent diarrhea, our leader Petr Brzak's pneumonia and an untypical injury when Hlavaček was badly bitten by an identified dog of the Kirgiz shepherds and had to be sent back to Prag to have rabies innoculations. Although the Ak-Su mountains do not reach the altitudes of the 7000-meter Pamirs farther to the east, it is a most attractive climbing area. Thanks to warm, stable, sunny weather, the lack of snow, relatively short approaches and particularly because of the quality of the granite, it can be considered one of the best rock-climbing areas not only in the USSR but all over the world. Its walls compare favorably with any in the Alps, Verdon and even Yosemite. The area surrounding 5300-meter Sabakch, which we could see to the west, promises to be equally attractive.

VLADIMÍR WEIGNER, *Czechoslovakia*

AUSTRALASIA

Irian Jaya

Carstensz Pyramid, Irian Jaya (New Guinea). This is the highest peak (5030 meters, 16,503 feet or 4884 meters,15,023 feet) in Australasia. We pursued it as a part of Pat Morrow's successful quest to climb the highest mountain on all seven continents. Access was complicated by the existence of Papuan nationalist rebel activity in the Indonesian province of Irian Jaya. No foreign climbing parties have received permission to climb Carstensz for some years. After 17 months of negotiation between Canada's External Affairs Department, Indonesia's Department of Social Cultural Affairs and the Indonesian Army, permission was obtained for a joint trip with the Mapala Club of the University of Indonesia. We flew to the transmigration settlement of Timika, traveled by Jeep to the mining town of Tembagapura at 6500 feet. There we added ten Moni and Dani porters and five local soldiers and proceeded up the aerial tramway to the Freeport Indonesia copper mine. We established camp at the foot of the Meren Glacier and then moved to the base of Carstensz in the Yellow Valley (13,500 feet). Carstensz resembles a giant rock flake of prickly limestone. We proceeded up the north face along Heinrich Harrer's 1962 first-ascent route. After three roped pitches and a scramble up a gully, we reached the knife-edged ridge. Working through notches, using three rappels and climbing out on the south face with moves up to 5.8, we reached the summit at 1:15 P.M. on May 7. The slow descent repeated the ridge line rappels and finished with three rappels after dark. The party consisted of Canadian Pat Morrow and his wife Baiba Morrow, Indonesians Adi Seno and Titus Pramono, and me.

STEPHEN FOSSETT

Book Reviews

EDITED BY JOHN THACKRAY

Mountain Light: In Search of the Dynamic Landscape. Galen Rowell. Sierra Club Books, San Francisco, 1986. 224 pages, 80 color photographs. $35.00.

I once read in a review of another of Galen Rowell's books the complaint that Rowell's photographs were, in fact, "fairly ordinary," that if you compared them with pictures taken by other mountaineering photographers, the final portfolios would be quite similar.

With the publication of *Mountain Light: In Search of The Dynamic Landscape,* Galen Rowell's photographic autobiography of twenty years of landscape photography, such deprecatory remarks must be silenced. The viewer is stunned into reverent silence by the collective power of eighty of Rowell's favorite photographs, including several of his strongest images, like the fabled, "Rainbow Over The Potala Palace, Lhasa, Tibet." These are captured jewels from nature's mixed palate of light, pictures taken by a masterful hand and eye, and superbly reproduced as only Dai Nippon can. They challenge our preconceptions of the limits of landscape photography. Warm light, cold light, artist's light, light-upon-light, all are carefully preserved by Rowell's skilled vision, the interpretive chemistry of photographic film and camera. Balancing the photographs is an informative text which makes fascinating reading all on its own and illuminates how each of the final images was achieved.

Fortunately Rowell's original idea of "—a little book of photographs and the stories behind them —" grew into this large-format book. With the photographs divided into eight exhibits, variously entitled "Magic Hour," "Figures on a Landscape," and "Unexpected Convergence," amongst others, Rowell also describes, in alternate chapters, his evolution from unknowledgeable amateur shutterbug to world-class photo-journalist, from childhood to the early 1970s in Yosemite and the High Sierra to the present day. The book resists being pigeon holed as an autobiography, a technical photo manual, or a philosophical treatise on photography. It is, rather, an agreeable blend of all three, that go into this account of Rowell's search for mountain light.

The photographer, like any artist, must also be a technician. But Rowell does not belabor the technical aspects of 35mm photography. Instead he describes technique only in relation to how it helps him capture the peak moments of mountain experience. His results are achieved by a near religious pursuit of technical proficiency and an identifiable personal vision. The roots of photographic style, Galen insists, lie in one's personal vision and not primarily in photographic techniques.

Photography for Rowell is a hunt and mountain light is the quarry. Through years of experience, practice, and patience, he consciously tries to place himself in strategic locations at "the magic hour," sunrise and sunset, when juxtapositions of unusual light occur naturally, particularly in high mountain settings where the air is sharp and clean. "There are only two variations of light anywhere in the world," writes Rowell, "the warming of direct light as it is transmitted through the atmosphere, and the cooling of indirect light by scattering and reflection." At sunrise and sunset, these two very different types of light meet and mingle, in "edges" of light. This unusual pattern of converging light, with the twilight wedge meeting the earth's shadow, is best exemplified by his image, "Twilight In The White Mountains, California."

Beyond their role of factually recording an event, pictures are not worth taking, Rowell continues, unless they involve both intellectual and emotional stimulation. In these days of computer-generated and manipulated photography, Rowell feels a stronger commitment than ever that his brand of outdoor landscape photography must preserve an inner-directed approach, or outwardly the resulting image will only portray a particular photographic technique. "Only those (photographs) based on the qualities of light and form will remain equally valid in whatever new technologies evolve," he observes. What gives Galen Rowell's photographs such vibrant life, after all, and their almost transcendental glow is the resulting inner communication which occurs between the photographer and viewer through the excitement of the image itself, through the picture's power to evoke an emotional or intellectual response from the viewer. With pictures like "Lynx in Alpine Flowers, Teklanika River, Alaska Range," "Climber on Mt. Dickey, Alaska Range," "Late Summer Snow under Mount Williamson, Southern Sierra, California," and others, Rowell spellbinds us with his art and craftsmanship.

It is only when internal and external events collide, with a measured dose of good luck (which in the final chapter Rowell does acknowledge to exist), that this "unexpected convergence" of creating a uniquely expressive image takes place. While these occasions of synthesis are indeed rare and by their nature essentially unrepeatable, that is their very attraction.

Luck, how important an ingredient is it in photography? Having attempted to repeat certain favorite photographs of my own, and failed, I was relieved to hear Rowell acknowledge the importance of luck in obtaining an exceptional image. What separates him from the crowd of landscape photographers is his ability to predict a unique situation well in advance, realize the scene's potential, and act swiftly to capture the fleeting moment.

His advice on photographic gear, tripods, time exposures, reciprocity failure, depth of field and the use of his favorite split-level, neutral-density filter all make excellent reading for interested outdoor photographers. The underlying theme of Chapter Six, "Operative Vision," is the constant creative need to shed the skin of old technical proficiencies, those comfortable, but ultimately restrictive habits, and learn anew.

"Chance favors the prepared mind," said Louis Pasteur, whom Rowell quotes on page 131. In *Mountain Light,* Galen Rowell reveals the painstaking preparation of his own mind for the capture of mountain light on film, and his truly extraordinary results. Your record collection wasn't complete without "Springsteen Live." The same can now be said of mountaineering libraries and *Mountain Light.* Treasure it.

ED WEBSTER

Moments of Doubt and Other Mountaineering Writings. David Roberts. The
   Mountaineers, Seattle, 1986. 237 pages. $13.95.

In the nearly twenty years since the publication of his first book, *The Mountain of My Fear,* David Roberts has become one of our finest interpreters of the mountaineering scene. He has written for widely disparate audiences, as this selection of twenty years of his work demonstrates. Some of the pieces are from mountaineering journals, including the *AAJ,* but most come from wider-circulating magazines, particularly *Outside,* which has offered him a valuable forum. They are surprisingly consistent in tone, and in the quality of the writing. The mountaineering articles are unusually personal, while the others are without condescension.

By his own account, Roberts has been fortunate in his editors: many have given him a free editorial hand and plenty of space. He complains, under-standably, about the exceptions—particularly about the *Backpacker* editor who "mangled" his article on Boulder and the Shawangunks into "a promo piece for rock climbing." A comparison of Roberts' manuscript, which he reprints here, with the published distortion explains his disgust and shows some of the difficulties of writing about climbing for a general audience. Some of *Backpacker*'s changes were the kinds of excision familiar in any space-pressured magazine. Others were irritating but minor: "fun" replaced "dissipation"; climb-ing "graybeards of almost forty" became "almost 50." Roberts seems most exasperated with the coarse context in which his piece was placed, and who can blame him? It is headed, "Think rock climbing is tame? [How many *Backpacker* readers thought that?] Then you don't know what's going on in these two hot spots." Doubtless such hype sells copies.

The *Backpacker* editor had a compulsion *to explain.* Thus his readers learned that the crux is "the most difficult section of a climbing route" and a belay, "the art of supporting or securing a climber by ropes." Alas, there was more: two separate sets of parentheses define free climbing as being ropeless—amazing news for the thousands of us who have fallen while climbing free.

The interpreter of mountaineering has, to be sure, deeper problems than explaining what a carabiner is. There is the abiding question of why people climb at all. Here Roberts' dual credentials as writer and major climber are particularly fitting: his explanations are embedded in his narratives. They hold us as the experiences must have held him. With its introduction and headnotes, the book is tantamount to an autobiography: an account not just of climbs—there are many good ones—but of attitudes toward climbing. Roberts is admittedly ambivalent about this "useless pastime," as he terms it; and these mixed feelings blend with accuracy and candor to give the book its binding strength.

Roberts has written an entire book about exploration hoaxes, and a faked first ascent is at the center of his novella, *Like Water and Like Wind*. But what more deeply fascinates him, I suspect, is the obverse: authenticity. His doubts and his fears—key words for him—permeate his narratives. The title piece is a harrowing rendition of observed mountain fatalities. The earliest of these—Roberts and his fallen companion were only eighteen—is an initiation story; it is told from the perspective of a later generation, yet recreates the experience of youth—the time when so many of us feel invulnerable to the hazards of the mountains. A moment's misstep and that is all gone. Roberts has a writer's eye, and ear, for the validating detail. As his unseen partner begins to fall, he notes "a soft but unmistakable sound, and my brain knew it without ever having heard it before. It was the sound of cloth rubbing against rock." After several more deaths, the essay ends on a characteristically divided note: a paean to the exaltation of climbing, but with a last word that is elegy as well as affirmation: "It was worth it then."

Roberts' ambivalence is both personal—the advent of married life and its responsibilities—and public. Both the author and climbing have greatly changed since he began. His critique of "the public climber" concentrates on a loss of uniqueness and of privacy. Points well taken; but I am not persuaded by his defense of his own role in the process: "There is a difference between writing without ulterior motive about one's pastime and signing on to be the star of a live TV ascent." No doubt. But even the writing popularizes our sport, makes it accessible and plausible to a larger audience.

The longest section of the book consists of vivid profiles of well known climbers like Messner and Wiessner, along with one fondly remembered bush pilot, Don Sheldon. All evoke their subjects as human beings, not automata in ascent. (Roberts complains about climbing autobiographies: "What is missing then? Virtually everything that signifies that climbers are real people, as well as climbers. All the internal things.") Several of the pieces return to old and fascinating controversies, with glimpses of viewpoints that are still largely private: Roskelley about Nanda Devi in 1976, Jack Durrance about K2 in 1939. While rightly warning that "a writer must not become dependent on the approval of his subjects," Roberts plainly admires, though not unreservedly, even the most prickly of the outstanding climbers he describes.

Roberts raises but does not fully explore the question of responsibility in the mountains. This issue is joined to his deepest themes: judgment, the linking symbolism of the rope, and above all, risk. In the mountains we all take chances—for ourselves, for the partners of our ropes, and even for those who will try to save us if we get into trouble. Roberts describes the search for two young climbers on Mount Washington in the winter of 1982. One of the rescuers was caught in an avalanche and killed. Such things happen in the mountains, as the victim must have known, but the question of responsibility—and its frequent inner corollary, guilt—remains. Roberts addresses the matter, but it gets displaced by his admiration for his spirited hero's return to hard climbing, without feet or lower legs. Nor is the question pursued in Roberts' accounts of other accidents, including those which he had witnessed. He experiences grief, even despair, but the urge to climb always overcomes these feelings. I wish he had explored this area of emotion more deeply.

Roberts is plainly worried about the direction that climbing is taking, particularly in this country. "The life-giving impulse behind our climbing has always been escapist, anarchistic, 'useless,' he contends with praise in one essay; and in the next (and most recent) he deplores "a modern drift toward narcissism and depersonalization." As our sport—or avocation, or obsession— becomes even more popular and more public, some of its joys may become transformed, or vanish. A distressing prospect: but fortunately David Roberts will continue to write about it, with his characteristic skill and perception.

STEVEN JERVIS

The Guiding Spirit. Andrew J. Kauffman and William L. Putnam. Footprint Publishing, Revelstoke, British Columbia, 1986. 256 pages, photographs, and proper maps. $16.00.

The Guiding Spirit is a biography of the well-known Swiss (and Canadian) mountaineering guide Edward Feuz Jr. Using the modern technique of tape recording of interviews, Andrew J. Kauffman, who did most of the writing, and William L. Putnam, who did much of the research, have preserved details of this guide's life and mountaineering history.

I have to admit that I did not begin at the beginning of the book, but plunged in at the middle. (You'll see why when you look at the contents.) Kauffman has chosen to center the narrative around Edward Feuz' words themselves, but digresses to include stories of Feuz' friends and associates, to a pleasing effect. There are many amusing stories and many chuckles in these pages, as well as dramatic and even horrifying incidents. The star of the show is clearly Edward Feuz himself, through his spoken words in the tape recorder.

The book also succeeds in conveying a sense of adventure active in the times in which Edward Feuz lived, and the adjustments which Feuz and his fellow professionals had to make (or failed to make in some cases) to the alien, wild environment of Canada in its latter days of exploration, in contrast to the settled, ordered world of Switzerland. Their business relation to the Canadian Pacific Railroad is also clarified, which reveals that while the railroad was a good employer in general, there were points of friction which developed during the early course of their employment.

This volume is well written, and will appeal most to those mountaineers who have experience in the Canadian Rockies and the Columbia Mountains (Interior

Ranges) of British Columbia, and who consequently have a little exposure to their history. A list of the dramatis personae is included in the appendices. It is a welcome change from sometimes dreary accounts of expedition logistics and comes with the reviewer's recommendation.

EARLE R. WHIPPLE

Painted Mountains: Two Expeditions to Kashmir. Stephen Venables. Hodder & Stoughton, London, 1986. 239 pages, color photographs, route diagram, maps, bibliography. £12.95.

For all the current celebration of the small, "alpine-style" expedition, it has not brought very many notable additions to mountaineering book shelves. An 8000-meter peak attacked by a phalanx of star mountaineers may have an inherent story value that a handful of noncelebrity climbers on a 6000-meter peak perhaps lack. At any rate, it takes unusual literary and journalistic skills to raise their story beyond the limits of the magazine article, where the record of most alpine-style ascents end up.

Stephen Venables' *Painted Mountains* tells of two trips to India, three years apart. The first to Kishtwar, where he and Dick Renshaw climbed the previously unnamed Shivling; the second, in 1985, to the Rimo peaks, in the Karakoram, with a much larger cast of characters from the UK and India, one of the first of the Indo-foreign expeditions that are now permitted near the Indian–Pakistani frontier there. Although the stories are very different, both give a wonderfully accurate picture of the climbing, the history of the regions, the flora of the Himalaya. Venables has a good documentary style. Candid without being confessional. Understated, but not self-consciously so. A reasonable, intelligent, wholesome character to be in the mountains with—that's how he comes across.

Readers will decide for themselves whether they prefer the Shivling account, where the two alpinists complete a model of the alpine style genre; or the Karakoram adventure, where the presence of nine other climbers, a roving geographer and a clownish liaison officer keep one well entertained. The Brits were lucky indeed to have teamed up with capable Bombay climbers, led by Harish Kapadia. It is rumored that recently arranged Indo-foreign expeditionary marriages in this region have had less felicitous results.

JOHN THACKRAY

White Limbo: The First Australian Climb of Mt. Everest. Lincoln Hall. Kevin Weldon, McMahons Point, 1985. 262 pages, color photographs, route diagrams, map, glossary. $40.00 (US).

The rich and varied lore of mountaineering literature devoted to Mount Everest ranges from the classic official accounts of the British expeditions to the mountain in the 1920s and 1930s to Walt Unsworth's definitive history, *Everest: A Mountaineering History.* One of the most recent entries in an already crowded field is *White Limbo,* the provocatively named account of the successful 1984 Australian ascent of the North Face by mostly a new line.

What is most appealing about this book is the unusually productive combination of superb mountain color photography and Lincoln Hall's excellent, tightly written account. In most books of this kind, either the writing or the photographs predominate. Here, there is a remarkable balancing of the two with—of all things—a nearly flawless tracking of photos and text event-by-event.

Hall writes from the compelling perspective of one who had strong ambitions for the summit, but was sensitive enough to his personal limits, due to old frostbite injuries, to turn back just below the Yellow Band. He could only watch three of his companions go on toward the summit. It must have been disappointing to Hall, but when the exhausted summiters returned to high camp, he provided the essential support that saw Greg Mortimer, the most seriously affected from the altitude, successfully down the mountain. Andy Henderson was not so fortunate. With severely frostbitten fingers, he turned back a mere fifty meters below the summit. Once back home, Henderson underwent extensive surgery on his damaged hands.

That the Australians ever got themselves in a position to make a summit push is remarkable. Early in the expedition, avalanches nearly wiped out their Camp II on the face and buried a cache of gear at its base. Tim McCartney-Snape had to resort to cross-country ski boots, establishing a unique altitude record for such footgear.

The Australian climb was carried out in the finest style above the highest fixed ropes at nearly 24,000 feet. No oxygen was used by any of the climbers, making it, after Messner's solo ascent, the only time a new route has been completed on Everest without the benefit of supplementary oxygen. Hall's book is more satisfying than simply another recounting of a successful climb, mainly because of the strong message one draws from the pages of *White Limbo:* It is possible to climb an Everest with a small group of friends who have an experience imbued with happiness and mutual respect.

JAMES WICKWIRE

First on Everest: The Mystery of Mallory and Irvine. Tom Holzel and Audrey Salkeld. Henry Holt, New York, 1986. 322 pages, black and white photographs. $19.95.

In 1971 when Tom Holzel first proposed his theory that George Mallory may indeed have reached the summit of Everest in 1924, the climbing establishment—particularly in England—scoffed at the idea. Aside from disbelief about the physical feat itself, Holzel was attacked for his suggestion that Mallory could have left his strong, but inexperienced young companion, Andrew Irvine, near the famous Second Step (28,280 feet) to make a solo bid for the top. This behavior, it was argued, was highly unlikely, if not inconceivable, when considering the ethics of the day.

Aside from an ice axe that Wyn Harris found in 1933, just *below* the first step (28,000 feet), a rock feature some lateral distance down the northeast ridge from the Second Step, no trace of Mallory or Irvine was ever found, that is, until rumors surfaced in the early 1980s of a Chinese sighting at 26,600 feet on the northeast ridge route of the dessicated body of a climber garbed in tattered, outdated clothing. Unfortunately, from the standpoint of mountaineering history, the Chinese climber, Wang Hong Bao, was not able to verify his claim to have seen the body of an "English" (as he referred to it) as Wang was killed in 1979 in an avalanche below the North Col during a Chinese–Japanese reconnaissance of Everest. Wang's alleged discovery, coupled with Messner and Habeler's first oxygenless ascent of the mountain in 1978 and subsequent other such ascents including Messner's astonishing solo in 1980 of a new route on the North Face, suddenly converted the wildly speculative to the possibly probable.

Holzel and Salkeld's well-written and documented account, however, is not merely a regurgitation of Holzel's earlier Mallory-ascent theory in the light of recent events. It is much more. Based partly on recently available letters and diaries, the authors delve more deeply into Mallory's background than his previous biographers, presumably in an effort to explain why it just might have been possible—even in 1924—for Mallory to have fulfilled his life's ambition. What emerges from the material that the authors weave together is something far more significant than demonstrating that Mallory possessed the sheer physical ability to climb Everest. It clearly appears he had that enormous wellspring of mental tenacity and drive that now is taken for granted as perhaps the most essential ingredient of successful high-altitude climbing.

Without question, Mallory was the dominating force on these early Everest expeditions. After two defeats (that is, if the brilliant reconnaissance of 1921 can be called a defeat), Mallory became convinced that his best chance to reach the summit was to use supplementary oxygen on his last attempt. The debate among British climbers in the 1920s whether oxygen should be used on Everest had been waged on both ethical and physical grounds depending upon one's point of view. In a letter to his wife, Mallory wrote:

> The gasless party has the better adventure [and] it is naturally a bit disappointing that I shall be with the other party. Still, the conquest of the mountain is the great thing, and the whole plan is mine . . . and will give me, perhaps, the best chance of all of getting to the top.

Significantly, Mallory goes on to confide to his wife that "it is almost unthinkable with this plan that *I* shan't get to the top; I can't see myself coming down defeated." [Emphasis in orginal.]

That Mallory possessed the requisite willpower to carry him that last thousand feet to the summit is reasonably clear. It now remains to subject Holzel's conjectural account of the events of June 8, 1924, at and above the Second Step, to a modicum of critical analysis. Whether it is credible that Mallory and Irvine separated after surmounting the Second Step is not easy to evaluate. It is entirely possible that this occurred, though, particularly when the earlier precedent on the same expedition is taken into account: Norton's solo attempt on the summit after an extreme sore throat and cough stopped Somervell. So for purposes of what follows, it is assumed that Mallory and Irvine agreed to separate.

First, what can we make of Holzel's assertion that the two climbers actually succeeded in climbing to the top of the Second Step? Odell's eyewitness account is to be given great weight, but even he is not entirely sure that he saw them on the Second, not the First Step. The author admits that the French attempt, via the northeast ridge in 1981, casts some doubt on his theory when Marmier, the French leader, told him that it may well have been the First Step on which Odell saw the pair because of a similar snow patch that the French encountered. Having opened the door to reevaluation of Odell's pivotal sighting, Holzel slams it shut by assuming, without further discussion, that it was the Second Step all along.

With due respect to the Chinese who climbed the Second Step with considerable difficulty in 1960, even at the cost of the lead climber's severely frostbitten toes because his boots were removed, and the nine-person Chinese team that repeated the climb in 1975, it can be assumed that Mallory's prowess as a rock climber exceeded the Chinese standards. As the 1975 Chinese left a wire ladder on the final steep section, the Japanese were able to use the ladder five years later, thereby negating any positive implications from their success on the Second Step. The only other team to climb the Second Step, the Catalans in the 1985 post-monsoon season, "were of the impression that it was perfectly feasible for Mallory and Irvine, climbing the ridge when relatively clear of snow, to have reached the summit." Although it is far from clear (based on personal experience on two expeditions in which I have been to 8000 meters and above on Everest's North Face in both the pre-monsoon and post-monsoon seasons) that pre-monsoon conditions are easier, the opinion of the Catalans should be weighed carefully. More snow cover on the rock portions of the Second Step is possibly offset by the Catalans climbing without oxygen at this extreme altitude. Thus, their experience may have been comparable to Mallory's.

Assuming that Irvine was assisted down the Second Step with the aid of a rope from Mallory, he reasonably could have descended along the northeast ridge past the First Step to the slabs where, if the evidence of the ice axe found in 1933 is to be accepted, he slipped and fell the thousand feet or so to the relatively gentle area near 26,600 feet where the Chinese climber spotted an "English" body eight years ago. This accounts for Irvine, but what about Mallory?

Holzel, who alone authored the first chapter, "The Mystery" and the last chapter, "The Clues," gets quickly past the first piece of business: Mallory's transfer of Irvine's partly used oxygen bottle to his own pack with the successful switch of the connecting hose from his own spent bottle to Irvine's. But, after getting Mallory above the Second Step, Holzel's conjecture is flawed by misunderstandings about the physical nature of the final pyramid and he resorts to unnecessary speculation about Mallory's last movements. These, ironically, have the effect of undermining his own theory. For instance, the ground above the Second Step is easy, particularly if one climbs diagonally across the final pyramid as the Chinese did in 1975, and presumably the Catalans in 1985. The precise route that the Chinese took in 1960 remains unclear.

That Mallory, with the aid of oxygen, could have reached the summit in a few hours is probable. In 1984, Phil Ershler (using oxygen) and John Roskelley (climbing without) took about eight hours to climb from our high camp at 26,500 feet to 28,000 feet at the base of the final pyramid. They had climbed at Roskelley's pace *sans* oxygen although they were delayed in climbing the steep Yellow Band that bisects the Great Couloir at 27,200 feet. Yet, when Roskelley turned back a scant thousand feet from the summit, Ershler was able to climb the last section (quite similar to what Mallory would have encountered) in an amazing one and one-half hours.

Holzel questions whether Mallory could have made it down the final pyramid safely and speculates about a possible glissade. He also suggests that Mallory would not have been able to make it down the Second Step because of frozen hands or lack of strength, forgetting that a few paragraphs earlier in his account, Mallory had a rope which he used to lower Irvine down the Step. The questions and speculation are unnecessary.

However kind subsequent events have been to the Mallory-success theory, all but one team that climbed the Second Step have endured a bivouac on the way down. Only the Chinese in 1975, who placed their highest camp above the Second Step, avoided this. Although still a matter of conjecture, it seems likely that Mallory died of exposure on the way down.

As related elsewhere in this issue of the *Journal*, the 1986 expedition that the authors mounted to search for the remains of Mallory and Irvine did not uncover any additional evidence, such as cameras with undeveloped film, to shed light on the greatest mystery in the history of mountaineering. Mallory and Irvine's final hours more than likely will remain just that.

James Wickwire

Island in the Sky: Pioneering Accounts of Mount Rainier, 1833-1894. Paul Schullery, editor. The Mountaineers, Seattle, 1987. 200 pages, black and white illustrations, 1 early map. $10.95 (paper).

Schullery, a former National Park Service seasonal naturalist/historian and the editor and/or author of several other books and numerous articles in outdoor-history journals, has here compiled accounts of fourteen selected explorations and ascents of Mount Rainier—plus a fabricated legend of an Indian's ascent—prior to establishment of the National Park in 1899. The literary style of the 1800s enhances the enjoyment of this thoughtful choice of accounts of those pioneering efforts, when the elements of discovery still prevailed in the first climbing done in the Pacific Northwest and in the new sport of mountaineering.

The volume begins with Dr. Fraser Tolmie's 1833 botanical excursion into the northwestern foothills of the present National Park, where, accompanied by several Indians, he became the first white man to enter the Park area and, probably, the first to document the existence of glaciers in the United States. Following this is the famous "Hamitchou's Legend," by young travel-writer Theodore Winthrop (author of *The Canoe and the Saddle*, 1862), who interweaves fiction with possible fact in his tale of an Indian's quest for material riches (in clam shells) at the top of the mountain, but who learns the pitfalls of greed.

Next comes the story of the two unknown whites who, while surveying the boundary of the newly established Yakima Indian Reservation in about 1852, hired Saluskin, a young Yakima, to lead them through the foothills and the eastern base of the mountain. From, probably, a camp near the lower margins of the Winthrop Glacier, they left the Indian and made a one-day round-trip ascent. Although the whites never documented their achievement, there's little reason to doubt the Indian's verbal account, given years later, in 1915, to historian Lucullus McWhorter.

The first well documented accounts of climbs on the mountain include those of Lt. A.V. Kautz in 1857, who got to within about four hundred feet of the summit, via the present Kautz Glacier, and the first formally recognized ascent to the peak's summit, via the Gibraltar Route, in 1870 by P.B. Van Trump and Hazard Stevens (son of Washington's first territorial governor). These two stories were well told and widely read, and they provided the first detailed documents of the entire journeys, from lowland forts and towns to the upper snows of the mountain. The accounts laid the groundwork—and showed the route—for a number of subsequent, late-1800 ascents of the mountain. Virtually all summit climbs in the next twenty years followed the Gibraltar Route, via an approach from the west along the Nisqually River valley and to timberline at Paradise Valley on the south. Among these are ascents described by George Bayley, a well travelled California mountaineer and frequent climbing companion of John Muir. With Van Trump, Bayley ascended the Gibraltar Route in 1883 and the Tahoma Glacier in 1892.

Some accounts describe rather casual trips made in a vacation spirit: ascents by neophyte mountaineers, who explored new approaches on the north and east sides of the mountain while on deer- and goat-hunting excursions. These led to climbs up the Winthrop Glacier on the northeast in 1884, documented by J. Warner Fobes, and an 1886 ascent partway up the Ingraham Glacier on the east, by a party of one white with a group of Indians, described by Allison Brown.

Completing the coverage are detailed descriptions of ascents, by John Muir (1888), by Fay Fuller (first woman to reach the top of Mount Rainier) in 1890, and by George Dickson (1892), Van Trump (1892) and Olin Wheeler (1894). All the accounts provide an atmosphere of exciting discovery of new lands and of both the beauties of the scenery and the labors and hazards of the climbs. Described are the many-day approaches through lowland forests and heavy undergrowth, battling mosquitoes, flies and yellow jackets, and eventually attaining timberline and open parklands that lead to the alpine world above.

These provide a sharp contrast to the stories of the modern mountaineer, who first touches the terrain at timberline parking areas and completes the adventure in two days.

These early chroniclers were disadvantaged by the lack of detailed maps and of formally accepted names of various geographic features. Several of the accounts fail to clearly define the routes taken above timberline. Nonetheless, these stories have provided the basis for some evidence of climatic changes that affect the mountain's snowfields. Even Van Trump was confused by changes in the mountain between his ascent in 1870 and several subsequent climbs. To this reviewer, there might have been some benefit in including the more scientifically oriented account of the 1870 ascent of the Gibraltar Route (second ascent) by S.F. Emmons and A.D. Wilson, world-renowned geologists then working on the Geological Survey of the Fortieth Parallel.

DEE MOLENAAR

Seven Summits. Dick Bass and Frank Wells, with Rick Ridgeway. Warner
    Books, New York, 1986. 336 pages, color photographs. $19.95.

The late, and much lamented, Tom Patey, had, as readers of his luminous book, *One Man's Mountains,* know, a fine ear for song. One of my favorites, to be sung to the tune of "Onward, Christian Soldiers," is entitled "Onward, Christian Bonington." Here is the first verse:

> Onward, Christian Bonington of the A.C.G.
>   Write another page of Alpine history.
>   He has climbed the Eigerwand, he has climbed the Dru—
>   For a mere ten thousand francs, he will climb with you:
> Onward, Christian Bonington of the A.C.G.
>   If you name the mountain, he will name the fee.

This verse came to mind as I read the twelfth and thirteenth chapters of this book, *Seven Summits.* I am sure that I don't have to remind the readers of our journal that the seven summits in question are the highest mountains on each of the seven continents and that these were climbed for the first time as a group by at least one of two of the authors of the so-named book. (This last sentence sounds like something out of a police report; but so be it.) The twelfth and thirteenth chapters have to do with the climb of Mount Vinson, the highest mountain in Antarctica on which the authors toiled in the company of none other than the above-mentioned Christian Bonington. What I liked about this chapter was that it was the only one in which one gets some sense of what this entire caper must have cost—although the costs that are discussed must represent— pardon the allusion—just the tip of the iceberg. Chapter Twelve opens with a conversation between one of the principals—Frank Wells—and a climber called Pat Morrow who, it turns out, is also trying to climb the seven summits. I have no idea whether it is a verbatim transcript of an actual conversation, but here is what is reported. It begins with Morrow:

"I've seen the *Fortune* article [a remarkably apt venue for an article on this enterprise] about you and Dick and I wondered if I might ask how you two are planning to get to Antarctica?"

"Do you have $200,000?" Frank asked.

"No."

"Well, that's what it takes."

That is, one gathers, what it took for starters. A fee of a mere $90,000 is tossed off for rebuilding an airplane. A description of this is followed by a wonderful exchange:

"They were halfway through the task [of rebuilding the plane] when Frank called Dick with yet another hurdle."

"Just got a call from Chile. They're having trouble down there finding enough money to keep the country going. The price of copper is so low they may scrap their whole Antarctic program. If that goes, our fuel drop goes, and if the fuel drop goes, we don't go."

That's what I call getting one's priorities straight. The Chilean economy be swiggered; it's the *goddamned fuel drop!*

Not long ago, I saw a Richard Pryor special. In it, he describes the occasions when his daughter brings home a galaxy of her nubile teen-age girl friends. Pryor finds himself all but consumed by animal urges and then, he says, they start to talk. Horrible teen-age honking sounds come out of their mouths and his libido collapses like a punctured inner tube. "It's the only thing that saves them," Pryor added with a wistful look. That is a little how I feel about this book. I have great admiration for the feat. It was a crazy and wonderful idea and then they start to talk. Much of what they say makes me cringe—like reading Mozart's letters to his cousin Bäsle. It is wheeling and dealing; Dallas in the mountains. We all know that climbers—usually rather pathetically—try to wheel and deal. But these people have raised wheeling and dealing in the mountains to an art form. I find that while I am impressed, I cannot work up much affection. Reading this book was, for me, a little like watching one of those television sports broadcasts between two teams, when one doesn't care which team wins. For Bass, who seems to have gone back to his oil and ranching interests in Texas, and for Wells, who has gone back to the film industry as the president of Walt Disney, the mountains were an interlude in their lives. One wishes that what they did, had been done by people with a deep, lifetime commitment of our activity.

JEREMY BERNSTEIN

Hypothermia, Frostbite and Other Cold Injuries: Prevention, Recognition and Prehospital Treatment. James A. Wilkerson, Cameron C. Bangs, John S. Hayward. The Mountaineers, Seattle, 1986. 105 pages, illustrations, color photographs, charts, diagrams, glossary, bibliography. $8.95 (paper).

The popularity of extreme climbing in winter or bad weather, and the increasing recognition that hypothermia can be as major a problem as hypoxia make this a valuable and important book. The authors are experts in both theory and practice and have been active in search and rescue activities on mountains and in the Arctic, as well as management of badly injured patients in hospitals. Written in language easily understood by the nondoctor, this is an excellent update on what we know (and don't know) about cold injury today. This book in strongly recommended for anyone expecting to be out in the cold, at high altitude or low down, or on the water.

CHARLES S. HOUSTON, M.D.

Medicine For The Outdoors; A Guide to Emergency Medical Procedures and First Aid. Paul S. Auerbach. Little Brown, Boston, 1986. 345 pages, profusely illustrated with line drawings; glossary, bibliography. $12.95 (paper).

This is a first-class paperback, an easy-to-carry handbook for the lay person, describing the signs, symptoms, cause, treatment and prevention of just about everything you might encounter away from (or even in) your backyard. Written in nontechnical language, with excellent illustrations, it's the simplified version of the comprehensive *Management of Wilderness and Outdoor Emergencies,* edited by Auerbach and Geehr in 1983 and designed for health professionals. An appendix on commonly used drugs, giving indications, dosage, and side effects and an excellent glossary defining medical terms add to the value of a brief chapter on ideal first aid kits. Problems encountered in scuba diving, climbing, eating wild plants, or being struck by lightning, bitten by snakes or spiders are well but simply discussed. This is an ideal companion on any trip of more than a few days—and good medical education for a lazy day in the sack.

CHARLES S. HOUSTON, M.D.

Avalanche Safety for Skiers & Climbers. Tony Daffern. Rocky Mountain Books, Calgary, 1983. 172 pages, black and white photographs, diagrams, glossary, bibliography. $11.50 (Canada).

Daffern directs this book to the mountaineer or back-country skier facing various types of avalanche hazards along the way. Using well-chosen case histories of mountaineering and wilderness skiing accidents, Daffern discusses the risks—including implications of decision-making—without resorting to sensationalism or preaching.

Daffern has gathered his snow studies and resource material from several respected sources and the technical sections are generally very good and up to date. However, I found a few of his drawings a little obscure, particularly the one describing heat gain/heat loss in the snowpack on pages 39 and 40. On the plus side, the section on field snow observations is the most complete of any current avalanche handbook. It includes many casual observations that can be made, while on skis, in addition to the more formal tests and snow structure studies.

Daffern does not fail to mention the particular uniqueness and subtleness of those delayed-action avalanches—those involving deep snow layers and those which occur after a storm or period of recent loading, perhaps several days later, and often in conditions of clear, calm weather. The problem with this type of avalanche is down-played in most other publications, yet this is the avalanche which results in the majority of skier avalanche deaths. A particularly telling photograph on page 141 is a good reminder.

There are the usual, but well-done chapters on route-finding and rescue. Of particular note is a discussion on what helicopters can and cannot do in the mountains, acknowledging that the helicopter is part of the mountain scene in many areas today.

An interesting and generous selection of photographs carries the information well. Many of the photographs are of climbing situations, as well as skiing. Of special note are the state-of-the-art snow crystal photographs by Ronald Perla.

In summary, *Avalanche Safety for Skiers & Climbers* is an excellent field-level avalanche handbook. For mountaineers, it is the best available.

PETER LEV

The Avalanche Book. Betsy Armstrong and Knox Williams. Fulcrum, Golden, Colorado, 1986. 212 pages, appendices, bibliography. $14.95.

Anyone whose encounters with snow tend toward the nonhorizontal should have a working understanding of avalanches. Until recently, this has been difficult to acquire due to a paucity of nontechnical information on the subject. In the last few years, however, an "avalanche renaissance" of sorts has produced several good books for the general reader, of which *The Avalanche Book* is the most recent and the most comprehensive. If there were an avalanche category of Trivial Pursuit, this book would have all the answers. What should you do at the moment of being buried by an avalanche? (Shout once to alert rescuers, then close your mouth to prevent it from being packed with snow.) How many buried victims have been recovered alive by avalanche dogs? (One.) What are the legal liabilities of a real estate developer who sites a house in an avalanche path? (Depends on whether you live in Colorado or Alaska.) But avalanches are anything but trivial, as this book's harrowing case histories and chilling statistics well attest.

Within the tightly-knit world of avalanche professionals, *The Avalanche Book* has generated a certain amount of controversy. Some feel that Armstrong and Williams give undue credit and attention to academically oriented researchers, while downplaying the contributions of the practical field workers who spend their days skiing over avalanche terrain with backpacks full of dynamite. Both authors are prominent researchers, and their emphasis, while galling to those they somewhat condescendingly refer to as "practitioners," in no way lessens the usefulness of their book for the general reader. Practical aspects of avalanche safety, avoidance, and rescue are covered in a clear and thorough manner. Of particular interest is a chapter on what to do if actually caught in an avalanche. This information, made unforgettable by vivid case histories, could save your life. A more prudent approach, however, would be to read with extra care the chapters on the causes of avalanches and the choice of routes to circumvent them.

Where *The Avalanche Book* departs most noticeably from its predecessors is the considerable attention devoted to some of the more esoteric areas of avalanche research, such as attempts to defeat snow slides through engineering. The Swiss, in particular, have pioneered the use of steel and concrete structures to impede, divert, or withstand the crushing forces of moving snow. They have also done a great deal of thinking about the legal limits of individual and community responsibility for avalanche safety. The chapter "Avalanches and the Law" offers a worldwide overview of this little known but increasingly important field.

The authors' background as editors of *The Snowy Torrents,* the ongoing chronicle of American avalanche accidents, gives their current book great historical depth. Case studies of avalanche disasters, from Hannibal's misfortunes in the Alps to the latest contemporary incidents, offer dramatic reading and a riskless substitute for experience, which in the case of avalanches is not the best teacher.

The climber or skier looking only for succinct, practical advice on avoiding avalanches may occasionally feel that he has gotten off route in deep snow as he makes his way through some of *The Avalanche Book's* more specialized chapters. On the other hand, there is an equal likelihood that he will discover a new interest in tactics of avalanche warfare, winter recreations of nineteenth-century miners, land-use planning in Swiss communes, or aerial delivery of explosives. Anyone who deals with snow will do so more knowledgeably after reading this lively and wide-ranging book—even practitioners.

KIM FADIMAN

East Coast Rock Climbs. John Harlin III. Chockstone Press, Denver, 1986. 397
    pages, black and white photographs, line drawings, maps. $22.00 (paper).

This is the third volume of John Harlin's ambitious *Climber's Guide to North America* series. It provides a comprehensive overview of the fifteen principal climbing areas on the eastern seaboard, ranging from Yellow Creek Falls in Alabama to Charlevoix in Quebec, Canada. The format is identical to the earlier Rocky Mountains and West Coast volumes, and has standardized introductory remarks about the purpose, scope, and use of the book; ratings; safety; style and ethics; and similar guidebook conventions. This is followed by informative essays on the nature of the climbing in the East and its colorful history.

Each major climbing area is covered in its own chapter, and there is even a separate chapter at the end of the book that briefly describes a scattering of smaller, less-heralded crags that the author encountered on his travels. A general selection of routes in all grades is included within each area, with the emphasis being on the most popular or accessible. The routes are mostly shown on a combination of photographs and line drawings (topos), but are further described when additional clarification is needed. Helpful comments about protection sometimes appear as well. Besides the routes, each chapter has a wealth of information on the area being considered, including highlights of the climbing, environment and local history; location maps; the availability of camping; the nature of the weather; a listing of local guidebooks, guide services and equipment stores; emergency services to contact in case of accident; public transportation; and, most important of all, restrictions and warnings.

An especially desirable theme that is echoed throughout the book is the need for climbers to minimize their impact on the environment, both on and off the rock. Harlin is right to declare that "damaging the rock [chopping holds] is the biggest transgression in American climbing" and that "littering is unthinkable in the outdoors." At the same time, he also should have condemned the equally destructive practice of placing bolts on rappel, but unfortunately, his sentiments do not run in this direction.

One of the biggest problems the author experienced when writing this book was to balance his limited amount of time with the book's vast geographical scope. Shortcuts necessarily had to be taken, and most of the information had to be obtained from existing guidebooks and local climbers, rather than personal experience. Inevitably, this has resulted in a certain number of errors. Perhaps the most obvious one is the use of topos in the Shawangunks. On cliffs where features are few and far between, topos are often effective, but in the Gunks, where the architecture is exceedingly complex, they simply do not work. Aerial photographs in conjunction with route descriptions would have been better. Elsewhere in the book, several of the photos are too dark (pages 53, 169, 195, 319, 324), while others are poorly cropped (page 314), out of focus (page 281), or of limited interest (page 241). A big disappointment is the use of numerous photos that have been published before, thus robbing everyone of the chance to see new faces in new places.

In terms of the accuracy of individual details, I can't speak for areas I am not familar with, but in the Connecticut Traprock section I noticed three worthy of note: Sam Slater was on the first ascent of "Superpower," not Sam Streibert; Bruce Dicks was not on the first ascent of "Thunderbolt"; and "Silmarillion" has one pitch, not two.

Despite these problems, *East Coast Rock Climbs* is well written and has been carefully organized and designed to be of maximum value to the traveling climber. Although some may argue against the usefulness of such a broadly based regional guide, everyone has to agree that the idea has proven to be immensely popular. Not only has the book opened up several "new" areas for climbers to enjoy, but it has also done a better job of documenting certain other areas than the local guidebook authors have done themselves. *East Coast Rock Climbs* is therefore highly recommended, and I hope John Harlin continues and improves the series.

KEN NICHOLS

The Gunks Guide: Rock Climbs in the Shawangunks of New York. Todd Swain. Alpine Diversions, New Paltz, 1986. 318 pages, black and white photographs, sketch maps. $20.00 (paper).

The Shawangunks is the finest rock climbing area in the Eastern United States and is internationally known for its spectacular overhangs and wide range of excellent climbs in every grade. It is one of the few places where beginners and experts alike can climb side by side on routes of equal quality but opposite extremes of difficulty. Recently there has been a surge of new route activity in the highest grades that has even given the Gunks undeniable world-class status.

Equalling the difficulty of these new routes has been the perennial problem of creating a guidebook that measures up to the excellence of the area. Unfortunately, the Gunks does not lend itself very well to guidebook treatment because of the almost monotonous uniformity of the rock, the size of the cliffs, and the wandering nature of many of the lines. To be successful, then, a guidebook must provide sufficient detail to sort out the confusion and, at the same time, be accurate and easy to use.

Various formats have been tried. Topos have been well-known failures because the Gunks has too many critical details in too small an area for symbols to be useful. Route descriptions by themselves have also proven to be inadequate because they are too prone to misinterpretation if the author has been less than meticulous with the English language. To use an old cliché, a picture is worth a thousand words, and Art Gran capitalized on this by using high-resolution photographs of the cliffs in conjunction with route descriptions in his 1964 guidebook. Dick Williams then successfully continued the trend in his 1972 guidebook. However, when Williams revised his guide in 1980, two major design flaws became immediately apparent. The book was too fat and couldn't be carried in your pocket on those esoteric multipitch routes, and there was no convenient cross-referencing system between the route descriptions and the photographs at the end of each section; instead, one had to laboriously flip back and forth to the index or search tediously through the text. Nevertheless, the strong point of the 1980 guidebook was its abundant and well-reproduced photographs, most large enough to reveal even the smallest detail.

Todd Swain, with the benefit of 20-20 hindsight, has thus had the opportunity to create a first-class guidebook by avoiding the mistakes of the past. So how does *The Gunks Guide* measure up to the old guides and the area?

On the positive side, *The Gunks Guide* miraculously fits in your pocket, despite containing nearly 1000 routes or roughly double that of the 1980 guidebook, so there is no need to rip it in half. Todd has also obviated the need to cross-reference the photos and route descriptions by interspersing the photos in the text near the descriptions rather than bunching them up at the end of each section. Both advantages will save everyone a lot of trouble.

Most climbers will also appreciate Todd's use of the 0-3 star quality rating system and letter grades G, PG, R, and X for protection. Todd may have been a bit conservative with his quality ratings, but he should be given credit for making a good-faith effort to steer visiting climbers away from horrid routes like "Ventre de Boeuf" and "Red's Ruin." On the other hand, Todd may not have been conservative enough with his protection ratings. Climbs such as "Blind Ambition," "Thunder and Frightening," "To Be or Not to Be," and "The Black-out," to name a few, are all probably more serious than indicated. Guidebook authors owe a special responsibility to climbers to be accurate in this respect, even more so than with difficulty ratings which are much more subject to individual variation.

Two other welcome additions have been Todd's use of   and   symbols instead of the awkward phrases "hard for the grade" and "easy for the grade" or the illogical a-b-c-d subdivisions, and his reintroduction of silly puns and slapstick humor to liven up the text. There is even a "trivial pursuit" page to amuse climbing historians on rainy days.

On the negative side, the biggest failing of *The Gunks Guide* is its lack of attention to detail. The book seems to have been rushed into production without much consideration for quality. Nowhere is this more apparent than with the photographs which are almost invariably too small, too dark, and poorly reproduced. Newcomers to the area will find them difficult to use for locating routes. And compounding the problem are a number of vague route descriptions, especially when second and third pitches are concerned.

The internal design of the book leaves much to be desired as well. Route and first-ascent information is jammed together in an unorganized fashion, and so much is crowded on each page that details are sometimes cut off at the margins. Running heads are often omitted at the tops of the pages, making it difficult to know where you are when casually flipping through the book. Even more distracting is the large number of misspellings (seven on the first five pages alone), the improper use of punctuation, and the conspicuous lack of hyphenation. One should expect better from a $20 guidebook.

Todd has also dropped the ball on the difficult subject of ethics. His brief discussion at the beginning does not convey the crisis that exists at the Gunks concerning such unethical practices as chopping holds and using aid to preplace protection on so-called "free" routes. While he does make a strong plea for preservation of the area (which is on private land), this should extend to the traditional standards of climbing as well, since such standards act to preserve the environment from unbridled Munich mechanization and the unnecessary proliferation of bolts.

The overall advantage of *The Gunks Guide* is that it concentrates most of the known routes on the four most popular cliffs in the Gunks in a single volume. A host of new routes has been opened up for climbers to enjoy. For this reason alone, *The Gunks Guide* is recommended, but don't throw away the earlier guidebooks, for their pictures are worth a thousand words.

KEN NICHOLS

Lumpy Ridge and Estes Park Rock Climbs. Scott Kimball. Chockstone Press, Denver,1986. 184 pages, black and white photographs, line drawings. $15.00 (paper).

This guidebook represents a compilation and updating of Scott Kimball's three earlier works: the unpronounceable *Thath-áā-ai-ātah* (with Chip Salaun), *Soli tary Summits,* and *Long's Peak Freeclimber*. It has a modern, professional appearance that is well organized and designed.

The main focus of the book is Lumpy Ridge, whose subalpine granite walls beckon with easy access to climbers first arriving in Estes Park. Several more obscure areas, with lengthy approaches but worthwhile climbs, are also included and are lumped into two sections called "Estes Valley Rocks" and "The Crags." At the tail end of the book are the popular alpine walls of Long's Peak, Hallett Peak, and Spearhead, but these, curiously, almost seem to have been added as an afterthought, perhaps to increase sales.

My first impression of *Lumpy Ridge* was favorable. The stylized indigo cover with its pattern of silver stars is quite original and attractive, and strongly evokes images of the Milky Way on a cold, clear Rocky Mountain night. The author's sensitivity to the environment is then pleasantly continued inside the book with a lengthy essay on the seasons, flora, and fauna, and complementary illustrations by his wife, Annegret. It's nice to see a guidebook that is more than just a mechanical recitation of routes, rocks, and ratings.

The crags are organized in a logical sequence from the rocks of Lumpy Ridge, north of Estes Park, to the remote walls in the Long's Peak area to the south. The 579 route descriptions are usually quite detailed and often provide helpful suggestions on protection and rope drag, but the language is disappointingly dry and lacks the tongue-in-cheek humor that enlivens many other guidebooks. Most of the descriptions are accompanied by a mixture of photographs and line drawings that often clarify when the descriptions confuse. All are conveniently cross-referenced with numbering systems except, oddly enough, those in the High Mountain section.

Kimball has adopted the use of the increasingly popular 0–3 star quality rating system and the shorthand R and X protection grades for routes containing serious runouts or dangerous moves. He has also elected to discard the NCCS roman numeral grade for overall commitment on the subalpine routes because they never were very practical and unnecessarily cluttered the text. These are all big plusses.

On closer inspection, however, there are numerous problems that tend to undermine the book's effectiveness. Although the writing is sometimes eloquent, all too often it is clumsy and hard to follow because of awkward phraseology and missing or incorrect punctuation. Literally scores of hyphens have been left out of such descriptive combinations as right-facing dihedral, 155-foot pitch, eight-legged creatures, etc. I gave up counting misspellings after finding twenty-three on the first twelve pages, including nine on page four alone! Inconsistency in usage also haunts the reader from one end of the book to the other.

When three items are listed and the word "and" connects the last two, sometimes a comma precedes "and" and sometimes it doesn't. Off-width appears as both two words and one. And the author never can decide whether Long's Peak has an apostrophe or not. While most of these errors are relatively minor, many obscure the meaning of what has been written and, together, they distract the reader and cost the author much loss of credibility.

Some of the illustrations depicting routes leave much to be desired as well. Excessively dark shadows on the photos and grainy reproduction too often obscure detail, and many of the line drawings are unclear, especially where the starts of routes are concerned. Because of the nature of the rock, photo treatment across the board would probably have been more successful. In addition, the use of squiggly little arrows to point out lines of ascent is unconventional and looks odd (see page 67). Continuous lines (solid, dashed, or dotted) would have been easier to follow and less confusing (see, for example, the bottom of the photo on page 87).

My final comment is concerned with the section on style and ethics, which is rather weakly entitled "Further Considerations." In the long run, this is one of the most important parts of the book. Every guidebook author has a heavy responsibility to use his or her influence as strongly as possible to maintain the traditional standards of the sport and prevent the wholesale desecration of the crags from indiscriminate bolting on rappel. And yet the author, whose concern for the environment is apparent throughout the book, lamely writes that "Climbers should proceed in any manner or style they deem appropriate, be it free or aid. . ." This phenomenal statement is then followed by a couple of willowy qualifications that defy definition. Kimball's strongest statement about the crisis that is polarizing American climbing is actually buried on page 50 in the route description for "Pizza Face!" Wisely, he did not give first-ascent credit to the perpetrators of this pizza farce.

Lumpy Ridge and Estes Park Rock Climbs is not a literary masterpiece, nor is it one of Chockstone Press's finer creations. But it is bound to be a successful guidebook anyway, because most climbers are more concerned with climbing than commas. And when all is said and done, the guidebook does, in fact, do a good job of describing the quality routes surrounding Estes Park, Colorado.

KEN NICHOLS

Devils Tower National Monument: A Climber's Guide. Steve Gardiner and Dick Guilmette. The Mountaineers, Seattle, 1986. 136 pages, black and white photographs. $6.95 (paper).

Devils Tower is a fantastic volcanic plug that erupts hundreds of feet into the sky above the gently rolling hills of northeast Wyoming. Its remarkable vertical columns provide climbers with classic corners and cracks that cannot be matched for purity of form anywhere else in the world.

Being somewhat off the beaten track, the Tower has been out of the mainstream of climbing until recently, but in the last ten years its superb quality has finally been recognized and the number of visiting climbers and new routes have risen dramatically. To meet the red-hot demand for information, Steve Gardiner and Dick Guilmette have put together an extremely attractive guidebook that has been carefully researched and well designed, and which conveys the mystique of the area.

The first thing that strikes you is the bold cover: a sunlit view of Devils Tower surrounded by molten red. The second thing is its colorful historical anecdotes, starting with the old Indian legend about the great bear clawing the flanks of the Tower. This is followed by the bizarre and entertaining account of William Rogers and Willard Ripley's 1893 ascent of the Tower via a 350-foot wooden ladder. Next comes the inspiring tale of the first ascent using modern rock-climbing techniques by Fritz Wiessner, William House, and Lawrence Coveney in 1937. And finally comes Charles Hopkins' epic 1941 parachute jump onto the summit and his ensuing rescue. One thing that was not mentioned, to the credit of the authors, is the commercialism surrounding the filming of "Close Encounters of the Third Kind," which I think is best forgotten.

The heart of the book, of course, is the 145 separately described routes and variations. All have been depicted on photographs that are appropriately spaced through the text, adjacent to the route descriptions. In addition the photos and descriptions are cross-referenced with a numbering system that totally eliminates any chance for confusion. Another nice feature in each description is the suggested list of equipment. This is always helpful on long routes when what is needed cannot be readily discerned from the ground.

Only a couple of minor problems are apparent in the book, both easily correctable in the next edition: the photo on page fifty-six is a bit too dark, and Lawrence Coveney's last name has mysteriously lost the second "e" whenever it appears. Other than these, my only other criticisms are subjective in nature. Two different grading systems have been mixed rather incongruously together. If   and   are used in the lower grades, why not in the upper as well? Also, I find it objectionable that certain climbers have arrogantly renamed aid routes they have purportedly freed. The routes haven't changed, only the manner in which they were climbed. Does this mean, then, that someone doing an even "purer" ascent (i.e., an unroped solo) has the "right" to change the name again? Although the authors are not to blame for this situation, they still must bear part of the responsibility for perpetuating it. At least they have made a conscientious effort to record the old names so they are not lost to future generations.

One suggestion for the future would be to include a 0–3 star quality rating system. To a limited extent, this has been done in the Note sections, but many two- and three-star routes such as "Mr. Clean," "Soler," and "Tulgey Wood" were not mentioned in this respect.

On an overall basis, *Devils Tower National Monument: A Climber's Guide* is highly recommended. Not only does it serve its purpose exceedingly well, but at $6.95 it has to be one of the greatest bargains ever.

KEN NICHOLS

Joshua Tree Rock Climbing Guide. Randy Vogel. Chockstone Press, Denver,
1986. 401 pages, black and white photographs, line drawings, maps. $25.00
(paper).

Joshua Tree National Monument is *the* winter playground of snowbound climbers from all over the U.S., and its exotic desert environment, unusual rock
formations, and endless number of routes make it one of the finest outdoor
gymnasiums in the world.

Randy Vogel has done a superlative job in capturing the flavor of Joshua
Tree with his monumental new guidebook that contains no less than 1374
routes! No effort was spared to make the book a pleasure to use and the routes
and rocks easy to find. Besides being well written and attractively designed, it
is profusely illustrated. Numerous maps are included that range from topo-
graphical reproductions of the overall area to detailed locations of the individual
formations. Most of the routes are carefully delineated on photos, which are
sometimes augmented by line drawings (topos) when additional details need to
be shown. All the illustrations and route names/descriptions are conveniently
cross-referenced and located adjacent to each other in each section. Route
names are bold-faced and even italicized to make them readily identifiable in
the text.

Other welcome features include a 0–5 star rating system for route quality;
the inclusion of top-rope routes, which are all too often ignored in less pro-
gressive guidebooks; an alphabetized checklist of the routes by grade (5.7 and
up); a definitive international grading comparison chart; and, perhaps most
unusual of all, a translation of the Summary into several languages (French,
Japanese, and German) for visiting foreign climbers.

One of the strongest points of the book is the excellent section on ethics and
local standards. For once, ethics and style have been clearly defined for all those
climbers who loosely bandy about the terms without understanding their difference. Vogel then goes on to mount a powerful and eloquent defense of traditional climbing standards and rightfully condemns the destructive and degrading
practices of chopping holds and placing bolts on rappel. It's nice to see an area
where the locals actively work to preserve the rock and the sport from the
excesses of the less competent. Bravo!

Only a few minor difficulties crept into the book, none of which detracts
from its overall excellence. On page nine, "prospective" and "uncomparable"
should probably have been "perspective" and "incomparable" instead. The use
of   and   and a-b-c-d subdivisions in the difficulty ratings seems oddly
inconsistent. Why not one or the other? Also, the use of 0–5 stars to indicate
quality seems a bit too excessive; perhaps the more commonly used 0–3 star
system would have been better.

Even if one does not like the modernistic lavendar cover, this guidebook is
certainly one of the two or three best ever published in the U.S. and is a great
credit to the author, the publisher, and the area. It is well worth the $25 price.

KEN NICHOLS

Rock Climbs of Tuolumne Meadows. Don Reid and Chris Falkenstein. Chockstone Press, Denver, 1986. 140 pages, black and white photographs, line drawings. $13.95 (paper).

This is an excellent revision of the authors' 1983 guidebook, and it should be well received by those who seek refuge from the summer waves of heat and humanity in Yosemite Valley below.

Several improvements have been made in this edition that are immediately obvious. Carolly Hauksdottir's inspired illustration of Tuolumne Meadows has been enlarged and moved to the title page. In its place on the cover is a striking wrap-around, color photograph of a climber dramatically silhouetted against a sea of water-streaked granite. The introductory material has been set in larger, easier-to-read 10-point typeface, and route names have been attractively bold-faced to make them readily distinguishable in the text. The biggest improvement has been the increased emphasis on photographs of the cliffs. The photos are more numerous than in the 1983 edition, and they have been spread conveniently through the book rather than bunched up in one place. This very practical idea makes the guidebook considerably easier to use.

Other noteworthy features are the inclusion of several newly discovered areas, the helpful comments on protection, and the retention of Tom Higgins' well written historical perspective. Higgins' eloquent plea for a return to traditional climbing style is especially thought provoking and should be read by every climber who contemplates murdering the impossible with questionable tactics.

Other than a few misspellings (guidebook is one word, for example), there is very little to criticize about this fine book. Only three relatively minor points come to mind, and two of these are purely cosmetic. Many of the route names in the captions for the illustrations are not lined up vertically with each other, which creates a rather ragged appearance on close inspection. Also, despite the great success of boldfacing throughout the book, it is almost overwhelming in the index; it probably would have been better to save the boldfacing for the relatively small number of formations listed there instead. And finally, it would have been nice to know what route is depicted on the cover so that visiting climbers could duplicate the shot if they so desired.

All in all, *Rock Climbs of Tuolumne Meadows* is an excellent investment. It is certainly one of the best guidebooks yet produced for any area in the United States and should whet the appetite of any climber who enjoys exhilarating runouts on endless sweeps of granite.

KEN NICHOLS

East Africa International Mountain Guide. Andrew Wielochowski. West Col Productions, Goring, 1986. 151 pages, photographs, line drawings, maps, bibliography. $25.00 (U.S.).

This is a welcome addition to climbing book shelves to sit alongside *Guide to Mount Kenya and Kilimanjaro* and *The Mountains of Kenya—A Hill Walker's*

Guide, both by the Mountain Club of Kenya. This guidebook also covers Mount Kenya and Kilimanjaro. But, in addition, it describes the Ruwenzori Mountains and many of the first-class rock climbs that abound in East Africa. As a bonus, cave exploration is included. The author spent eight years gathering the information for the book and has done most of the climbs and some first ascents himself.

Apart from the Ruwenzori and Kilimanjaro, the guide concentrates on Kenya. The author first deals briefly with its geography and people, then its flora and fauna. He gives a short discourse on the Swahili language, from which, he says, an ungrammatical but understandable speaking knowledge can be gained. He also discusses transportation, health, weather and climbing hazards and gives a bibliography and a list of useful maps—unfortunately, hard to obtain at present. Driving directions to the climbs are included, together with information on garages and the availability of gasoline.

The rock climbs are graded by the UIAA system and the ice climbs by the Scottish method. The length of the climbs is given in meters (the book is in the metric system only) and times are given for the mountain routes. The quality of a climb is also rated with one, two or three stars. The rock climbs are of a high standard, many being Grade IV–V (5.0–5.6), with many more of VI- to VII- (5.8–5.10c).

I have done several of the mountain routes and can attest to the accuracy of the descriptions, which have roughly the same detail as Beckey's guidebook.

The updated information on the Ruwenzori is valuable and, while in Kenya, climbers should be tempted to try some of the rock climbs and walking routes described. Some important climbs, however, are excluded, such as Mawenzi. Good walking areas, such as Mount Elgon and the Abedare Mountains are also not included. In this respect, *A Hill Walkers Guide* is better.

MICHAEL D. CLARKE

Maps of Nepal. Harka Gurung. White Orchid Books, Bangkok, 1983. 100 pages, 28 color and black and white maps, many sketches and geological information.

The author has been engaged in large-and small-scale planning, not only in his native Nepal but for international organizations as well, and has published books and articles about the physical sciences, and the economy and politics of tourism in Nepal. He has collected twenty-eight maps, ranging from one by Kircher in 1666 to the 1981 Landsat map of Nepal, and has annotated them skillfully. There are brief chapters on the history of mapping in the Himalaya, panoramas, and fascinating summaries of geological and geomorphological studies, in addition to a short bibliography and a list of major peaks along Nepal's northern boundary (which will doubtless intrigue climbers). Though the modern maps are too small in scale to be helpful to the traveller, the book is a must for anyone interested in the history of exploration, geopolitics, and mapping in Nepal, and by extension much of the Himalaya.

Like a number of similar unusual books, this one is available through Akio Horiuchi, Bookseller, A-102 2-12-23 Motomachi-kyose, Tokyo 204, Japan.

CHARLES S. HOUSTON, M.D.

Living on the Edge. Cherie Bremer-Kamp. Peregrine Smith Books, Layton, Utah, 1987. 213 pages, 33 color photos, 6 maps and diagrams. $19.95.

There are risks in writing about climbing that mirror the risks of the sport itself. The intensely personal nature of the struggle, and of our concepts of life and death, set the writer a delicate task. Cherie Bremer-Kamp, during the course of a deliberate life, has embraced both varieties of risk with fervor; in both cases, unfortunately, the hazards seem to have gotten the upper hand.

Ms. Bremer-Kamp and the late Chris Chandler first met during the 1978 American K2 Expedition. This book tells of their subsequent years and adventures together, culminating in the tragedy of their lonely winter attempt on Kanchenjunga in 1985, when Chris died of altitude-related illness and Cherie herself nearly failed to make it back down with their single Nepali helpmate.

The book begins promisingly, with a provocative account of an epic sea journey in a sailboat that the two of them had crafted in their spare time. This engaging introduction is then left behind for a gossip-laden account of their participation in the K2 expedition; and the reader is soon left in a state of unrequited curiosity as husband, children, and the rest of the author's former life are apparently forgotten in order to pursue a love and a set of ideals that remain inadequately explicated. We are never treated to the background material that might serve to explain Chris and Cherie's willingness to sacrifice so much for their great loves: climbing and each other. Dreams hide within these pages; we catch glimpses of them but their substance escapes. Brief, passing references to Cherie's former spouse (who was also a member of the K2 expedition) do little to illuminate for us the power of emotions that can lead to such a complete disruption of one's life, or the end of life itself.

Simultaneously paean and apologia, this book has great tragedy and the intense passions that lead up to it as its themes. There are moments of great honesty and insight, but in the end to read it is a saddening experience, not only for what it relates but also because the reader must ultimately come to grips with the fact that passion alone does not give a book substance. The depth and universality of the emotions dominating *Living on the Edge* are belied by their brief and anecdotal treatment; on the other hand, events and situations that should have been able to speak for themselves are either spoken for or treated so cursorily that they have no voice.

The author has taken upon herself a monumental task, essaying to draw the reader into the vortices of a very personal and tortuous relationship, and to show us what it means to confront the mountains at their most hostile with that relationship as shield and weapon. But the expository sections of the book are inadequate as a preparation for what is to come, and the climax—Chris's death—serves only to bring the book to a hasty close. At this point, where it is most needed, Cherie's introspective voice seems most at a loss for something meaningful to say.

The book seems to have been assembled hurriedly and (understandably) under great stress; the author herself acknowledges the essential support of family and friends in writing it. She has labored under the additional handicap of insensitive and careless editing; the reader's empathy flows less freely around the obstacles of syntax and spelling that are thrown in his path. Especially annoying are the ubiquitous parenthetical conversions from metric to English measurements, present even during the most emotionally charged moments.

One can see that this book carries with it a lot of the author's emotional sensibilities; the writing of it was, no doubt, a painful act of catharsis. Unfortunately the reader is apt to be an unsympathetic lout, and require a bit more guidance to understanding than Ms. Bremer-Kamp was able to give. There is too much of the author here, and too little of that painful world of hope, despair, and tragedy that she inhabits. And, inevitably, there is too little of Chris Chandler himself; but that, now, will always be the case.

RON MATOUS

In Memoriam

HENRY SNOW HALL, JR.
1895-1987

A very proper Bostonian, in every positive sense of the word, Henry Hall has been the most important single figure in the maturity of the American Apline Club.

Born June 3, 1895, Henry was educated at Saint George's School in Newport, Rhode Island and graduated from Harvard College with the Class of 1919. He was in infantry officer in World War I. He is survived by his wife, Lydia, and daughter, Edith Overly.

Our first Honorary President served the Club in various capacities, Counsellor, Secretary, President and Honorary President, since becoming a member in 1918. While he partook of many interests in his life, including a prominent part in community and public service endeavors in the Greater Boston area, the ongoing interest of Henry's life has been mountaineering, which he took up as a teenager on a visit to Switzerland, and The American Alpine Club.

The Club's accomplishments during Henry's long membership became one with his own and are best summed up in his own words, "Mountaineering is now recognized as a legitimate sport for thousands of people. The AAC was instrumental in making it a respectable pastime."

To him, our Club's greatest single accomplishment came in 1941, when he, and the other Club officers, convinced General George Marshall that the United States would have to have trained mountain troops before the war could be won in Europe and perhaps elsewhere. This was the genesis of the 87th Mountain Infantry Regiment, which saw service in the Aleutian Islands in 1943. It then became part of the 10th Mountain Division, which broke the "Gothic Line," was the first unit to reach the Po River and forced the surrender of the German troops in Italy, initiating the collapse of Hitler's rule in 1945. Having stimulated the formation of mountain troops, Henry set out to help recruit members for it, including a variety of Harvard mountaineers, and others, for whom he wrote one of the required three letters necessary for acceptance into this elite corps.

Henry's serious climbing activities began before World War I and continued until well after World War II. First in the Bernina Alps and later in the Valais, he returned year after year to the mountains of his youth. But his greatest accomplishments in mountaineering were in North America, in Alaska and British Columbia. Henry's list of first ascents include little known peaks such as Mount Hallam in the Monashees, and well known ones like the North Peak of Mount

HENRY SNOW HALL, JR.
1895-1987

Waddington, in the Coast Range and a new route on formidable Mount Robson. Along the way have been dozens of other ascents, first and otherwise. He was not among the summit team on the first ascent of Mount Logan as he volunteered to help another member, who had frozen his feet, down the mountain from 17,000 feet.

Of them all, the Coast Range of British Columbia was probably Henry's favorite haunt, and his living room, for fifty years, was adorned by a painting of the area done for him by Belmore Browne. He made several visits to these mountains, sometimes approaching from the sea, and other times from the Interior, often in company with Don and Phyllis Munday, and packer Batise Dester. While he knew he did not possess the technical skill to climb the higher South Peak of Waddington, he noted it as "one of the most remarkable culminating points of any mountain range in the world."

Henry's climbing record also included ascents in New Zealand, Mexico, the Caucasus, Japan, Columbia, besides many parts of the United States. New country was his specialty, opening new vistas by backpacking and horse-train ventures. Others were to follow later and make other ascents, but Henry's were always the unique and opening moves. Some of his "bear stories" were priceless, but this is not the place for them. Between climbs, Henry was a hiker, sometimes walking dozens of miles each day, and routinely climbing Mount Monadnock in southern New Hampshire.

While he enjoyed an almost lifetime association with the AAC (being six years older than the Club, itself) Henry was also the founder and guiding light of the oldest collegiate mountaineering organization in the country, the Harvard Mountaineering Club, in 1924. His persistent support of this group enabled many of its members to become among the most prominent alpinists of the country, and provide leadership to countless other mountaineering ventures.

The Hall residence in Cambridge was always open to visiting alpinists, from all over the world. Countless Club members have been guests there, planned expeditions while sitting around his living room floor, studied the records and maps in his enormous library, and picked his brains on approaches, sources of supply, people to look up and the myriad trivia of getting set to go into new country. Invariably, Lydia Hall (née Storer), who married Henry in 1921, would receive us with that same gentle graciousness she displayed to the entire American Alpine Club when finally elected a member. Lydia had long met all the Club's criteria for membership, with several seasons among glacier-hung peaks and numerous prominent ascents to her credit, but she had always preferred to leave the alpine spotlight to shine alone on her generous husband. In 1982, the Club's Board of Directors decided she had been under wraps long enough.

Henry Hall was honored at home and abroad for his persistent support of alpinism in all its forms, of which the most prestigious was being elected to Honorary membership in the Alpine Club in 1962 (after 38 years as a member). But to the American Alpine Club, and American mountaineering of which he has been the most persistent and generous supporter in history, the Club's *An-*

gelo Heilprin Citation, given Henry at our 1985 Annual Meeting, said it best: ". . . always quiet, always in the background, but always ready to help. Without Henry modern American expeditionary mountaineering would never have grown to its present stature. Yet no one, perhaps not even Henry himself, will ever know precisely where he assisted and by how much. Minya Konka? Nanda Devi? K2 in 1938 and several times later? Mount Everest? The laurels went to the climbers. Henry remained in the shadows. Only the poor and simple alpinists of this world, like Ed Feuz, have ever expressed their gratitude and appreciated the greatness of his generous anonymity."

Edward Feuz, Jr. (1884-1981), Swiss guide of Canada, climbed with Henry Hall on many occasions, starting to do so at the insistence of Henry's father, in 1916. His judgment, rendered in 1924, was: "I'll bet he'll do more for mountain climbing than all the guides and climbers who've been out here in Canada put together." How well he saw the future!

But Feuz was not alone in visualizing the place in alpinism of our loving and generous Honorary President. Fritz Wiessner knew; "Henry has been one of the most active and important members of the AAC and other mountain clubs in the world. His intense interest and correspondence with other leaders in the field made him probably the best informed American alpinist." And from a co-founder of the Harvard Mountaineering Club, William Osgood Field: "Henry personally knew just about everybody in the mountaineering field in North America and many more at the Alpine Club in London and on the Continent."

Our distinguished past President, Professor T.C.P. Zimmerman summed it up, too: "Throughout all the achievements of our national mountaineering organization runs the thread of Henry Hall's continuous and often anonymous generosity."

Henry Hall was a thoughtful and generous catalyst, who made possible many of the works of the American Alpine Club, most particularly visible in the renowned quality of our *Journal*. Without him, the American Alpine Club will never be the same.

WILLIAM LOWELL PUTNAM

FRITIOF MELVIN FRYXELL
1900-1986

Fritiof M. Fryxell, geologist, professor, writer and mountaineer, died December 19, 1986 at his home in Rock Island, Illinois. He had been a member of the American Alpine Club for 56 years and was elected to honorary membership in 1981. Professor Fryxell's professional life was rich and varied. Born April 27, 1900, in Moline, Illinois, he attended Augustana College, Rock Island, earned an MA in English from the University of Illinois and a Ph.D. in geology from the University of Chicago in 1929. His dissertation on the glacial features of Jackson Hole was the first expression of what would become a lifelong passion: the mountains of the west. He interpreted them scientifically, in professional papers and lectures, and poetically, in the descriptions and metaphors of his well-known book *The Tetons: Interpretations of a Mountain Landscape* (now in its sixth edition). He served as the first Ranger-Naturalist for the Grand Teton National Park (1929-34), later (1935-1939) was a member of the museum planning staff of the National Park Service, and initiated (1946) the cooperative research arrangement between the National Park Service and the US Geological Survey which flourishes today.

In 1923 Fryxell joined the faculty at Augustana College, and during his 50-year tenure created and taught in its nationally recognized department of geology. A museum and endowed chair in the department now bear his name. During World War II Fryxell served as assistant chief of the Military Geology Unit, which was responsible for analyzing the terrain of projected battle sites. In 1948 the death of his professional colleague and friend (and AAC member), François Matthes, redirected his efforts for some seventeen years to the editing and completing five of Matthes' projected books on Yosemite and the Sierra Nevada.

Fryxell initially developed his interest in the west and the Teton range through perusal of railroad guidebooks which his father brought back to Illinois after working in California. One of these, *The Pacific Tourist,* contains a replica of the early W.H. Jackson photograph of the Grand Teton as well as an illustration from the Langford 1873 article in *Scribner's Magazine,* which described the climb (or attempt) on the Grand Teton. This book also contains numerous engravings by Thomas Moran and an article by F.V. Hayden on the Yellowstone. All these topics became subject matter for his prolific writings, in several books and numerous articles.

In the summer of 1924 he hitchhiked from West Yellowstone to Tetonia on the west side of the range, obtaining his first close-up view of the Tetons. That time he got only into the foothills from the west. The summer of 1926 was Fryxell's first of many summers in the Teton mountains, when he began work on his geological thesis. An impromptu attempt to climb the Grand Teton that first summer failed, but his climbing record began in 1927 with successes on the East Prong of Mount Owen and the Grand. The second high Teton summit, Buck Mountain, he reached the following summer during four additional weeks of geological field work.

But it was the summer of 1929, after the opening of the newly created Grand Teton National Park, that Doc, as he was known to almost all of his younger friends, began his outstanding sequence of pioneering first ascents in the range, commonly with his fellow ranger, Phil Smith. Within a one-month period Doc, sometimes solo but mostly with Phil, climbed Woodring, Grand Teton, Teewinot, Rockchuck, St. John, Symmetry Spire, Wister, Hunt, and the Middle Teton; seven of these were first ascents! As members of the small ranger staff, Doc and Phil were expected by the park superintendent to be available for duty twenty-four hours a day, seven days a week. Great energy and some ingenuity

JOHN L. J. HART
1904-1986

FRITIOF MELVIN FRYXELL
1900-1986

were required to get away for these climbs, making the accomplishments all the more impressive. The next two summers were equally productive, with first ascents of Nez Perce, Bivouac Peak, Mount Owen, Cloudveil Dome, East Horn of Moran, and Storm and Ice Point. After a summer in the Colorado Rockies in 1932, where he climbed a dozen 14,000ers, Doc returned to the Tetons for the following three summers, adding first ascents of Rolling Thunder, Prospectors, and Ranger Peak. It was a glorious period in Teton history and Doc made the most of it.

These climbs, together with extensive canyon hiking and glacier study, were largely exploratory in nature, rather than for the goal of overcoming of sheer difficulties as seems more common now. But three, at least, of Doc Fryxell's climbs still rank as significant technical achievements. The first ascent of Mount Owen in 1930 with Underhill, Henderson and Smith was a landmark climb, for the peak remains today as perhaps the most difficult of the Teton peaks. His second ascent, in one day, of the east ridge of the Grand Teton in 1934 with Fred Ayres, with little or no information on the route, still seems a remarkable accomplishment.

But truly impressive in imaginative pioneering was his climb of the north ridge of the Grand Teton with brilliant Robert L.M. Underhill. In this climb they were perhaps a generation ahead of their time. It was a clear technical step forward, the most difficult alpine ascent yet completed in the United States. It stands today as *the* classic among a dozen great Teton alpine climbs. To comprehend fully the accomplishment of Underhill and Fryxell in 1931, let a modern climber try the ascent with their equipment: Underhill used Tricouni nailed boots, while Doc's smooth-soled work boots had one composition sole and one leather sole. It was an extraordinary climb, and Underhill, in writing of the climb, related that Fryxell ". . . raced up the rocks of the grandstand in his usual fashion, showing the same dexterity and speed that on our frequent ropeless climbs had regularly left me well in the rear."

Such stories as these only partially reveal the energy and enthusiasm which carried Doc Fryxell throughout his long life with his love of nature, the mountains, the west, and its history. His particular talent was the ability to convey this enthusiastic sense to students and all who came within his purview. His evening campfire talks in the early Grand Teton National Park days are now legendary. As well described in the *American Alpine News,* Doc Fryxell was the eloquent interpreter *par excellence*. This talented and gifted man compounded a profound understanding of geology and the natural scene, with an extraordinary skill in the English language. A reader of his *Interpretations of a Mountain Landscape* cannot fail to appreciate the careful craftsmanship of his descriptive phrases. Equally remarkable, the same care in the selection of words highlighted his correspondence and even informal conversation.

A complementary and permanent contribution of Doc Fryxell to the Teton scene is found in the numerous creative and mellifluous place names he attached to the mountains and lakes, waterfalls and glaciers. Who else could have produced Cloudveil Dome and Symmetry Spire, Rolling Thunder Mountain and Lake of the Crags?

With the passing of Fritiof Fryxell we have lost one of the last and finest links to the pioneer era of American mountaineering. Fryxell was in the forefront of those who brought the Tetons from their obscurity in the 1920s to the prominent place they now occupy as a primary climbing center in the United States. Yet this was done without a trace of self-promotion. His old-school modesty was as ingrained as his gentlemanly tendency to say only good things about others. Perhaps these words of his convey not only his mountaineering ethic but his approach to life itself: "Each trip into the mountains was sheer delight, however great the labor and whether it led to a peak ascent or not."

LEIGH N. ORTENBURGER

NOEL E. ODELL
1890-1987

The distinguished climber, geologist and friend, Noel E. Odell, died on February 21, 1987, as we were about to go to press. He became a member of the American Alpine Club in 1928 and was made an honorary member in 1936. A complete obituary will appear in the *American Alpine Journal* in 1988.

VITALY MIKHAILOVICH ABALAKOV
1906-1986

With good reason Vitaly Abalakov was known as "The Father of Soviet Mountaineering." One of the first to pursue serious mountaineering within the socialist system, he contributed much to the development of Russian climbing: as the indomitable leader of first ascents; fertile inventor of ironmongery; advocate and example of extreme physical conditioning; efficient director of international climbing camps; delegate to the UIAA and its belaying commission; and esteemed member of the first Soviet team to visit the United States. He was made an honorary member of the American Alpine Club in 1976.

At an early age he began scrambling on rock formations near Krasnoyarsk, the Siberian city of his birth. In the early 1930s he shot to prominence, accomplishing many notable ascents in the Pamirs, Tien Shan, Altai, and Caucasus. His partners included wife Valentina, the finest Soviet woman climber of her time, and brother Eugene, the first person to attain the summit of Pik Kommunizma, highest in the Soviet Union.

Vitaly stopped climbing in 1936 after suffering frostbite on Khan Tengri in the Tien Shan; one-third of his left foot and parts of fingers on both hands had to be amputated. Rebounding from this setback, he embarked on a formidable exercise program that presaged Buhl, Gill, and Messner in its intensity. Dispensing with gloves in winter tempered his hands against the cold. Gymnastic workouts strengthened arms and fingers (he could execute one-arm pull-ups on each arm). And ski racing developed his cardiovascular system to the efficiency of a professional athlete.

After World War II he returned to high-altitude mountaineering, leading a major expedition almost every year until the early 1960s. Among his best achievements were "north face" routes in the Caucasus; a seven-peak traverse of Pik Lenin, Pik 19, and others in the Pamirs; and the first ascent of Pik Pobedy in the Tien Shan, second highest Soviet summit.

A mechanical engineer by profession, Abalakov developed various kinds of climbing equipment, many of them constructed of lightweight titanium. The bulk of his talent, however, was invested at the Central Scientific Research Institute for Sport, where for twenty years he held the position of laboratory director. Here he specialized in constructing devices to monitor athletic performance in different sports. His work has been credited with improving athletic training methods in the USSR and other socialist countries.

The years brought many awards from the Soviet state: Honored Master of Mountaineering (1934), Honored Master of Sport (1943), Honored Trainer of the USSR (1957), Order of Lenin (1957), Order of the Badge of Honor (1972), Order of Friendship Among Peoples (1982).

Not until recent years did American mountaineers become personally acquainted with the man. In 1974, Abalakov acted as climbing director of the international camp attended by a large contingent of Americans. The tragic events of that summer, which included the loss of American Gary Ullin and a group of Soviet women, were described by Robert Craig in *Storm and Sorrow in the Pamirs*. The following year, the American Alpine Club invited a Soviet team to tour the United States, and Abalakov was sent as a kind of honorary leader; he took little part in the actual climbing. Even at the age of 69 he was remarkably fit and possessed the physique of a man years younger. His character left a lasting impression, too. An unquenchable spirit and patient wisdom shone through his modest demeanor.

A mild stroke finally put an end to active mountaineering, yet Abalakov's last years were anything but inactive. He worked on equipment for the successful Soviet expedition to Everest in 1982 and lectured around the country, encouraging young people to get involved in mountaineering organizations. He also canoed the rivers of northern Russia and enjoyed life as a great-grandfather.

PIETER CROW

JOHN L. J. (JERRY) HART
1904-1986

John Lathrop Jerome (Jerry) Hart, President of the American Alpine Club from 1970 until 1973, died April 27, 1986 at his home in Laguna Niguel, California at the age of 81. He is survived by his wife Jane, his three children,

Dr. Kate Zimmerman, Sally Whiting, and Jack Hart, four grandchildren, his brother Stephen H. Hart, a member of the American Alpine Club, and his sister Margot Hart Tettemer.

Jerry was born in Denver, Colorado on August 15, 1904 of a pioneer Colorado family. He was admitted to Harvard University at the age of 15. After graduation from Harvard he was awarded a Rhodes Scholarship and obtained three graduate degrees at Oxford.

In 1929, Jerry was admitted to the Colorado Bar and practiced law for many years in Denver where he was a senior partner in the firm of Holland and Hart together with his brother Steve. He was active in many clubs and civic organizations and was one of the founders of the University Corporation for Atmospheric Research located in Boulder, Colorado.

Jerry was a pioneer Colorado climber. His interest in mountaineering began before he was ten years old at the family summer home in Buffalo Creek, Colorado. He first taught himself, then his brother Steve, the art of climbing. In September 1922, Jerry planned to make the first ascent of the East Face of Longs Peak but his proposed route was climbed by Professor J.W. Alexander of Princeton a few days before Jerry, Carl Blaurock, Dudley Smith and other friends made it. He also made early ski-mountaineering ascents of various peaks in the Rockies. Jerry was an early member of the Colorado Mountain Club and Editor of its magazine, *Trail and Timberland*. In 1925, at age 20, he wrote the authoritative classic on Colorado's mountains, *Fourteen Thousand Feet, A History of the Names and Early Ascents of the High Colorado Peaks*. He prepared a revised second edition, which was published in 1931 and reprinted in 1972. In fact, Jerry was so synonymous with Colorado mountaineering that the author of a juvenile pot boiler, *Climb to the Top,* called his wise adult counselor "Mr. Hart." One suspects this name was not picked at random from the Denver telephone directory.

Jerry's mountaineering interests went far beyond the borders of his native state. He did winter climbs in Huntington and Tuckerman Ravines on Mount Washington, rock climbs in Wales, and various climbs in the Alps including a traverse of the Grand and Petit Dru with Sir Douglas Busk, guided by two of the most famous alpine guides of all time, Armand and Georges Charlet.

Besides being an active climber, Jerry was a student of mountaineering literature and a collector of mountaineering books. He amassed a significant mountaineering library which he donated to the University of Colorado Library where they form the foundation of that institution's mountaineering collection.

He was a charter member of the Harvard Mountaineering Club and the "Honorary Secretary" of the Oxford Mountaineering Club. He also belonged to The Alpine Club and the French and Swiss Alpine Clubs as well as the Groupe de Haute Montagne. He joined the American Alpine Club in 1925, dropped out in 1938, but rejoined the Club in 1949.

Jerry had the misfortune to preside over the affairs of the American Alpine Club in an era in which such matters were conducted at an unprecedentedly high decibel level. He did a remarkable job as president while constantly being criticized by those who did not understand what he was doing, as well as by those who did understand what he was doing. But he always retained his sense of humor. I still have memories of leaving yet another board meeting in which the air had been filled with everything except chairs, and after the inevitable discussion of what had just hit us, Jerry would begin to regale me with another one of his amusing stories from a seemingly inexhaustible store. For it was a tribute to his great decency and integrity that even his most vociferous critics were very fond of him. The most recent tangible expression of this affection was at the last Club dinner in Denver at which Jerry was awarded the Angelo Heilprin citation for service to the Club and American mountaineering. It was the first time the award had been made posthumously.

Jerry made many contributions to American and international mountaineering, but his greatest contribution was the establishment of the exchange program between Soviet and American mountaineers and obtaining permission for American mountaineers to climb anywhere in the Soviet Union. It took Jerry and his wife, Jane, years of unremitting effort and numerous trips to the Soviet Union to accomplish this, but Jerry's ingenuity, perseverance, and diplomacy did it; the first U.S. delegation of climbers went to the Pamirs in 1974. Undoubtedly, it was this experience that led to his interest in promoting world peace which he pursued so avidly in recent years.

During many years of close association with Jerry, the most indelible incident I experienced with him which best showed his character, enthusiasm, and zest for life, took place not in the mountains, nor in the boardrooms of alpine clubs, but in the Los Angeles Coliseum. It turned out that this Rhodes scholar, prominent lawyer, distinguished citizen, and staid elder statesman of the mountaineering world, was a track-and-field nut. In 1968, he flew out from Denver to Los Angeles to watch the final tryouts for the United States track-and-field team which was going to compete in the Mexico City Olympics. Jerry insisted that my wife and I join him, so the three of us sat in the large crowd in that vast stadium watching the confusing spectacle on the field while Jerry tried to explain some of the finer points to us. Suddenly a crimson sweatshirt could be spotted in the swarming array of athletes below us. Without warning, a "Yea, Harvard" blasted past my ear, rolled across the field, seemingly bounced off the opposite side, and came back at us. While I struggled to regain my composure, a thousand faces turned towards us and began to grin as the solitary Harvard contestant stopped dead in his tracks, looked up, and smiled. The mood in the crowd seemed a lot lighter after that. So perhaps the best way one can sum up such a remarkable person as John L. J. Hart is in a variation of that simple cheer— Yea, Jerry.

NICHOLAS B. CLINCH

LILLIAN GEST
1898-1986

Lillian Gest, last surviving member of a prominent Philadelphia family, died in January, 1986, at age eighty-eight. Many years before, on her graduation from Vassar, she had set out to get a job, but had been stopped by her family, who said that getting a job would deprive some man who needed it. Accordingly she turned to volunteer social work, where she was very active for the rest of her life, especially with the Philadelphia Children's Bureau, which she served as president. Lillian was always active out-of-doors too, and helped to start the Philadelphia Trail Club.

However, most of Lillian's climbs were made in the Canadian Rockies, although she did some minor climbing in the Alps in 1929. Her love affair with the mountains started with Caroline Hinman on packtrips which crisscrossed Jasper and the Canadian Rockies, using outfitter Jim Boyce and hunting guide Charlie Hunter.

She attended many of the summer camps of the Alpine Club of Canada and the Skyline Hikers of the Canadian Rockies, climbing after camp with her favorite guides, Christian Hasler and Eduard Feuz. She joined forces with Katie Gardner on several major first ascents in 1937: Mount Bryce complete from Rice Brook, Queant and Trident. She was very pleased at climbing Mount Columbia from the ACC camp in 1938.

She was one of the most knowledgeable Canadian Rockies enthusiasts and was continually consulted. After her active climbing days she became interested in research and wrote of three favorite areas: *History of Lake O'Hara*, 1961; *History of Moraine Lake*, 1970; and *History of Mt. Assiniboine*, 1979.

Lillian was a member of the American Alpine Club for over fifty years, serving on the council from 1947-1949. She was also the originator and first editor of the *A.A.C. News*, a publication that speedily became a valuable way to inform and unite the Club's widely separated membership.

Lillian was a longtime friend, tentmate and climbing companion over a period of fifty years. Her hobbies were birding, photography and skating. In later years she was usually to be found during the summer at Lake O'Hara Lodge, where she was much in demand for her early memories and beautiful slide shows.

Always helpful, with her practical good sense and cheerfulness, Lillian will be sorely missed by her many friends in the United States and Canada.

POLLY PRESCOTT

LAWRENCE IRVING GRINNELL
1889-1985

Lawrence Grinnell was not perhaps one of our most outstanding climbers, but rather an all-around outdoorsman, who enjoyed mountaineering, mountain hiking and whitewater river running for his personal pleasure and satisfaction. He also liked to share his enjoyment with others as his numerous articles in *Appalachia* and the *American Alpine Journal* attest. He developed an early interest in birds and became a professional ornithologist.

Lawrence I. Grinnell was born in Flushing, New York on June 14, 1889, and was educated at Pomfret School, and Harvard College from which he graduated in 1912. After three years in the publishing business he joined a National Guard cavalry unit, and then, when cavalry was deemed unsuitable for trench warfare, served in a field artillery unit in World War I. Following the end of the war he returned to the publishing business and became editor of a trade journal for some five years until he shifted his attention to the real-estate field. Eventually he established his own firm from which he retired in 1938. He moved to Ithaca, New York to pursue his studies in ornithology, receiving an SM degree in 1943 and a PhD in 1947 from Cornell in that field.

He married Julia Temple in New York City on September 27, 1930 and they had a daughter, Sarah, born in 1931. With his wife, who was also an avid outdoorswoman (see *A.A.J.*, 1961, page 348), he did a great deal of climbing and whitewater canoeing. The two of them set about ascending all the state high points in the lower forty-eight, a feat about which he wrote in the *A.A.J.*, 1944 on pages 212 to 221. This writer well remembers leading a party, of which he was a member, up Gannett Peak, the highest point in Wyoming, which involved a long day's climb requiring twice crossing the continental divide by a high pass.

He wrote many articles for *Appalachia*, both on his climbing and his whitewater canoeing, the latter in an endeavor to popularize the sport in the New York area, starting originally with an article on the *Rivers Within 100 Miles of New York,* and later covering the rivers of central New York state after his removal to Ithaca. These finally led to the publishing in book form his magnum opus on the subject, *Canoeable Waterways of New York.*

After receiving his doctorate from Cornell, he became a Research Associate at the Cornell Laboratory of Ornithology, and indulged his love of music by playing the violin in the Cornell University Orchestra and the Ithaca Chamber Orchestra. Many of his later travels were in pursuit of his profession as an ornithologist and included rafting trips on big rivers. Although he has been inactive for the last few years, the Club lost one of its oldest and most interesting members upon his death on December 22, 1985.

KENNETH A. HENDERSON

L.C. "JACK" BALDWIN
1921-1986

The mountaineering world lost a great leader when, on June 26, Jack Baldwin suffered a fatal heart attack at age 65. Jack was born in Hood River, Oregon and was a descendent of a pioneer Hood River family. He was educated at Oregon State University as an engineer and was owner of the L.C. Baldwin Construction Company. He served with distinction as a Sea-Bee in the South Pacific during World War II.

Jack was an avid and devoted mountain man from adolescence until the time of his death. He climbed hundreds of peaks in the Cascades and Olympics. He became a member of the American Alpine Club in 1955 and was a founding member of the Alpinees, a Hood River climbing and mountain rescue organization, serving as president for many terms. As an engineer, Jack designed and developed a cable rescue system widely used in the Northwest. He was developer and operator of the Cooper Spur Ski Area on Mount Hood.

Jack was a strong and versatile climber and woodsman. He carried huge packs with ease over rough country. If you fell into a stream and your camera was soaked, Jack would pull out of the side pocket of his pack a jeweler's kit and a vial of alcohol and, two hours later, you had a dry and working camera. If a pack-strap rivet stripped, presto—a rivet kit appeared. If a boot started to come apart, he would dig in his pack and find an awl and thread.

Obviously, Jack was an expedition man par excellence. He was quartermaster of the American Quitana Roo Expedition of 1967, which crossed on foot 170 miles of previously unexplored jungle in Yucatán, Mexico. They discovered significant Mayan ruins en route. He served in the same capacity in the 1978 penetration of the great and previously unexplored canyon of the Río Mesquital between the Mexican states of Durango and Nayarit.

No one could match Jack for pure strength and determination. He was a man who enjoyed the mountains or the jungles to the fullest. The mountain winds and snows exalted him. The jungle Morpho butterflies challenged him.

The Alpinees have established the Jack Baldwin Memorial Fund to assist in financing young climbers and explorers in their efforts to "look behind the ranges." (Address: Alpinees, c/o Carrol Davis, Hood River, Oregon 97031.)

Jack is survived by his wife Virginia, a son Donald, both of Hood River and a daughter Jan Panfilio of Portland, Oregon.

ROBERT LEE

THOMAS GORDON GOMAN
1944-1986

Tom Goman died on Mount Hood May 14 while leading a climbing group from the Oregon Episcopal School. Father Tom, as he was called by his students, was born in 1944 in Corvallis, Oregon. He graduated from the University of Puget Sound in 1966 and went on to Oregon State University to do graduate work in chemical physics and spectroscopy. This led to geophysics and gravity field studies of Mount Saint Helens and the Wenatchee Mountains. Goman then concentrated on his interest in theology and enrolled in Harvard University Divinity School, graduating Magna Cum Laude in 1970. He was ordained in the Episcopal Church in 1972 and taught physics, chemistry and ethics at various institutions from 1970 to 1978 while also serving as vicar and chaplain for missions of the Episcopal Church. In 1978, Father Tom joined the Oregon Episcopal School. He continued to teach mathematics, physics and ethics as well as being Chess Team coach and coordinator of student climbing and outdoor activity.

Tom first climbed at age 13 and subsequently made multiple ascents of most of the major Oregon and Washington peaks along with innumerable rock climbs. He enjoyed the outdoors and, along with climbing, took equal pleasure in scrambling and hiking mountain trails. He joined the American Alpine Club in 1982.

His students have provided ample testimony to his sound instruction and leadership. Teaching calculus in high school and simultaneously giving classes in leadership and ethics was a large order, but he still saved time to write on purely religious subjects.

Father Goman is survived by his wife, Mar, whom he married in 1968, his mother, LaVerne Goman, as well as his brother, Jon and sister, Sybil.

LEWIS L. MCARTHUR

STEVEN GEOFFREY SCHWARTZ
1961-1986

The central Ohio climbing community was saddened by Steve's death during a solo ascent of the north face of Les Courtes in the Mont Blanc Range on March 16, 1986. His demise ended a potential life-time of commitment and contribution to mountaineering.

Steve chose to develop his climbing skills and interest in the sport as a member of The Ohio State University Mountaineers Club. His development in technique, experience and leadership soon saw him teaching and presenting lectures to the membership. He was further active on issues of access to climbing areas. As a founding member of the Ohio Climbers Association, Steve worked very hard to retain climber access to neighboring J. Bryant State Park or the Clifton Gorge climbing area. His contributions were greatly appreciated at the time and are sorely missed now.

In addition to numerous climbs in the Ohio area, Steve climbed at Seneca Rocks, West Virginia, and made ascents of Mount Temple, Deltaform (Super Couloir), and Houndstooth (Bugaboos Group) in the Canadian Rockies. At the time of his passing, he planned to further develop his climbing skills in Europe.

JOHN GRIMSON LYON

WALDO H. HOLCOMBE
1912-1986

Waldo H. Holcombe became interested in mountains when he spent a year at school in Switzerland, and his enjoyment of them never left him. While in college he climbed and skied in the White Mountains and on Katahdin, and one summer did some climbs in the Rockies. His only major ascent was in 1934 in the Fairweather Range of Alaska, where with Bradford Washburn and

Adams Carter he reached the summit of Mount Crillon, a peak that had thwarted previous attempts. For some years afterward he flew his small plane west to climb in the Wind River Range, the Tetons or the Canadian Rockies. If the weather was not good in one area, he would fly to a better one.

For several years after graduating from Harvard, Waldo taught at the Brooks school in North Andover, Mass. Though he left it to work for the Sigma Instrument Co. in Boston, his connection with Brooks, later mainly as a trustee, lasted for over 50 years. Waldo, before his retirement, became Director of Planning for the Museum of Science in Boston, where he also gave a highly regarded course open to the public in celestial navigation. After retirement he gave distinguished service to the Boston Metropolitan Planning Council and won awards from the Environmental Protection Agency and the Massachusetts Audubon Society.

Waldo and Ruth (Wood), his wife of nearly 50 years, were keen on skiing and sailing. These sports gradually gained precedence over mountaineering in their vacations, though both managed to do some climbing. Their three sons, daughter, and ten grandchildren have been brought up to enjoy the mountains as well as the sea.

ROBERT H. BATES

HERBERT J. KOTHE
1906-1986

Herbert J. Kothe died on April 1, 1986 at the age of eighty. He joined the American Alpine Club in 1943. At that time he lived in New York. He later moved to Connecticut and in the early 1970s to Sarasota, Florida. He is survived by his wife Margaret, two daughters and two grandsons.

He greatly enjoyed rock climbing along the Hudson and in the Shawangunks. Most of his mountain climbing was in the Canadian Rockies though he also climbed in the Dolomites and Alaska.

The Religious Society of Friends was an important part of his life. His hobby was amateur photography, at which he spent many happy hours, doing his own darkroom work. Professionally he was a research chemist in the Fleischmann Laboratories.

KERMITH F. ROSS
1910-1986

Kermith Ross, known to some friends as "Lefty", died of cancer on December 23 in Denver. He began climbing about 1948, in Colorado, and also climbed extensively in Wyoming and California. He participated in expeditions to Canada, Alaska, Peru, Ecuador, and Mexico. Among climbers he will be especially remembered as a member of the group which made the first ascent of the east ridge of Mount Logan in 1957, and as a member of an American expedition to the Cordillera Blanca of Peru in 1959. On that trip he made with others the second ascent of Toсllaraju, the third ascent of Chinchey, and a new route on Pucaranra. He also took part in several probable first winter ascents in Colorado and Wyoming, including Sunlight, Windom, and Fremont; and he climbed all of the fourteen-thousand-foot peaks in Colorado.

Born in Missouri in 1910, he was a patent attorney by profession. He received his law degree from Georgetown University, after an undergraduate degree in chemistry at Kirksville, Missouri. During World War II he was an ordnance officer in the navy, and also taught swimming and gymnastics. His back flips, somersaults and dives were a treat to watch. He remained in the Naval Reserve for years and retired with the rank of Commander. After the war he worked for General Motors, at Los Alamos on the Manhattan Project, at NASA, and at China Lake, California, for the Navy. He retired from the law after many years as a partner in a private Denver firm. Never married, he is survived by one sister, Mae Belt of Atlanta, Missouri.

An inveterate traveler whether at work or leisure, Kermith's sojourns also included wildlife watching in Canada, trekking to the base of Everest, mountaineering in New Zealand, and touring Europe and China. He liked to fish, usually kept camera at hand, and shared his experiences with a wide circle of friends on return. He had a tremendous sense of humor, with an endless supply of jokes, and a trip with him was always enjoyable. It was also unusually safe. In our 40 years of shared mountaineering, I know of no serious accident ever happening to a party with which he was climbing. He combined a good nature with great endurance and good technical ability. Those who climbed with him will always remember him with fondness.

DON MARKS

PHILIP P. UPTON
1919-1984

In 1964, as a fledgling glaciology student from Ohio State University, I spent my first North American summer in the St. Elias Mountains in the Yukon. The OSU contingent was part of a larger group participating in the Arctic Institute of North America's Icefield Ranges Research Project which had been created by Dr. Walter Wood in 1961. Philip Upton was the principal pilot, having been with the project since its inception. During 1964, I came to realize how much the glacier-based research carried out within IRRP depended on the air support provided by Phil and the AINA/AGS heliocourier. In those early days glaciologist-pilot R. H. (Dick) Ragle also played a significant role on the air logistics scene. It was he who checked Phil out on the machine as I remember it.

How clearly I recall standing many times on the Hubbard-Kaskawulsh Divide gazing in awe at the overpowering bulk of Mount Logan, 35 kilometers away. Little did I realize that Upton and Ragle had discussed several times the possibility of landing up on the plateau at 17,500 feet.

Four years passed before I returned to Kluane to carry out a topographic survey of Logan. Phil and the "helio" were still the mainstay of the Icefields operation: in the meantime Phil had pioneered the skillful feat of landing on the plateau with the now turbo-charged "helio." The medical HAPS project was already well underway with Dr. Charles Houston as director.

Then, in 1974, I began a series of surveys on Logan which were to culminate in the recovery of a 103-meter core from the northwest col in 1980. In order to accomplish this we relied entirely on the logistics provided by Phil and his protegé, Andrew Williams, flying the two turbo-charged "helios." By then, the HAPS project had wound down and we were fortunate to have the fullest atten- tion of the pilots in 1980 as well as 1981 when the final evacuation of drill and core was made. Most of the ice core was flown to Whitehorse, direct from the mountain, above the freezing level. That core is the most valuable item I have ever handled in my life.

Charles Houston, I and many others who carried out research on Mount Logan and in many other parts of the St. Elias Mountains were totally dependent on the skill of both AINA pilots. Even the local aviators regarded these two as being in a special class. The four IRRP volumes, the HAPS project tome and my papers describing the ice-core results (with more to come) all owe their exis- tence to the dedication of Phil Upton. In addition to providing the logistics for scientific projects in the St. Elias, Phil also supported a large number of purely climbing or skiing expeditions.

I last flew with Phil in the summer of 1983 not realizing that his time was near. The end of his "era" was recorded by him and published in the 1984 *Canadian Alpine Journal* at the time of his death. A postscript to that account is provided by Christopher Shank: "If Canada is looking for a folk hero, Phil Upton seems to be a likely candidate."

In recognition of the achievements of this remarkable man, a plaque was made to perpetuate his memory. The bronze plaque measures 15cm × 22cm. It has been attached by rock bolts to the solid granodiorite rock which crops out on the 5475-meter pass between AINA Peak and Prospector's Peak. This pass provides access from the upper "Football" field of the King Trench route to the plateau and is frequently travelled. Only 15 meters lower than Mount St. Elias and with this mountain as its magnificent backdrop, it is probably by far, the highest memorial plaque in Canada. It sits in its lofty granite perch in fitting tribute to this great Canadian-American aviator. It should be there long, long after we have all gone. From all of us, thanks Phil.

GERALD HOLDSWORTH

GEORGIA ENGELHARD CROMWELL
1906-1986

Born in New York City, November 19, 1906, Georgia was an adept pho- tographer, her father having achieved considerable prominence in the field. She practiced her profession for various commercial entities, on both sides of the camera.

Georgia Engelhard took up serious alpinism in 1926 and joined the American Alpine Club two years later, the youngest age of admission for a woman to that date. She continued a very active climbing career with lengthy visits to the mountains of western Canada—specializing in the Rockies and Purcells—almost every summer until interrupted by the American involvement on World War II. Her record of thirty-two first ascents is one of the most outstanding ever developed in that area.

Her record of ascents in the Alps was longer lived, but started with her spectacular performance in 1935 when she made forty-four ascents, many of them guideless and all of prominent peaks. Most of those ascents were traverses of the summits, some multiple.

Georgia did not neglect the more prominent peaks of the United States. She did several of the "Fourteeners" of Colorado and most of the Cascade volcanos; Mount Baker in 1929 and the others in 1937 (back when St. Helens was a longer and more legal trip).

Just prior to American involvement in World War II, she met and later married Oliver Eaton Cromwell, an equally distinguished alpinist who participated as deputy leader in the, ill-fated, 1939 American expedition to K2.

Georgia was a great favorite with the Swiss guides employed by the Canadian Pacific Railway, in particular Ernst Feuz (1889-1960), with whom she made a number of her better climbs and several first ascents. In their reminiscences, it appears that she was regarded as a difficult, but distinguished client—difficult because she would carry as much as any man in the party and often showed up the less sturdy male members of any party; and distinguished because she was unique in this attribute among the women climbers of the day.

She died two months before her eightieth birthday, in Interlaken, where she and Tony Cromwell had lived for the past thirty years. Georgia is survived by her husband, who now resides in Bryn Mawr, Pennsylvania and two stepchildren, O. Eaton Cromwell, Jr. of Haverford, Pennsylvania and Camilla C. Anderson of Noblesville, Indiana.

WILLIAM L. PUTNAM

Club Activities

EDITED BY FREDERICK O. JOHNSON

A.A.C., Alaska Section. 1986 proved to be an excellent year for the Alaska Section. Successes included the annual Ice Climbing Festival in Valdez, the first winter ascent of Mount Logan, numerous first ascents of local waterfalls, ski traverses, and the successful completion of the first half of the Soviet-American Climbing Exchange.

Hosted in February by Andy Embick, the annual Ice Climbing Festival in Valdez was visited by climbers from around the state and Japan. We are happy to report that Masaki Matsumoto, leader of the Japanese climbing team that visited Alaska in 1985, is now an A.A.C. member of our Section.

Later in March, Section members George Rooney, Willi Hersman, and Vern Tejas along with John Bauman, Steve Koslow and Todd Frankiewicz made the first winter ascent of Mount Logan via the Trench Route. With the spring sunshine the Soviets arrived, polished off Denali in a week, and spent the remainder of their visit traveling across Alaska. Highlights included halibut fishing and kayaking in Kachemak Bay and visits to Barrow and Fairbanks. Much of the credit for the success of the Soviet visit lies in the individual efforts of Section members, family, friends, and the unselfish generosity of local businesses. Special thanks to Lowell Thomas, Markair, Neil Bergt, John Markel, Sam Barber, Judy Lehman, Chuck and Vera McClain, Dana Anderson, Carolyn Borjon, and the communities of Talkeetna and Homer.

The Alaska Section annual meeting was held in October at the Stuckagain Heights restaurant. The setting which overlooks Anchorage and Cook Inlet was breathtaking. Before the banquet the business meeting was conducted, during which Charlie Sassara was elected Chairman and Mike Howerton Newsletter editor. The topics of discussion included the annual Denali climbing report by Ranger Bob Seibert, new routes of local interest, the pharmacology of Decadron, the current Soviet-American Exchange, and recent climbs in the Soviet Union by Gary Bocarde, Susan Havens, and Pete Panarese.

CHARLIE SASSARA, *Chairman*

A.A.C., Blue Ridge Section. The Blue Ridge Section reorganized in 1986 with the election of new officers. The Section wishes to extend its invitation to other Club members to take advantage of our location in "Lobby City, U.S.A.," for pursuing climbing-related issues with Congress and the various federal agencies located here. Our intent is to help others with logistics, i.e., rides from the airport, lodging, directions around the Washington bureaucracy. Because of increasing pressure on climbers to respond to matters ranging from liability to access, we feel the need to voice our opinions in Washington as well as in the local jurisdictions where the issues arise. Our Section hopes to make it easier for others to come to Washington to plead their causes where it counts.

The Section was also vaguely active climbing in an unorganized way. Several members had fine mountaineering accomplishments to their credit in 1986. Plans for 1987 include membership expansion and more active climbing involvement in the community.

Other Sections and climbing groups who wish to make enquiries concerning assistance in Washington, D.C., are encouraged to write or call the Section secretary, Stuart Pregnall, 214 13th Street S.E., 2, Washington, D.C. 20003; phone 202-543-3988.

RANDY STARRETT, *Chairman*

A.A.C., Cascade Section. Forty-two consecutive days without rain in the Cascades during July and August coupled with a beautiful fall made for outstanding local climbing for the Cascade Section. As usual, our members compiled an impressive list of new routes and ascents in our local mountains and in other ranges of the world.

Our 1986 activities started with the annual banquet, attended by 150 members and guests. This nearly record crowd enjoyed Dr. Andy Embick's presentation on climbing and kayaking in the Karakoram Range of Pakistan. Other programs in 1986 included Nick Clinch on the first ascent of Ulugh Muztagh in China, Jim Frush on Cho Oyu, and Mark Dale on Mount Foraker.

A very special activity that involved considerable Section resources and effort by our members was the Soviet visit in May. The 10-member Soviet team was given royal treatment while in Seattle: sailing, sightseeing, and shopping. The Mountaineers hosted a public showing of the team's slides attended by nearly 200 people. Although the Section received no financial support from the Club for this activity, we hope to be able to continue to do this type of thing in the future.

Other Section activities centered around access problems associated with lowland rock-climbing areas in the state and volunteer trail maintenance projects. The Peshastin Pinnacles, a popular sandstone area near Leavenworth, was closed to climbers in August by the private landowners. The Cascade Section has been an active member of a committee of local clubs formed in an effort to re-open the area. For the first time the Section has adopted a trail, Mount Pugh, abandoned by the Forest Service. The Mount Pugh trail is a popular conditioner and viewpoint in the Central Cascades. Nearly 100 man-hours were spent in 1986 on its maintenance. The Section also spent nearly 200 man-hours and substantial financial resources on the construction of a cable crossing of Slesse Creek in the North Cascades. This ambitious project has long-term benefits for hikers and climbers in this popular area. Five newsletters were published in an effort to increase communications within the Section and with Club headquarters. The Section added 18 new members in 1986.

Our goals for 1987 are to continue our high level of communication within the Section; maintain our number of annual Section activities, both social and project-oriented; and to continue to solicit support from and improve our relationship with the national Club.

DONALD J. GOODMAN, *Chairman*

A.A.C., New York Section. After a brief respite for rest and rehabilitation following the Club's 83rd Annual Meeting, the New York Section continued with a busy schedule of events in 1986. Illustrated lectures were presented by such well known climbing celebrities as Dave Breashears, Gordon Wiltsie, and Rick Ridgeway. In addition Olaf Sööt presented a memorable multi-media slide show commemorating the 50th anniversary of Waddington's first ascent. These lectures are followed by a social hour, giving members an opportunity to expand their circle of climbing acquaintances.

The Annual Dinner, a black-tie affair at the Union Club, has become the principal event on the Section calendar, regularly attracting a capacity audience of 150 members and guests, many from outside the New York area. This year's featured speaker was Peter Habeler, Austria's leading climbing personality. Departing from the usual expedition narrative, Habeler, in a noteworthy address, sought to explain the recent rash of disasters in the Himalayas including the series of accidents on K2 this summer that claimed 13 lives and some of Europe's finest climbers. Among the causative factors he identified was a general loss of respect for the mountain, leading to an overly casual attitude towards the debilitating effects of remaining at high altitude for long periods of time. Also to blame was the increased prevalence of a self-centered mountaineering ethic which leaves little room for the kind of team spirit demonstrated by the gallant 1953 American K2 Expedition. Finally, solo climbing in the Himalayas is totally reckless, as proved by the death of Renato Casarotto, who perished in a crevasse on K2.

As is customary, the Dinner was run as a fund-raiser for a needy Club cause. This year's beneficiary was the Library. Proceeds from the affair will be used to expand the collection in a number of important areas including guidebooks, periodicals, and the establishment of the country's largest and most complete collection of climbing videos. In addition, funds will be used to help preserve and restore the Library's collection of rare and antiquarian books, a very vital and necessary task.

On the climbing front two especially noteworthy achievements by Section members should be signaled. On October 5 M. Girard (Gerry) Bloch reached the summit of El Capitan by the Nose route as part of a three-person team, thus realizing a long-time goal. At age 68½ Gerry is by far the oldest person to have climbed El Capitan, after having spent four days and three nights on the wall. Another member, Lynn Hill, proved conclusively that she is one of the finest women rock climbers in the world by finishing second in the European Rock Climbing Championships and an easy first in the French Championships at Troubat in the Pyrenees.

PHILIP ERARD, *Chairman*

A.A.C., Oregon Section. 1986 was an eventful year for the Oregon Section, although we had few actual climbs to report. Our most time-consuming activity was the continuing and almost successful effort to have Mount Saint Helens opened to climbers. This was brought to a head when Jim Angell filed a formal appeal with the chief of the Forest Service in Washington, D.C. He supported the club position on all points but one, and the Mount Saint Helens staff announced in December that the mountain would soon be open to climbers. "Soon" has not come to pass, and Jim is again boiling the pot. The Section continued the annual trail work party at Smith Rock State Park with the cooperation of the State Parks Division. The 1987 work date is Saturday, March 28, and all rock climbers are encouraged to participate.

Oregon has been saddened by two tragedies in the past year. The first was the death in May of the Episcopal School climbers including A.A.C. member Tom Goman. The second was the loss of Alan Pennington and John Smolich on K2. Both were in the process of joining the Club before they left for the Himalaya. In the wake of the loss on Mount Hood, the Section has been active in the effort to improve coordination and communication between the various groups involved in search and rescue.

Climbing continues on a local level with Beacon Rock and Smith Rock among the more attractive spots. There is also some activity on the coast on sea stacks and shoreline rocks. The Section has had evening meetings with both slides and video cassettes as well as our regular December outing to the Snow Shoe Cabin on the north side of Mount Hood. In the winter, the three-mile, uphill ski trip provides a welcome seclusion.

At our annual meeting the following officers were elected: Section Chair, Jim Angell; Vice-Chair, Tim Carpenter; Secretary, Kurt Wehbring; Treasurer, Jim Angell. As Jim Angell is now commuting to Los Angeles, he resigned as Chairman in December, but remained as Treasurer. Tim Carpenter succeeded Jim as Chairman.

LEWIS L. MCARTHUR

Colorado Mountain Club. The Colorado Mountain Club has about 7500 members in groups throughout the state. The largest is the Denver Group with about 4600 members. There are also the Denver Wilderness Kids Group for families with pre-teenagers and the Denver Juniors for teenagers. Other Groups are in Aspen, Boulder, Colorado Springs, Fort Collins, Glenwood Springs, Durango, Estes Park, Grand Junction, Longmont, Pueblo, and a new group in Crested Butte-Gunnison.

The club had over 2000 scheduled trips in 1986, with a wide range of activities. They ranged from easy to strenuous one-day hikes and climbs to multi-day outings, mostly in Colorado, including a two-week in-state outing. Winter trips included cross-country and downhill skiing, snowshoe trips, and ice-skating.

Out-of-state trips included outings to Alaska, Arizona, California, Washington, and Wyoming. International trips featured bicycle trips to Ireland and Corsica-Sardinia-Italy, a canoeing trip to Canada, a climbing trip to Mexico, and a hiking-climbing trip to the Swiss and Austrian Alps.

The C.M.C. has been instrumental with volunteer trail crews, working with the Forest Service, in the construction of The Colorado Trail, some 350 miles long, from Denver to Durango. We expect to complete this in 1987.

Our Conservation Committee continues efforts to cooperate with the Forest Service in long-range planning, and to monitor logging and mining activities in the mountain areas, as well as water projects.

ALBERT OSSINGER, *President*

Iowa Mountaineers. The club completed another active year in 1986, with membership at 1100. Nearly 840 members participated in one of the many instructional courses, the mountaineering camps, or the foreign expeditions that were one to four weeks long. The courses and mountain camps were again offered for University of Iowa credit, if desired. Under the instruction of Jim and John Ebert, 63 members finished the concentrated one-week basic rock-climbing courses at Devils Lake State Park, Wisconsin, and 521 members completed the weekend rock-climbing courses offered to University of Iowa students. Three general weekend outings were held at Devils Lake with an average attendance of 50.

In December, 20 members made a seven-day cross-country skiing trip to the Collegiate Range in Colorado. Here they built and lived in snow shelters and skied throughout the Tennessee Pass area. In January, a small group skied in the Jackson Hole area of Wyoming.

Twenty-three members hiked and climbed from January 18 to February 17 throughout New Zealand's North and South Islands, including the Milford and Routeburn Tracks. The weather generally was very good. John Ebert was leader.

The club sponsored a one-week hiking trip in March to the Grand Canyon and Havasupai in Arizona. Jim Ebert was the leader for this trip that attracted over 50 people.

The club's annual banquet on May 1 featured the African film made by John and Jim Ebert showing the club ascents of Kilimanjaro and Mount Kenya and climbing in the Ruwenzori of Uganda. Over 100 people attended.

In June the club again offered an intermediate rock climbing course on Devils Tower in Wyoming, during which 13 ascended by the Durrance route. Also in June 17 members journeyed to the volcanic peaks in the Northwest, where ascents were made of Mount Adams and Mount Rainier.

John and Jim Ebert led a group of 42 to the Peruvian Andes, where Base Camp was located in the Quebrada Quilcayhuanca from June 28 to July 26. During this period 33 members ascended Jatunmontepuncu (17,765 feet), 19 ascended Maparaju (17,475 feet), and 17 the north peak of Maparaju. Robert Wilson and Hans Steyskal ascended Chopiraju (18,087 feet) and Pucaranra (20,168 feet). Joe Burleson was in charge of an ascent of Nevado Huascarán (22,208 feet). Ten out of the group of 14 reached the summit. The weather was excellent throughout the trip except for two days when it snowed 10 to 14 inches. The club will return to Peru in 1989 to the Quebrada Shallap.

In August Jim Ebert led two outings in Wyoming. In the Wind Rivers 12 people climbed Gannett Peak, Wyoming's highest, and 13 climbed Fremont Peak. Later in the month a five-day mountaineering outing was held in the Tetons. Seventeen people attempted the Grand Teton and Teewinot, but were unsuccessful because of the steady rain and wind during the ascent days.

In 1987 the club will again sponsor eight one-week basic rock-climbing courses at Devils Lake State Park, Wisconsin, during May, June and August. An ascent of Devils Tower is planned during the intermediate rock climbing course from June 8 to 11. The main trip will be to Alaska to climb and hike along the Alaska Highway. The mountaineering camps will start with 10 days in the Colorado Chimney Peak area from July 7 to 17, followed by a 10-day camp in the northern Wind Rivers from July 21 to 31. The main summer mountaineering camp will be in the Sawtooths of Idaho from August 4 to 14. The final outing will be held in the Tetons from August 17 to 21.

In coming years the main foreign expeditions will be to East Africa to climb Kilimanjaro and Mount Kenya from June 25 to July 24, 1988; New Zealand from January 14 to February 20, 1989, to ascend peaks on both the North and South Islands and to hike the Milford and Routeburn Tracks; the Peruvian Andes from June 24 to July 22, 1989 to climb in the Quebrada Shallap followed by climbs of Nevado Huantsán and Nevado Huascarán. Finally, in 1990 a European outing is planned for from June 29 to July 22 to climb the highest and most famous peaks in six Alpine countries.

JIM EBERT, *Vice President*

Memphis Mountaineers. Based in the Memphis, Tennessee area, the Memphis Mountaineers promote mountaineering sports among Mid-Southerners. They provide various types of mountaineering activities, the opportunity to meet climbing partners, and climbing instruction. The membership is informed of club activities through the monthly *Memphis Mountain News*. The club meets at the Highland Branch of the Memphis Public Library on the second Monday of every month from seven to nine P.M.

In 1986, informative programs on climbing areas as diverse as Ireland and Colorado supplemented club business at the monthly meetings. Other activities included social events, such as the annual Christmas party, and physical training sessions on backyard climbing gymnastic equipment. Nineteen weekend outings provided rock climbing from North Carolina to Missouri. A longer Thanks-giving climbing trip went to Enchanted Rock, Texas. In addition to running a large introduction to rock climbing seminar at Pinnacle Mountain, Arkansas, experienced club members also instructed courses at Memphis State University for recreation students and Park Ranger trainees.

Six members participated in the 1986 expedition to southern Arizona in March. Noteable ascents included the southeast arête of Baboquivari, and the first ascent of an unnamed spire at Cochise's Stronghold. Paul Diefenderfer, president of the Arizona Mountaineering Club, was most helpful in planning this trip. Another small expedition, to Zion National Park, Utah, is slated for March, 1987.

Membership in 1986 included 42 regular members (local) and associate members (from as far away as Hong Kong). Officers included Jim Detterline (president), Scott Hall (vice president), Richard Bennett (secretary), Cynthia McKinnon (treasurer), Rick Guerrieri (Baboquivari expedition leader), and Larry Mallory (Zion expedition leader). For more information, write: Memphis Mountaineers, Inc., P.O. Box 11124, Memphis, TN 38111.

JIM DETTERLINE, *President*

Potomac Appalachian Trail Club, 1986 was a big year for the Potomac Appalachian Trail Club's Mountaineering Section. At the beginning of the year we set out to accomplish a few things: increase membership, establish new trip leader and safety guidelines to meet the liability demands on our club, finalize the efforts in progress to open Bull Run Mountain to hiking and climbing, and finally, increase our activities in climbing, socializing, trash removal in climb-ing areas, but above all, climbing. The section is proud to report that we have been very successful in all our efforts.

We were also involved with a number of other activities during the year. The President's Commission on American Outdoors came to an open house at P.A.T.C., and we gave them our views on issues related to climbing. Our efforts to assist flood victims in West Virginia following the November 1985 disaster were continued. Toward that end, we assisted in the rebuilding of the access bridge at Seneca Rocks, worked with the Forest Service in planning a new climbers' campsite at Seneca, and provided financial and material assis-tance to families in the area. We co-sponsored two guest speakers in 1986. John Harlin spoke to us and the Ski-Touring Section, and Rosie Andrews gave her slide show on Women Climbers in the 80s to us and the Washington Women Outdoors. The section sent a representative to the American Alpine Club's annual meeting in Denver.

Time was also found to extend the section's horizons with respect to climb-ing, with members climbing all over much of the world. There were two trips to Africa's Mount Kenya and Mount Kilimanjaro, both successful, and some of the excellent rock climbing to be found in Africa was enjoyed as well. Alaska also received a visit or two, with Denali being ascended and other areas explored for future trips. Several members climbed in the Alps, South American ranges, and the Canadian Rockies. Closer to home, trips were made to the Tetons in Wyoming and to California's Yosemite, Mount Whitney area, and some of the smaller crags in the San Francisco Bay area. New England also received much of our attention both in winter and summer. Locally, the section climbed every weekend, with trips to the Gunks, Seneca Rocks, Stone Mountain, the New River Gorge, and other areas. Although the list of regulars may at times have seemed small, when viewed over the year, we accomplished quite a bit of climbing.

For the future, section activities look good. We have embarked on another guidebook, this time for Carderock. The Great Falls Guide has gone into its second printing within a year of publication. Membership will continue to be a key focus, as will our access and conservation activities. And, of course, we plan to continue to climb as often and in as many places as possible. Visitors to the Washington, D.C., area are encouraged to contact us, P.A.T.C. Mountaineering Section, phone 202-638-5306, 7-10 P.M. weekdays.

STUART PREGNALL, *Chairman, Mountaineering Section*

AAC PUBLICATIONS

THE AMERICAN ALPINE JOURNAL, edited by H. Adams Carter.

THE AMERICAN ALPINE JOURNAL INDEX
1929-1976, Edited by Earlyn Church.
1977-1986, Edited by Patricia A. Fletcher.

ACCIDENTS IN NORTH AMERICAN MOUNTAINEERING, edited by John E. Williamson

ACONCAGUA, Topographic map by Jerzy Wala, Text by Carles Capellas and Josep Paytubi.

CLIMBING ICE, by Yvon Chouinard.

CLIMBING IN NORTH AMERICA, by Chris Jones.

THE COLUMBIA MOUNTAINS OF CANADA—CENTRAL (The Interior Ranges of B.C.), by Earle R. Whipple, Roger Laurilla and William L. Putnam.

THE COLUMBIA MOUNTAINS OF CANADA—WEST (The Interior Ranges of B.C.), Earle R. Whipple and William L. Putnam.

THE GREAT GLACIER AND ITS HOUSE, by William L. Putnam.

THE INTERIOR RANGES OF BRITISH COLUMBIA—SOUTH, by Robert Kruszyna and William L. Putnam.

MOUNTAIN SICKNESS, by Peter Hackett, M.D.

THE MOUNTAINS OF NORTH AMERICA, by Fred Beckey.

MOUNTAINS OF THE MIDDLE KINGDOM, by Galen Rowell.

THE RED ROCKS OF SOUTHERN NEVADA, by Joanne Urioste.

THE ROCKY MOUNTAINS OF CANADA—NORTH, by Robert Kruszyna and William L. Putnam.

THE ROCKY MOUNTAINS OF CANADA—SOUTH, by Glen W. Boles, with Robert Kruszyna and William L. Putnam.

SHAWANGUNK ROCK CLIMBS, by Richard C. Williams.

SURVIVING DENALI, by Jonathan Waterman.

TAHQUITZ AND SUICIDE ROCKS, by Chuck Wilts.

TOUCH THE SKY: The Black Hills in the Needles of South Dakota, by Paul Piana.

TRAPROCK: Rock Climbing in Central Connecticut, by Ken Nichols.

A WALK IN THE SKY, by Nicholas Clinch.

WASATCH ROCK CLIMBS, by Les Ellison and Brian Smoot.

WHERE THE CLOUDS CAN GO, by Conrad Kain.

YURAQ JANKA: The Cordilleras Blanca and Rosko, by John Ricker.

Prices and order forms on request from The American Alpine Club, 113 East 90th Street, New York NY 10128-1589.

INDEX

Volume 29 ● Issue 61 ● 1987

Compiled by Patricia A. Fletcher

This issue comprises all of Volume 29

Mountains are listed by their official names and ranges; quotation marks indicate unofficial names. Ranges and geographic locations are also indexed. Unnamed peaks (e.g., P 2037) are listed following the range or country in which they are located.

All expedition members cited in major articles are included, whereas only the leaders and persons supplying information in the **Climbs and Expeditions** section are listed.

Titles of books reviewed in this issue are grouped as a single entry under **Book Reviews.**

Abbreviations used: Article: *art.;* Bibliography: *bibl.;* Obituary: *obit.*

A

Abalakov, Vitaly Mikhailovich, *obit.,* 348-49
Abi Gamin (Garhwal Himalaya), 258-59
Absaroka Range (Montana), 181-82
Accidents: Annapurna, 250; Annapurna III, 253; Ardver Sar, 289; Broad Peak, 278; Chacraraju, 193; Chiring, 288; Cho Oyu, 242; Denali National Park, 143-45; Dhaulagiri, 255, Dhaulagiri II, 256-57; Diran, 288; Everest, 234-35, 300-301; Gangotri, 261; Gasherbrum II, 279; Hidden Peak, 278; Himalchuli, 249; Himalchuli North, 247; K2, *art.,* 1-4; 12-13, 16, 271-74, 276; Kangchungtse, 226; Kommunizma, 310, 311, 312; Korzhenevskoi, 311; Kumbhakarna, 222; Lhotse Shar, 233; Logan, 182; Makalu, 223-24; Manaslu, 246; Meru North, 264-65; Satopanth, 259; Shivling (Garhwal), 262; Tilitso, 249; Torre, Cerro, 104; Utah, 73

Aconcagua (Argentina), *art.,* 136-40; 205, 215, 218; *altitude of,* 140; *ascents of,* 136-40; *clean-up of,* 205; *map of,* 138-39; *routes on,* 136-40
Adela Sur (Patagonia), 215
Admiralitek (Turkestan Range, USSR), 312
Adrspach-Teplice (Czechoslovakia), 218
Africa, 218
"Aguilera" (Patagonia), 206
Aikes, Jorge, 137
Aimara (Cordillera Real, Bolivia), 202
Ak-Su Glavnoye (Turkestan Range, USSR), 312
Ak-Su Mountains (Turkestan Range, USSR), 312-13
Ak-Su Skalnoye (Turkestan Range, USSR), 312
Aktiubek (Turkestan Range, USSR), 312
Alaska, *arts.,* 81-90, 91-96; 142-62, 218
Alaska Range, *art.,* 81-90; 142-54, 218
Aleksandre Bloka (Turkestan Range, USSR), 312